W9-ADD-877

# THE BIBLE in MILTON'S EPICS

# THE BIBLE
# in
# MILTON'S EPICS

*James H. Sims*

UNIVERSITY OF FLORIDA PRESS
*Gainesville*
*1962*

TO BETTY

*"My other self, the partner of my life"*
and to our children



*A University of Florida Press Book*

PUBLISHED WITH ASSISTANCE
FROM
THE FORD FOUNDATION


LIBRARY OF CONGRESS CATALOGUE CARD NUMBER: 62-20738
PRINTED BY ROSE PRINTING COMPANY, INC.
TALLAHASSEE, FLORIDA

# Preface

THIS STUDY is in large part the result of the effect of the intellectual stimulation of Milton's thought and art upon one whose background and interests have caused him to be receptive particularly to that Christian tradition which is firmly based on the Bible. Due largely to my parents, my interest in the Bible and in Christian faith and thought go back beyond memory; the stimulation of that interest by contact with literature generally and with Milton specifically came about, primarily, through two of my teachers: Professor Thomas B. Stroup, now of the University of Kentucky, and Professor Ants Oras. This particular study of Milton was first projected in 1955 when an idea, initiated in a seminar all but unconsciously, was crystallized and made articulate by a sentence from Harris Francis Fletcher's *The Use of the Bible in Milton's Prose*. Professor Fletcher wrote, "Another important aspect in the study of Milton's use of the Bible in his prose works is the evidence it affords of the need for a re-evaluation of his use of the Bible in his poetry." While it is not claimed that the present work sufficiently satisfies the need of which Professor Fletcher spoke, it is hoped that the need is partially met and that the way is cleared for a more adequate and inclusive study.

I wish to acknowledge help received from many sources; a few deserve special mention here. Part of the work done on this study was made possible by a grant from the Southern Fellowships Fund, Chapel Hill, North Carolina. The director and staff of the University of Florida libraries have been especially cooperative and helpful. In addition to the inspiration he has provided as a teacher, Professor Ants Oras has been a patient and painstaking guide, an encouraging friend, and perhaps most important, a keen critic. The advice of Professor T. Walter Herbert was invaluable in the initial shaping and condensing of the mass of material to be dealt with as well as in the later stages of the writing. Professors Joseph Brunet and Ernest Cox are largely responsible for the accuracy of form of the foreign languages and of the English respectively; any inaccuracies are wholly mine. Professors Edwin C. Kirkland and Thomas Pyles have, through their reading and criticism, contributed greatly to whatever is of value in the content and form of this study. Finally, the greatest debt I owe is to my wife and children, who have ungrudgingly allowed me to give a disproportionate share of the past five years of my life to scholarship in general and to Milton and the Bible in particular.

J. H. S.

## Contents

*Introduction*—1

I

*Authoritative Reality*—8

II

*Linguistic Versatility*—64

III

*Dramatic Effectiveness: Setting and Action*—103

IV

*Dramatic Effectiveness: Language and Character*—151

V

*Epic Unity of Theme*—216

*Conclusion*—250

*Bibliography*—255

*Index of Biblical References*—259

*Index of Selected Subjects*—279

# Introduction

A SYSTEMATIC STUDY of the use of the Bible in Milton's epic poems is a mountainous task involving much time spent in checking references, turning the pages of several Bibles and concordances almost simultaneously, and noting references previously pointed out by Milton's editors and commentators. It is also the kind of study which seems almost pointless, since everyone knows that Milton's Biblical knowledge was as thorough as his classical knowledge and that his epics are classical in form and Biblical in content. What else is there to be said? The epics are saturated with the Bible, and, since that is such an obvious fact, there seems little point in launching a study whose only conclusion can be that the epics are, indeed, saturated with the Bible.

These two factors—the immensity of the bulk of the Biblical material in the poems and the feeling that not much worth discovering would be yielded by a study of such Biblical material—may be primary factors in the neglect by modern scholars of this particular kind of study of Milton. Yet bodies of material as vast and vaster (and duller) have been dealt with successfully, and many attempts have been made to explain both the obscure and the obvious. That the Biblical saturation is obvious in Milton does not imply that the nature, extent, and effect of that saturation are obvious, and the analysis of these is the task undertaken in this study of *Paradise Lost* and *Paradise Regained.*

Another cause for the neglect of a systematic study of Milton's poetic use of the Bible is, of course, the growing ignorance of and lack of interest in the doctrines and even the once-familiar stories of the Bible. In an age when not a single member of a graduate class in English in a major state university can identify Keats' allusion to Ruth's standing "in tears amid the alien corn" and when only a handful of students in a large freshman class can recognize the story of the Prodigal Son when it is read to them from a modern English translation, there is not much hope that a poet who depends on a general sensitivity to Biblical allusion on the part of the literate public will be very popular reading even in academic circles. There seems even less hope for the success of a secondary study elucidating Biblical references in Milton and analyzing the aesthetic effect on, and the ethical insight gained in, the mind of the reader. Both poet and critic are increasingly in danger of finding themelves without even a few to make up a "fit audience." But the very danger indicates the need for such a study.

None of these factors, however, prevented editors of an earlier age from noting and commenting at length on certain references, nor did the feeling that the Biblical references would be obvious to Milton's readers prevent these editors from discussing the effect gained by his artistic use of the Bible. The possibility that such use or their comments on it might have neither meaning nor interest for the literate public was not seriously considered by his editors, at any rate not by those of the seventeenth and eighteenth centuries; and at least one modern editor, Merritt Y. Hughes, has followed in their train by refusing to allow such a possibility to deter him from supplying many original notes on the Biblical elements in *Paradise Lost* and *Paradise Regained.* That most of the Biblical allusions discussed in this study were noted by the editors of centuries earlier than the nineteenth and that the identification of Biblical references by modern editors (from Masson onward—with the notable exception of Professor Hughes) has been, for the most part, mere repetition of matter supplied by earlier editors are made clear by the "Index of Biblical References in Milton's Epics" at the end of this book. The editions of Patrick Hume (1695) and Bishop Newton (1749) list between them more Bible references to *Paradise Lost* than the others combined, although it should be stated that Bishop Newton drew on several collaborators and predecessors. Altogether 1,364 individual citations to Scripture have been recorded by Milton's editors from

Hume to Hughes. Yet none of the editors, commentators, or scholars have attempted to bring together and systematize Milton's use of the Bible in his major poems; this is the task I have undertaken here, and I have, in the process, added 816 Biblical citations to particular lines of the two epics.

The various editors of Milton from 1695 through the eighteenth century held differing views of Milton as a man, as an artist, and as a Christian, but, in spite of the random nature of their references, they were practically unanimous in their praise of his use of the Bible and in their feeling that his poems, being "taken out of Sacred Story," as Hume said, were superior to the classics because, as Todd put it, they were "based on real histories and matters of fact"; most of them, however, did not go so far as Gillies, who announced his purpose to be "to show *this only,* that Paradise Lost owes its chief excellence to the Holy Scriptures."[1] Gillies' statement is certainly the opposite of the prevailing modern attitude towards Milton and his epics, the attitude that the Biblical material and the theology are unpleasant and ineffective medicines which, although they have a certain antiquarian appeal, are made palatable only by the phonetic sweetness and richness of the poetry. The point of view of this study is neither the one nor the other but is at a mid-point between the two. The Bible contributes a great deal to the music and imagery of the poetry, and Milton's great and transforming mental powers make the Scriptural material he uses peculiarly his own, fitted within the dramatic and epic context of his "great Argument." *Paradise Lost* does not owe its chief excellence to the Bible, but rather to Milton's skillful poetic use of the Bible; the Bible, on the other hand, does not derive its authority and convincing power from the poem, but rather brings them into the poem via Milton's catalytic mind. The Biblical elements in the epics, therefore, cannot be ignored any more than the classical elements; even for purposes of appreciating the cosmic sweep and organ tones of Milton's poetry, one must, if one is to

1. Quotations from Milton's editors are taken from Ants Oras, *Milton's Editors and Commentators from Patrick Hume to Henry John Todd* (London, 1931), pp. 32, 223, 297. Professor Oras' work is a thorough survey of the methods, characteristics, and idiosyncrasies of Milton's commentators on Biblical and other literary matters.

base appreciation on anything concrete, take into account the Biblical tone and idiom which permeate the epics. And if one turns from the sound to examine the sense, an acquaintance with the Bible, it is hoped the following pages will make clear, is often the *sine qua non* of a full understanding of the poet's statements and suggestions.

One of the major problems faced at the outset of this study was that of determining which versions of the Bible to use. Professor Fletcher's work was of help here, for he has conclusively shown, as far as Milton's prose is concerned, that the "agreement of the majority of his quotations in English with the Authorized Version is markedly apparent."[2] The percentage of quotations agreeing with the Authorized Version almost doubles after Milton's blindness; Professor Fletcher's figures show 47.7 per cent before and 80.4 per cent after. "There is but one real class of variants discernible after his blindness, and this is represented by the quotations that present a reading for or a translation of the original Hebrew or Greek which is Milton's own production."[3] With the tentative hypothesis, based on Professor Fletcher's work with the prose, that Milton's Biblical references and allusions in his major poems would be predominantly from the Authorized Version and that variants would be explained largely by Milton's own translations from the original languages of the Bible, there still remained to be settled the question of which edition and printing of the Authorized Version and which text of the Hebrew Old Testament and the Greek New Testament to use.

Professor Fletcher's identification of Milton's English Bible as a 1612 printing by Robert Barker was based on a precedent set by the British Museum authorities in 1884[4] and has been followed for purposes of this study. As the reader progresses through the following chapters, he will doubtless be convinced by the over-

2. Harris Francis Fletcher, *The Use of the Bible in Milton's Prose* (Urbana, 1929), p. 20.

3. *Ibid.*, p. 94.

4. Wynne E. Baxter ("Milton Bibles," *N&Q*, III [1911], 109-110) summarizes the evidence on all the Bibles associated with Milton and his wives and concludes that the British Museum Bible is the only one extant which we can be reasonably sure that Milton used. The only other extant Bible connected with Milton is a Geneva version of 1588 owned by his third wife,

whelming evidence of agreement between Milton's poetry and the 1612 printing of the Authorized Version (the first quarto, Roman letter printing) that it is indeed the version Milton most frequently used and had most indelibly in his mind. For the Hebrew and Greek versions, since there is no evidence connecting any particular editions with Milton, the Antwerp Polyglot, printed by Christopher Plantin in 1584 and mentioned by David Daiches[5] as a widely known Bible available to the King James Version translators and to others interested in studying the original Scriptures, has been used. The text of the Antwerp Polyglot is based on the Complutensian Polyglot of 1520, the product of the most famous of the trilingual colleges of the sixteenth century, Alcalà (called Complutum by the Romans), Spain. The Antwerp Polyglot is listed in Jacques Charles Brunet's *Manuel du Librairie* (fifth edition) as having gone through five printings from 1572 to 1657 (at Antwerp, Geneva, and Leipzig) and is called "la plus belle et la plus estimée" of Christopher Plantin's Bibles. For the Latin references in the poems, the Vulgate has seemed closer than the Junius-Tremellius Latin Bible which was used by Milton in his prose.[6] The spellings have been maintained in quotations from all the versions referred to, but typography has been modernized ("j" has been substituted for "i," as in "iustice," "u" for "v," and a few others in the English version, and scribal abbreviations in the Hebrew and Greek texts have been discarded in favor of separate characters). Bibliographical data on the Bibles used will be found in the bibliography.

---

Elizabeth Minshull Milton, and autographed by her in 1664 (no evidence of use by Milton of the Geneva Bible has been discovered in his poetry). The story, perhaps apocryphal, of the acquisition of Milton's Bible by the British Museum is interestingly told by George Potter ("Milton Bibles," *N&Q*, III [1911], 70): "I believe it was [Thomas] Kerslake who told me that when he was staying at a hydropathic establishment at Matlock, a fellow-visitor told him he had an old Bible in his bedroom that had belonged to Jo. Mitton, the sporting man. Kerslake asked to see it, and, on its being brought, exclaimed: 'Why, this belonged to John Milton, the poet!' to which the owner replied: 'If it only belonged to a poet, it ain't no good.' The result was that Kerslake obtained it for a trifling sum, and later very liberally handed it to the British Museum authorities at the same price." Further information on Milton's Bibles may be found in Frank Allen Patterson, ed., "Notes on Milton's Bibles," *The Works of John Milton* (New York, 1931), XVIII, 559-65.

5. *The King James Version of the English Bible* (Chicago, 1941), pp. 146-48.

6. Fletcher, p. 21; see also Patterson, XVII, 430.

The quotations from Milton's poetry and prose are from the text of the first editions as given by Frank Allen Patterson in his *Student's Milton* (1947). Biblical chapter and verse references are incorporated into the text in parentheses as are line references to Milton's epic poems; all other documentation is included in the footnotes. Abbreviations of the names of the books of the Bible and of Milton's poems are confined to the notes and references and are those which are generally familiar.

As this study progresses, there is an ascending order of importance in the chapters, each succeeding chapter being more directly related to and shedding more light upon Milton's art. Milton is first seen as a Christian poet, believing in the Biblical basis of his subject and communicating the conviction of Biblical authority, of superhistorical reality, of Truth to his audience. Then the Milton of vast learning in the classical and Biblical languages is portrayed as he alludes to the Hebrew, Greek, and Latin Scriptures, with transliterations which he could depend on a select number of his "fit audience," those trained in the trilingual tradition of Oxford and Cambridge especially,[7] to recognize. Next Milton is presented as the epic dramatist, enhancing the dramatic force of his epics beyond anything that could have been accomplished on the stage by following to some extent the tradition of Biblical allusion for dramatic effect as it had been established on the Elizabethan stage by Marlowe and Shakespeare, and before them by the mystery plays. Finally Milton's peculiarly epic uses of the Bible are shown as aiding him in his achievement of the sublimity, variety, and thematic unity so vital to the literary epic. If the reader has occasionally been disconcerted by having to shuttle between the two epics in the earlier chapters, the revelation in this last chapter of the chain of thematic unity linking the two epics, together with the evidence of each preceding chapter that Milton's patterns of Biblical allusion are essentially the same in both, should assure him that the shuttling is a necessary evil which culminates in an appreciation of the two quite different poems as really two unified facets of Milton's one great justification of God's ways to men.

7. Daiches, *The King James Version*, pp. 142-43.

Appended is an index to the Biblical references in both epics with an indication of the editors who have noted each reference. The index has been made as complete as time, knowledge, and diligence allowed; it may well be the most useful part of this study for the student of Milton.

One question remains to be answered: What can the reader hope to gain from Milton's epic poems as a result of his perusal of this study? The answer is fourfold.

(1) A clearer sense of the aura of truth which Milton achieves by reference to Biblical authority both in those clearly Biblical parts of his epics and those invented parts imaginatively developed from germinal Bible texts.

(2) An increased aesthetic pleasure from and ethical insight into the poems resulting from recognition of Milton's linguistic knowledge and skill in alluding to the Bible in its original languages and in Latin.

(3) A more sensitive awareness of the dramatic power with which Milton used Biblical language in establishing setting and mood, conducting the present action and foreshadowing future action, and delineating character. (It is especially hoped that a sharper insight into the character and motivation of Satan, the Son, Adam, and Eve may result.)

(4) A greater appreciation of Milton as a creative artist building upon solid, traditional foundations of form and content two great literary works which are original in the best sense of the word (i. e., firmly rooted in the past while thrusting forth more highly and nobly than anything of its kind before or since) and which demonstrate a successful amalgamation of classical, Biblical, and original elements into a superbly unified epic style.

And now to a detailed consideration of Milton's poetic use of that

> truth
>
> . . . . . . . . . . . . . . . . . . . .
>
> Left onely in those written Records pure,
> Though not but by the Spirit understood.

# I

## *Authoritative Reality*

AMONG the many problems Milton faced in composing *Paradise Lost* and *Paradise Regained* were two which called upon his highest powers both as a poet and as a man of Biblical learning. These were the problem of making the persons seem real, even those whose otherworldly character removed them from the ordinary experience of the reader, and the problem of giving the stories a prevailingly Scriptural authoritativeness even when the poet's imagination took him far afield from actual Scripture.

The informed belief in the Bible held by practically everyone with any claim to literacy in the seventeenth century provided a remarkable opportunity for Milton to achieve the illusion of reality for his readers. Basil Willey has described this unique literary potential: "The traditional sources of poetry were running dry; mythologies were exploded and obsolete; no poet with Milton's passion for reality could pour all the energies of his nature into such moulds any longer. But there still remained one source, and one only, from which the seventeenth century protestant poet could draw images and fables which were not only 'poetic' but also 'true': the Bible. . . . Milton, together with nearly everyone else in his century, felt all proper contact with biblical material to be, in quite a special sense, contact with Truth."[1]

Although the modern reader has quite a different attitude, Milton can still achieve an illusion of reality and a persuasion of truth for one who will acquaint himself rather closely with the Bible and make a poetic "suspension of disbelief" which was once less necessary. It is especially true of *Paradise Lost,* but also true of *Paradise Regained,* that the convinced Christian who has a knowledge of the Scriptures as well as a cultivated literary taste will re-

1. *The Seventeenth Century Background* (New York 1953), pp. 226-227.

ceive the most instruction and delight from Milton. As Professor L. A. Cormican of Cambridge has said, "To endeavor to read him without any close acquaintance with the Bible is to evade the kind of preparation which he assumed." [2] Then, he adds: "The parallel between Milton and the Bible is true to this extent that it is only by an intensification of the religious spirit, as well as by expanding experience, that we can come to grasp the complexity of the great Psalm 22, the Lord's Prayer, or *Paradise Lost;* can we come to see explicitly what was before only implicit to our less developed religious sensibility." [3] Reading Milton with no knowledge of the Bible and no personal religious experience, continues Professor Cormican, is comparable to a child's reading *Romeo and Juliet;* having had no acquaintance with the passions of real love, the child is baffled. But there is this difference: though the child cannot enter imaginatively into an emotion which he has never experienced, there are even atheists and agnostics who have the necessary intellectual and aesthetic maturity to enter imaginatively into Milton's attempt to "justifie the wayes of God to men," and, if willing to suspend their disbelief in the dependability of the Bible, they may do so. Most modern readers who have such maturity and willingness to suspend disbelief however, lack knowledge of the Bible; and Biblical allusions can produce an effect only when recognized. By helping Milton's readers to recognize his allusions, this discussion may help Milton to achieve his effects for modern readers, and such readers may respond to a technique capable of persuading their imaginations of a reality like that of immediately important history.

Milton made his epics such virtual mosaics of Biblical echo, paraphrase, allusion, idiomatic structure, and tone that a reader steeped in the English Bible is subject to the illusion (received either consciously or unconsciously) that the author speaks with textual authority backing every phase of his poems. Thus, aside from providing the basic stories, the Bible and Biblical allusion work for Milton as means of making his action, characters, and

2. "Milton's Religious Verse," in *A Guide to English Literature: From Donne to Marvell,* ed. Boris Ford (London, 1956), p. 181.

3. *Ibid.,* p. 185.

setting believable, probable, and real, even in the invented parts of his great poems.

Milton's achievement in this respect is so successful that even unorthodox implications may be unnoticed. C. S. Lewis has remarked that generations of orthodox Christians have read *Paradise Lost* without realizing that it includes heretical doctrines, and one Roman Catholic sister has defended the orthodoxy of Milton's long epic from the point of view of a strict Trinitarian. Professor Lewis says, "Heretical elements exist in it, but are only discoverable by search: any criticism which forces them into the foreground is mistaken and ignores the fact that this poem was accepted by many generations of acute readers well grounded in theology."[4] Sister Miriam Joseph, C. S. C., says, "With respect to the three Persons of the Trinity and the work of creation . . . *Paradise Lost* seems in harmony with the teachings of Catholic theologians. Especially in expressing the equality of the Son with the Father, the poem appears to accord with Catholic dogma; at least, it would hardly lead the ordinary reader to suspect its author of the heresies he had set forth in *De Doctrina Christiana.*"[5] Milton's use of familiar Biblical language, especially in the speeches by and about the Father and the Son, probably accounts for such a reader's acceptance of *Paradise Lost* as orthodox.

Statements, phrases, or ideas which immediately suggest their Scriptural origin are abundant in both the epics. In the opening thirteen lines of *Paradise Lost,* for example,

> Of Mans First Disobedience, and the Fruit
> Of that Forbidden Tree, whose mortal tast
> Brought Death into the World, and all our woe,
> With loss of *Eden,* till one greater Man
> Restore us, and regain the blissful Seat,
> Sing Heav'nly Muse, that on the secret top
> Of *Oreb,* or of *Sinai,* didst inspire
> That Shepherd, who first taught the chosen Seed,
> In the Beginning how the Heav'ns and Earth
> Rose out of Chaos: or if *Sion* Hill
> Delight thee more, and *Siloa's* Brook that flow'd

4. *A Preface to Paradise Lost* (London, 1942), p. 81.
5. *Orthodoxy in Paradise Lost* (Quebec, 1954), p. 258.

> Fast by the Oracle of God; I thence
> Invoke thy aid to my adventrous Song,

there are allusions to no less than fifteen familiar Biblical passages.[6] These allusions develop early in the epic an aura of authoritative reality by placing the reader in contact with events belonging to particular places and persons in Scripture (Oreb, Sinai, Sion, Siloa, That Shepherd, chosen Seed, greater Man, Eden) and suggesting some of the central doctrines of Christianity (the Fall and consequent death, redemption by Christ, and an inspired revelation of God in the Bible). By concentrating in these opening lines references to such widely separated persons as Adam and Christ, Israel (the "chosen Seed" descended from Abraham and an ancestor of Christ who was himself called the "seed of the woman") and Moses, Milton is appealing to his readers to make a kind of connection which they were accustomed to make when they read the Bible or heard it expounded from the pulpit: a vertical or figural connection between events not horizontally or causally connected except as they were seen as stages in the history of man's salvation. For example, the disobedience of Adam in Eden, the receiving of the Law by Moses on Sinai, and the placing of the Ark of the Covenant in the Temple on "*Sion* Hill" are not causally connected as a horizontal chain of events, but the divine scheme of salvation as seen by centuries of Christians seeking to align the Old Testament with the New had vertically connected these events as successive stages in God's plan for man's redemption. Adam in Eden, Moses on Sinai, and the Temple on Sion are connected because each represents a particular phase of God's providential dealings with mankind: the Fall and its results, the Law which seals man's condemnation because he cannot keep it, and the Temple which represents a way of bringing sinful man and God into reconciliation. Erich Auerbach has happily phrased the force of such figural connections in the traditional concept of Old Testament unity: "The greater the separateness and horizontal disconnection of the stories and groups of stories in relation to one another, compared

6. Rom. 5:12, 19; Gen. 2:17; I Cor. 15:45, 47; Ps. 23:3; Exod. 34:2, 3; Exod. 3:1; Exod. 24:12-18; Gen. 1:1; John 1:1; Neh. 3:15; Isa. 8:6; Ps. 28:2; Ps. 2:6; Deut. 4:10; Exod. 19:18.

with the *Iliad* and the *Odyssey,* the stronger is their general vertical connection which holds them all together and which is entirely lacking in Homer. Each of the great figures of the Old Testament, from Adam to the prophets, embodies a moment of this vertical connection. God chose and formed these men to the end of embodying his essence and will—yet choice and formation do not coincide, for the latter proceeds gradually, historically, during the earthly life of him upon whom the choice has fallen."[7]

Thus in his opening lines Milton is establishing the atmosphere for the whole poem: an atmosphere in which on apparent Biblical authority every action, every speech, every description is part of a great system reaching back into the past of Chaos, Creation, and the Fall and forward into the working out of God's providence in Redemption and Restoration.

## *PARADISE LOST*

### *The Devil-Deities*

Biblical language adds authoritative reality to the theory that the fallen angels became the heathen deities of Hebrew antiquity. The devils assemble around Satan as "Powers that earst in Heaven sat on Thrones,

> Though of their Names in heav'nly Records now
> Be no memorial, blotted out and ras'd
> By thir Rebellion, from the Books of Life.
> Nor had they yet among the sons of *Eve*
> Got them new Names, till wandring ore the Earth,
> Through Gods high sufferance for the tryal of man,
> By falsities and lyes the greatest part
> Of Mankind they corrupted to forsake
> God their Creator, and th' invisible
> Glory of him, that made them, to transform
> Oft to the Image of a Brute, adorn'd
> With gay Religions full of Pomp and Gold,
> And Devils to adore for Deities:
> Then were they known to men by various Names,
> And various Idols through the Heathen World.
> (*P. L.*, I, 360-375)

7. *Mimesis: The Representation of Reality in Western Literature* (New York, 1957), p. 14.

Although there is no statement in the Bible that the fallen angels became heathen gods, Milton's use of the traditional explanation is acceptable to those who believe that the Biblical Jehovah is the only true God, and important to acceptance of this explanation are the Biblical language and allusions. The concept of a Book of Life out of which one's name may be blotted is Biblical. The Biblical statement, however, concerns those who overcome temptation or defilement and thus will *not* have their names blotted out; Milton simply reverses the situation to make it appropriate to the fallen angels. The emphasis upon the names has an ironic effect when one remembers that the Biblical overcomers of evil are given new names in Heaven (Rev. 3:12b), while these fallen angels "Got them new Names" upon earth through the evil of pagan idolatry. "Thou hast a few names even in Sardis, which have not defiled their garments, and they shall walk with me in white: for they are worthy. He that overcometh, the same shall be clothed in white raiment; and I will not blot out his name out of the booke of life, but I will confess his name before my Father, and before his Angels" (Rev. 3:4, 5). Another reference (l. 361) includes the idea of the destruction of even the memory of the names cast out by God. "Thou hast rebuked the heathen, thou hast destroyed the wicked; thou hast put out their name for ever and ever.... Their memoriall is perished with them" (Ps. 9:5, 6b). The phrase "wandering ore the Earth, / Through Gods high sufferance for the tryal of man" recalls the story of God's suffering Satan in his wanderings "to and fro in the earth" to try Job's patience and faith (Job 1:7; 2:2); the fact that the greatest part of mankind, unlike Job, was corrupted and forsook God for these devilish deities is more understandable when Milton's phrase "the Sons of *Eve*" is considered together with his earlier statement (l. 36) that it was the "Mother of Mankinde" who was deceived by the serpent. The Pauline explanation of pagan deterioration from the knowledge of the true God to beast worship is alluded to in lines 367-371; the Gentiles, says Paul, "changed the glory of the uncorruptible God, unto an image made like to corruptible man, and to birds, and fourefooted beasts, and creeping things... [and] changed the trueth of God into a lie, and worshipped and served the creature more than the Creatour" (Rom. 1:23, 25). But Milton's crowning Biblical authority in this passage from *Paradise Lost* is suggested by the alliterative line "And Devils to adore for Deities," for here he alludes to a clear Scriptural precedent for identifying heathen gods with devils. From the Biblical passage the idea could be deduced that idolatry resulted from the activity of devils. Moses spoke of those who had turned from Jehovah to other gods as those who "sacrificed unto devils, not to God" (Deut. 32:17), and Paul added New Testament force to the idea by contrasting the worship of Christians with the worship of Gentiles. "The things which the Gentiles sacrifice, they sacrifice to devils, and not to God: and I would not that yee should have fellowship with devils. Ye cannot drinke the cup of the Lord, and the cup of devils: ye cannot bee partakers of the Lords Table, and of the table of devils" (I Cor. 10:20-21).

It is only after having made this strong appeal to Biblical authority that Milton turns to his Muse in a parenthetical invocation for the knowledge of these devils' names; and, of course, since they are provided by the Spirit, the names and the descriptions correspond to the most prominent false gods in Scripture. But "After these" (l. 476) appear those whose Scriptural authority is not so clear: the "bleating Gods" of Egypt, Belial who has no temple or altar of his own, and "Th' Ionian Gods, of *Javans* Issue held / Gods" (ll. 508-509). Milton carefully separates that which is based on reasonable Biblical authority from that which has no authority or doubtful authority. Although Javan's (son of Japheth) issue "held" as "Gods" the Olympian crew, Biblical grounds are insufficient for Milton to commit himself unreservedly to the proposition that the Ionian gods were among the crew in Hell. In the description of the Greek gods, therefore, there is no appeal to authoritative reality as there is in the description of gods clearly mentioned in the Bible—or even of those not mentioned (Osiris, Isis, Orus) when it may be reasonably assumed that the worship of such deities in Egypt resulted in Israel's worship of the golden calf on Mount Horeb. Yet because of Ezekiel's reference to him (Ezek. 8:13-14) even Thammuz (Adonis) takes his place among the devil-deities.

Biblical truth, and thus Biblical authority, comes sometimes from strange lips. Satan and his cohorts often pervert the Scriptures, as might be expected; but they sometimes speak the truth, and Milton gives the Biblical clues that communicate the conviction that truth is being spoken. When Beelzebub, Satan's second in command, rises to present the Satanic policy of indirect war by guile, he refers to

> another World, the happy seat
> Of som new Race call'd *Man,* about this time
> To be created like to us, though less
> In power and excellence, but favour'd more
> Of him who rules above; so was his will
> Pronounc'd among the Gods, and by an Oath,
> That shook Heav'ns whol circumference, confirm'd.
> (*P. L.*, II, 347-353)

The statement that God's will to make man was confirmed by an oath which shook Heaven has the authority of Biblical language: "Wherein God willing more abundantly to shewe unto the heyres of promise the immutabilitie of his counsell, confirmed *it* by an oath" (Heb. 6:17); "Whose voice then shooke the earth, but now hath promised, saying, Yet once more I shake not the earth only, but also heaven" (Heb. 12:26). Milton has here combined the language of two texts which in themselves have no connection with the creation of the world or of man. The first text refers to God's promising Abraham a blessing upon all his posterity, and the second to the consummation of all things at the return of Christ to the earth; both are taken out of context to add to the authoritativeness and convincing power of Beelzebub's speech. There is an allusion here, however, to another text which does concern the making of a man, a text which, if it is considered a Messianic prophecy, adds dramatic irony to Beelzebub's speech: "I will make a man more precious than fine gold; even a man than the golden wedge of Ophir. Therefore I will shake the heavens" (Isa. 13:12-13). This reference is not noted by any of Milton's editors, although it seems more appropriate to Beelzebub's speech than others which are noted.

Beelzebub, "Majestic though in ruin," is frank and straightforward, facing the truth that war against Heaven cannot prevail and that God will not ignore the devils' efforts to build up a rival empire. Of God he says,

> For he, be sure
> In highth or depth, still first and last will Reign
> Sole King, and of his Kingdom loose no part
> By our revolt, but over Hell extend
> His Empire, and with Iron Scepter rule
> Us here, as with his Golden those in Heav'n.
> (*P. L.*, II, 323-328)

This is Biblical truth and it is truth spoken in Biblical language. "I am Alpha and Omega, the beginning and the end, the first and the last" (Rev. 22:13); "Thy throne (O God) *is* for ever and ever: the sceptre of thy kingdome is a right sceptre" (Ps. 45:6); "Thou shalt breake them with a rod of yron; thou shalt dash them in pieces like a potters vessell" (Ps. 2:9): these texts are echoed in Beelzebub's official statement of the fallen host's future line of attack, a statement which defines the scope and limitations of the future action of God's enemies and convinces the reader as well as the devils, but on a different level: the reader recognizes, through Biblical allusion, the truth that God will ultimately vanquish evil, while the devils are unaware of it. Even Beelzebub's final barb, shot at the preceding speakers, though it is meant to prick them into agreement, is feathered with Biblical language that makes it lethal to the devils' hope of success.

> Advise if this be worth
> Attempting, or to sit in darkness here
> Hatching vain Empires.
> (*P. L.*, II, 376-378)

The psalmist speaks of "such as sit in darknesse and in the shadow of death: being bound in affliction and yron: because they rebelled against the words of God: and contemned the counsel of the most high" (Ps. 107: 10-11). For the devils Beelzebub's conclusion sums up in a vivid image the ridiculousness of Mammon's counsel, which has so recently seemed superior to that of Moloch and Belial; for the reader the conclusion suggests the ultimate fate of all rebels against God. After having thus suggested that Beelzebub's counsel will also, in time, be vain, Milton carefully states:

But their Spite still serves
His glory to augment.
(*P. L.*, II, 385-386)

This is the *ad majorem Dei gloriam* theme stated in non-Biblical language; as a Christian truth it is easily acceptable to those familiar with the psalmist's words, "Surely the wrath of man shall praise thee: the remainder of wrath shalt thou restrain" (Ps. 76:10), and with the words Joseph spoke to his brothers upon confronting them years after they had sold him into slavery, "But as for you, ye thought evil against me: *but* God meant it unto good" (Gen. 50:20a).[8]

*The Holy Trinity*

Biblical allusion gives the authority of reality to scenes other than those in Hell and to characters other than those seen there. As individuals in the vast drama of *Paradise Lost,* even the Persons of the Trinity require authentic credentials. Both statements and implications made about the Holy Spirit in the opening of Book I are soundly Scripture-based.

And chiefly Thou O Spirit, that dost prefer
Before all Temples th' upright heart and pure,
Instruct me, for Thou know'st; Thou from the first
Wast present.
(*P. L.*, I, 17-20)

"Temples" recalls the Biblical image of man's body as the temple of the Spirit: "your body is the Temple of the Holy Ghost, *which is* in you, which ye have of God" (I Cor. 6:19). Paul said that his instructor was the Spirit; he wrote his epistles "not in the words which man's wisdome teacheth, but which the holy Ghost teacheth" (I Cor. 2:13). The Spirit alone knows the things of God (I Cor. 2:11b) and was present from the beginning (Gen. 1:2). Thus Milton's phrasing strikes a responsive chord in the mind of the reader who knows the Bible, and, subliminal or not, the reader's

8. The allusions pointed out in Beelzebub's speech characterize the speaker, foreshadow future action, and provide thematic statement as well as give authority to the speech; such overlapping of function, to be expected in the work of a master of the Bible like Milton, sometimes causes categorization of his allusions to be arbitrary. A definite pattern is discernible, however, and provides the basis for the organization of this study.

response is made as to one who speaks not fancifully but authoritatively. Further, when Milton refers to the Spirit as one from whom neither Heaven nor Hell can hide anything (I, 27-28), the words of the psalmist to the Spirit of God may be recalled: "If I ascend up into heaven, thou art there; if I make my bed in hell, behold, thou *art there*" (Ps. 139:8).

Restating the theme of his own ultimate victory over Satan, God the Father addresses his "Onely begotten Son" (l. 80; John 1:18) and says of Satan:

> bent he seems
> On desperat revenge, that shall redound
> Upon his own rebellious head.
> (*P. L.*, III, 84-86)

The Biblical expression is so common as to be unmistakable.[9] Such an expression is, "His mischiefe shall returne upon his owne head, & his violent dealing shal come downe upon his owne pate" (Ps. 7:16). When God says of man,

> I made him just and right,
> Sufficient to have stood, though free to fall,
> (*P. L.*, III, 98-99)

He is exonerating himself from any fault in the forthcoming Fall in the language of the Preacher of Ecclesiastes, "God hath made man upright: but they have sought out many inventions" (Eccles. 7:29).

In all the utterances of both the Father and the Son in Book III much specifically Scriptural language is used. Prophesying the Resurrection and his triumph over death and the grave, the Son says:

> Though now to Death I yeild, and am his due
> All that of me can die, yet that debt paid,
> Thou wilt not leave me in the loathsom grave
> His prey, nor suffer my unspotted Soule
> For ever with corruption there to dwell;
> But I shall rise Victorious, and subdue
> My Vanquisher, spoild of his vanted spoile;
> Death his deaths wound shall then receive, & stoop

9. I Sam. 25:39; II Chron. 6:23; Neh. 4:4; Esther 9:25; Ezek. 9:10, 11:21; Joel 3:4; Judg. 9:57.

Inglorious, of his mortall sting disarm'd.
I through the ample Air in Triumph high
Shall lead Hell Captive maugre Hell, and show
The powers of darkness bound. Thou at the sight
Pleas'd, out of Heaven shalt look down and smile,
While by thee rais'd I ruin all my Foes,
Death last, and with his Carcass glut the Grave.
(*P. L.*, III, 245-259)

The words of a Messianic psalm in which David, in the person of Christ, prophesies, "For thou wilt not leave my soule in hell; neither wilt thou suffer thine Holy one to see corruption" (Ps. 16:10) are here blended with Paul's statement that Christ "spoyled principalities and powers . . . triumphing over them" (Col. 2:15), with Paul's image of sin as "the sting of death" (I Cor. 15:56), with his portrayal of Christ in his ascension as having "led captivity captive" (Eph. 4:8), with his statement that the "last enemy *that* shall bee destroyed, *is* death" (I Cor. 15:26), and with his description of all the powers opposing God as the "powers of darknesse" (Col. 1:13). Then, a few lines later, the Son concludes with another allusion to the same Messianic psalm when he says to the Father that he will ultimately enjoy "in thy presence Joy entire" (l. 265), alluding to "In thy presence is fulnes of joy" (Ps. 16:11). Of course, one may not recognize all these references as one reads, but the origin of one's conviction that truth has been expressed lies in the poet's careful interweaving of Biblical language.

The hymns of the angels include a great deal of Biblical allusion. After God the Father has given a résumé, practically all in Biblical phraseology, of Christ's work from the Fall to the rising of the New Heaven and New Earth, the angels "introduce / Thir sacred Song" (ll. 368-369).

Thee Father first they sung Omnipotent,
Immutable, Immortal, Infinite,
Eternal King; thee Author of all being,
Fountain of Light, thy self invisible
Amidst the glorious brightness where thou sit'st
Thron'd inaccessible, but when thou shad'st
The full blaze of thy beams, and through a cloud
Drawn round about thee like a radiant Shrine,

Dark with excessive bright thy skirts appeer,
Yet dazle Heav'n, that brightest Seraphim
Approach not, but with both wings veil thir eyes.
Thee next they sang of all Creation first,
Begotten Son, Divine Similitude,
In whose conspicuous count'nance, without cloud
Made visible, th' Almighty Father shines,
Whom else no Creature can behold; on thee
Impresst the effulgence of his Glorie abides,
Transfus'd on thee his ample Spirit rests.
(*P. L.*, III, 372-389)

In the portion of this angelic hymn addressed to the Father (ll. 372-382), Milton has combined the song of the heavenly multitude in the Apocalypse, "Alleluia: for the Lord God omnipotent reigneth" (Rev. 19:6), with Paul's doxologies "unto the King eternal, immortal, invisible" (I Tim. 1:17) "who only hath immortalitie, dwelling in the light, which no man can approach unto, whom no man hath seene, nor can see" (I Tim. 6:16), and with Isaiah's vision of the wing-veiled seraphim before the throne of God (Isa. 6:2). Then the Son is hymned (ll. 383-389) in phrases reminiscent of Paul's description of Christ as the one in whose face the knowledge of the glory of God shines (II Cor. 4:6) and of John's phrase "onely begotten Sonne" (John 1:18, 3:16). From John also come the ideas of God's being visible only through the Son ("No man hath seene God at any time: the onely begotten Sonne, which is in the bosom of the Father, he hath declared him" [John 1:18]) and of Christ's having the fullness of the Spirit ("For God giveth not the Spirit by measure *unto him*" [John 3:34]).

*Eden and Its Inhabitants*

In the first three books of *Paradise Lost* details of scenery are authoritatively established. Hell's burning lake, chains, and darkness are all, of course, based on the Bible picture of Hell; Heaven's golden streets (so closely viewed by Mammon), God's throne, the angels' harps, and the sea of jasper are likewise Scriptural. It is in Book IV, however, that Milton shows to greatest advantage his ability to permeate a scene and its characters with an air of immediate Biblical reality while using his creative imagination as freely as he had done in the scenes in Heaven and in Hell. There Eden is first seen through the eyes of Satan, and described both through him and directly by the poet, it becomes a real place, with key points in the description firmly tied to the authority of Genesis.

T. S. Eliot has commented on the vagueness and generality of Milton's description of Eden, a generality which Mr. Eliot praises for its effect on the reader while he censures Milton (by implication at least) for not having had greater powers of visual description. Mr. Eliot seems to feel that Milton's faults became his virtues (which shows one way of revising one's critical opinions about a great poet without having to retract any specific criticisms of his poetry); Milton's "limited interest in human beings . . . turns out to be a positive virtue, when we visit Adam and Eve in Eden," and his "weakness of visual observation," while it keeps us from seeing Eden clearly, results in an emphasis on sound of which the end is "the unique versification that is the most certain sign of Milton's intellectual mastership." As for Eden, "a more vivid picture of the earthly Paradise would have been less paradisiacal. For a greater definiteness, a more detailed account of flora and fauna, could only have assimilated Eden to the landscapes of earth with which we are familiar. As it is, the impression of Eden which we retain is the most suitable, and is that which Milton was most qualified to give: the impression of *light*—a daylight and a starlight, a light of dawn and of dusk, the light which, remembered by a man in his blindness, has a supernatural glory unexperienced by men of normal vision."[10]

Actually Milton has given the Garden of Eden a convincing reality for the Bible-oriented reader by using highly specific detail drawn from the Genesis account and expanded by his imagination. (Certainly the Genesis account contains about as little as any artist ever had to go on, short of having no model at all except in his mind.) Compared to the Garden of Genesis, the poet's is anything but vague and general. From a sun-based astronomer's telescopic view of Earth, Paradise, and Adam's bower, Milton brings Satan (and the reader) gradually closer untill the individual kinds of

10. *Milton: Annual Lecture on a Master Mind,* in Proceedings of the British Academy, XXIII (London, 1947), 11-12.

trees ("Cedar, and Pine, and Firr, and branching Palm" [l. 139]) can be identified, still closer so that the brilliant, "gay enameld" colors of the blossoming and fruit-bearing trees can be seen, and even closer until the "balmie spoiles" (l. 159) can be smelled. Disdaining to enter the gate, the "first grand Thief" leaps over the wall of trees into "Gods Fould"; once he is inside, the description begins to take on Scriptural authority. Satan alights atop the Tree of Life, described as the "middle Tree and highest there that grew" (l. 195), since the Biblical account places the Tree of Life in the "midst of the garden" (Gen. 2:9). Here Biblical authority adds weight to a Miltonic idea. The Bible does not describe the Tree of Life as the highest; yet the description seems right because of its conjunction with "middle." The poet, giving careful attention to the text, makes a distinction that many preachers did not (and do not) make: the Garden is not identical with Eden, it is *in* Eden:

> for blissful Paradise
> Of God the Garden was, by him in the East
> Of *Eden* planted.
>
> (*P. L.*, IV, 209-211)

"And the LORD God planted a garden Eastward in Eden" (Gen. 2:8).

Remembering that the meaning of the Hebrew word transliterated "Eden" is "pleasant," Milton says:

> in this pleasant soile
> His farr more pleasant Garden God ordained;
> Out of the fertil ground he caus'd to grow
> All Trees of noblest kind for sight, smell, taste;
> And all amid them stood the Tree of Life,
> High eminent, blooming Ambrosial Fruit
> Of vegetable Gold; and next to Life
> Our Death the Tree of Knowledge grew fast by,
> Knowledge of Good bought dear by knowing ill.
> Southward through *Eden* went a River large
> . . . . . . . . . . . . . . . . . . . .
> and with many a rill
> Waterd the Garden; thence united fell
> Down the steep glade, and met the neather Flood,
> . . . . . . . . . . . . . . . . . . . .

And now divided into four main Streams,
Runs divers, wandring many a famous Realme.
(*P. L.*, IV, 215-223, 229-231, 233-234)

How carefully this description is based on Scripture and how beautifully the poet visualized and expressed the Scriptural account are evident when the poetry is compared with the original: "And out of the ground made the LORD God to grow every tree that is pleasant to the sight, and good for food; the tree of life also in the midst of the garden, and the tree of knowledge of good and evill. And a river went out of Eden to water the garden, and from thence it was parted and became into foure heads" (Gen. 2:9-10). Although this passage is followed in Genesis by an account of the four streams and the lands through which they flowed and one can imagine the wonderfully sonorous passage he could have created with the names of the rivers, lands, and minerals of Genesis 2:11-14, Milton exercised restraint because of these things one "here needs no account" (l. 235). Since the account needed is "to tell how, if Art could tell, / . . . the crisped Brooks, / . . . Ran Nectar, visiting each plant, and fed, / Flours worthy of Paradise" (ll. 236-237, 240-241), the poet's love of sound is not allowed to deflect him from his main purpose. And it is not just the sound that Milton gives up by omission; more authoritativeness could be given his poetic account by a listing of the Biblical rivers and the lands they watered. But attention is to be focused on the Garden, on Paradise, not on lands outside, and enough authority is provided without sacrificing that focus. A slight touch like "Flours of all hue, and without Thorn the Rose" (l. 256) communicates the necessary reality, for the reader (whether or not he consciously thinks of it) knows that "thorns . . . and thistles" were the result of the Fall (Gen. 3:18).[11]

Satan also furnishes the first view of Adam and Eve. As a supernatural being, lately a resident of Heaven, and consequently a better judge of man's Godlikeness than the poet or the reader,

11. G. W. Whiting has shown in his note, "And without Thorn the Rose," *RES*, X (1959), 60-62, that Milton's precedent for this idea had been set by St. Basil and St. Ambrose, who used the thornless rose as a symbol of the sinless state of man before the Fall. "The rose with thorns is a symbol of the troubles, anxieties, the pains that inevitably and justly afflict man in his fallen condition" (p. 62).

he recognizes immediately "in thir looks Divine / The image of thir glorious Maker" (ll. 291-292), a phrase which echoes "So God created man in his owne Image, in the Image of God created he him; male and female created he them" (Gen. 1:27). Then, as in the Genesis account where the general statement of the creation of mankind as male and female is followed by a detailed account of the creation of Adam and Eve, Milton follows the general statement that the image of God shone in both Adam and Eve by a detailed explanation of the person of each. The repetition of "seemd" (ll. 290, 291, 296) keeps the reader conscious that Satan is the observer; the "seemd" is then dropped and the poet himself speaks of the difference in the outward appearance of the pair, a difference which symbolizes man's superior nature: "Hee for God only, shee for God in him" (l. 299). As in his description of the Garden, Milton gives the reader a visual impression of the human pair to be maintained throughout the poem; thus he emphasizes man's headship over woman with an image of the two which stresses the appearance of their hair. The Puritans of Milton's "fit audience" certainly would not have missed the point here, and neither does the modern reader who knows the Bible. Adam's "Hyacinthin Locks / Round from his parted forelock manly hung / Clustering, but not beneath his shoulders broad" (ll. 301-303). Of Eve, Milton says,

> Shee as a vail down to the slender waste
> Her unadorned golden tresses wore
> Dissheveld, but in wanton ringlets wav'd
> As the Vine curles her tendrils, which impli'd
> Subjection.
>
> (*P. L.*, IV, 304-308)

In the New Testament Paul stated that woman's subjection is symbolized by her long hair. "But I would have you know, that the head of every man is Christ: and the head of the woman is the man, and the head of Christ is God. . . . The woman is the glory of the man. . . . Neither was the man created for the woman: but the woman for the man. For this cause ought the woman to have power [Authorized Version margin, 'That is, a covering in signe that she is under the power of her husband'] on her head, because of the Angels.... Doeth not even nature it selfe teach you, that if a man have long haire, it is a shame unto him? But if a woman have long haire, it is a glory to her: for her haire is given her for a covering" (I Cor. 11:3, 7, 9-10, 14-15). By reference to the Bible, Milton makes the reader aware of the divine order of the sexes and thus foreshadows the means by which Satan will manage to separate them. After her Satan-induced dream in which she imagines herself eating the forbidden fruit, it is Eve's unwillingness to remain subject to and dependent upon Adam that causes her to leave his side and to have to face alone the Tempter's wiles.

In alluding thus to a passage of Scripture stating that the hair length of men and women is symbolic of the divine order of male and female, Milton is, of course, projecting New Testament standards, and seventeenth century Puritan standards, back to the innocent pair in the Garden of Eden before the Fall; but by so doing, he communicates all that has been indicated and perhaps more. Certainly by such a projection he could, for his generation, add to the description not only Biblical authority but also reality: Adam and Eve are the perfect, sinless example of what a Christian husband and wife should be. The poet similarly projects New Testament standards back to the Garden of Eden when he describes the connubial love of the innocent pair, who

> eas'd the putting off
> These troublesom disguises which wee wear,
> Strait side by side were laid, nor turnd I weene
> *Adam* from his fair Spouse, nor *Eve* the Rites
> Mysterious of connubial Love refus'd.
> (*P. L.*, IV, 739-743)

"Rites / Mysterious" recalls Paul's statement, "For this cause shall a man leave his father and mother, and shalbe joyned unto his wife, and they two shalbe one flesh. This is a great mysterie: but I speake concerning Christ and the Church" (Eph. 5:31-32). Perhaps because of his own experience, perhaps not, Milton is assuming that our first parents maintained by instinct and mutual love a principle Paul laid down for Christian marriage. "The wife hath not power of her owne body, but the husband; and likewise also the husband hath not power of his owne body, but the wife.

Defraud you not one the other, except *it bee* with consent for a time, that ye may give yourselves to fasting and prayer, and come together againe, that Satan tempt you not for your incontinencie" (I Cor. 7:4-5).

Throughout the indignant indictment of those who bid men abstain from marriage and throughout the apostrophe to wedded love which follow the scene in which Adam and Eve retire for the night, appropriate allusions add Biblical authority to Milton's views on marriage. Especially interesting are the statements used to defend his placing of the sexual relationship in Paradise against those hyprocrites who "austerely talk / Of puritie and place and innocence" (ll. 744-745) and against those who assign sexual love to the period after the Fall rather than before. When Milton says, "Our Maker bids increase, who bids abstain / But our Destroyer, foe to God and Man?" (ll. 748-749) he is presenting an allusion to God's command which antedated both Temptation and Fall, "Be fruitfull and multiply" (Gen. 1:28), apparently considering this command a more important argument for including wedded love in Paradise than the statement that Adam knew Eve after their expulsion (Gen. 4:1) is for excluding it. He all but quotes Scripture. Speaking of "wedded Love," he says,

> Farr be it, that I should write thee sin or blame,
> Or think thee unbefitting holiest place,
> Perpetual Fountain of Domestic sweets,
> Whose Bed is undefil'd and chast pronounc't,
> Present, or past, as Saints and Patriarchs us'd.
> (*P. L.*, IV, 758-762)

The writer of the Epistle to the Hebrews says, "Marriage *is* honorable in all, and the bed undefiled" (Heb. 13:4), and that Milton interprets the statement as pronouncing the marriage bed chaste for present or past shows that his projection of New Testament standards of Christian morality back to Paradise, though anachronistic, is deliberate. The last part of Hebrews 13:4—"but whoremongers and adulterers God will judge"—may have inspired Milton's condemnation of "the bought smile / Of Harlots" (ll. 765-766) which immediately follows his praise of married love.

Such allusions placing Adam and Eve's relationship in alignment with New Testament (and seventeenth century Christian) concepts of the order of the sexes and the marriage relationship were doubtless intended to suggest to Milton's audience a convincing contemporary reality. At the same time, these allusions to the "Rites / Mysterious" establish a vertical or figural connection between the pair in Paradise and Christ as the Bridegroom of his bride, the Church.

### *Raphael's Narration*

For his initial description of communication between heavenly beings and those of earth, Milton seems to depart from the Genesis account in which God is the first communicant with man (Gen. 2:16-17) because earliest in the poem comes the conversation between Adam and the angel Raphael. In the total scheme of *Paradise Lost,* however, Milton does follow Genesis, for Adam later reveals to Raphael (Book VIII) that his first conversation with a heavenly being was with God. In artistically unfolding the great drama, Milton chose to build towards a climax by revealing the human pair conversing, then the communication between man and the "sociable Spirit" Raphael, and finally the conversation between Adam and his Maker.

In the poem the visit of Raphael serves many purposes: it presents God as giving man every possible forewarning of the danger of disobedience, it prepares the reader for more extraordinary contact between human and divine actors, it provides a means for describing the events leading up to Satan's fall, and, perhaps most important, it provides Biblical authority for a fundamental philosophic assumption of the poem: that divine events must be described in material terms. Raphael says,[12]

12. James Holly Hanford (*A Milton Handbook* [4th ed.; New York, 1954], p. 205) says of Raphael's speech: "The philosophic assumption which underlies the narrative and indeed Milton's whole conception of his poem, is given in lines 563-577. Spiritual facts can only be so represented to human sense, but there is also a real analogy between earth and Heaven, the former being, according to the Platonic doctrine of ideas, an imperfect replica of the latter, and this analogy justifies the phrasing of divine events in material terms." Milton has behind him, in addition to Plato, the authority of the writer of Hebrews, whose description of the earthly temple and priesthood in comparison to the heavenly sanctuary and Christ as the eternal Priest is in terms of "the example and shadow of heavenly things" (Heb. 8:5).

> what surmounts the reach
> Of human sense, I shall delineate so,
> By lik'ning spiritual to corporal forms,
> As may express them best, though what if Earth
> Be but the shaddow of Heav'n, and things therein
> Each to other like, more then on earth is thought?
> (*P. L.*, V, 571-576)

To provide a rationale for this assumption Milton has Raphael partake of a meal with Adam and Eve; the angel's capacity for material food demonstrates his own materiality, though it is of a different consistency from Adam's. It is interesting to trace Milton's Biblical allusions in support of a doctrine of spiritual materiality.

When God calls Raphael to Him and sends him to forewarn Adam, the archangel is described, in accord with the familiar story in the Apocrypha, as "the sociable Spirit, that deign'd / To travel with *Tobias,* and secur'd / His marriage with the seaventimes-wedded Maid" (*P. L.*, V, 221-223). Here Milton is using the authority of canonical Scripture in contrast to the Apocrypha. Wishing to establish the basic material similarity of men, angels, and all created things, he alludes to the Apocryphal story often used to deny just such material similarity of angels and men. The reason for such an allusion becomes evident when Milton, who has already drawn on Scriptural authority by references to the angels' visit to Abraham when Sarah prepared food for them and "they did eat" (Gen. 18:1-8; *P. L.*, V, 299-313, 359-360), refers to "the common gloss / Of Theologians" (ll. 435-436) that angels do not really eat but merely seem to do so. For such a gloss the theologians usually depended on Raphael's statement to Tobias, "I did neither eat nor drinke, but yee did see a vision" (Tob. 12:19). Raphael's denial of having really assimilated food was accompanied by the solemn declaration, "I am Raphael, one of the seven holy Angels, which present the prayers of the Saints, and which goe in and out before the glory of the Holy one" (Tob. 12:15). Since this declaration did not prevent Milton's portrayal of the same angel as really eating the fruits of Paradise just as Adam ate them, it is clear that the poet rejected the authority of the Apocryphal story.

So down they sat,
And to their viands fell, nor seemingly
The Angel, nor in mist, the common gloss
Of Theologians, but with keen dispatch
Of real hunger, and concoctive heate
To transubstantiate.[13]

(*P. L.*, V, 433-438)

After their meal Adam inquires further about the comparative quality of human and angelic feasts, giving Raphael opportunity to discourse on the relationship of body and spirit.

O *Adam*, one Almightie is, from whom
All things proceed, and up to him return,
If not deprav'd from good, created all
Such to perfection, one first matter all
Indu'd with various forms, various degrees
Of substance, and in things that live, of life;
But more refin'd, more spiritous, and pure,
As neerer to him plac't or neerer tending
Each in thir several active Sphears assignd,
Till body up to spirit work, in bounds
Proportiond to each kind. So from the root
Springs lighter the green stalk, from thence the leaves
More aerie, last the bright consummate floure
Spirits odorous breathes: flours and thir fruit
Mans nourishment, by gradual scale sublim'd
To vital Spirits aspire, to animal,
To intellectual, give both life and sense,
Fansie and understanding, whence the soule
Reason receives, and reason is her being,

13. An excellent summary discussion of the background of Milton's doctrine that angels actually eat and assimilate human food into their bodies is that by Robert H. West in his *Milton and the Angels* (Athens, Ga., 1955), pp. 164-169. Professor West sees Milton as, like Robert Fludd, using this point in angelology "to support a contention larger than angelology": that nature's scale rises in a telescoping succession in which the higher comprehends the lower and the whole of the lower may be translated into the higher. If man had not fallen, he might have eventually turned "all to Spirit," Raphael tells Adam (V, 497), and with such a conception of the universe, it is to Milton's advantage to picture Raphael assimilating human food. His reference to "the common gloss / Of Theologians" is shown by Professor West to be a glance at the Church Fathers and practically all their successors, both Catholic and Protestant, except Robert Fludd, since all of them had felt it necessary to explain away the angels' eating at Abraham's tent (Gen. 18:1-8) by reference to Raphael's explanation to Tobias that his eating was not actual but merely visionary (Tob. 12:19).

Discursive, or Intuitive; discourse
Is oftest yours, the latter most is ours,
Differing but in degree, of kind the same.
Wonder not then, what God for you saw good
If I refuse not, but convert, as you,
To proper substance; time may come when men
With Angels may participate, and find
No inconvenient Diet, nor too light Fare:
And from these corporal nutriments perhaps
Your bodies may at last turn all to Spirit,
Improv'd by tract of time, and wingd ascend
Ethereal, as wee, or may at choice
Here or in Heav'nly Paradises dwell;
If ye be found obedient, and retain
Unalterably firm his love entire
Whose progenie you are.

(*P. L.*, V, 469-503)

This passage begins with an allusion to the Biblical statement that "of him, and through him, and to him, are all things" (Rom. 11:36) and expands that idea into a conception of an unbroken continuum of matter "Differing but in degree, of kind the same," except, of course, for the exclusion of that which is "deprav'd from good" from returning to God.

In Henry John Todd's edition of *Paradise Lost*, Bishop Newton is quoted as saying that this passage, though probably based on the fifteenth chapter of First Corinthians, contradicts the principle of boundaries between species or kinds. Commenting on lines 478 and following, the bishop says: "This notion of matter refining into spirit is by no means observing *the bounds proportion'd to each kind.* I suppose, he meant it as a comment on the doctrine of a natural body changed into a spiritual body, as in I Cor. xv, and perhaps borrowed some of it from his systems of divinity. For Milton, as he was too much of a materialist in his philosophy, so he was too much of a systematist in his divinity."[14] But if one understands Milton's qualification to the continuum from body to spirit ("if not deprav'd from good") and if it is remembered that I Corinthians 15 is written not to the innocent Adam but to fallen men who have been redeemed, one can harmonize this passage

14. *The Poetical Works of John Milton* (London, 1801), II, 385. (Note on *P. L.*, V, 478 ff.)

with Paul's contrast of the earthly and the heavenly; if sin had not entered, and death by sin, Raphael's prediction might well have come true. And the message of Pauline Christianity is that through Redemption and Resurrection, "as we have borne the image of the earthly, we shall also beare the image of the heavenly" (I Cor. 15:49), thus fulfilling Raphael's prediction ultimately, although not by the means of human obedience. The Biblical allusions of Raphael's discourse implicitly foreshadow the grace of God bringing good out of the sin of man. When Raphael says, "Your bodies may at last turn all to Spirit . . . If ye be found obedient" the reader realizes, as he recognizes the allusion to I Corinthians, that in spite of man's disobedience, through God's grace and the obedience of Christ on behalf of man, the body of a believer who dies "is sowen a naturall body, it is raised a spirituall bodie" (I Cor. 15:44). The image of the root, stalk, leaves, and flowers in Raphael's discourse may have been suggested by the Biblical image of the Resurrection: "that which thou sowest, thou sowest not that body that shall be, but bare grain, it may chance of wheat, or of some other graine: but God giveth it a body as it hath pleased him, & to every seed his own body" (I Cor. 15:37-38).

Bishop Newton apparently read the chapter from Paul's epistle as setting up a dichotomy between body and spirit, natural and spiritual, terrestrial and celestial, earthly and heavenly, while Milton read it as suggesting the possibility of rising from a lower form to a higher. Since God has promised, in the Bible, such a possibility of ascension in form to fallen and redeemed man, it is logical to assume, as Milton did, that such a possibility was held out to unfallen man. Finally, the reminder to Adam of his own dignity and divine origin in the phrase "Whose progenie you are" echoes Paul's "For we are all his offspring" (Acts 17:28b), stated in a sermon on the Resurrection. The general effect of the Biblical allusions here is a feeling of sadness (since it is known that man will not be obedient) at the thought of what "might have been" for Adam and his posterity; this sadness, however, is mixed with intimations of hope for a better future for redeemed and resurrected man. Perhaps more important to the reader's acceptance of the material war of spirits to be related in Books V and VI, the philosophical basis on which spiritual forms are to be likened to corporal forms, the possibility that "Earth / Be but the shaddow of Heav'n, and things therein / Each to other like, more then on earth is thought," has been given some degree of Biblical authoritative reality.

When the Son of God goes forth to war on the third day of the battle in Heaven, his chariot ("The Chariot of Paternal Deitie") is described by Raphael in the language of Ezekiel's vision by the river Chebar.

> Wheele within Wheel undrawn,
> It self instinct with Spirit, but convoy'd
> By four Cherubic shapes, four Faces each
> Had wondrous, as with Starrs thir bodies all
> And Wings were set with Eyes, with Eyes the Wheels
> Of Beril, and careering Fires between;
> Over thir heads a chrystal Firmament,
> Whereon a Saphir Throne, inlaid with pure
> Amber, and colours of the showrie Arch.
> (*P. L.*, VI, 751-759)

In Ezekiel's vision "the spirit of the living creature *was* in the wheeles" (Ezek. 1:20), the four living creatures "every one had foure faces" (1:6), their bodies were in appearance like "burning coles of fire" that "went up and downe among the living creatures" (1:13), "their rings were ful of eyes" (1:18) and the wheels "like unto the colour of a Berill" (1:16), over their heads was a firmament "as the colour of the terrible chrystal" (1:22), and above that "the likenesse of a Throne, as the appearance of a Saphyre stone" (1:26) with the "colour of amber" (1:27) and the appearance of "the bow that is in the cloud in the day of raine" (1:28). Later, inside the Temple, Ezekiel saw the same creatures and their "whole body, and their backes, and their hands, and their wings, and the wheeles, *were* full of eyes round about" (10:12). Thus a Biblical representation of the glory of God revealed in judgment upon a disobedient nation is woven into Milton's description of the Son's avenging chariot, and yet the nature of the image and its visionary source suggest a spiritual meaning to the Son's conquest as well as a literal one. Raphael's narration, through "measuring things in Heav'n by things on Earth" (l. 893), and through the

Biblical allusions involved in the earthly yardsticks used, has been made with authority and reality and, at the same time, with the suggestion that none of the details need be interpreted with complete literalness. That Satan rebelled and was consequently expelled from Heaven by the power of the Father through the agency of the Son is, however, to be taken literally to teach "By terrible Example the reward / Of disobedience" (l. 912).

Raphael's account of the Creation is often taken almost verbatim from the Authorized Version of the Bible. Most of the variations from it result from the work of composing poetry from the prose of Genesis, although some variations result from Milton's own translations of the original Hebrew and Greek Scriptures. In the account of the six days of Creation Milton follows the English Bible very closely and yet skillfully works in personal interpretations, supporting them with allusions to books of the Bible other than Genesis. For example, his famous image of the "golden Compasses" used by the Son to circumscribe a section of the boundless deep for the creation of Heaven and Earth is taken from one of the texts upon which Milton based his theory of Creation as not *ex nihilo* but as the voluntary putting forth of God's goodness to bring order into a section of chaotic but eternal matter, and Scripture gives authority to his theory. The allusion in the lines,

> in his hand
> He took the golden Compasses, prepar'd
> In Gods Eternal store, to circumscribe
> This Universe, and all created things,
> (*P. L.*, VII, 224-227)

is to the Authorized Version of Proverbs: "When hee prepared the heavens I was there: when hee set a compasse upon the face of the depth" (8:27).[15]

Although Milton's explanation of how the forming of the sun

15. Harris Francis Fletcher (*Milton's Rabbinical Readings* [Urbana, Ill., 1930], p. 102) argues that the A. V. translation of חוג, "compasses," was not sufficient authority for Milton and that he went to "the commentaries of the rabbis in the Proverbs passage in Buxtorf"; George Newton Conklin (*Biblical Criticism and Heresy in Milton* [New York, 1949], pp. 47-49), however, has shown convincingly that the use of the word in the A. V. was supported by the standard lexicons of Milton's day and that there is no need to look further than the A. V. for the source of the compass image.

could have been delayed until the fourth day of Creation when light had sprung forth on the first day is apparently original with him, it is not cut loose entirely from textual authority.[16] He is careful to use appropriately suggestive language when he describes what happened:

> Let ther be light, said God, and forthwith Light
> Ethereal, first of things, quintessence pure
> Sprung from the Deep, and from her Native East
> To journie through the airie gloom began,
> Sphear'd in a radiant Cloud, for yet the Sun
> Was not; shee in a cloudie Tabernacle
> Sojourn'd the while. God saw the Light was good;
> And light from darkness by the Hemisphere
> Divided: Light the Day, and Darkness Night
> He nam'd. Thus was the first Day Eev'n and Morn.
> (*P. L.*, VII, 243-252)

The main body of this passage is from Genesis: "And God said, Let there be light: and there was light. And God saw the light, that it was good: and God divided the light from the darknesse. And God called the light Day, and the darknesse he called Night. And the evening and the morning were the first day" (1:3-5). But by reference to the light sojourning in a "cloudie Tabernacle" until the sun was created, the poet indicates support for an idea to be expatiated on when he describes the fourth day and the creation of the sun; the Scripture passage is from Psalm 19: "The heavens declare the glory of God; and the firmament sheweth his handie-work.... Their line is gone out through all the earth, and their words to the end of the world. In them hath he set a tabernacle for the Sunne"(19:1, 4). Then after the account of the fourth day (again quoting almost verbatim from the Authorized Version), which includes his explanation of how the sun's orb was created porous so as to receive and retain "by farr the greater part" of light, Milton alludes again to Psalm 19 when he says,

16. Bishop Newton, as quoted in Todd's edition of *P. L.*, indicates originality when he speaks of Milton's "different hypothesis," but he warns: "Let it be remembered that this is all hypothesis and that the Scripture determines nothing one way or the other" (Todd, *Poetical Works,* III, 34). In spite of his not convincing the Bishop, it is clear that Milton sought to support his theory by subtle Biblical allusion.

First in his East the glorious Lamp was seen,
Regent of Day, and all th' Horizon round
Invested with bright Rayes, jocond to run
His Longitude through Heav'ns high rode....
(*P. L.*, VII, 370-373)

The psalmist speaks of the sun "as a bridegrome comming out of his chamber, *and* rejoyceth as a strong man to run a race. His going foorth *is* from the ends of the heaven, and his circuit unto the ends of it" (Ps. 19:5-6). Thus Milton's own interpretations are subtly supported and fidelity to Genesis is maintained.

Raphael's narration of the Creation contains some of Milton's most beautiful visual images: the "Fish that with thir Finns & shining Scales / Glide under the green Wave," "the Swan with Arched neck / Between her white wings mantling proudly, Rowes / Her state with Oarie feet," the insects "In all the Liveries dect of Summers pride / With spots of Gold and Purple, azure and green," and the lion being brought forth from the earth "pawing to get free / His hinder parts, then springs as broke from Bonds, / And Rampant shakes his Brinded main." Yet none of the images are overly extravagant or fanciful, many have their origin in Scriptural phrases, and what might be regarded as simply beautiful poetry is really beautiful poetry firmly based on the Bible.

*The Creation of Adam*

Raphael's description of the creation of man in Book VII is confined to a comparatively few lines and is not very detailed. In Book VIII this lack of detail is explained: Raphael and other angels were serving as a security watch at the gates of Hell when Adam was created. Thus Milton prepares the way for Adam to tell of his own creation.

Earlier in Book VIII Raphael has referred to the starry heavens as

the Book of God before thee set,
Wherein to read his wondrous Works, and learne
His Seasons, Hours, or Days, or Months, or Yeares.
(*P. L.*, VIII, 67-69)

The idea of the created universe as a Book of God is based on the psalmist's view that the heavens give testimony in a universal language to the existence and glory of God: "The heavens declare the glory of God: and the firmament sheweth his handieworke. Day unto day uttereth speech, and night unto night sheweth knowledge. *There is* no speech nor language, *where* their voyce is not heard" (Ps. 19:1-3). In the New Testament, Paul used this idea to demonstrate the inexcusability of heathen idolatry. All created things speak to man of a Creator, a Maker, and should lead him to worship the Creator and not the creature. "For the invisible things of him from the creation of the world, are clearly seene, being understood by the things that are made, *even* his eternall Power and Godhead, so that they are without excuse" (Rom. 1:20).

Such allusions in Raphael's statement prepare the way for Adam's explanation of his arrival at the idea of a Maker; following the reasoning that any rational being could follow, he concluded from the world around him and from his own existence the existence of God. Adam's process of reasoning leads him to wish to know and adore the One responsible for his being. Delighted by his own body and mind, the surrounding flora and fauna, and his power to speak and name whatever he sees, Adam says to the natural universe:

> Tell, if ye saw, how came I thus, how here?
> Not of my self; by some great Maker then,
> In goodness and in power præeminent;
> Tell me, how may I know him, how adore,
> From whom I have that thus I move and live,
> And feel that I am happier than I know.
> (*P. L.*, VIII, 277-282)

Adam's unfallen intellect provides him with a philosophical starting point which is a step farther along than Descartes' *cogito ergo sum;* Adam is saying, in effect, *sum ergo Deus est.* The Biblical reminiscence of the line "From whom I have that thus I move and live" likens Adam to the pagan philosophers of Athens for whom Paul identified their "unknown God" as the One in whom "we live, and move, and have our being" (Acts 17:28). Adam's experience illustrates Milton's conviction that knowledge of God can be arrived at by reasoning from the nature of man's mind and the beauty of the universe, even when God is not known through special revelation in a book or through a missionary; any detailed knowledge of God, however, beyond the fact of his Godhead, power, and goodness is attainable only by revelation.

Although Adam arrives at the knowledge of God by reason, he wants to know more of Him and to know how to worship Him, and therefore God comes to him in a personal revelation.[17] The passage in which the "Presence Divine" first speaks to Adam has a Biblical resonance of a particularly important nature.

> One came, methought, of shape Divine,
> And said, thy Mansion wants thee, *Adam*, rise,
> First Man, of Men innumerable ordain'd
> First Father, call'd by thee I come thy Guide
> To the Garden of bliss, thy seat prepar'd.
> So saying, by the hand he took me rais'd,
> And over Fields and Waters, as in Aire
> Smooth sliding without step, last led me up
> A woodie Mountain.
>
> (*P. L.*, VIII, 295-303)

Here there is figural foreshadowing of future relationships between God and man. The stress on Adam as "First Man" and "First Father" recalls both "Of Mans First Disobedience" of the first line of the poem and the contrast between "The first man Adam" and the "last Adam" in Scripture (I Cor. 15:45). The Creator uses other Biblical phrases which suggest His own future incarnation as "the last Adam" to overcome the effects of the Fall, through his ministry and death, and to restore man to his "blissful Seat" (*P. L.*, I, 5). Although there is dramatic irony for the reader because he knows "the Garden of bliss" will be lost, there is also a vertical connection, by means of the Biblical allusions, to God's eternal

17. In his prose treatise on doctrine Milton says, "The Deity has imprinted upon the human mind so many unquestionable tokens of himself, and so many traces of him are apparent throughout the whole of nature, that no one in his senses can remain ignorant of the truth. There can be no doubt but that every thing in the world, by the beauty of its order, and the evidence of a determinate and beneficial purpose which pervades it, testifies that some supreme efficient Power must have pre-existed, by which the whole was ordained for a specific end. . . . No one, however, can have right thoughts of God, with nature or reason alone as his guide, independent of the word, or message of God. . . . Such knowledge of the Deity as was necessary for the salvation of man, he has himself of his goodness been pleased to reveal abundantly." "The Christian Doctrine," trans. Bishop Sumner, in *The Student's Milton*, ed. Frank Allen Patterson (New York, 1947), pp. 923, 924.

purpose to bring good out of evil. This "Mansion" will be lost, but the Son of God is to make and keep the promise, "In my Fathers house are many mansions; if it were not so I would have told you: I goe to prepare a place for you" (John 14:2). Such Biblical allusions help identify the "Presence Divine" who converses with Adam in Book VIII as the Son rather than the Father.

When Paradise is committed to Adam's care, Biblical language lends an immediate power to his account and, simultaneously, maintains the identity of the Deity who speaks as the Son.

> Rejoycing, but with aw
> In adoration at his feet I fell
> Submiss: he rear'd me, & Whom thou soughtst I am,
> Said mildely, Author of all this thou seest
> Above, or round about thee or beneath.
> This Paradise I give thee, count it thine
> To Till and keep, and of the Fruit to eate:
> Of every Tree that in the Garden growes
> Eate freely with glad heart; fear here no dearth;
> But of the Tree whose operation brings
> Knowledg of good and ill, which I have set
> The Pledge of thy Obedience and thy Faith,
> Amid the Garden by the Tree of Life,
> Remember what I warne thee, shun to taste,
> And shun the bitter consequence: for know,
> The day thou eat'st thereof, my sole command
> Transgrest, inevitably thou shalt dye;
> From that day mortal.
> (*P. L.*, VIII, 314-331)

Adam falls prostrate before the glorious appearance of his Maker much as John fell at the feet of the risen Christ on Patmos (Rev. 1:17) and as Ezekiel fell upon his face before "the appearance of the likenesse of the glory of the LORD" (Ezek. 1:28), and, like John and Ezekiel, Adam is raised to his feet to hear the Word of God. Furthermore, the Creator couples the Biblical "I am" of Deity with the term "Author" (a term caught up and repeated by Adam, who is seeking an appropriate name for his Maker). One of the most serious charges the Pharisees brought against Jesus, that he had claimed to be God, was based on his use of the term "I am" ("Before Abraham was, I am" [John 8:58]), a term used by God Himself in the Old Testament as a name for the God of the Hebrews (Exod. 3:14). The name "Author" is identified with Christ in the New Testament, where he is described as "the author of eternall salvation" (Heb. 12:2). Milton's lines, "Author of all this thou seest / Above, or round about thee or beneath," connect Adam's Maker with the Biblical Christ, by whom "were all things created, that are in heaven, and that are in earth" (Col. 1:16). Yet, in spite of the testimony of such allusions, the fact that the Son is the agent who creates all things, including man (in Book VII), and Milton's consistent portrayal of the Father as communing with man either through an angel (as in Books V, VI, XI, and XII) or through the Son (as in Book X), at least one leading scholar persists in the view that the Deity represented in Book VIII is the Father.

Professor Maurice Kelley makes one of his strongest arguments against the Trinitarian interpretation of *Paradise Lost* depend on the "Presence Divine" in Book VIII being the Father rather than the Son. He speaks of the failure of Trinitarian scholars to "recognize that in Book VIII of the epic, Milton clearly repeats the Arian dogma of the *De Doctrina.* In his reply to God, Adam states:

> No need that thou
> Shouldst propagat, already infinite;
> And through all numbers absolute, though One.
> (VIII, 419-421)"[18]

Granted that in his prose treatise Milton robs the Son of coequality with the Father by making the generation of the Son contingent upon the Father's will (since He had no natural necessity to propagate), to call these lines from *Paradise Lost* "Arian dogma" is to misunderstand the dramatic situation, the *personae* involved, and the essential differences between systematic theology and poetry. Milton's Adam has asked for a companion, and, in reply to God's suggestion that he be content alone like his Maker, he is pleading his own inferiority as the basis of his need of "social communication" in contrast with the Son's perfect being. If the Deity here is the Father, would he say, ". . . for none I know / Second to mee or like, equal much less" (VIII, 406-407), when the Father has called the Son "Second Omnipotence" (VI, 684)? On the other hand, it

18. *This Great Argument* (Princeton, 1941), pp. 120-121.

may be objected, neither would the Son say this with reference to the Father. Although Milton's consistent portrayal of the Son as the one through whom the Godhead directly communes with men and his use of Biblical allusions which identify the divine speaker in Book VIII with the Christ of the Gospels make it seem clear that the Son is the speaker of the lines quoted above, it is possible that the relation between Father and Son is being disregarded here and that the Son speaks merely as God to man rather than in the capacity of any particular Person of the Godhead. The allusions discussed in the text above, together with those to be discussed later in connection with the character of the Son (Chapter Four), do, however, seem to make a clear figural or typical connection between this Person in Book VIII and the One who became the incarnate Son of God, Jesus Christ.

The rest of the speech quoted above (*P. L.* VIII, 314-331) follows the Authorized Version of Genesis except for the textual variation "Till" for "dress" (l. 320; Gen. 2:15), a variation based on Milton's own interpretation of the Hebrew word involved (the same word translated "till" in Genesis 3:23). "And the LORD God tooke the man, and put him into the garden of Eden, to dresse it and to keepe it. And the LORD God commanded the man, saying, Of every tree of the garden thou mayest freely eate. But of the tree of the knowledge of good and evill, thou shalt not eate of it: for in the day that thou eatest thereof, thou shalt surely die" (Gen. 2:15-17). The poet suggests, almost imperceptibly, his own interpretation of the reason why Adam and Eve did not die on the day that they ate the forbidden fruit; in the midst of the Son's speech to Adam, as he explains the "bitter consequence" of eating the fruit, are the words "From that day mortal" (l. 331). Man's death turns out to be a "long day's dying," for Adam and Eve live long and have children after the Fall; Milton's explanation is that they became mortal and began to die from the day of disobedience. Thus Milton justifies this particular phase of God's way with men, a phase in which it appears that God's threat of punishing disobedience with death on the same day was not carried out.

*The Temptation of Eve*

As the book in which "mans First Disobedience" is treated, Book IX is the pivotal book of *Paradise Lost.* All that precedes it points forward to the seduction of Eve by the Tempter and all that follows it is a direct consequence of man's fall from innocence. Milton suggests the centrality of this book and its events by his explicit statement, "I now must change / Those Notes to Tragic" (IX, 6), by his repetition of the first Biblical allusion made in the epic (Rom. 5:12, 19—"as by one mans disobedience . . ."), and by his comparison of his own epic to the great epics of the world as "Not less but more Heroic" because of a higher "Argument." His subject is not the wrath of Achilles, nor the rage of Turnus, nor the ire of pagan gods and goddesses; it is of "Anger and just rebuke, and judgment giv'n" by the Almighty God, Maker of Heaven and Earth, against the "foul distrust, and breach / Disloyal on the part of Man." Since Milton so heavily underscores the importance of this book in his own epic within the context of the great Greek and Latin epics, one may expect an even greater use of Biblical allusion here than in the earlier books. Actually, however, Book IX includes fewer allusions to the Bible than do some other books, and those used turn out to be almost all for the achievement of dramatic effects. Here we can see, however, how Milton communicates Scriptural reality through his imaginative presentation: he follows the Bible in certain crucial statements by the two chief actors in the temptation scene. The reader feels, as Basil Willey says, that "the persons have the solidity of real persons; the events have the air of having really happened."[19] This feeling is the result of the truthfulness of Milton's portrayal of human nature, especially feminine human nature, and the power transmitted by the Biblical language in the dialogue between Eve and the Serpent.

Although the Genesis account makes no mention of Eve's surprise at the ability of the Serpent to speak, nor of the Serpent's claim to have already eaten of the forbidden fruit, Milton presents these as important motivating forces which explain Eve's gullibility. He makes it clear (ll. 86, 560) that he is using the Scriptural statement of the Serpent's superior subtlety as a basis for his presentation

19. *The Seventeenth Century Background,* p. 248.

of a progressive temptation (flattery, awaking desire for the fruit by lying before revealing the source of the fruit, leading Eve to the very foot of the forbidden tree before the realization that sin is involved has dawned upon her). Once Eve has been won to confidence in the Serpent's truthfulness and is within reach of the fruit of the "Tree / Of prohibition" (ll. 644-645), the language of the two becomes basically Scriptural, though Milton varies the order of the speeches (in Genesis the Serpent first questions Eve concerning God's command; in *Paradise Lost* Eve states the command and then the Serpent asks his question with its insinuation of God's injustice). Eve says to the Serpent

> Serpent, we might have spar'd our coming hither,
> Fruitless to me, though Fruit be here to excess,
> The credit of whose vertue rest with thee,
> Wondrous indeed, if cause of such effects.
> But of this Tree we may not taste nor touch;
> God so commanded.
>
> (*P. L.*, IX, 647-652)

The Tempter inquires, as though surprised,

> Indeed? hath God then said that of the Fruit
> Of all these Garden Trees ye shall not eate,
> Yet Lords declar'd of all in Earth or Aire?
>
> (*P. L.*, IX, 656-658)

Eve has taken the Serpent's bait enough so that when he impugns the goodness of God by his sly suggestiveness, she responds by exaggerating the nature of the command God had given. In Genesis, as in *Paradise Lost*, the command was not to eat of the fruit; nothing was said about not touching it or the tree. Since Milton follows the Authorized Version almost exactly both for God's original command and for Eve's exaggeration of it, he deems it necessary to designate Eve as "yet sinless" (l. 659) at this point. The sin does not lie in the temptation nor even in the tendency of the tempted to succumb; it lies only in the act of open revolt, of disobeying God. Therefore, although Eve replies,

> Of the Fruit
> Of each Tree in the Garden we may eate,
> But of the Fruit of this fair Tree amidst

> The Garden, God hath said, Ye shall not eate
> Thereof, nor shall ye touch it, least ye die,
> (*P. L.*, IX, 659-663)

she is "yet sinless"; but the Tempter knows that he is gaining ground. He plays the part of an impassioned orator indignant over injustice to man and, even using the *Areopagitica* argument that evil should be met and known in order to be shunned (ll. 697-699), he launches into a persuasive speech which is interwoven with the language of Genesis.

> Queen of this Universe, doe not believe
> Those rigid threats of Death; ye shall not Die:
> How should ye? By the Fruit? It gives you Life
> To Knowledge? By the Threatner, look on mee,
> Mee who have touch'd and tasted, yet both live,
> And life more perfet have attaind then Fate
> Meant mee, by ventring higher then my Lot.
> . . . . . . . . . . . . . . . . . . . . . .
> Why then was this forbid? Why but to awe,
> Why but to keep ye low and ignorant,
> His worshippers; he knows that in the day
> Ye Eate thereof, your Eyes that seem so cleere
> Yet are but dim, shall perfetly be then
> Op'nd and cleerd, and ye shall be as Gods,
> Knowing both Good and Evil as they know
> (*P. L.*, IX, 684-690, 703-709)

The whole dialogue between Eve and the Tempter has such dramatic reality and Biblical authority about it that one can be sure of exactly where Milton deviates from Genesis only by comparing the two accounts. The Biblical record is briefer and less dramatically conceived, but Milton has built practically his whole structure on the text and its connotations. "Now the serpent was more subtill then any beast of the field, which the LORD God had made, and hee said unto the woman, Yea, hath God said, Yee shall not eate of every tree of the garden? And the woman said unto the serpent, We may eat of the fruite of the trees of the garden: But of the fruit of the tree which *is* in the midst of the garden, God hath sayd, Ye shall not eat of it, neither shall ye touch it, lest ye die. And the serpent said unto the woman, Ye shall not surely die. For God doth know, that in the day ye eate thereof, then your eyes shall be opened, and ye shalbe as Gods, knowing Good and evill" (Gen. 3:1-5).

Building upon this authority, Milton portrays Eve as seduced through all five senses to allow her desire for the fruit (and for the divinity it allegedly bestows) to usurp power over right reason. She has looked upon the fruit, the sight of which "Might tempt alone" (l. 736), she has heard the "perswasive words" (l. 737) of the Tempter, the smell of the fruit (l. 740) has aroused in her a desire to touch and taste (l. 742); therefore, she trusts the Serpent as "Friendly to man, farr from deceit or guile" (l. 772), and, with him as her chief proof that "Here grows the Cure of all, this Fruit Divine" (l. 776), she sums up her reasons and acts. The fruit, especially since "the hour of Noon" (l. 739) draws on, is

> Fair to the Eye, inviting to the Taste,
> Of vertue to make wise: what hinders then
> To reach and feed at once both Bodie and Mind?
> So saying, her rash hand in evil hour
> Forth reaching to the Fruit, she pluck'd, she eat.
> (*P. L.* IX, 777-781)

Likewise in the Scriptural account Eve hears the Serpent speak, she sees the fruit as "pleasant to the eyes," her appetite is awakened, perhaps by the smell suggesting taste, for she sees that the tree is "good for food," and she touches and takes the fruit and eats thereof (Gen. 3:6). One is almost surprised to find in the Bible no mention of the smell of the fruit or of the hour of noon, because every detail in the poem seems appropriate to the situation and seems either based on or clearly suggested by the Bible text.[20]

20. A hint provided by Professor Edwin C. Kirkland in a private conversation and followed up by the writer reveals the strong possibility that Milton's setting Eve's temptation near the hour of noon (and placing one of the temptations of Christ at that hour also [*P. R.*, II, 292]) may have textual authority. Psalm 91:6 speaks of "the destruction *that* wasteth at noonday." The Vulgate is even more suggestive of influence in its rendering: *ab incursu daemonio meridiano.* A connection between Satan and destruction is made in *P. L.*, IX, 55-56, 473-479. Aldous Huxley's essay on "Accidie," the midday demon of medieval superstition, is an interesting discussion of the evolution of the literary concept of the demon's influence. See Houston Peterson (ed.), *Great Essays* (New York, 1954), pp. 367-371.

*The Judgment in the Garden*

The scene in Book X in which Adam, Eve, and the Serpent are judged has authoritative reality as the result of the speeches of both Judge and judged being taken almost bodily from Genesis with brief dramatic additions and some poetic inversions in word order. Milton has retained much of the divine simplicity and brevity of the Biblical speeches. The Judge and Adam talk more at length in Milton's poem, but the additions increase the dramatic unity and coherence of this part of the poem with what has gone before. To God's "Where *art* thou?" (Gen. 3:9) of Scripture Milton adds eleven lines (ll. 103 ff.), but the man's answer,

> I heard thee in the Garden, and of thy voice
> Affraid, being naked, hid my self,
> (*P. L.*, X, 116-117)

makes use, with a few omissions, of the words of the Bible: "I heard thy voyce in the garden; and I was afraid, because I *was* naked, and I hid my selfe" (Gen. 3:10). The reply of the "gracious Judge" in its last two and one-half lines is verbally identical with Genesis 3:11:

> that thou art naked, who
> Hath told thee? hast thou eaten of the Tree
> Whereof I gave thee charge thou shouldst not eat?
> (*P. L.*, X, 121-123)

The Biblical Adam, sore beset, replies with a statement which appears to be an attempt to shift the blame from himself; Milton's Adam, however, explains that he blames Eve simply because it is the truth that Eve gave him of the fruit and he knows the uselessness of trying to hide the truth from God. The implication of Adam's words in Scripture—"The woman whom thou gavest *to be* with me, shee gave mee of the tree, and I did eate" (Gen. 3:12)—is almost to cast blame upon God for giving him the woman in the first place, and Milton expatiates on this briefly by having him explain (he forgets, perhaps, how he begged God for a mate in Book VIII):

> This Woman whom thou mad'st to be my help,
> And gav'st me as thy perfet gift, so good,
> So fit, so acceptable, so Divine,

That from her hand I could suspect no ill,
And what she did, whatever in it self,
Her doing seem'd to justifie the deed;
Shee gave me of the Tree, and I did eate.
(*P. L.*, X, 137-143)

One can imagine the satisfaction with which the poet included this last line of the confession; verbally identical with Scripture, it is also metrically perfect and, in spite of Adam's previous side-stepping, it ends with the naked truth: "I did eate." As Milton describes the sin, although the man was "fondly overcome with female charm," he made a deliberate decision to eat of the fruit; taken intact from Scripture, this line carries connotations consistent with Milton's view of and portrayal of the Fall, and is at the same time an integral part of the poem's artistry. Even the regular movement of the monosyllables in the line is appropriate to the mood of Adam's confession, and the Judge picks up Adam's initial stress on "shee" to ask, "Was shee thy God?"

Similarly, Eve's confession consists of one line from the text of Genesis with only one change in word order: for the Bible's "The Serpent beguiled me and I did eate" (3:13), Milton has "The Serpent me beguil'd and I did eate" (l. 162).

The judgment pronounced upon Adam is much closer in vocabulary and word order to the Authorized Version than those pronounced upon the Serpent and Eve, although the latter, too, follow Biblical wording. The judgment upon Adam in Genesis, here arranged in eleven lines to correspond to Milton's lines, is:

Because thou hast hearkened unto the voyce of thy wife,
and hast eaten of the tree of which
I commanded thee, saying, Thou shalt not eate of it:
cursed *is* the ground for thy sake: in sorrow
shalt thou eate of it all the dayes of thy life;
Thornes also and thistles shall it bring forth to thee:
and thou shalt eate the herbe of the field:
In the sweat of thy face shalt thou eat bread,
till thou returne unto the ground: for
out of it wast thou taken,
for dust thou *art*, and unto dust shalt thou returne.
(Gen. 3:17-19)

The parallel is almost exact:

Because thou hast heark'nd to the voice of thy Wife,
And eaten of the Tree concerning which
I charg'd thee, saying: Thou shalt not eate thereof,
Curs'd is the ground for thy sake, thou in sorrow
Shalt eate thereof all the days of thy Life;
Thornes also and Thistles it shall bring thee forth
Unbid, and thou shalt eate th' Herb of th' Field,
In the sweat of thy Face shalt thou eate Bread,
Till thou return unto the ground, for thou
Out of the ground wast taken, know thy Birth,
For dust thou art, and shalt to dust returne.
(*P. L.*, X, 198-208)

The question may well arise, Why do Milton's Biblical allusions become almost exact quotations in this particular part of *Paradise Lost* rather than in any other part? The answer involves Milton's conception of the chief problem man faces in maintaining a right relationship with God: that problem is, stated as a question, How can man avoid disobedience to God? The answer is that man must know his own part and person, he must have "self-esteem grounded on just and right" (*P. L.*, VIII, 572), and he must not allow his passion (the main object of which in *Paradise Lost* is Eve) to get the better of his reason (the logical result of right reason being that life must be devoted to the love and service of God above all others). To be deceived, as Eve was, is to be guilty of "foul distrust" of God (*P. L.*, IX, 6); to put allegiance to any other being ahead of obedience to God, as Adam did, is "breach / Disloyal on the part of Man" (IX, 6-7). Only judgment can follow such transgressions, and Milton has given the judgment scene an extraordinary measure of Biblical reality because the scene is of such significance in his view of "the wayes of God to men."

*Michael and Adam*

When Michael turns from portrayal of the future by pageant and comment in Book XI to straight narration in Book XII, the appeal to Biblical authority results in a greater frequency of references in the latter book than in any other. Hardly a line is without one reference and in many lines the references are multiplied. Although the whole narrative from the flood to the new heavens and new earth is made authoritative by Biblical allusion, perhaps the most significant passage is Adam's final summation of the duty of man as he sees it after the knowledge that has been committed to him by Raphael and Michael (and by his own experience) has been assimilated. Having his fill of knowledge, "what this vessel can containe," Adam says,

> Henceforth I learne, that to obey is best,
> And love with feare the onely God, to walk
> As in his presence, ever to observe
> His providence, and on him sole depend,
> Merciful over all his works, with good
> Still overcoming evil, and by small
> Accomplishing great things, by things deemd weak
> Subverting worldly strong, and worldly wise
> By simply meek; that suffering for Truths sake
> Is fortitude to highest victorie,
> And to the faithful Death the Gate of Life;
> Taught this by his example whom I now
> Acknowledge my Redeemer ever blest.
> (*P. L.*, XII, 561-573)

By the aid of the heavenly prophet, the first man has learned the wisdom which only through the long slow process of ages was to be revealed to his children; he knows what Samuel was to seek, unsuccessfully, to teach self-willed Saul: "Behold, to obey, *is* better than sacrifice" (I Sam. 15:22). Adam has reached the conclusion to which wise Solomon came only after years of vain searching for the meaning of life, "Feare God, and keepe his Commandements" (Eccles. 12:13), and he has added to it the New Testament insight that to love God is to keep his commandments (John 14:15). He has learned to depend completely upon God, "casting all [his] care upon him" as Peter did later (I Pet. 5:7); he has learned long before the psalmist that God's tender mercies are "over all his works" (Ps. 145:9). He knows that a positive principle of God's providence is to do what He asks his children to do, to "overcome evill with good" (Rom. 12:21); he has learned from Michael what Paul later taught by inspiration, that "God hath chosen the weake things of the world, to confound the things which are mighty: and base things . . . which are despised, hath God chosen . . . to bring to nought things that are" (I Cor. 1:27-28); he has learned that suffering precedes victory because Michael has revealed to him that which was later to be revealed to Peter, that "Christ . . . suffered for us, leaving us an example, that yee should follow his steps" (I Pet. 2:21), and that the Christ pictured by Michael in both Death and Resurrection is the one who will reward those who are "faithful unto death" with a "crowne of life" (Rev. 2:10); all of this Adam has learned through the example of Christ "who is over all, God blessed forever" (Rom. 9:5).

Milton's Adam has learned his lesson well, for Michael praises him for having attained "the summe / of wisdom" (ll. 575-576); yet the angel gives the man one more piece of Scriptural advice:

> onely add
> Deeds to thy knowledge answerable, add Faith,
> Add Vertue, Patience, Temperance, add Love
> By name to come call'd Charitie, the soul
> Of all the rest: then wilt thou not be loath
> To leave this Paradise, but shalt possess
> A Paradise within thee, happier farr.
> (*P. L.*, XII, 581-587)

Michael's advice is based on Peter's exhortation—in the light of the "great and precious promises" by which men "might be partakers of the divine nature, having escaped the corruption that is in the world through lust"—to all Christians to "adde to your faith vertue; and to vertue knowledge; and to knowledge, temperance; and to temperance, patience; and to patience, godlinesse; and to godlinesse, brotherly kindenesse; and to brotherly kindenesse, charitie. For if these things bee in you and abound, they make you that ye shall neither be barren nor unfruitful" (II Pet. 1:5-8). Just as Paradise was first lost inwardly and later became an "Iland salt and bare" (XI, 834), Paradise is to be first regained inwardly, and the inner man must be a fruitful garden before Paradise is to be regained outwardly. Michael's statement, especially when one understands the Biblical allusion, points forward to the "greater Man" who shall restore us to the "blissful Seat"; to Christ and *Paradise Regained.*

## *PARADISE REGAINED*

In *Paradise Regained,* as in *Paradise Lost,* Milton uses Biblical allusions to establish an atmosphere of authoritative reality; in the shorter epic, however, his action, setting, cast of characters, and range of mood are so much more limited that the range of allusion is also limited. And then Milton did not face the same problems in both poems. For one thing, there is a much clearer Scriptural record of the temptation of Christ by Satan than of the subject matter of *Paradise Lost.* The character of Satan, the war in Heaven, the Son of God himself, the details of Eve's transgression and Adam's disobedience, the presence of Satan in the Serpent —all are described on the basis of more or less traditional conjecture about widely separated texts in the Bible rather than on the basis of clear statements. Authority for Milton's portrayal of Christ and Satan in the wilderness could be drawn from Matthew, Mark, and Luke, who were contemporaries and who told (with varying emphasis and order) basically the same story, whereas in *Paradise Lost* Milton had to draw his material from sources as widely separated in space, time, and tone as Genesis and Revelation. Nevertheless, though the problems were different and less difficult and the sources more homogeneous, Milton used basically the same methods of Biblical allusion for the same effects in *Paradise Regained* as in *Paradise Lost.*

### *The Person of Christ*

*Paradise Regained,* after Milton's introduction and invocation, opens with Satan's frank appraisal of events leading up to and including the baptism of Jesus. Satan tells the truth in spite of himself, for his Biblical allusions are accurately used although he occasionally interjects doubt. After outlining Christ's birth and growth to manhood, Satan says:

> Before him a great Prophet, to proclaim
> His coming, is sent Harbinger, who all
> Invites, and in the Consecrated stream
> Pretends to wash off sin, and fit them so
> Purified to receive him pure, or rather
> To do him honour as their King; all come,
> And he himself among them was baptiz'd,
> Not thence to be more pure, but to receive
> The testimony of Heaven, that who he is
> Thenceforth the Nations may not doubt; I saw
> The Prophet do him reverence, on him rising

> Out of the water, Heav'n above the Clouds
> Unfold her Crystal Dores, thence on his head
> A perfect Dove descend, what e're it meant,
> And out of Heav'n the Sov'raign voice I heard,
> This is my Son belov'd, in him am pleas'd.
> His Mother then is mortal, but his Sire,
> He who obtains the Monarchy of Heav'n,
> And what will he not do to advance his Son?
> His first-begot we know, and sore have felt,
> When his fierce thunder drove us to the deep;
> Who this is we must learn, for man he seems
> In all his lineaments, though in his face
> The glimpses of his Fathers glory shine.
> (*P. R.*, I, 70-93)

Satan's slurs, like "Pretends to wash off sin," and "what e're it meant," and his insinuation that God's motives are like those of any doting father with a son to advance, do not detract from the picture of Christ that the allusions in Satan's speech give. Actually the device of having an enemy report Scriptural facts about Christ heightens the glory of Christ more than would that of having a friend, John the Baptist for example, make the report. Satan's speech to his "gloomy Consistory," like Beelzebub's speech in Pandaemonium (*P. L.*, Book II), includes Biblical truth which condemns the speaker the more for seeking to fight what is bound to be a losing battle against God. Milton has already stated that Christ will come forth "By proof the undoubted Son of God" (*P. R.*, I, 11), but Satan's allusions to the baptism of Christ recorded in Matthew 3:13-17, Mark 1:9-11, and Luke 3:21-22, and especially the allusion to "the glorie of God in the face of Jesus Christ" (II Cor. 4:6), add authoritative reality to the person of Milton's hero.

*The Virgin Mary*

Mary, the mother of Christ, is realistically portrayed in Book II. As she thinks of her missing son and reviews details of their hardships since his birth, she progresses from the mild impatience expressed by her ironic reference to her "favour'd lot, / My Exaltation to Afflictions high" (ll. 91-92) to the calm peace reflected in her words, "But I to wait with patience am inur'd" (l. 102). Her meditative soliloquy, while it repeats some aspects of Christ's story, adds new incidents heretofore unmentioned. Grounded in Biblical language, these incidents remind the reader of Christ's unusual and supernatural youth. Mary enumerates the sorrows and fears with which she has been advanced beyond the lot of other women: her son's birth in a cold season when only a stable could be found for her and a manger for him; the wrath of Herod and the slaughter of the innocent children; the flight into Egypt; the return (after Herod's death) to the homeland but settlement in Nazareth; her child, now grown to manhood, baptized by John, and "own'd from Heaven by his Father's voice" (l. 85). After mention of this last event, Mary says,

> I look't for some great change; to Honour? no,
> But trouble, as old *Simeon* plain fore-told,
> That to the fall and rising he should be
> Of many in *Israel*, and to a sign
> Spoken against, that through my very Soul
> A sword shall pierce, this is my favour'd lot,
> My Exaltation to Afflictions high;
> Afflicted I may be, it seems, and blest;
> I will not argue that, nor will repine.
> But where delays he now? some great intent
> Conceals him: when twelve years he scarce had seen,
> I lost him, but so found, as well I saw
> He could not lose himself; but went about
> His Father's business; what he meant I mus'd,
> Since understand; much more his absence now
> Thus long to some great purpose he obscures.
> But I to wait with patience am inur'd;
> My heart hath been a store-house long of things
> And sayings laid up, portending strange events.
> Thus *Mary* pondering oft, and oft to mind
> Recalling what remarkable had pass'd
> Since first her salutation heard, with thoughts
> Meekly compos'd awaited the fulfilling.
> (*P. R.*, II, 86-108)

Mary uses the very language of Simeon as recorded by Luke: "And Simeon blessed them, and said unto Mary his mother, Behold, this child is set for the fall and rising againe of many in Israel: and for a signe which shall bee spoken against, (Yea a sword shall pearce thorow thy owne soul also) that the thoughts of many hearts may be revealed" (2:34-35). The allusion here serves the immediate purpose of substantiating Mary's expectation that more trouble, rather than more honor, will be connected with Heaven's recognition of her son, but it also points into the future beyond the temptation to the preaching ministry of Christ so bitterly opposed by the Pharisees, to martyrdom (and hope of resurrection) for his followers, and to the sorrow which Christ's own death would bring to Mary. Yet she finds comfort in this time of separation from her son, even though she is ignorant of his whereabouts, through the memory of her experience in having lost him once before when he was twelve—an experience which proved to her that "He could not lose himself." "And it came to passe, that after three dayes they found him in the Temple, sitting in the midst of the Doctours, both hearing them, and asking them questions. . . . And when they saw him they were amazed: and his mother said unto him, Sonne, why hast thou thus dealt with us? Behold, thy father and I have sought thee sorrowing. And he said unto them, How is it that ye sought me? wist ye not that I must bee about my Fathers businesse? And they understood not the saying which he spake unto them" (Luke 2:46, 48-50).

Mary's statement that she now understands after having mused over Christ's saying is given authority by allusion to the statement that "his mother kept all these sayings in her heart" (Luke 2:51), and the reference to Mary's "pondering oft" has the support of Scriptural testimony that "Mary kept all these things, and pondered them in her heart" (Luke 2:19). Although there is nothing in the Bible about Mary's attitude of mind during the time Jesus was away in the wilderness being tempted of the Devil, Milton has presented her realistically by the use of Biblical allusion.

## *IMAGINATIVE EXPANSION OF TEXTS*

As already indicated, there are elements in both *Paradise Lost* and *Paradise Regained* which have a certain degree of authoritative reality although they involve events, objects, and persons which do not actually appear in the Bible as they do in the poems. These elements are appropriate in Milton's Biblical epics because they are founded upon Scripture: they involve a logical extension from and expansion of a textual starting point. Those in *Paradise Lost* which are so striking as to demand special comment are the allegory of Sin and Death, the bridge built by Sin and Death, and Limbo and the stairs to Heaven; those in *Paradise Regained* include the description of Jesus among the wild beasts in the desert and the revised order and purpose of the last of Satan's temptations of Christ.

*Sin and Death*

Dr. Samuel Johnson selected Milton's allegory of Sin and Death as the target of one of his severest criticisms of *Paradise Lost;* according to him, it is "one of the greatest faults of the poem; and to this there was no temptation, but the author's opinion of its beauty."[21] There was, however, the additional temptation of certain Bible texts about sin and death which provided Milton with both the idea and the authority for concretizing as persons these abstract terms. The purpose here is not to argue the consistency or appropriateness of the allegory but rather to analyze the Biblical basis which makes Milton's picture of Sin and Death convincing and gives authority to his account of their origin and function.

Sin and Death are first seen through the eyes of their Author and, like him, the reader only gradually comes to realize who these beings are. Seeking to leave Hell on the first leg of his long journey up to light, Satan sees two horrible shapes at the gates.

> Before the Gates there sat
> On either side a formidable shape;
> The one seem'd Woman to the waste, and fair,
> But ended foul in many a scaly fould
> Voluminous and vast, a Serpent arm'd
> With mortal sting.
> . . . . . . . . . . . . . . . . .
>
> The other shape,
> If shape it might be call'd that shape had none
> Distinguishable in member, joynt, or limb,
> Or substance might be call'd that shadow seem'd,
> For each seem'd either; black it stood as Night,

21. "Milton," *Lives of the English Poets,* ed. George Birkbeck Hill (London, 1905), I, 186.

Fierce as ten Furies, terrible as Hell,
And shook a dreadful Dart; what seem'd his head
The likeness of a Kingly Crown had on.
(*P. L.*, II, 648-653, 666-673)

The reader is given specific Biblical clues to the identity of these shapes before their names are mentioned. Milton does not name them in the "Argument," but causes the reader to share Satan's ignorance of their identity up to a point; beyond that point the reader knows and watches with suspense to see how Satan will react to the news that his rebellion has brought about the existence of these two foul monsters. Sin's being described as "a Serpent arm'd / With mortal sting" recalls first the Serpent in Genesis and then the New Testament comparison of sin to a sting: "The sting of death is sinne" (I Cor. 15:56). In the description of Death, "shadow" and "black . . . as Night" are reminiscent of the Scriptural phrase "the shadow of death" (as in Ps. 23), and the "Kingly Crown" he wears identifies him with Death as he is personified in Revelation: "And I saw, and behold a white horse: and he that sate on him had a bowe, and a crowne was given unto him" (6:2a); "And I looked and behold a pale horse, and his name that sate on him was Death, and hell followed with him" (6:8). Speaking of the death of the wicked, Bildad told Job, "His confidence shall be rooted out of his tabernacle, and it shall bring him to the king of terrours" (Job 18:14).[22] When Sin intervenes as Death and Satan are about to clash, she refers to Satan as "Father" and to Death as "Son," titles Satan cannot understand since he does not recognize his offspring; the reader, however, understands that here is a grimly ironic parody of the Trinity. Sin's account to Satan of how she sprang full-grown from his head (as Pallas Athene sprang from the forehead of Zeus) and of how their relationship brought forth Death is largely the result of Milton's classical learning and great imaginative powers—and yet the account is based on a Scriptural starting

22. Milton's image of Death begetting yelping Hell-hounds upon his mother, Sin, and of their returning at will into her womb to howl and gnaw (ll. 790-802) may be based on Job 18:13, "It shall devoure the strength of his skin: *even* the first borne of death shall devoure his strength," with a change of sex for Sin. The conception of Sin as a woman may be based on the strange woman of Proverbs, whose "house inclineth unto death, and her paths unto the dead. . . . Her feet goe downe to death; her steps take hold on hell" (2:18, 5:5).

point from which the details are logically expanded. The suddenness of Sin's appearance is indicated by the Old Testament statement, interpreted to be God's words to Satan, "Thou *wast* perfect in thy waies from the day that thou wast created, till iniquitie was found in thee . . . thou hast sinned: therefore I will cast thee as prophane out of the mountaine of God" (Ezek. 28:15-16). In *Paradise Lost* the iniquity found in Satan which results in his bringing forth Sin is vividly described by her.

> All on a sudden miserable pain
> Surpris'd thee, dim thine eyes, and dizzie swumm
> In darkness, while thy head flames thick and fast
> Threw forth, till on the left side op'ning wide,
> . . . . . . . . . . . . . . . . . .
> Out of thy head I sprung: amazement seis'd
> All th' Host of Heav'n; back they recoild affraid
> At first, and call'd me *Sin*.
> (*P. L.*, II, 752-755, 758-760)

The description of the sudden means by which Sin was brought forth from Satan is followed by the description of how Death was conceived. Sin says,

> I pleas'd, and with attractive graces won
> The most averse, thee chiefly, who full oft
> Thy self in me thy perfect image viewing
> Becam'st enamour'd, and such joy thou took'st
> With me in secret, that my womb conceiv'd
> A growing burden. (*P. L.*, II, 762-767)

Death's birth in Hell, Sin having been cast out with the rebellious host from Heaven, is related next.

> Pensive here I sat
> Alone, but long I sat not, till my womb
> Pregnant by thee, and now excessive grown
> Prodigious motion felt and rueful throes.
> At last this odious offspring whom thou seest
> Thine own begotten, breaking violent way
> Tore through my entrails, that with fear and pain
> Distorted, all my nether shape thus grew
> Transform'd; but he my inbred enemie
> Forth issu'd, brandishing his fatal Dart
> Made to destroy. (*P. L.*, II, 777-787)

The conception and birth of Sin and the eventuation of Sin in Death are according to the pattern of Scripture. When it is remembered that Satan, earlier in the poem, has accused God of tempting him and the other angels to attempt God's throne (I, 642), the context of the Scripture which explains how sin and death come about is especially striking. "Let no man say when he is tempted, I am tempted of God: for God cannot bee tempted with evil, neither tempteth hee any man. But every man is tempted, and when he is drawn away of his owen lust, and entised. Then when lust hath conceived, it bringeth forth sinne: and sinne when it is finished, bringeth forth death" (Jas. 1:13-15).[23]

The mythological echoes of Milton's allegory are exceeded by its Biblical reminiscences. Although Sin, like Pallas Athene from the forehead of Zeus, springs "heav'nly fair, a Goddess arm'd" (l. 757) from Satan's head, it is not from his forehead she springs but from "the left side op'ning wide" (l. 755)—and even this has its Biblical connotations in *Paradise Lost,* since Milton (adding to the Genesis account, which merely relates that God took a rib from man without specifying which side) has Eve created from a rib removed from Adam's left side. (*P. L.*, VIII, 465-466).

One function of having Sin and Death so personified in the epic is to provide a dramatic, figural foreview of Satan's temptation of Eve. Sin is a woman; she has been given a commandment by God to keep the gates of Hell unopened, although she has a key that will open them. Eve, commanded to abstain from the forbidden fruit, has the free will to disobey and eat. Sin is won to open the gates by the "suttle Fiend," who knows how to indulge in smooth flattery and exalting promises of future bliss. Eve is won to trust the Serpent through his flattery and his lying promises of godly powers to be hers once she disobeys God. Sin can open the gates but she cannot shut them. Eve can transgress but cannot undo what once is done (IX, 926). Sin is woman and serpent combined and has in her power the "Sad instrument of all our woe" (II, 872).

23. "Bringeth forth" (Jas. 1:15) is translated, in its first use, from *ἀποκυέω*, meaning to bear forth young, or to beget young, used only here and in James 1:18 in the New Testament; in its second use, it is translated from *τίκτω*, which is always used in the N. T. in connection with childbirth, variously translated in the A. V. "bring forth," "be delivered of," and "travail in birth."

Eve is "perhaps" identified with "the Serpent, whom they calld / *Ophion* with *Eurynome,* the wide- / Encroaching *Eve*" (X, 580-582), and Adam in his bitterness over the Fall calls Eve "thou Serpent" (X, 867) because she misused her power to eat of the tree which was the "root of all our woe" (IX, 645). Milton does much to mitigate woman's sin by his sympathetic picture of Eve (she initiates the repentance of the sinful pair, for example), but there is no way to soften the Biblical fact that she "being deceived, was in the transgression" (I Tim. 2:14) and Milton hardens it if anything.

The allegory also provides a vivid illustration of Milton's theme text: "As by one man sin entered into the world and death by sin ..." (Rom. 5:12). This is true also of the universe; it is by one angel that Sin is born, and the same proud, ambitious lust that brought forth Sin conjoins with her to bring forth Death. That angel then comes to earth, tempts and deceives Eve into a sin like his (transgression through proud ambition) and the consequence is sin and death for all mankind. Satan brings forth sin and sin brings forth death—in Heaven, in Hell, and on the earth.

It is fitting, then, that Heaven, Hell, and Earth be joined together; and Milton found in the Scriptures the basis for the allegorical image of a tremendous bridge and stairway to do just that.

*The Bridge of Sin and Death*

It is practically certain that the image of a "bridge of wondrous length," "a broad and Beat'n way," paved by Sin and Death from the gates of Hell to the New world "soon after when man fell" (II, 1021-1030) was inspired by the words of Jesus, "wide is the gate, and broad is the way that leadeth to destruction, and many there be which goe in thereat" (Matt. 7:13). Milton's image of the gates of Hell left standing wide open after Sin had used the key committed to her is based on the same verse of Scripture; it is possible that the same text was the origin of the figure of "a Bannerd Host / Under spread Ensigns... / With Horse and Chariots rankt in loose array" (II, 885-887) which, Milton says, might march through the gates, "So wide they stood." By Book X (ll. 235-304) when the details are given of the building of the

"Pontifice" over the vast stretches of chaos to this universe, the Biblical language by which the bridge was first described has made acceptable to the Bible-centered reader Milton's device for portraying in graphic form the results of man's disobedience. Not even Milton's anti-Catholic pun about the "wondrous Art / Pontifical" by which Sin and Death connect the new universe and Hell with "this new wondrous Pontifice" (X, 312-313, 348) can detract from the reader's admiration for the magnificent sweep of Milton's imagination (the pun may well have increased the average seventeenth century Englishman's admiration) which could expand a brief Bible text into such a breathtaking image.

*Limbo and the Stairs to Heaven*

One element in *Paradise Lost,* also aimed at Catholicism, although lacking specific authority, is made to dovetail with the image of the broad way leading to destruction and the stairs leading to Heaven, both of which do have Scriptural authority. That is the "Paradise of Fools" (III, 496) or Limbo. Allusions to the kind of people who wind up there are included (Pharisees, III, 451-454, Matt. 6:5; the Giants of antediluvian times, III, 463-465, Gen. 6:4; the builders of Babel, III, 466-468, Gen. 11:2-4), but there is no Biblical basis for such a place unless it is the "outer darkness" into which hypocrites and unprofitable servants are cast (Matt. 22:11-14, 25:29-30). Milton is using "Limbo" in its literal meaning of "border, edge"; it is the border country, the no man's land, which stands just between this world and the next. Having arrived at the bare outside of this world by the route to be made a permanent causeway to Hell, Satan passes through the area to be known later as Limbo, and he soon finds himself at the foot of the golden stairs joining this universe with Heaven (III, 501-509). As Satan views the stairs ascending to the gate of Heaven, he sees also

> A passage down to th' Earth, a passage wide,
> Wider by farr, then that of after-times
> Over Mount *Sion,* and though that were large,
> Over the *Promis'd Land* to God so dear.
> (*P. L.,* III, 528-531)

Thus, in Book X, when Sin and Death have finished the bridge from Hell, the "three sev'ral wayes" are in sight of each other:

> and now in little space
> The Confines met of Empyrean Heav'n
> And of this World, and on the left hand Hell
> With long reach interpos'd; three sev'ral wayes
> In sight, to each of these three places led.
> (*P. L.*, X, 320-324)

Three ways—the way to Hell, the way to Heaven, the way to Earth —meet on the outside rim of this universe. Those who are to land in Limbo are confident that they will ascend the golden stairs, but when they lift their feet to go up, "loe / A violent cross wind from either Coast / Blows them transverse ten thousand Leagues awry" (III, 486-488).

The stairs to Heaven are given authority by comparison with those "whereon *Jacob* saw / Angels ascending and descending. . . . And waking cri'd, This is the Gate of Heav'n" (III, 510-511, 515), an allusion to Genesis 28:12, 16-17 and to the words of Jesus in the New Testament, "Hereafter ye shall see heaven open & the Angels of God ascending and descending upon the Sonne of man" (John 1:51). The latter verse of Scripture explains Milton's statement that "Each Stair mysteriously was meant" (III, 516). Jacob's ladder as well as Milton's stairway is a symbol of the way to Heaven, the Way, the Truth, and the Life (John 14:6), Jesus Christ, the Son of Man. When all the symbolic passages are brought together in Book X (ll. 320 ff.), Hell is seen on the "left hand," giving a pictorial emphasis of cosmic immensity to the words to be pronounced by the Son as Judge "unto them on the left hand, Depart from me, ye cursed, into everlasting fire, prepared for the devill and his angels" (Matt. 25:41).

### *Jesus Among the Beasts*

Some incidents in *Paradise Regained* are extensions of a brief text in the Bible. For example, the only mention of the temptation of Christ in the Gospel of Mark is put very concisely in two verses; yet an element is included which is recorded by neither Matthew nor Luke in their otherwise more extended accounts, and upon this element Milton builds a striking image of the Son of God as having been in the wilderness for forty days without food or hunger, and then, when he begins to feel hunger, as still in control of himself and his surroundings. Mark's account of the temptation is: "And immediately the Spirit driveth him into the wildernesse. And he was there in the wildernesse fourtie dayes tempted of Satan, and was with the wild beasts; and the Angels ministered unto him" (1:12-13). The following passage shows how much Milton adds to his account on the authority of the phrase "with the wild beasts," while at the same time he ventures to add no description of how Jesus spent the forty days, for it "is not reveal'd":

> Full forty days he pass'd, whether on hill
> Sometimes, anon in shady vale, each night
> Under the covert of some ancient Oak,
> Or Cedar, to defend him from the dew,
> Or harbour'd in one Cave, is not reveal'd;
> Nor tasted humane food, nor hunger felt
> Till those days ended, hunger'd then at last
> Among wild Beasts: they at his sight grew mild,
> Nor sleeping him nor waking harm'd, his walk
> The fiery Serpent fled, and noxious Worm,
> The Lion and fierce Tiger glar'd aloof.
> (*P. R.*, I, 303-313)

The mildness and harmlessness of the beasts in the presence of Christ emphasize his power over nature. When the Israelites, having been delivered from Egypt, began to complain against God's provision for them in the wilderness, God "sent fiery serpents among the people, and they bit the people; and much people of Israel died" (Num. 21:6); but when Christ walks the wilderness in humble submission to his Father, the fiery serpent flees his path. Even the man-eaters, the lion and the tiger, stand aloof from the Son of God. An animal instrument will not serve Satan in his temptation of this Man, and Satan is soon to learn that no disguise can hide his identity from Christ (*P. R.*, I, 356). These, and more, connotations Milton suggests through his expansion of the Biblical statement that Christ "was with the wild beasts."

*The Order of the Temptations of Christ*

Milton bases his order of the various temptations in *Paradise Regained* on Luke's account rather than on Matthew's; therefore the placing of Christ on the pinnacle of the Temple occurs last in the poem, and the poet's treatment provides artistic justification for the order of Luke. Everything builds to the climax on the highest spire of the Temple where Christ stands while Satan falls, defeated in the air, his own boasted sphere of conquest (*P. R.*, I, 45-46, IV, 563-571). Yet, in spite of the fact that having the last scene take place on the spire is more effective dramatically, it is highly probable that if Milton had not had the authority of Luke's example, rather than depart from Scriptural order, he would have followed the order of Matthew, in which Satan's condition that Christ fall down and worship him is stated last. Although it cannot be demonstrated from Milton's writings, it is probable that he chose Luke's account not for artistic and dramatic reasons primarily, but for two Scriptural reasons.[24] In the first place, Luke prefaces his Gospel with a statement that he, "having had perfect understanding of all things from the very first," is writing down the events "in order" (1:3), a claim that Matthew does not make. In the second place, Luke closes his account of the temptation, after the Temple scene, with the words, "And when the devill had ended all the temptation, he departed from him for a season" (4:13), a statement implying that the pinnacle test was the final test of all those applied by Satan in the wilderness. Milton inserts the stormy night between Christ's rejection of the kingdoms of the world, including worldly knowledge, and the Temple scene. When he comments, at the close of the temptation on a high hill and the beginning of the stormy night before the temptation on the pinnacle, that Satan "to the Wilderness

24. Elizabeth Marie Pope, in her comprehensive and highly readable summary of the traditional accounts of the temptation known in the seventeenth century, assigns other reasons for Milton's adoption of Luke's order than I have here suggested; she admits, however, that "the difficulty about the order of the temptations was a very minor one. Luke's arrangement might not be so satisfactory as Mathew's, but it was there in the Bible, and hence quite authoritative enough to be used by any writer who needed it." (*Paradise Regained: The Tradition and the Poem* [Baltimore, 1947], p. 102.) Her chapter entitled "The Temptation of the Tower" is especially valuable in its placing of the scene on the pinnacle of the Temple in proper perspective with the other temptations and with the triple-equation of religious tradition about the temptation: the world, the flesh, the devil.

/ Brought back the Son of God, and left him there, / Feigning to disappear" (*P. R.*, IV, 395-397), he is apparently alluding to Matthew's account, which says, after the high mountain scene, "Then the devill leaveth him" (4:11).

Luke's words, "when the devill had ended all the temptation," can be interpreted as indicating finality, as it seems Milton did interpret them; he may have also thought of this statement, together with Paul's saying that Jesus was "in all points tempted like as we are, yet without sinne" (Heb. 4:15), as his justification for including a much greater variety of approach for Satan in his poem than Satan is given in the Scripture (such scenes, for example, as that of the lavish banquet table and the vision of "*Athens* the eye of Greece"), thus giving Christ opportunity to prove himself able to "resist / All his sollicitations, and at length / All his vast force, and drive him back to Hell" (I, 151-153). Finally, Milton uses the temptation story as a starting point from which to project the ultimate victory to be won over Satan, Sin, and Death by Christ as suffering Redeemer, resurrected and ascended Lord, and returning King. That overcoming the temptations of Satan is merely the beginning of Christ's work and not by any means its completion is stated by the Father (I, 150-167), by the Son himself (I, 259-267), and by the angels (IV, 616-625, 633-635).

Through Biblical allusion, Milton was able to achieve an atmosphere of authoritative reality for events and persons described explicitly in the Bible and to support his own imaginative additions and inventions with the same reality by basing them on Bible texts and keeping his elaboration within the limits of what could be logically extended or expanded from such texts. As we have seen, there is yet another dimension to the Biblical reality of *Paradise Lost* and *Paradise Regained:* the vertical, figural connection established between the present event (or person) and the future working out of the ultimate plan of God for man and the world.

In order to achieve poetic and didactic effects within such a universal scope, Milton summoned all his powers of expression in other languages as well as in his native language. The result was a deepening and broadening of the beauty and meaning of his epic poems, a result to be analyzed in the following pages.

# II

## *Linguistic Versatility*

MILTON'S Greek and Latin poems, his translations of Hebrew psalms, and the copious references in both his Latin and his English prose, especially in *De Doctrina Christiana* and the divorce tracts, amply testify to his proficiency in the three Biblical languages: Hebrew, Greek, and Latin. The Greek and Hebrew Scriptures are utilized most in Milton's epics, although he sometimes finds the Latin Bible more appropriate to his poetic purpose and meaning. But Milton's knowledge of the original Scriptures and his ability as a textual critic of them are revealed most fully in his prose. Professor Harris Fletcher in *The Use of the Bible in Milton's Prose* has carefully and adequately analyzed the various uses Milton makes of Biblical citation; that Milton's religious beliefs grew out of his thorough knowledge of the original languages and his own scholarly methods of Biblical criticism and exegesis is demonstrated by George Newton Conklin in *Biblical Criticism and Heresy in Milton.* The purpose here, however, is neither to analyze the critical method by which Milton arrived at translations different from those of the Authorized Version nor to discuss in detail the doctrinal implications of his uses of the original languages of the Bible; rather it is to provide insight into the poetic effects Milton achieves through his linguistic versatility in the use of Biblical allusion. These poetic effects are, chiefly, the aesthetic one of heightening the pleasure of the Biblically informed reader (today, more than ever, "fit . . . though few") and the didactic one of instructing through the illumination of Bible passages translated into poetry, an instruction necessary to Milton's general purpose to "assert Eternal Providence, / And justifie the wayes of God to men" (*P. L.*, I, 25-26).

Milton used the Greek, Hebrew, and Latin Bibles as sources for allusions in his epics (1) by transliterating Greek or Hebrew into English and following or preceding the transliteration with a translation, (2) by providing variant translations of certain texts, and (3) by following the words or phrasing of the Latin Bible. [1]

## *TRANSLITERATIONS WITH TRANSLATIONS*

The practice of transliterating classical Greek words, often with a translating phrase, was common in works of the sixteenth and early seventeenth century.[2] Milton continues the traditional practice and expands it to include New Testament Greek words and Old Testament Hebrew words. In the tradition of such writers as Edmund Spenser, Robert Burton, and Sir Thomas Browne, his description of the four "infernal Rivers" of Hell provides the literal meanings of the Greek words used.

> Abhorred *Styx* the flood of deadly hate,
> Sad *Acheron* of sorrow, black and deep;
> *Cocytus,* nam'd of lamentation loud
> Heard on the rueful stream; fierce *Phlegeton*
> Whose waves of torrent fire inflame with rage.
> (*P. L.*, II, 577-581)

1. Since it is too difficult to attach to specific Bible texts, Milton's use of foreign idiom and syntax is excluded; this aspect of Milton's language, frequently commented upon from Addison to Eliot, includes much that is not Biblical but classical. Dr. Johnson, commenting on Addison's judgment that "our language sunk under him," complained that Milton formed "his style by a perverse and pedantick principle. He was desirous to use English words with a foreign idiom" ("Milton," *Lives of the English Poets,* ed. G. B. Hill [London, 1905], I, 190). Eliot compares *P. L.* to *Finnegans Wake* because both are "great books by blind musicians, each writing a language of his own based upon English." (Quoted in *Milton Criticism: Selections from Four Centuries,* ed. James Thorpe [New York, 1950], p. 323.)

2. A few titles exemplifying the practice of transliterating and translating are Thomas Watson's *Hekatompathia, or a Passionate Century of Sonnets,* John Bodenham's *Politeuphuia, or Wits Theatre,* Everard Guilpin's *Skialethia, or the Shadow of Truth,* and John Lyly's *Euphues: The Anatomy of Wit.* Such words were even more commonly used without the translation, as in Thomas More's *Utopia,* Edmund Spenser's *Prosopopoia,* Samuel Daniel's *Musophilus,* and Roger Ascham's *Toxophilus.* In the seventeenth century the practice was continued both in titles and in the main body of the work. Sir Thomas Browne, for example, says in *Religio Medici,* "Nay further, we are what we all abhor, Anthropophagi and cannibals, devourers not only of men but of ourselves," and later he speaks of "those *noctambuloes* and night walkers." (*Seventeenth Century Prose and Poetry,* ed. Robert P. Tristram Coffin and A. M. Witherspoon [New York, 1946], pp. 363, 373.)

Styx comes from στυγεῖν, "to hate or fear"; Acheron from ἀχέρων, means "river of woe"; Cocytus is derived from κωκυτός, "a wailing"; and Phlegethon is a transliteration of the present participle of φλεγέθην, "to blaze or burn." Other examples are "*Eurynome*" used with "wide-Encroaching" (*P. L.*, X, 580-582), "Nocturnal and Diurnal rhomb" followed by "Wheele / Of Day and Night" (*P. L.*, VIII, 134-136), and "*Hecatompylos*" translated "hunderd gates" (*P. R.*, III, 287).

Since the transliterations Milton uses are words in use in English during and before his time, their coinage is not here being attributed to Milton, although there is at least one which is Milton's original contribution to English: "*Pandaemonium*" (*P. L.*, I, 756), derived from πᾶν and δαίμων as the name for "the high Capital" of Hell. But the point here is not Milton's originality but that his use of a word transliterated from Greek (or Hebrew) and followed or preceded by an English translation makes the reader conscious of the origin of the word, while it assures his understanding of the meaning of it. For example, the word *baptize* was originally a transliteration of the Greek verb βαπτίζω. If the statement "The minister is to baptize John today" appears, the reader thinks of the word as an English word with varying meanings according to denominational interpretations. But if the statement appears as "The minister is to baptize John today, completely immersing him in water," the reader (assuming that he knows a little Greek), aided in recalling that the English word *baptize* is a transliteration of the Greek (literally meaning "to immerse"), has a specific rather than a vague image of what is to happen to John. Thus when Milton speaks (through Michael) of "Baptizing in the profluent streame" all who believe in Christ as a "signe / Of washing them from guilt of sin to Life / Pure" (*P. L.*, XII, 442-444), a gloss from the *De Doctrina* is not necessary to an understanding of Milton's interpretation of baptism.[3]

3. It is interesting, however, to see how closely this passage in *P. L.* parallels Milton's definition of baptism in the *De Doctrina* (Bishop Sumner's translation) as "the first of the sacraments commonly so called . . . *wherein the bodies of believers who engage themselves to pureness of life, are immersed in running water* [in profluentem aquam], *to signify their regeneration by the Holy Spirit, and their union with Christ in his death, burial, and resurrection*"; again Milton answers by an illustration those who argue that to baptize is to sprinkle: "in washing we do not sprinkle the hands, but immerse them" ("The Christian Doctrine," in *The Student's Milton*, ed. Frank Allen Patterson [New York, 1947], pp. 1029, 1031). Milton's "washing" in both *P. L.*

In Book I Satan emphasizes Beelzebub's former high state (and, consequently, Satan's former even higher state) by speaking to his inferior in the language of Isaiah 14, where God addresses Satan, and by describing him in comparison with the other spirits of Heaven as one who "Cloth'd with transcendent brightnes didst outshine / Myriads though bright" (I, 86-87). A few lines later Satan refers to the "Innumerable force of Spirits arm'd" (I, 101) that had revolted under his leadership against the Almighty. The Authorized Version translation for the plural form of the Greek μυριάσιν is "innumerable multitude" (from τῶν μυριάδων, used as a plural subject in Luke 12:1) or "Innumerable company" (Heb. 12:22); Milton has Satan follow his plural "Myriads" with "innumerable force." Since it is not stated until Book II that Satan actually led only one third of the angels in revolt, the reader familiar with that Bible fact recognizes Satan's claim to have drawn away from God an innumerable force as a magnificent lie before the progress of the poem reveals it as a lie. Within Book I Satan numbers the host in Hell (l. 571), and yet he persists in referring to his "Myriads of immortal Spirits" (l. 622), even claiming to have "emptied Heav'n" (l. 633). A knowledge of the English Bible is sufficient for identifying the Devil as a lying braggart, but a recognition of Milton's use of the Greek New Testament to reveal Satan as a liar heightens the pleasure the reader derives from Milton's art and guides him earlier into the adoption of a definite attitude towards Satan.

Milton sometimes uses a transliteration more than once before coupling it with a translation, as though giving the reader time for recognition of the Greek before providing the transliteration and its translation together. He refers early in the poem to "the vast Abyss," (I, 21) using a familiar transliteration from Greek ἄβυσσος. The word appears again in Satan's oration to his followers:

> For this Infernal Pit shall never hold
> Cælestial Spirits in Bondage, nor th' Abysse
> Long under darkness cover.
>
> (*P. L.*, I, 657-659)

---

and the *De Doctrina* recalls the A. V. translators' criticism of the "scrupulositie of the Puritans, who leave the olde Ecclesiasticall words . . . as when they put *washing* for Baptisme" ("The Translators to the Reader," *The Holy Bible* [London, 1612], n. p.).

This time the reference to "Infernal Pit" comes closer to identifying "Abysse" with the bottomless pit of the Apocalypse. Then in Book II when Beelzebub, having won the devils' full assent to his plan to attack God through his creatures, asks,

> who shall tempt with wandring feet
> The dark unbottom'd infinite Abyss
> And through the palpable obscure find out
> His uncouth way, or spread his aerie flight
> Upborn with indefatigable wings
> Over the vast abrupt, ere he arrive
> The happy Ile [?] (*P. L.*, II, 404-410)

the use of "Abyss" (ἀ, "no," plus βύσσος, "bottom") with "unbottom'd" completes the identification of this area where Hell is located and through whose infinite reaches the rebels have fallen as the "bottomless pit" (τὴν ἄβυσσος) into which John saw "the dragon, that old Serpent, which is the Devil, and Satan" cast bound, but to be "loosed a little season" (Rev. 20:1-3). The horror of the fallen angels' situation is deepened as the identification of their location with the Biblical bottomless pit suggests that, though he will be "loosed a little season," Satan's final eternal doom in the lake of fire and brimstone, described in the same chapter of the Bible (Rev. 20:10), is inevitable.

Although all the names Milton uses in *Paradise Lost* are appropriate to their bearers and to their bearers' dramatic functions,[4] the use of some names is so extraordinary as to invite discussion here: the use of a transliterated name, a translation being provided at a

4. Examples of the appropriate use of names, according to the meaning of the original words, abound. Among the elect angels are *Uriel*, "God is light," *P. L.*, III, 648, I Chron. 6:24; *Gabriel*, "God is mighty," *P. L.*, IV, 549, Dan. 8:16; *Uzziel*, "God is strong," *P. L.*, IV, 782, Exod. 6:18; *Ithuriel* (from *Ithiel*, "God is," plus *ur*, "light"), *P. L.*, IV, 788, Neh. 11:7; *Zephon*, "dark, wintry," *P. L.*, IV, 788, Num. 26:15; *Raphael*, "God is to be feared," *P. L.*, V, 221, Tob. 3:17; *Abdiel*, "servant of God," *P. L.*, V, 805, I Chron. 5:15; *Michael*, "who is like God?" *P. L.*, VI, 44, Dan. 10:13; *Zophiel*, "God is watcher," *P. L.*, VI, 535, I Chron. 6:26 (from *Zophai*, "watcher"). Among the fallen angels there are *Adramelec*, "honor of the king," *P. L.*, VI, 365, II Kings 17:31; *Ariel*, "lion of God," *P. L.*, VI, 371, Isa. 29:1; *Arioc*, "lion-like," *P. L.*, VI, 371, Gen. 14:1, Dan. 2:14; *Ramiel*, "God is high," *P. L.*, VI, 372, Ezek. 10:35; *Nisroc*, "eagle, hawk," *P. L.*, VI, 447, II Kings 19:37; *Lucifer*, "shining one," *P. L.*, VII, 131, Isa. 14:12. The fallen angels' names, of course, add to the irony of their rebellion against God; when they follow

crucial point in the poem after the name has been mentioned several times without translation. The Devil is first referred to in *Paradise Lost* as "Th' infernal Serpent" (I, 34) and then a few lines later as "th' Arch-Enemy, / And thence in Heav'n call'd Satan" (I, 81-82). The name *Satan* is a phonetic rendering in English of the Hebrew שָׂטָן, used in the Old Testament not only of the Devil but of any adversary; for example, Rezon, who reigned over Syria, is called "an adversary [שָׂטָן] to Israel all the dayes of Solomon" (I Kings 11:25). In its first occurrence in *Paradise Lost* the name is almost but not quite translated; the word itself does not indicate a superior enemy or "Arch-Enemy." The name is used several more times (I, 271, 757; II, 5, 300, 380, 427) with no reference to its meaning. But when Satan has begun his journey towards the new world and man, Milton emphasizes the meaning of the name in the lines:

> Mean while the Adversary of God and Man,
> *Satan* with thoughts inflam'd of highest design,
> Puts on swift wings. (*P. L.*, II, 629-631)

This is the appropriate moment for a statement of the full significance of the name: Satan is not merely an adversary, he is "the Adversary of God and Man" both. He is in Hell because of his opposition to God; he is seeking to leave Hell in order to oppose and ruin man. The transliteration alone carries little force because of its familiarity as the name of the Devil, but Milton's translation at this crucial point in the action brings to the reader's consciousness the literal meaning, a meaning not likely to be forgotten henceforth when Satan appears.

The names of the chief human characters are treated similarly. The names *Adam* and *Eve* are transliterations of the Hebrew words for "man" and "to live, to be": אָדָם, *adam,* and חַוָּה, *havah,* respectively. The literal meanings of both names are mentioned in *Paradise Lost* before the familiar names are associated with

---

Satan, they belie their names and, consequently, their names are blotted out in Heaven (*P. L.*, I, 361-363). The new names which they acquire as devils are such names as *Beelzebub,* "lord of the fly," *P. L.*, I, 81, Matt. 10:25; *Chemosh,* "fire," *P. L.*, I, 406, Num. 21:29; *Dagon,* "fish," *P. L.*, I, 462, Judg. 16:23; and *Belial,* "worthless, lawless," *P. L.*, I, 490, Deut. 13:13.

the literal renderings. One who is conscious of the meaning of Adam's name associates him immediately with the second word of the poem ("Of Mans First Disobedience...") and, consequently, the "greater Man" with the second Adam who will restore what the first man lost. Satan refers early to God's purpose to build a new world and "therein plant / A generation" (I, 652-653) but does not use the name *man*; that is reserved for Beelzebub, who elaborating on Satan's former hint about the "fame in Heav'n," refers directly to "som new Race call'd *Man*" (II, 348). In the opening scene of Book III, in which the Son volunteers to become an obedient man to die in the place of disobedient man, "Man" is on the lips of both Father and Son a total of fourteen times and "mankind" three times within 176 lines (III, 64-240); thus attention is focused on the means by which mankind, to lose Paradise in the first Adam, will be restored to Paradise in the second Adam. After his journey from Hell, Satan seeks from Uriel directions for seeing and admiring all God's wondrous works "but chiefly Man" (III, 663); Uriel becomes the first to use the name of the first man when he says,

> That spot to which I point is *Paradise,*
> *Adams* abode, those loftie shades his Bowre.
> (*P. L.*, III, 733-734)

Once inside the Garden of Eden, Satan views for himself the object of his evil purpose, "*Adam* the goodliest man of men since borne" (IV, 323), a phrase in which the poet very effectively brings together the transliterated name and its meaning. It is Satan, however, who brings together all the possible meanings of Adam's name and adds to them his own resentful interpretation:

> this new Favorite
> Of Heav'n, this Man of Clay, Son of despite,
> Whom us the more to spite his Maker rais'd
> From dust: spite then with spite is best repaid.
> (*P. L.*, IX, 175-178)

Fairly spitting out spite, Satan's speech alludes to the meaning of אָדָם as "man," "of the ground," both meanings connected with this Hebrew word. Although Satan is wrong to assign the motive of spite to God in his epithet "Son of despite" (a Hebraism reminiscent of the phrase "Son of Belial" in the Old Testament), there is ironic truth in his disdainful title "Man of Clay," for it is by the fall of the first Adam, the man formed of the dust of the ground, that Paradise shall be lost and man return unto dust in death. Even in this dark and tragic Book IX, however, one does not forget the second Adam who has volunteered to become man, to take up a "darksom House of mortal Clay" (as Milton expressed it in "On the Morning of Christs Nativity," l. 14), in order that "Death his deaths wound" should receive (*P. L.*, III, 252).

Eve is first mentioned as "The Mother of Mankinde" who was deceived by the "infernal Serpent" (*P. L.*, I, 36), an allusion to the Biblical reference to "the Serpent [who] beguiled Eve through his suttiltie" (II Cor. 11:3) as well as to Adam's having "called his wifes name Eve: because she was the mother of all living" (Gen. 3:20), "existence," or "life," being involved in the meaning of her name. In *Paradise Lost* the name *Eve* is first used when the description of the fallen angels begins; they are the ones who corrupted the greatest part of "Mankind," "the Sons of *Eve*," to forsake God and worship devils. Yet in spite of the stress from the beginning of the poem on Eve's part in the entrance of sin and death, her name is mentioned also, like Adam's, with overtones of hope and promise: Milton calls the Virgin Mary "second *Eve*" when Raphael comes to warn Adam and Eve (V, 387) and again when the Son judges the Serpent for his part in the Fall (X, 183). Thus Eve and Adam carry in their names connotations of disobedience, sin, and death, together with suggestions of the promise of redemption and life through the second Eve and the second Adam. When Michael sums up the meaning of Eve's name (as Satan earlier summed up the meaning of Adam's), his salutation crystallizes into a statement the connotations of her name already suggested by allusion to the Hebrew word involved.

> Haile to thee
> *Eve* rightly call'd, Mother of all Mankind,
> Mother of all things living, since by thee
> Man is to live, and all things live for Man.
> (*P. L.*, XI, 158-161)

In addition to such allusiveness in the names of persons, there are interesting uses of transliterated place names in *Paradise Lost.* Milton uses the term *Tartarus* twice as a designation for Hell (II, 858; VI, 54) and twice as an adjective: "*Tartarean* Sulphur" (II, 69) and "tartareous . . . dregs" (VII, 238). An examination of these passages indicates that the allusion here is not so much to the Greek Hell referred to in the *Iliad* as to the Greek verb ταρταρόω, used in the New Testament only once, with the meaning "cast down to hell": εἰ γὰρ ὁ Θεὸς ἀγγέλων ἁμαρτησάντων οὐκ ἐφείσατο, ἀλλὰ σιροῖς ξόφου ταρταρώσας παρέδωκεν εἰς κρίσιν τηρουμένους (Πετρου β′ 2:4).

One of Sin's reasons for opening the gates of Hell to let Satan out is that she owes everything to him, her father and husband, and owes nothing to God, who, she says,

> hath hither thrust me down
> Into this gloom of *Tartarus* profound
> To sit in hateful Office here confin'd.
> (*P. L.*, II, 857-859)

Although apparently the reference is only to the place called Tartarus, the lowest Hell, the expression "thrust me down / Into . . . *Tartarus*" is almost certainly an allusion to the Biblical "cast down to hell," translated from ταρταρώσας (II Pet. 2:4). Again Milton has transliterated a Greek word, and, by his translation, connected Sin's statement with the New Testament text which uses a verb derived from the noun Τάρταρος, a text which speaks of the "angels that sinned" as "cast down to hell." "Tartarus" is used also by the Father when he commissions Michael and Gabriel to drive the fallen angels from Heaven

> Into their place of punishment, the Gulf
> Of *Tartarus,* which ready opens wide
> His fiery *Chaos* to receave thir fall.
> (*P. L.*, VI, 53-55)

Here again the reference is to the deepest Hell, but, although no translation is provided, a downward fall is closely associated.

In the use of both adjectival forms, "Tartarean" and "tartareous," the allusion is to the Greek verb, used in the New Testament to express downward thrusting motion. In Raphael's account of the Creation, he says,

Darkness profound
Cover'd the Abyss: but on the watrie calme
His brooding wings the Spirit of God outspred,
And vital vertue infus'd, and vital warmth
Throughout the fluid Mass, but downward purg'd
The black tartareous cold infernal dregs
Adverse to life. (*P. L.*, VII, 233-239)

The Spirit purges downward to the depths the dregs which are not only black, cold, infernal, and adverse to life, but are also "tartareous," that is, they go downward by their very nature. There is nowhere for such dregs to go but to the lowest depths of the bottomless abyss; that is where Hell is and that is where those angels who have sinned go by nature.

It is only in the light of these later uses of "Tartarus" and its derivatives that one fully grasps the fallacy of Moloch's speech in Book II. Of his projected "open Warr" on God, Moloch says,

he shall hear
Infernal Thunder, and for Lightning see
Black fire and horror shot with equal rage
Among his Angels; and his Throne it self
Mixt with *Tartarean* Sulphur, and strange fire,
His own invented Torments. But perhaps
The way seems difficult and steep to scale
With upright wing against a higher foe.
Let such bethink them . . .
. . . . . . . . . . . .
That in our proper motion we ascend
Up to our native seat; descent and fall
To us is adverse.
(*P. L.*, II, 65-73, 75-77)

Moloch argues that the "proper motion" of heavenly spirits is upward, and he is right; however, he and the other rebels are no longer heavenly spirits. They have grown so gross by sinning that they did not even have to be pursued by the Son in their fall to Hell (*P. L.*, VI, 880 ff.). They were not really forced down to Hell; their nature is now that which goes down rather than up. While Moloch speaks of using "*Tartarean* Sulphur" against God, he is unconscious of being himself a part of the "tartareous... dregs" that have been purged downward from Heaven. Furthermore, Satan's journey disproves Moloch's thesis that "Th' ascent is easie." Once Satan leaves Hell, it is hard work for him to make headway upward towards light; hitting a "vast vacuitie . . . plumb down he drops / Ten thousand fadom deep" (*P. L.*, II, 932-934).[5] Moloch pictures the rebel armies as mixing God's own throne with "*Tartarean* Sulphur and strange fire," not realizing that where he and his armies now are is where they will end after the final Judgment Day. His use of the expression "strange fire" adds powerful irony too; it was for offering "strange fire before the LORD which he commanded them not" (Lev. 10:1) that Nadab and Abihu, the sons of Aaron, were devoured by fire which came out from the Lord.

The keynote for the atmosphere of suspense which pervades Book IV of *Paradise Lost*—suspense created through the idyllic bliss of Paradise and its human inhabitants being described while the Evil One who is to blast all this beauty lurks around and in the Garden—is the poet's wish that a warning voice like that which John the Revelator heard upon Satan's being cast out as man's Accuser might now warn "our first Parents" of "The coming of their secret foe" (IV, 6-7), "The Tempter ere th' Accuser of man-kind" (IV, 10). The blissful and beautiful background that

5. Moloch's assumption that ascent will be easier than descent for him and his fellow rebels is not the only fallacy in his speech. He says,

> Who but felt of late
> When the fierce Foe hung on our brok'n Rear
> Insulting, and pursu'd us through the Deep,
> With what compulsion and laborious flight
> We sunk thus low? Th' ascent is easie then.
> (*P. L.*, II, 77-81)

Edward S. Le Comte has shown by collating the parallel references to the fall of the rebel angels that Moloch is continuing the lie or error of Satan in *P. L.*, I, 169, 326, an error repeated by Chaos (II, 996): that is, the error that the rebels were pursued by the elect angels. The true version of the matter is given by Raphael (VI, 880): single-handed the Son drove the devils out through the "mural breach" of Heaven and returned to the Father before the eyes of all his saints "who silent stood / Eye witnesses of his Almightie Acts" (VI, 882-883). Le Comte quotes the Richardsons, early editors of Milton, as saying of the devils, "They Imagin'd they were persu'd by Millions . . . but were Too much Terryfied to look Behind them, and Too much Confounded to Judge of what was doing Above them" (*Yet Once More* [New York, 1953], p. 145). To the Richardsons' comment it may be added that Moloch is too incensed with wrath and cast down by defeat to be a competent judge of what is easy or hard.

the innocent Garden of Eden forms for the author of all evil is intensified by Miltons' indication of the literal meaning of the Hebrew עֵדֶן, transliterated Eden and meaning "pleasant," "pleasure," or "delight." Sitting atop Mount Niphates "in prospect of Eden" (*P. L.*, IV "Argument"), just before beginning his soliloquy which ends in the determination "Evil be thou my Good" (IV, 110), Satan views both Earth and Heaven.

> Sometimes towards *Eden* which now in his view
> Lay pleasant, his grievd look he fixes sad,
> Sometimes towards Heav'n and the full-blazing Sun,
> Which now sat high in his Meridian Towre.
> (*P. L.*, IV, 27-30)

Atop Mount Niphates is an appropriate place for Satan's soliloquy since it gives him a view of both Heaven, where he attempted to lead the angels in revolt against God (with partial success), and Earth, into which he is now planning to bring upon man disobedience and death. And this is an appropriate place in the poem to emphasize that Eden, as a place altogether pleasant, stands in sharpest contrast with Hell, the place of torment and pain from which Satan has come. But the view is still from without the Garden. Once Satan is inside, sitting like a cormorant atop the Tree of Life, the Garden is seen to be a "farr more pleasant" spot in the area of "pleasant soile" called Eden:

> for blissful Paradise
> Of God the Garden was, by him in the East
> Of *Eden* planted; *Eden* stretchd her Line
> From *Auran* Eastward to the Royal Towrs
> Of Great *Seleucia,* built by *Grecian* Kings,
> Or where the Sons of *Eden* long before
> Dwelt in *Telassar*: in this pleasant soile
> His farr more pleasant Garden God ordaind.
> (*P. L.*, IV, 208-215)

In the description of Eden and then of the Garden (a concentrate of Eden's best pleasures), poetic appeal is made to the senses of sight (it is a seat of "various view"), taste (the fruit is of "delicious taste"), touch (the sun "warmly smote" and the rose is "without Thorn"), hearing ("murmuring waters fall / Down the slope hills"), and smell ("vernal aires, / Breathing the smell of field and grove"); Milton's description of sensations felt by a person in Eden is as much in accord with the literal meaning of *Eden,* "pleasure," "delight," as poetry can make it. And the realization that Satan, the one through whom these sensations are primarily communicated, is out to rob Eden of all its pleasant aspects intensifies both the unattainable (for sinful man as for Satan) bliss of the Garden and the suspense of the drama as the temptation of Eve and man's Fall is anticipated.

Later, in Book VIII, a play on words in the speech of the Creator to Adam takes on more significance for the reader who has recognized Milton's use of *Eden* with its Hebraic connotations of a completely pleasant place. When Adam, wishing a mate, pleads his need of companionship, God gently chides him for his determination to taste "No pleasure, though in pleasure, solitarie" (*P. L.*, VIII, 401-402). That is, Adam, as long as he is alone, finds no pleasure in Eden, although to be in Eden is to be in pleasure, since *Eden* means "pleasure" or "pleasant." Discussing her desire to work separately from her husband on the fateful day of the Fall and, by a technique the reverse of that just illustrated in the speech of God, Eve uses the name *Eden* and lets the meaning be understood as she somewhat petulantly comments that if she and Adam are not safe either "single or combin'd":

> Fraile is our happiness, if this be so,
> And *Eden* were no *Eden* thus expos'd.
> (*P. L.*, IX, 340-341)

Although the roses in Eden are "without Thorn," an even more extraordinary and exotic flower, transplanted from Heaven to the place of earthly pleasure, blooms there by the Tree of Life; after man's sin, however, the heavenly flower is returned to Heaven where it shades the fountain of life. Milton's transliteration and translation of the name for this flower, the amarant, appear in the scene in Book III of *Paradise Lost* in which the elect angels bow in reverent adoration to the Son who has volunteered to die for man and to the Father who has prophesied that a new creation shall be the result of Christ's work of redemption.[6]

6. Milton had made effective use of this transliteration from the Greek word for "unfading" much earlier, in *Lycidas.* Calling on the flowers, through

With solemn adoration down they cast
Thir Crowns inwove with Amarant and Gold,
Immortal Amarant, a Flour which once
In Paradise, fast by the Tree of Life
Began to bloom, but soon for mans offence
To heav'n remov'd where first it grew, there grows,
And flours aloft shading the Fount of Life,
And where the river of Bliss through midst of Heavn
Rowls o'er *Elisian* Flours her Amber stream;
With these that never fade the Spirits Elect
Bind thir resplendent locks inwreath'd with beams,
Now in loose Garlands thick thrown off, the bright
Pavement that like a Sea of Jasper shon
Impurpl'd with Celestial Roses smil'd.
(*P. L.*, III, 351-364)

Milton has here taken the name "Amarant" applied by Pliny and Clement of Alexandria to an unfading, purple-velvet-colored flower and has placed both flower and name in Heaven; but he seems to have done this not so much on the authority of the Church Fathers as on the basis of two Bible texts—although he doubtless was familiar with other references to the amarant.

The first text, from Peter's first epistle, speaks of the "inheritance incorruptible, and undefiled, and that fadeth not away" reserved in Heaven for the elect: *κληρονομίαν ἄφθαρτον καὶ ἀμιάντον, καὶ ἀμάραντον, τετηρημένην ἐν οὐρανοῖς εἰς ὑμᾶς* (*Πετρου α'* 1:4). The second text, also from I Peter, speaks specifically of "a crown that fadeth not away": *τὸν ἀμαράντινον τῆς δόξης στέφανον* (*Πετρου α'* 5:4). The transliteration "Amarant" from *ἀμάραντον* is accompanied by the adjective "Immortal" (in the sense of "undying"), and a few lines later the reader is told that the elect spirits bind their locks with crowns or garlands of amarantine flowers "that never fade" (l. 360).[7] The

the "*Sicilian* Muse," to mourn for Lycidas, he says, "Bid Amaranthus all his beauty shed" (l. 149): i. e., let the flower which never fades wither for Lycidas' sake.

7. Don Cameron Allen ("Milton's Amarant," *MLN*, LXXII [April, 1957], pp. 256-258) has shown that the idea of the translation to Heaven of the "Immortal Amarant" comes from Clement of Alexandria's *Paedagogus*, Lib. 2, Cap. 8, in a context describing the crowns one might win through a faithful Christian life. Although Professor Allen quotes I Peter 1:4 as a possible source for "Amarant," he does not refer to I Peter 5:4, which associates the never-fading amarant with the crown to be conferred upon faithful ministers

image of the angels casting down their crowns is taken from the Apocalypse. "And round about the Throne . . . I saw foure and twentie Elders sitting, clothed in white raiment; and they had on their heads crownes of gold. . . . And before the throne there was a sea of glasse like unto Chrystal. . . . The foure and twentie Elders fall down before him that sate on the Throne, and worship him that liveth for ever and ever, and cast their crownes before the Throne" (Rev. 4:4, 6, 10).

Those who consider Milton lacking in powers of visual imagery should compare such colorful passages as the one quoted above from Book III of *Paradise Lost* with their sources, such as this passage from Revelation. Beautiful and sublime as the Scriptural passage is, Milton's image of the flowers "inwreath'd with beams" and impurpling the sea of jasper results in a much more vivid scene before God's throne. Later, when God, in order to tell them of His judgment upon fallen man, has a trumpet convene the angels "from their blissful Bowrs / Of *Amarantin* Shade" (XI, 77-78), the reader associates "Amarant" with the immortal, unwithering, unfading beauties of Heaven enjoyed by those who remain faithful, an association in sharp contrast with the curse soon to fall upon Paradise because of man's disobedience.

Milton uses "panoplie" as a transliteration of the Greek πανοπλίαν, "whole armour," of Ephesians 6:11, 13. The word is first used with reference to the entire angelic host:

> Now when fair Morn Orient in Heav'n appeerd
> Up rose the Victor Angels, and to Arms
> The matin Trumpet Sung: in Arms they stood
> Of Golden Panoplie, refulgent Host,
> Soon banded.
>
> (*P. L.*, VI, 524-528)

The allusion is to Paul's exhortation, "Put on the whole armour of God, that ye may be able to stand against the wiles of the devil" (Eph. 6:11). The phrase "the whole armour" is the Authorized Version translation of the Greek phrase τὴν πανοπλίαν. The elect angels in *Paradise Lost* stand "in Arms" against the wiles of Satan and the fallen angels, not knowing of the newly invented cannon that are

---

by the Chief Shepherd. This latter reference seems more closely related to Milton's use of "amarant" in *P. L.*, III, 352-353, 360-361.

soon to throw them into confusion. But this reference to the armor of the angels is primarily preparatory to the description of the armed might of the Son of God. The accompanying chariots and "Cherubic shapes" are drawn from the imagery of Ezekiel, but the description of Christ's person is in terms of the New Testament.

> Hee in Celestial Panoplie all armd
> Of radiant *Urim,* work divinely wrought,
> Ascended.
>
> (*P. L.*, VI, 760-762)

This time a fuller translation is given than for the transliterated "Panoplie" of the angels. The Son, not merely "in Arms" like the angels, is "all armd," and that in the whole armor of Urim, the mysterious precious stones of Aaron's high-priestly breastplate by which the Israelites knew the will of God (Exod. 28:30, I Sam. 28:6).

The same Greek word is used in one other place in the New Testament. The reader who associates "panoplie" and "whole armour" with the Biblical Christ's defense of his own power in casting out devils will think it particularly appropriate that the transliteration and translation is used in *Paradise Lost* (VI, 760-762) where the Son is presented as casting out all the devils from Heaven before the foundation of the world. Speaking of Satan as "a strong man" and of himself as "stronger than he," Christ defends his power as from God and not from Beelzebub in the following words. "When a strong man armed keepeth his palace, his goods are in peace; but when a stronger than hee shall come upon him, and overcome him, he taketh from him all his armour wherein he trusted, and divideth his spoils" (Luke 11:21-22). Milton's allusion to the Greek New Testament contrasts "all his armour" in which Satan has trusted (τὴν πανοπλίαν αὐτοῦ) with "the whole armour of God" (τὴν πανοπλίαν τοῦ Θεοῦ) by which the Son of God overcomes and drives from Heaven Satan and his hosts. Recognition of the parallel uses of the word in the New Testament increases the appreciation the reader has for the Son as the one to whom "all power is given . . . in heaven and in earth" (Matt. 28:18). Just as the armor of the elect angels could not protect them against Satan's arms (the cannon), all of Satan's armor in which he trusted cannot protect him against the whole armor of the Son of God. By means of such Biblical allusion, Raphael's account of the war in Heaven becomes not only a narration of past conquest of Satan by Christ but also a prophetic foreview of the future conquests of Satan by Christ in his earthly ministry (as celebrated in *Paradise Regained*), in his death and resurrection, and in his ultimate victory at his return as King of Kings.

Milton's use of a translated transliteration provides an indication of the identity of the Muse he invokes. In his invocation to Urania at the beginning of Book VII of *Paradise Lost,* he states explicitly that the meaning of the name is of most importance.

> Descend from Heav'n *Urania,* by that name
> If rightly thou art call'd, whose Voice divine
> Following, above th' *Olympian* Hill I soare
> Above the flight of *Pegasean* wing.
> The meaning, not the Name I call: for thou
> Nor of the Muses nine, nor on the top
> Of old *Olympus* dwell'st, but Heav'nlie borne.
> (*P. L.*, VII, 1-7)

He requests Urania, who has guided him up into the Heaven of heavens, to continue to guide him in his relation of things pertaining to the earth: "still govern thou my Song, / *Urania,* and fit audience find, though few" (VII, 30-31). Having hinted at the "meaning" of the name in his reference to her birth ("Heav'nlie borne"), the poet states the meaning of *Urania* near the close of the invocation: "thou art "Heav'nlie" (l. 39). Here he is using *Urania* not as an epithet for Aphrodite, nor as the name of the Greek Muse of astronomy; he calls on the meaning of οὐράνιος, which is translated "heavenly" in such passages as Matthew 6:14, 26, 32, usually descriptive of God the Father. Thus Urania is the "Heav'nly Muse" invoked at the opening of *Paradise Lost* as the one who inspired Moses with the knowledge of "how the Heav'ns and Earth / Rose out of *Chaos*"; it is fitting that the Muse should again be invoked at the opening of Book VII with its quite detailed account of the six days of Creation, following Genesis. Milton's reference to Urania as the sister of "Eternal wisdom" alludes to Proverbs 8, in which wisdom is a personified attribute of God. At one point in Wisdom's self-description, she says, "I wisdome dwell with prudence, and finde out knowledge of wittie inventions" (Prov. 8:12). It is possible that in Book VII Milton is invoking a heavenly prudence (to be communicated by the Spirit) that will give a spiritual appropriateness to his artistic presentation of affairs described at some length in the Bible. Up to this point in the epic Milton has dealt primarily with actions in Heaven and in Hell which are scarcely dealt with at all in the Scriptures; since he is now to deal with the Creation, which is described more fully in the Bible, he has even more need of the safe guidance of his heavenly Muse, lest, having successfully "drawn Empyreal Aire" and presented with unflagging art and almost constant Biblical authority matters outside the "visible Diurnal Spheare," he should now "from this flying Steed unrein'd . . . fall / Erroneous, there to wander and forlorne" (VII, 17-20). Since he has a mortal voice, Milton can now sing more safely "Standing on Earth, not rapt above the Pole" (l. 23), but he still needs the aid and control of heavenly prudence not only to assure himself of an appropriate audience but also to prevent the "barbarous dissonance" of his age from drowning out his heroic song. The poet implores:

> still govern thou my Song,
> *Urania,* and fit audience find, though few.
> But drive farr off the barbarous dissonance
> Of *Bacchus* and his Revellers, the Race
> Of that wilde Rout that tore the *Thracian* Bard
> In *Rhodope,* where Woods and Rocks had Eares
> To rapture, till the savage clamor dround
> Both Harp and Voice; nor could the Muse defend
> Her Son. So fail not thou, who thee implores:
> For thou art Heav'nlie, shee an empty dreame.
> (*P. L.*, VII, 30-39)

Whether Milton meant to invoke prudence or some other virtue, however, is not of first importance in this passage; if it had been, Milton would have made it clear. What is primary is that Milton recognizes his need for heavenly (ὁ οὐράνιος) guidance and control in his imaginative presentation of matters which have been revealed from Heaven. Even though his method will circumscribe his audience to one "fit . . . though few" and his Biblical subject risks rejection by many even of his own age, Milton intends, with heavenly direction, to continue his assertion of Eternal Providence and his justification of the ways of God to men in terms of His revelation to men in the Bible.

At the close of Book VII the angels sing, praising God for His power to bring good out of evil,

> Witness this new-made World, another Henv'n
> From Heaven Gate not farr, founded in view
> On the cleer *Hyaline,* the Glassie Sea;
> Of amplitude almost immense, with Starr's
> Numerous, and every Starr perhaps a World
> Of destind habitation; but thou know'st
> Thir seasons: among these the seat of men,
> Earth with her nether Ocean circumfus'd,
> Thir pleasant dwelling place.
> (*P. L.*, VII, 617-625)

*Hyaline* is a transliteration of *ὑαλίνη,* literally "of glass," used only twice in the New Testament, each time with *θάλασσα,* "sea" (Rev. 4:6, 15:2). The scenes in the Apocalypse in which these uses occur are both in Heaven and one is specifically located as "before the Throne" of God (Rev. 4:6). The angels mean, then, not that the "new-made World" is founded on the sea of glass but rather that it is now founded in view of those who stand on the glassy sea before the throne of God and that now it can be seen constantly as a witness to His power to bring good out of evil. In both Bible passages the scene is one magnifying God. In the first (Rev. 4:6) the glory of God as Creator is being hymned, as the context shows. "Thou art worthy, O Lord, to receive glory, and honour, and power: For thou hast created all things, and for thy pleasure they are and were created" (Rev. 4:11). Since the angels are praising God as Creator in the passage from the epic, the appropriateness of Milton's allusion to this Biblical context is evident.

In the second New Testament passage in which the phrase *θάλασσα ὑαλίνην,* "sea of glass," is used, the glory of God in the justice of His judgments is being praised. "Great and marveilous *are* thy works, Lord God Almighty: just and true *are* thy waves, thou King of Saints . . . Who shall not feare thee, O Lord, and glorifie thy Name? . . . For thy judgments are made manifest" (Rev. 15:3-4). Thus God is being praised by the angels as they view from the "cleer *Hyaline,* the Glassie Sea" the "pleasant dwelling place" that the Almighty has fashioned for "Thrice happie men": happy in their worship of God, in their position of rule over the works of God, and in their ability to multiply a "Race of Worshippers" of God. But the sea of glass, more than simply a vantage point for viewing the Glory of God as manifest in His Creation, is also a place from which God's judgments upon a disobedient world are surveyed in the Apocalypse; and when the angels of *Paradise Lost* sing of men as "Thrice happie if they know / Thir happiness, and persevere upright" (VII, 631-632), the *if* carries powerful dramatic irony for any reader, but for the reader who recognizes *hyaline* as an allusion to a Biblical Heaven rejoicing in the works of God and yet anticipating His wrath upon a disobedient world, there is also the foreshadowing of the opening of Book IX with its view of a Heaven alienated from and angry with disobedient man.

Similar uses of transliterated words from the original Scriptures are made in Milton's shorter epic poem. *Paradise Regained,* like *Paradise Lost,* opens with an invocation to the Spirit to inspire the poet. After a statement of the theme, that Christ through his obedience recovered what Adam had lost through disobedience, and "*Eden* rais'd in the wast Wilderness," Milton prays:

> Thou Spirit who ledst this glorious Eremite
> Into the Desert, his Victorious Field
> Against the Spiritual Foe, and broughtst him thence
> By proof the undoubted Son of God, inspire,
> As thou art wont, my prompted Song else mute,
> And bear through highth or depth of natures bounds
> With prosperous wing full summ'd to tell of deeds
> Above Heroic, though in secret done.
> (*P. R.*, I, 8-15)

As shown in the first chapter, Milton based his poem on the accounts of Christ's temptation as given in Matthew, Mark, and Luke, with the order and much of the detail drawn from Luke. Each of the Synoptic Gospels refers to Christ as having been led of the Spirit into the wilderness, and each uses the word ἔρημος, translated in the Authorized Version "wilderness" and by Milton "desert" (Matt. 4:1, Mark 1:12, Luke 4:1). Milton's reference to Christ as an "Eremite" is based on the Greek word for "wilderness" or "desert," the solitary, desolate place in which the Son of God met all the temptations of Satan and, repulsing them all, "Recover'd Paradise." The first Adam faced Satan's advances, through his wife, in the midst of bliss and plenty and was conquered; the term "this glorious Eremite" emphasizes the fact that the last Adam faced Satan's wiles in a place of hardship and privation and yet defeated the Tempter.

A more familiar title for Christ, with the translation following, is used in the second book of *Paradise Regained.* This is the transliterated Hebrew word *Messiah,* followed by the translation into English "Anointed" (II, 50).[8] Like the movement of Mary's thoughts from impatience to patience (II, 66-104, discussed in the preceding chapter) is the movement of the plaints of Jesus' newly baptized disciples from doubt to faith and from impatience for God to act to a patient willingness to wait on His providence, a movement which depends, in part, on the disciples' association of the term *Messiah* with its literal meaning, "anointed."

> God of *Israel,*
> Send thy Messiah forth, the time is come;
> Behold the Kings of the Earth how they oppress
> Thy chosen, to what highth thir pow'r unjust
> They have exalted, and behind them cast
> All fear of thee, arise and vindicate
> Thy Glory, free thy people from thir yoke,
> But let us wait; thus far he hath perform'd,
> Sent his Anointed, and to us reveal'd him,
> By his great Prophet, pointed at and shown,
> In publick, and with him we have convers'd;
> Let us be glad of this, and all our fears
> Lay on his Providence; he will not fail.
> (*P. R.*, II, 42-54)

The disciples begin their complaint at line 30 of Book II in despair; the name "Messiah" is mentioned twice (II. 32, 43), the second time as they impatiently call upon God to act. Then, as though suddenly remembering that the literal meaning of מָשִׁיחַ

8. The name "Messiah" for the Son appears often in the major epic, especially in Raphael's account of the rebellion and war in Heaven. The transliterated term is accompanied by translation in the Father's proclamation that his Son is to be worshipped (*P. L.*, V, 664) and in a reference to the incarnation of the Word at Bethlehem (XII, 359). The best example of Milton's use of the combination for special poetic effect seems, however, to be that discussed above (*P. R.*, II, 43, 50).

(Dan. 9:25, 26), transliterated "Messiah," is "Anointed," they take new hope that one whom God has so signally pointed out publicly as His Anointed One will not be withdrawn nor recalled but will return to them and finish the work he has begun. Beginning in despair, they end with "hope" and "joy" on their lips (l. 57), the turning point coming with the remembrance that God has performed so far as to send One who is anointed for a certain task; and their knowledge of the Old Testament principle that one who is anointed for a specific duty will surely fulfill it brings renewed hope to them. Their assurance that "he will not fail" may spring from a remembrance of such Old Testament examples as David, anointed by the prophet Samuel (I Sam. 16:13), undergoing many dark days as he fled for his life from the mad Saul (I Sam. 21:10), and finally crowned king in fulfillment of the prophecy involved in the anointing (II Sam. 5:4).

After Christ has emerged complete victor over the temptations of Satan, a "fiery Globe" of angels minister to him and hymn his praises; but to Satan the angels say:

> hereafter learn with awe
> To dread the Son of God: he all unarm'd
> Shall chase thee with the terror of his voice
> From thy Demoniac holds, possession foul,
> Thee and thy Legions, yelling they shall flye,
> And beg to hide them in a herd of Swine.
> (*P. R.*, IV, 625-630)

The reference to "Legions" of devils begging to enter into swine connects this passage in the poem with Mark's account of Christ's casting out devils from a man in the country of the Gadarenes. Christ is recognized as the Son of God by the evil spirits; after hailing him as such and causing the demoniac man to identify himself as "Legion" because there are so many devils in him, the devils ask for and are given permission to go into a herd of swine when they are cast out. The man, now healed, is identified as δαιμονιζόμενον, "him that was possessed with the devill" (Mark 5:15). An allusion to this story in the hymn of the angels is appropriate because it provides a future proof of the victory Christ has now won over Satan in the wilderness; the story demonstrates that the devils can no longer doubt Jesus' deity, his power over them, or that their ultimate fate is defeat at his hands and torment forever in the deep. As a part of the allusion, and as a final example of Milton's subtlety in using transliterations from the Greek New Testament, "Demoniac" is based on the Greek δαιμονιζόμενον and then explained as "possession foul." Both the Bible story and the terms in which Milton alludes to it highlight mankind's miserable state of sin because of one man's loss of Paradise and at the same time emphasize the "glorious work" upon which Christ has qualified himself to enter, the work by which Paradise is regained. Further implications are that one who has surrendered his will and inner peace to Satan is in Hell though he be in Paradise, and that one who, through the power of Christ, has his inner peace restored by being liberated from Satanic influence is in Paradise though he be in the wilderness.

## *VARIANT TRANSLATIONS*

Sometimes Milton's linguistic skill in the use of Biblical allusion is reflected in his own variant translations into English from the original Hebrew and Greek Scriptures without transliteration. Of the examples selected for discussion here, however, three are akin to Milton's practice of giving both transliteration and translation; these are passages in which Milton gives his own variant translation along with the Authorized Version translation of the same words within the same poetic context. Such double references help make clear the particular Bible text to which he is alluding. At the same time they afford the hint that Milton often gives his own translation with no indication, by a parallel use of the Authorized Version translation, that his translation is a variant from the standard English version. Three examples of Milton's use of his own and Authorized Version translations within the same passage are in *Paradise Lost;* no examples of this particular practice have been discovered in *Paradise Regained.* There are, however, many examples in both epics of Milton's use of his own translation for individual Greek and Hebrew words, examples which are discoverable when the allusion to a particular passage in Scripture is otherwise made clear.

When Raphael has closed his discussion of astronomy at the beginning of Book VIII with the advice to Adam that he "be lowlie wise" (l. 173) and leave high matters "to God above" (l. 168), Adam replies:

> How fully hast thou satisfi'd mee, pure
> Intelligence of Heav'n, Angel serene,
> And freed from intricacies, taught to live,
> The easiest way, nor with perplexing thoughts
> To interrupt the sweet of Life, from which
> God hath bid dwell farr off all anxious cares,
> And not molest us, unless we our selves
> Seek them with wandring thoughts, and notions vaine.
> (*P. L.*, VIII, 180-187)

Under Raphael's guidance, Adam further concludes that "to know / That which before us lies in daily life, / Is the prime Wisdom" (ll. 192-194); anything else is fume which renders us unpracticed and unprepared in things that most concern us, leaving us "still to seek" (l. 197). The allusion is to the part of Christ's Sermon on the Mount in which he exhorts his disciples to trust completely in the Father's day-by-day care and not to indulge in anxiety about the future. After giving examples of the Heavenly Father's provision for the living creatures and vegetation of nature, Christ says: "Therefore take no thought, saying, What shall we eat? or, what shall we drinke? or, wherewithal shall we be clothed? . . . But seeke yee first the kingdome of God and his righteousnesse, and all these things shalbe added unto you. Take therefore no thought for the morrow: for the morrow shall take thought for the things of it selfe: sufficient unto the day is the evill thereof" (Matt. 6:31, 33-34). Again, as he has been seen doing earlier in this study, Milton is projecting New Testament concepts back into the Garden of Eden. If God is the same "yesterday, today and forever," then His bidding, through His Son, to His children not to indulge in worry about external affairs of life is as applicable at one time of human history as at another, and Adam can speak in Biblical language of "Life, from which / God hath bid dwell farr off all anxious cares" without anachronism. The important point here, however, is that "to have anxious care" is a literal translation of the Greek verb μεριμνάω as it appears in Matthew 6:25, 27, 31, 34, translated in the Authorized Version each time as "to take thought" (negatively, with μή, as "take no thought"). Thus Adam's conclusion is in language which suggests Christ's injunction against "taking thought" as it appears in the English version (with the Miltonic addition to "thoughts" of the adjectival participles "perplexing," and "wandring," but with the added force of the Greek New Testament which makes it clear that it is not merely *thinking* which is proscribed but rather it is indulging in *anxiety* (the Vulgate has *anxiemini*), or being overly careful to the point of worry about things which are external to man's chief concern: to know God and practice righteousness day by day.

It is especially appropriate that Adam allude to this passage of Scripture in Book VIII. It is in this book that preparation is made for the chain of events which leads to the Fall; Adam admits to Raphael that Eve's beauty is such that "Authoritie and Reason on her waite" (l. 554) and is gently rebuked for being transported so by "an outside" (l. 568). It is precisely Adam's overanxious solicitude for his wife's happiness that leads him to neglect his place of authority as husband (thus neglecting the right order which God has ordained) and to allow Eve to work alone in the Garden on the day of the temptation, as described in Book IX. Having recognized in Biblical language that "to know / That which before us lies in daily life, / Is the prime Wisdom," Adam neglects his own responsibility of authority in the family, letting Eve venture out alone to face the Tempter. In his judgment, after the Fall, the Judge tells Adam that his place was "to beare rule, which was thy part / And person, had'st thou known thyself aright" (X, 155-156). Adam's words in Book VIII, then, are prophetic; his neglect of his place of authority, coupled with his anxious care for the pleasure of his wife,[9] renders him "Unpractis'd unprepar'd, and still to seek" that which most concerns him on the fatal day when sin enters the world and death by sin.

It is evident that Milton, though basing Adam's statement about

9. See I Corinthians 7:32-33 for a Pauline passage, certainly known by Milton, which seems to support the interpretation set forth above, particularly in the Greek version: "But I would have you without carefulnesse. He that is unmarried careth for the things that belong to the Lord, how he may please the Lord: but he that is married careth for the things that are of the world, how he may please his wife." The root word for "carefulnesse" and the verb "careth" in this passage is the Greek μεριμνάω.

"anxious cares" on both the English and the Greek versions of Matthew 6, makes an application different from the Biblical source; the thoughts involved in the gospel passage are about the material needs of life: food, drink, raiment. In *Paradise Lost* "perplexing thoughts" about astronomical and other scientific matters are, in Milton's view, as detrimental to Adam in Paradise as worries about the material needs of life are spiritually detrimental to Christians redeemed from the Fall and therefore committed to a life of trust in God. Adam could not be worrying about the need for food and clothing in the midst of the bounteous and sinless pleasures of Eden, but he does need to concern himself with God and His righteousness rather than with vain speculations about the universe; the New Testament Christian is not forbidden to learn whatever he can about God's creation, but his main concern, which is, like Adam's, to "seek first the kingdom of God and his righteousness," must not be neglected in the vain and anxious pursuit of mundane things. The situation of Adam is far different from the situation of those to whom Christ preached the Sermon on the Mount, but the basic problem is similar: How can man best please God? Milton's answer is twofold: Don't be anxious, but trust God to take care of difficult matters of the body or the mind; and keep first things first, putting the major emphasis on spiritual responsibility to God rather than on bodily needs or intellectual curiosity.

Milton's description of the evening in which God enters the Garden of Eden to pronounce judgment upon Adam and Eve for disobeying His command is beautiful both for its poetry and for its portrayal of the Son of God as loving and mild even in judgment upon those who have sinned.

> Now was the Sun in Western cadence low
> From Noon, and gentle Aires due at thir hour
> To fan the Earth now wak'd, and usher in
> The Eevning coole when he from wrauth more coole
> Came the mild Judge and Intercessor both
> To sentence Man: the voice of God they heard
> Now walking in the Garden, by soft windes
> Brought to thir Eares, while day declin'd, they heard,
> And from his presence hid themselves among
> The thickest Trees, both Man and Wife, till God

Approaching, thus to *Adam* call'd aloud.
Where art thou *Adam*[?]
(*P. L.*, X, 92-103)

The description is based on the account in Genesis 3:8-9. "And they heard the voyce of the LORD God, walking in the garden in the coole of the day: and Adam and his wife hid themselves from the presence of the LORD God amongst the trees of the garden. And the LORD God called unto Adam, and said unto him, Where art thou?" The word "coole" in the Authorized Version is translated from the Hebrew רוח, which is translated in the margin for this text, also in the Authorized Version, as "winde." The word is translated in the text of the Authorized Version 90 times as "winde" and only a single time (in the present text) as "coole." Milton's explanation of the translation "coole" is that in the evening "gentle Aires" are waked and cool the atmosphere. The fact that the same Hebrew word is translated some 232 times in the King James Version of the Old Testament as "spirit" probably influenced Milton's taking the "Eevning coole" as being indicative of the mood of God, Who comes "from wrauth more coole" than the cool winds of evening.

There is beauty in the poetry here and, consequently, delight for the reader; but equally important, if not more important in Milton's plan to "assert Eternal Providence," is the instruction for the reader. A literal translation of the Hebrew word is made the basis for emphasizing the time of man's judgment as a time of "gentle Aires" and "soft windes," and the Authorized Version translation is used to portray the Son as "coole" and "mild" in his sentence upon poor fallen man; he is the "gracious Judge without revile" (X, 118). Not only do the literal winds make the evening cool and carry the voice of God to the ears of the sinning pair, but the gentle spirit of the Son leads him to judge man in accord with the words spoken by the Father as the Son left Heaven:

Easie it may be seen that I intend
Mercie collegue with Justice, sending thee
Mans Friend, his Mediator, his design'd
Both Ransom and Redeemer voluntarie,
And destin'd Man himself to judge Man fall'n.
(*P. L.*, X, 58-62)

A final example of Milton's use of the Authorized Version translation of a Hebrew word coupled with his own variant and more literal translation occurs in his account of the second day of Creation.

> Again, God said, let ther be Firmament
> Amid the Waters, and let it divide
> The Waters from the Waters: and God made
> The Firmament, expanse of liquid, pure,
> Transparent, Elemental Air, diffus'd
> In circuit to the uttermost convex
> Of this great Round: partition firm and sure,
> The Waters underneath from those above
> Dividing: for as Earth, so hee the World
> Built on circumfluous Waters calme, in wide
> Crystallin Ocean, and the loud misrule
> Of *Chaos* farr remov'd, least fierce extreames
> Contiguous might distemper the whole frame:
> And Heav'n he nam'd the Firmament: So Eev'n
> And Morning *Chorus* sung the second Day.
> (*P. L.*, VII, 261-275)

The Genesis account of the second day of Creation is Milton's source. "And God said, Let there bee a firmament in the midst of the waters: and let it divide the waters from the waters. And God made the firmament; and divided the waters, which *were* under the firmament from the waters, which *were* above the firmament: and it was so. And God called the firmament, Heaven: and the evening and the morning were the second day" (1:6-8). It is immediately apparent that Milton has followed the Genesis statement of what occurred; his variation in the account is for the sake of explanation. As a part of his explanation of the Biblical "firmament," Milton uses a literal translation of the Hebrew word רָקִיעַ (Gen. 1:6), translated in the Authorized Version "firmament," and meaning, literally, "expanse." This does not mean, however, that Milton was accepting the idea of infinite space beyond this universe. The firmament, to him, is an "expanse," but of "liquid, pure, / Transparent, Elemental Air" composing a "Crystallin Ocean" as a shock absorber and insulator between this world and the realm of Chaos. The expanse is further explained as forming a "partition firm and sure."

Perhaps the most famous of Milton's independent translations from the Hebrew, a variant from all English versions, is his "brooding" for the Hebrew verb רחף instead of the Authorized Version translation "mooved" in Genesis 1:2. This Miltonic translation appears in two passages, both having to do with the work of the Holy Spirit in the Creation.

Thou from the first
Wast present, and with mighty wings outspread
Dove-like satst brooding on the vast Abyss
And mad'st it pregnant. (*P. L.*, I, 19-22)

Darkness profound
Cover'd th' Abyss: but on the watrie calme
His brooding wings the Spirit of God outspred,
And vital vertue infus'd, and vital warmth
Throughout the fluid Mass.
(*P. L.*, VII, 233-237)

Both of these passages are based on the Genesis statement, "And the earth was without forme, and voide; and darknesse *was* upon the face of the deepe: and the Spirit of God mooved upon the face of the waters" (1:2). The Hebrew word given above, rendered by Milton as "brooding" in *Paradise Lost* and as *incubabat* in *De Doctrina Christiana,* is used only three times in the Hebrew Bible. In the Authorized Version, it is rendered by a different English word each time: "mooved" here in Genesis, "flutter" in Deuteronomy 32:11, and "shake" in Jeremiah 23:9. The latter text, a reference to the quaking of Jeremiah's bones at the horror of his own prophecies, seems to have no connection with Milton's translation of the Genesis text. The occurrence of the same Hebrew word in Deuteronomy, however, was certainly known to a Bible scholar like Milton. Referring to God as an eagle, Moses said of the Israelites ("Jacob"): "As an Eagle stirreth up her nest, fluttereth over her young, spreadeth her wings, taketh them, beareth them on her wings: so the LORD alone did lead him [i. e., Jacob], and *there was no* strange god with him" (Deut. 32:11-12), "Fluttereth" here is a translation of the Hebrew רָחַף, *rachaph.* This picture of God as an eagle preparing a nest for His chosen people, fluttering (perhaps "brooding") and bringing forth the young nation, and then spreading out over them his wings of protection is quite similar to Milton's image of the winged, brooding Spirit.

Whatever Milton's source for his translation of *rachaph* it is peculiarly his, since it is not used in any English translation of the Genesis passage. By his use of the term "brooding" Milton suggests the importance he gave to the work of the Spirit in Creation; the Spirit is seen not as merely moving about surveying the scene but as the powerful, life-giving force that brought Heaven and Earth out of Chaos. In Milton's scheme the creation of the universe is by command of the Father (*P. L.*, VII, 163-167), by the agency of the Son (VII, 225-233), and by the organizing and ordering power of the Spirit (VII, 233b-242). It is difficult to see how a thoroughgoing Trinitarian poet could have more carefully arranged his account to avoid minimizing the role of any Person of the Trinity, and it is clear that Milton, particularly through the figure of the brooding Spirit with mighty outstretched wings, gives the Spirit a more prominent place in the Creation than Trinitarian translators of English versions of the Bible have done.

Amidst the description of the beauties of Eden in Book IV of *Paradise Lost* appears a lovely poem. It is Eve's tribute to Adam, her "Author and Disposer," the one she loves and obeys. Nine lines beginning "Sweet is the breath of morn" are followed by nine repetitive lines beginning "But neither the breath of Morn . . ." (IV, 641-656) and ending with repetition of the first word, "sweet." In the first part Eve speaks of her love for the sights, smells, and sounds of Nature which surround her; in the second part, she places Adam above them all—none of these wonders of Paradise can charm her without Adam. Yet she is puzzled that the night should be so beautiful when there is no one abroad to enjoy the "walk by Moon, / Or glittering Starrlight" (ll. 655-656); she is like the Bride in the Song of Solomon who desires to rise "by night . . . and go about the citie" (3:1-2). And like the Bride in the Song of Songs, she speaks of the rising of the morning as "the breath of morn." Here again one must look to Milton's knowledge of Hebrew for the source of his phrase. The Authorized Version has the Bride of Solomon say: "Untill the day breake, and the shadowes flee away: turne, my beloved, and be thou like a Roe or a young Hart, upon the mountains of Bether" (Song of Sol. 2:17). The verb "breake" is a translation of the Hebrew פּוּחַ *puach*, "to breathe," also translated in the Authorized Version as "blow," "puff," "utter," and "speak." The Biblical Bride is thinking of the day, or morning, as breathing soft airs as it rises; Eve speaks of the breath of morn in its rising, accompanied by the "charm of earliest Birds" wafted on gentle breezes. This brief Hebraic phrase, used just before Adam and Eve retire, is followed, after Eve's Satanically induced dream, by Adam's awaking Eve in Book V (ll. 17-25) in language strongly reminiscent of the Bridegroom's words to the Bride in the Song of Solomon 2:10-13. Helen Darbishire has commented on the peculiar linguistic appropriateness and semantic significance of the phrase "charm of earliest Birds" in the passage quoted from Book IV,[10] and the Hebraic image of the rising of the morning as a "breathing" is no less appropriate; the movement of both image and language, by their repetition, impress one indelibly with the sweet freshness of time's daily progression in the natural surroundings of the first human lovers, and the soft sounds emphasize the gentle, yielding (even when questioning) dependency of woman at her loveliest.

Satan is referred to as "the Evil one" at crucial points in both epic poems; in *Paradise Lost* the expression occurs immediately preceding Satan's temptation of Eve, while in *Paradise Regained* Christ uses the term as he rejects Satan's offer of the kingdoms of the world. Such an epithet for Satan does not appear in the King James Version. When ὁ πονηρός is used in the Greek New Testament, however, it may be translated as "evil," "the evil," or even "the evil one." In such a passage as the following (from the Lord's Prayer, after "lead us not into temptation") the evil involved may be personal rather than abstract: ῥῦσαι ἡμᾶς ἀπὸ τοῦ πονηροῦ, "deliver us from the evil (one)" (Matt. 6:13a).

10. "Milton had a true taste in country words. . . . I was alive suddenly to the true meaning of 'the charm of earliest birds' that delighted Milton's Eve, when I heard the word on the lips of an old country woman on Boar's Hill . . . : 'I can hear the charm of the birds out here.' (It then struck me that the Old English *cierm* is the word for the buzzing of bees or twittering of birds.)" (*Milton's Paradise Lost* [London, 1951], p. 12.)

For the reader familiar with this possibility of reading τοῦ πονηροῦ, literally "the evil," as "the Evil One," Eve's peril is intensified when Satan finds her alone in the garden and thus open to his temptation.

> Her graceful Innocence, her every Aire
> Of gesture or lest action overawd
> His Malice, and with rapine sweet bereav'd
> His fierceness of the fierce intent it brought:
> That space the Evil one abstracted stood
> From his own evil, and for the time remaind
> Stupidly good, of enmities disarm'd
> Of guile, of hate, of envie, of revenge.
> (*P. L.*, IX 459-466)

The Hell within Satan soon ends his delight, and then of course his hate is the more excited for having been allayed momentarily.

A similar use of "Evil one" occurs in *Paradise Regained,* but here, instead of the poet, Christ himself identifies Satan as the full and consummate personification of evil; the Tempted recognizes his Tempter. (Although Satan has been recognized by Christ in all the various forms he has assumed, when he offers the kingdoms of the world to Christ if Christ will worship him, Satan appears manifestly as the personification of all blasphemy, fraud, and evil.) Christ asks,

> Wert thou so void of fear or shame,
> As offer them to me the Son of God,
> To me my own, on such abhorred pact,
> That I fall down and worship thee as God?
> Get thee behind me; plain thou now appear'st
> That Evil one, Satan for ever damn'd.
> (*P. R.*, IV, 189-194)

Earlier in *Paradise Regained* Satan reports on the childhood and youth of Christ in the language of Scripture.

> His birth to our just fear gave no small cause,
> But his growth now to youths full flowr, displaying
> All vertue, grace and wisdom to atchieve
> Things highest, greatest, multiplies my fear.
> (*P. R.*, I, 66-69)

Satan's words follow those of Luke in the Authorized Version: "And Jesus increased in wisdome and stature, and in favour with God and man" (2:52). In at least one respect the language is closer to the original Greek than to the English version. The word translated "favour" in the Authorized Version is χάρις, meaning "grace." But more is involved here than Milton's preference for the more literal translation. The idea, though expressed by Satan, that Christ displayed increasing grace as well as virtue and wisdom as he grew to manhood is consistent with the picture of Christ which Milton gives in *Paradise Regained:* Christ has the limitations of man, for God the Father is opening up his mission to him step by step; he has not all the answers from the beginning. As Christ meditates, he says:

> And now by some strong motion I am led
> Into this wilderness, to what intent
> I learn not yet, perhaps I need not know;
> For what concerns my knowledge God reveals.
> (*P. R.*, I, 290-293)

The King James Version translators may have feared that using "grace" for χάριτι in Luke 2:52 would too closely identify Christ with ordinary men who are dependent upon God's grace and who must gradually increase in grace as they increase in wisdom or stature. Milton, since he did not feel that such identification with humanity detracted from the dignity or Godhead of the Son, would have had no such fears. The speech of Satan reflects both Satan's marked respect toward Christ as an adversary and Milton's conviction that the incarnate Son of God is human in every sense except that he is not of the seed of Adam. In both Milton's epic poems the view of Christ is more like that of the Epistle to the Hebrews—that of a divine being who became obedient man and was made perfect through suffering in order to be both Saviour and Succourer to those who are tempted—than the view of Christ given in the Fourth Gospel. Such a humanized Christ seems reflected in Milton's use of the word "grace" instead of the weaker "favour."

In both epics Milton, by using his own variant translation of a Greek verb, alludes to a text in Romans which refers to the ultimate victory of God over Satan. When in the major epic Satan is called the one whom the Son "shall tread at last under our feet" (*P. L.*, X, 190), and when the angels in the last book of the shorter epic say to Satan, "thou shalt fall from Heav'n trod down / Under his feet"

(*P. R.*, IV, 620-621), the reference is to Romans in the Greek New Testament: ὁ δὲ Θεὸς τῆς εἰρήνης συντρίψει τὸν σατανᾶν ὑπὸ τοὺς πόδας ὑμῶν ἐν τάχει (Πρὸς Ρωμαίους 16:20). "And the God of peace shall bruise Satan under your feet shortly" (Rom. 16:20). In the Authorized Version "bruise" is translated from the future form of the Greek verb συντρίβω, rendered in the margin as "tread." Milton prefers and uses "tread" in *Paradise Lost* and "trod" in *Paradise Regained.* This is at first surprising, since both epic passages are connected (the first explicitly, the second implicitly) with the Genesis prophecy that the seed of Eve would *bruise* the head of the Serpent. Milton's choice of "tread," while it indicates the consistency of his effort to stay near the literal meaning of the original languages of the Bible, may well have been based primarily on the image of Christ's victory that is involved. Rather than an image of Christ violently stamping upon Satan to bruise him, Milton conveys an image of Christ, in majestic dignity, walking over a prostrate and utterly defeated Satan. Thus both the coolness of the sentencing Judge in *Paradise Lost,* Book X, and the calmness of the tempted but victorious Saviour in *Paradise Regained,* Book IV, are maintained and emphasized as the same mood of quiet deliberation with which Satan will be finally doomed.

## *THE LATIN BIBLE*

Despite Milton's love for Latin and Latinized English, very little in *Paradise Lost* and nothing in *Paradise Regained* can be confidently designated as reflecting his use of the Latin Bible. When it is remembered that Milton considered Roman Catholicism the "only or the greatest heresy,"[11] one need not be surprised that he made so little use of the Vulgate in his major poetry. The examples chosen for discussion here are English words which show evidence of the influence of specific texts in the Latin Bible; syntactic constructions in *Paradise Lost* which may echo Latin constructions in the Vulgate are not considered.

Milton describes, in Book II of *Paradise Lost,* the damned as being tormented alternately in fire and in ice.

11. "Of True Religion, Heresy, Schism, Toleration; And What Means May Best Be Used Against the Growth of Popery," in *The Student's Milton,* ed. Frank Allen Patterson (New York, 1947), p. 915.

Thither by harpy-footed Furies hail'd,
At certain revolutions all the damn'd
Are brought: and feel by turns the bitter change
Of fierce extreams, extreams by change more fierce,
From Beds of raging Fire to starve in Ice
Thir soft Ethereal warmth, and there to pine
Immovable, infixt, and frozen round,
Periods of time, thence hurried back to fire.
(*P. L.*, II, 596-603)

Where the Authorized Version of Job 24:19—"Drought and heate consume the snow waters"—appears to have no connection with Milton's passage, the Vulgate reading of the same text suggests a transfer from fire to snow, from heat to cold: "Ad nimium calorem transeat ab aquis nivium."[12]

Like the translators of the King James Version before him, who had referred to Catholicism in their dedication as "some thicke and palpable cloudes of darknesse [which] would so have overshadowed this Land, that men should have been in doubt which way they were to walk," when Milton thought of an extraordinarily thick darkness, he thought of that plague of supernatural darkness which Moses had caused to descend upon the land of Egypt; and both the Puritan poet and the translators, surprisingly, expressed their thought of such darkness in the language of the Vulgate. In *Paradise Lost* Michael, foretelling the plagues upon Egypt, says, "Darkness must overshadow all his bounds, / Palpable darkness, and blot out three dayes" (XII, 187-188). The allusion is to the Vulgate account of God's judgment of darkness over Egypt as "tenebrae super terram Ægypti tam densae, ut palpari queant" (Exod. 10:21). The earliest reference in the epic to such a "felt darkness" is in Beelzebub's description of the arduous journey awaiting a volunteer daring enough to spy out the new creation:

who shall tempt with wandring feet
The dark unbottom'd infinite Abyss

12. Cf. Shakespeare's *Measure for Measure* (III, i, 121-122), in which Claudio, contemplating the horrors of Hell as he faces death, says that the sinner may have

To bathe in fiery floods or to reside
In thrilling region of thick ribbed ice.

And through the palpable obscure find out
His uncouth way.
(*P. L.*, II, 404-407)

Although such a word as "tangible" would substitute for the awkward "which may be felt" clause of the English version, Milton chose "palpable" in order to express his meaning perfectly, briefly, and in a recognizably Scriptural way.

One passage annotated by Patrick Hume, followed by Henry John Todd, as reflecting the influence of the Greek New Testament seems actually to reflect the influence of the Latin Vulgate instead.[13] Milton's description of the Son of God as one in whom "all his Father shon / Substantially express'd" (III, 139-140) certainly alludes to the portrayal of Christ in the Epistle to the Hebrews as "the express image of [God the Father's] person" (1:3), but the Greek phrase in this passage, χαρακτὴρ τῆς ὑποστάσεως αὐτοῦ (literally, "the character of his substance"), probably did not influence Milton's phrase as strongly as the Vulgate's "figura substantia ejus." He doubtless knew the Epistle to the Hebrews in all the languages involved, but his words in the epic are a poetic combination of the English version's "express" and the Vulgate's "substantia" rather than a literal translation of the Greek phrase. Had Milton desired to allude to the Greek original rather than to the Latin, he could not have failed to recognize that a form of the transliterated word "hypostasis," although known to his fit audience as well as "substantia," would be impossible to fit into a blank verse line in conformity with the Miltonic style.

The invocation to Urania at the opening of Book VII provides evidence of the Latin Bible's influence upon Milton's choice of a word for the pre-Creation activity of Urania.

Before the Hills appeerd, or Fountain flow'd,
Thou with Eternal wisdom didst converse,
Wisdom thy Sister, and with her didst play
In presence of th' Almightie Father, pleas'd
With thy Celestial Song. (*P. L.*, VII, 8-12)

The English version of Proverbs is drawn upon here: "When there were no fountains abounding with water, before the mountains

13. *The Poetical Works of John Milton*, ed. Henry John Todd (London, 1801, III, 194. (Note on *P. L.*, III, 139-140).

were settled, before the hills was I brought forth.... Then I was by him, as one brought up with him: and I was daily his delight, rejoicing always before him" (8:24-25, 30). Instead of the "rejoicing" of the Authorized Version, however, Milton uses "play" (l. 10), translating *ludens* from the Vulgate version of Proverbs 8:30—"Cum eo eram cuncta componens; et delectabar per singulos dies, ludens coram eo omni tempore."[14]

The animal life created on the sixth day ranges from "*Behemoth* biggest born of Earth" (*P. L.*, VII, 471) to the small "Insect or Worme" (l. 476), and of the latter, Raphael says,

> These as a line thir long dimension drew,
> Streaking the ground with sinuous trace; not all
> Minims of Nature; some of Serpent kinde
> Wondrous in length and corpulence involv'd
> Thir Snakie foulds, and added wings.
> (*P. L.*, VII, 480-484)

To emphasize that not everything described as "Worme" was small, the poet uses an anglicized form of *minima* from the Proverbs passage concerning the four things upon earth which are, though little, exceedingly wise: "Quattor sunt minima terrae, et ipsa sunt sapientiora sapientibus" (30:24). The wise man of Proverbs goes on to discuss the ants, conies, locusts, and spiders to show how, though they are *minima*, they accomplish much. In Milton's passage the "Worme" family are not all "Minims," neither in size, nor strength, nor wisdom; some are "of Serpent kinde," and a few lines further on appears an ominous line that is to grow more ominous through repetition: "The Serpent suttl'st Beast of all the field" (l. 495).

Presented with Eve, Adam identifies her with himself, names her, and prophesies concerning man's relationship with his wife, all in the language of the English version of Scripture—except for one key word from the Vulgate and a Miltonic interpretation.

> I now see
> Bone of my Bone, Flesh of my Flesh, my Self

14. The Hebrew word translated "rejoicing" in the Authorized Version of Prov. 8:30 is *sachaq*, translated "play" ten times in the Old Testament, notably as "before the LORD" (II Sam. 6:21, I Chron. 13:8), may be Milton's source.

> Before me; Woman is her Name, of Man
> Extracted; for this cause he shall forgoe
> Father and Mother, and to his Wife adhere;
> And they shall be one Flesh, one Heart, one Soule.
> (*P. L.*, VIII, 494-499)

Consistent with his impassioned pleas that mental and spiritual, as well as physical, compatibility is necessary in marriage, Milton adds "one Heart, one Soule." And his word for the union of man and woman, a union which comes before all filial ties, is "adhere." The word alludes to the Latin rendering of Genesis 2:24—"Quamobrem relinquet homo patrem suum, et matrem, et adhaerebit uxori suae: et erunt duo in carne una." Milton may have been using the Vulgate reading with the older meaning of "adhere" in mind, a meaning used by Shakespeare (as in "Nor time nor place / Did then adhere" [Macbeth, II, i, 51-52]): "to be consistent with, in accord or agreement with, appropriate to." Such a meaning is consistent with Milton's view that true marriage is a union of agreeable minds and spirits as well as of bodies; it is consistent also with his addition of "one Heart, one Soule" to the Biblical "one Flesh." "Cleave," the word used of the union of man and wife in the Authorized Version, would not have provided such connotations of Milton's views.

Preparing to send Michael to expel Adam and Eve from Paradise, the Father refers to his previous judgment upon the "peccant Angels," a phrase which associates his speech with a text in the Latin New Testament.

> But let us call to Synod all the Blest
> Through Heavn's wide bounds; from them I will not hide
> My judgments, how with Mankind I proceed,
> As how with peccant Angels late they saw;
> And in thir state, though firm, stood more confirmed.
> (*P. L.*, XI, 67-71)

The allusion is to Peter's argument (II Pet. 2:4-9) that "If God spared not the angels that sinned" ("Si enim Deus angelis peccantibus non pepercit"), nor the antediluvian world, except for Noah and his family, nor the cities of Sodom and Gomorrah, except for Lot, then God knows "how to deliver the godly out of temptations, and to reserve the unjust unto the day of Judgment to be punished." That is, Peter argues that God's past judgments give assurance that His future judgments will be just; Milton portrays God as manifesting the righteousness of all His judgments to the entire heavenly host. The Biblical passage alluded to, therefore, is appropriate to the context in *Paradise Lost,* and the phrase "peccant Angels," derived from "angelis peccantibus," identifies the specific Bible passage.

To the authoritative reality achieved for his readers by his use of the English Bible, Milton added the weight of references to the languages of the original Scriptures and to the Latin Bible. By the method (familiar to his contemporaries) of transliterating foreign words and giving their English equivalents, by showing his familiarity with problems of translation in certain texts and giving his own rendering, and by occasionally echoing words or phrases from the Latin Scriptures, Milton gave impressive proof of his linguistic versatility in Biblical exegesis and interpretation and thus of his right to be heard on subjects of such tremendous importance as the assertion of "Eternal Providence," the justification of God's ways to men, and the exaltation of Christ as the Son of God through whom lost Paradise was regained. In serving this purpose, Milton's allusions to the English, Hebrew, Greek, and Latin Scriptures also add to the dramatic effect of the characterization, language, setting, and action of his epics; a more detailed examination of his dramatic uses of Biblical allusion follows.

# III

## *Dramatic Effectiveness*
## *Setting and Action*

SINCE Milton projected his greatest literary work originally as an epic, later as a drama, and finally again as an epic, that he makes use of dramatic devices to a greater degree than is usual in an epic writer is not surprising and has been commented on frequently by Milton scholars. A full discussion of the probable trend of the poet's thinking from epic to drama and back to epic as the medium of his greatest work is found in Masson's edition of Milton's poetry,[1] Verity's edition of *Paradise Lost*,[2] and Hanford's handbook on Milton.[3] One modern editor has even gone so far as to suggest that the longer epic became more dramatic as it changed in Milton's imagination from a drama to an epic.[4] The student of Milton will agree that the best lyric and choric effects which the drama might have contained are in the epic poem, while the extreme demands upon the reader's credulity and patience that would have been made by the representation of supernatural beings by human actors and by the presentation of long narratives as episodes in a play are avoided.

Although, had he written his drama of the Fall, Milton would probably have followed either the morality play he left plans for or the classical drama he was to follow later in *Samson Agonistes*, his dramaturgy could hardly have escaped the influence of the Elizabethan dramatic tradition. And in writing his epic, he drew much from that tradition. His skillful use of such dramatic tech-

1. *Milton's Poetical Works*, ed. David Masson (London, 1910), III, 81-85.
2. *Milton: Paradise Lost*, ed. A. W. Verity (London, 1936), II, xxii-xliii.
3. James Holly Hanford, *A Milton Handbook*, 4th ed. (New York, 1954), pp. 177-193.
4. *Paradise Lost*, ed. Merritt Y. Hughes (New York, 1935), p. xliii.

niques of characterization, establishment of setting, and ironic foreshadowing of action as were used by the Elizabethans has been remarked on briefly by Douglas Bush[5] and more at length by James Holly Hanford.[6] Professor Hanford says, "Milton's ultimate decision to adopt the epic form must have resulted from a perception that neither the one element [the human action] nor the other [the wide sweep of the divine action] could receive its full development within the contracted limits of tragedy. In epic there was ample scope for all. But the epic which would include them would differ radically from any that Milton had previously contemplated on typically heroic themes. For it would retain a core of drama inherited from the original conception and would be subject to the influence of the dramatic quite as much as of the epic tradition."[7] In discussing the dramatic element in *Paradise Lost,* Professor Hanford shows many parallels in technique between Milton's epic and the plays of Marlowe and Shakespeare; one parallel, the use of the dramatic soliloquy by a villain, commented on by both Professors Bush and Hanford, may be expanded here in order to show its relation to a further dramatic technique inherited by Milton from the great Elizabethans as they inherited it from the mystery plays: the use of Biblical allusion for dramatic effect.

Edward Phillips' testimony that *Paradise Lost* was first designed as a tragedy is borne out by the evidence of the Trinity Manuscript containing, in rough outline, plans for a five-act drama first entitled "Paradise Lost" and afterward "Adam unparadiz'd." According to Phillips, the soliloquy of Satan which appears near the opening of Book IV of *Paradise Lost* was written as the exordium to Milton's projected tragedy. The soliloquy begins:

> O thou that with surpassing Glory crownd,
> Look'st from thy sole Dominion like the God
> Of this new World; at whose sight all the Starrs
> Hide thir diminisht heads; to thee I call,
> But with no friendly voice, and add thy name

5. *Paradise Lost in Our Time* (Gloucester, Mass., 1957), p. 65 ff. (first published, 1947).
6. "The Dramatic Element in *Paradise Lost,*" *SP,* XIV (1917), 178-195.
7. *Ibid.,* p. 193.

O Sun, to tell thee how I hate thy beams
That bring to my remembrance from what state
I fell.

(*P. L.*, IV, 32-39)

Professor Hanford has pointed out parallels between later utterances of Satan in this soliloquy and statements from Marlowe's Mephistophilis[8] and Faustus and Shakespeare's Richard III and Claudius of *Hamlet*.[9] What has not been pointed out is that in such soliloquies, as in other dramatic speeches, Milton, following the practice of the Elizabethan dramatists, uses Biblical allusions to intensify the dramatic effect. Satan's "which way shall I flie . . . Which way I flie is Hell" (*P. L.*, IV, 73, 75), like Faustus' "Whither should I fly? / If unto God, he'll throw me down to Hell" (*Dr. Faustus*, V, 76-77), involves an allusion to the Bible: "Whither shall I flie from thy presence? If I ascend up into heaven, thou *art* there: if I make my bed in hell, behold, *thou art* there" (Ps. 139:7b-8). The cry of the psalmist is one of faith in God's omnipresence and provident care for him and his welfare—God is even in Hell and loves him; Satan and Faustus both make it a cry of despair—wherever they go is Hell and Hell hurts. The allusion increases the reader's awareness that each speaker is condemned in his own self-will.

Examples abound of such dramatic use of the Bible in Elizabethan drama. When Machiavelli opens Marlowe's *The Jew of Malta* with a prologue, Biblical allusions are used to dramatic advantage: Machiavelli's sneer at the proverb, "Birds of the air will tell of murders past!" as "foolerie" alludes to the Biblical warning against cursing the king or the rich even in secret, "for a bird of the air shall carry the voyce, and that which hath wings

8. Cf., e. g., Satan's "my self am Hell" (*P. L.*, IV, 75) and Mephistophilis' "Where we are is Hell" (*Dr. Faustus,* V, 122); Satan's self-torturing remorse is generally similar to Marlowe's devil.

9. See Satan's "all Good to me is lost; / Evil be thou my Good" (*P. L.*, IV, 109-110) with Richard III's "since I cannot prove a lover, / To entertain these fair well-spoken days, / I am determined to prove a villain, / And hate the idle pleasures of these days" (*Richard III*, I, i, 28-31). See also Satan's "is there no place / Left for Repentance, none for Pardon left? . . . *Disdain* forbids me" (*P. L.*, IV, 79-80, 82) with Claudius' "What rests? / Try what repentance can: what can it not? / Yet what can it, when one can not repent?" (*Hamlet,* III, iii, 64-66).

shall tell the matter" (Eccles. 10:20); this allusion sets the stage for Barabas' mocking reversals of Biblical texts all through the play.[10] When *Othello* begins with Iago's remarking of the Moor to Roderigo (and to the audience), "I follow him to serve my turn upon him; / We cannot all be masters, nor all masters / Cannot be truly followed" (I, i, 42-44), Iago reveals his evil purpose to get revenge on Othello for not preferring him in the lieutenancy, but he uses, at the same time, language recognizable to a Bible-centered audience as allusive to Scripture: "My brethren be not many masters, knowing that we shall receive the greater condemnation. For in many things we offend all" (Jas. 3:1-2a). The perversion of a Bible text intensifies the malicious character of Iago and foreshadows the "greater condemnation" to come upon Othello because of his being the master of and having given offense to such a man as Iago.

The various responses made by a spectator to a stage performance or by a reader to a work of literature result from the interaction of four indispensable elements: setting, action, language, and character. Since responses are made to none of these elements in isolation but to the interaction of two or more of them, separating the elements for discussion is an artificial task and, indeed, if the dramatic power of the play or other work of literature is to be described and explained, it is an impossible task. There is always overlapping: discussing setting, one finds that the discussion suddenly involves action or character or both. And, of course, everything involves language. Still, there seems no better way to examine Milton's dramatic use of Biblical allusion than to group the allusions around the function served, whether it is primarily establishing *setting* (including psychological mood or atmosphere as well as physical setting), contributing to or foreshadowing the direction of the movement of the *action*, calling special attention to the irony or other special effect gained by what and how a character, or the poet, says in *language*, or adding further dimensions to the delineation of principal *characters*.

10. In a paper entitled "Marlowe's Looking-Glass View of Scripture," read before the Southeastern Renaissance Conference at Chapel Hill, N. C., in April, 1958, I have discussed more fully the uses Marlowe made of Biblical allusions in the two plays *The Jew of Malta* and *Dr. Faustus*.

## *SETTING*

### *Hell*

The action of *Paradise Lost* "hasts into the midst of things, presenting Satan and his Angels now fallen into Hell" ("Argument," Book I), and before Satan is seen or heard, a Biblical description of the setting is given. The brief mention of the part of the action "past over," Satan's rebellion and ejection from Heaven with his rebel hosts, prepares the way for Milton's portrayal of Hell by giving a picture of Satan

> Hurld headlong flaming from th' Ethereal Skie
> With hideous ruine and combustion down
> To bottomless perdition, there to dwell
> In Adamantine Chains and penal Fire,
> (*P. L.*, I, 45-48)

lines which recall Christ's words, "I beheld Satan as lightning fall from heaven" (Luke 10:18), John's apocalyptic vision of the "bottomless pit" in which Satan is chained (Rev. 20:1, 2), and both Peter's and Jude's references to the "chains" with which the fallen angels are bound (II Pet. 2:4, Jude 6). But after nine days and nights of oblivion, his doom having "Reserv'd him to more wrath" (I, 54) just as a reserved judgment awaits the fallen angels in II Peter and Jude, Satan finds himself in "Torments" as "round he throws his baleful eyes" (I, 56) much like Dives, who "in hell ... lift up his eyes, being in torments" (Luke 16:23). Hell flames as one great furnace, "yet from those flames / No light, but rather darkness visible" emanates (I, 63), following Job's description of the land of death as a land "without any order [Milton's Hell is in Chaos] and where the light is as darknesse" (Job 10:22). Milton varies the Biblical wording while basing his description on the Bible: his "fiery Deluge" (I, 68) and "burning Lake" (I, 210) is later called the "Lake of Fire" (I, 280) and is identifiable with the "lake of fire" of Revelation 20:15; his "ever-burning Sulphur unconsum'd" (I, 69) is the Biblical "brimstone" with which the lake of fire burns continually (Rev. 21:8).

Nor is there any doubt about the origin of this terrible setting. Milton says,

> Such place Eternal Justice had prepar'd
> For those rebellious, here their Prison ordain'd
> In utter darkness, (*P. L.*, I, 70-72)

following the words of Christ, who spoke of a place of "everlasting fire, prepared for the devill and his Angels" (Matt. 25:41), and of a place of "outer darknesse" (Matt. 22:13). It is only after having established the setting in Hell in Biblical language alluding to specific texts that Milton includes classical ideas of the abode of the damned with his listing of the "four infernal Rivers": Styx, Acheron, Cocytus, and Phlegethon. Even the description of the "adventrous Bands" of fallen spirits who roved in "confus'd march forlorn" through the dark and dreary vales of Hell "and found / No rest" (II, 614-618) reflects the Biblical comment of Jesus about the unclean spirit who "walketh through dry places, seeking reste, and findeth none" (Matt. 12:43, Luke 11:24). Any reader, of course, recognizes the setting and knows that the action of Books I and II takes place in Hell, for he is told this explicitly. It is the reader who knows and recognizes the Biblical descriptions of Hell, however, who feels at once the horror of the place and the powerful irony involved in Satan's bombast about "Better to reign in Hell then serve in Heav'n" (I, 263).

As Hell is characterized by darkness, Heaven is characterized by light, and the contrast is utilized to make the transition from Hell to Heaven dramatically effective. Long before Milton's invocation to light at the opening of Book III, in which he establishes the setting for the scenes in Heaven, he has been preparing the way for the transition from the "darkness visible" of Hell and the "ancient Night" of Chaos to the brilliant light of the new universe and of Heaven. Within the first two lines of his first utterance in Hell, Satan refers to the "happy Realms of Light" (I, 85) from which he and his armies have fallen. The contrast darkens Hell the more, and the darkness is deepened when the evil angels rise from the lake of fire like the locusts that darkened the land of Egypt in Moses' day (I, 340-343). The contrast between the Devil and his darkness and God and his light is brought together in one line when the future blasphemies of these fallen angels are being described: "And with their darkness durst affront his light" (I, 391).

In the assembly of devils, Belial holds out the hope that "This horror will grow milde, this darkness light" (II, 220), and Mammon asks, "cannot we his Light / Imitate when we please?" (II, 269-270). When Beelzebub's counsel of indirect revenge by an attack on God's new creation, man, has been accepted by the devils, Beelzebub holds out the future possibility of their dwelling in "some milde Zone . . . not unvisited of Heav'ns fair Light" (II, 397-398). Finally, Satan sums up the vast distance from darkness to light, from Hell to Heaven, from the Devil to God in the lines:

> long is the way
> And hard, that out of Hell leads up to Light.
> (*P. L.*, II, 432-433)

After the reader has made his exit from Hell with Satan, has struggled with him up through Chaos to "A glimmering dawn" (II, 1037), and catches a glimpse of Heaven and of "This pendant world," he is abundantly prepared for the beautiful invocation to light which opens Book III. The invocation provides a sharp contrast to the Biblical darkness of Hell, establishes the Biblical setting of pure light for Heaven, and foreshadows, through references to nature, the setting of Book IV in the earthly Paradise in Eden.

*Heaven*

It is not only a setting of physical light as opposed to physical darkness that Milton seeks to establish at the opening of Book III. It is also a setting of light as representative of God and of righteousness as opposed to the evil represented by Satan and his angels in the first two books. This spiritual contrast has already been referred to, but many Scriptural allusions in the invocation to light make this contrast, as well as the contrast in physical setting, more emphatic. "Hail holy light, ofspring of Heav'n first-born" (*P. L.*, III, 1) alludes to the first words spoken by God in the Genesis account of Creation, "Let there bee light" (1:3); and when the poet asks if he may without blame refer to light as "of th' Eternal Coeternal beam," he immediately quotes "God is light" (III, 3; I John 1:5) and, by referring to God as one who "never but in unapproached light / Dwelt from Eternitie" (III, 4), alludes to the Pauline statement that God "only hath immortalitie, dwelling in the light which no man can approach unto" (I Tim. 6:16). Then alternatively it is suggested that light is

> Bright effluence of bright essence increate,
> Or hear'st thou rather pure Ethereal stream
> Whose Fountain who shall tell?
> (*P. L.*, III, 6-8)

Reference is made here to the Apocryphal statement that wisdom is "a pure influence flowing from the glory of the Almighty . . . she is the brightness of the everlasting light" (Wisd. of Sol. 7:25, 26) and to God's question to Job, "Where is the way where light dwelleth?" (Job 38:19). Allusion is made again to the Divine *Fiat lux* which preceded the creation of the firmament, or Heaven, and even the sun, when Milton says to light:

> before the Sun,
> Before the Heavens thou wert, and at the voice
> Of God, as with a Mantle didst invest
> The rising world of waters dark and deep.
> (*P. L.*, III, 8-11)

An additional allusion is made to a psalm which speaks of God as one "who coverest *thyself* with light as *with* a garment" (Ps. 104:2). Having identified light with God, Milton proceeds to describe the Father as enthroned above all height with angels as "thick as Starrs" around Him and "on his right / The radiant image of his Glory" (III, 60-63). God is hymned by the angels in terms of light:

> Fountain of Light, thy self invisible
> Amidst the glorious brightness where thou sit'st
> Thron'd inaccessible, but when thou shad'st
> The full blaze of thy beams, and through a cloud
> Drawn round about thee like a radiant Shrine,
> Dark with excessive bright thy skirts appeer,
> Yet dazle Heav'n, that brightest Seraphim
> Approach not, but with both wings veil thir eyes.
> (*P. L.*, III, 375-382)

Thus light and light imagery are associated with God and Heaven as the appropriate divine setting just as darkness has been associated with Satan and Hell as the appropriate diabolic setting, and in the establishment of both settings, Milton makes liberal use of Biblical allusion. Soon, in Book IV, the earth, man's abode, is to be the center of attention and there are found both the powers of light and the powers of darkness; Gabriel and his angelic guard are in Eden for man's welfare while Satan enters the Garden to seek man's destruction. After the antithesis set up between light and darkness, it comes as no surprise that Satan's preliminary attempt on Eve (in a dream) takes place at night. But aside from the opposition of light and darkness, Milton also prepares in the invocation to light in Book III for the description of the earthly Paradise to follow in Book IV.

Turning from light in its essence as eternal and divine, Milton describes, in his invocation in Book III, some of the effects of physical light; he can feel the "sovran vital Lamp," although he cannot see its "piercing ray" (III, 21-24). Yet he does not forget nor neglect the beautiful sights that light makes manifest, such as "Cleer Spring, or shadie Grove, or Sunnie Hill" (III, 28). Although, like the Nightingale, he "Sings darkling" and never catches "sight of vernal bloom, or Summers Rose, / Or flocks, or herds, or human face divine" (III, 43-44), and although Nature's works are erased for him since he cannot see them in the physical light, he can still trust inner illumination of the divine light to make it possible for him to "see and tell / Of things invisible to mortal sight" (III, 54-55). The things which the inward shining of the "Celestial light" (l. 52) will reveal to him, though they are invisible to mortal sight, are not merely the Heavenly things of Book III: God, the Son, the angels, the sea of glass. They are also the clear springs, shady groves, and sunny hills, the vernal bloom and summer's rose, the animals, and above all, the "human face divine" of Paradise to be described in Book IV. Milton's invocation to light sets the stage, then, for his portrayal not only of Heaven but also of Earth. The eyes which Milton prays may be planted in his mind are to see more than the physical eye could see; they are the kind of eyes Paul prayed for on behalf of the Christians at Ephesus: "The eyes of your understanding being enlightened" (Eph. 1:18).

*The Garden of Eden*

The Biblical allusions used in describing the Garden of Eden and its inhabitants have been discussed in an earlier chapter. It seems worth while here, however, to emphasize that the setting (both physical and psychological) for the great drama of man's temptation and the Fall is based firmly on a Biblical description of the Garden. The Scriptural opposition between darkness and light is continued, with appropriate Biblical allusions, throughout the description of Paradise, where, from Book IV forward, there are the prince of darkness, angelic ministers of light, and the human pair which have become the focal point in the attention of Hell and Heaven—and the reader. It has been mentioned that Eve's bad dream takes place at night, and Biblical allusion is utilized in connection with that night and its aftermath.

Just before Adam and Eve retire on the night that Satan is to make his initial attempt, they speak thus in their devotions to God: "Thou also mad'st the Night, Maker Omnipotent, and thou the Day" (IV, 724-725). This allusion to the declaration of the psalmist that "The day is thine, the night also is thine" (Ps. 74:16a) makes it clear that God still controls things, even though a fateful night is falling. Only by God's permission could Satan raise his head from the burning lake in Book I, and it is only by His permission that Satan has succeeded in escaping Hell, getting into Paradise, and using the night for his own devilish purposes. He is caught in the act of seeking to raise in the mind of Eve "inordinate desires / Blown up with high conceits ingendring pride" (IV, 808-809) by the angelic guards and expelled from the Garden. Although God has control of both night and day, in poetic consistency with the opposition of light and darkness in the setting, when Satan flees, the shades of night flee with him (IV, 1015). Immediately following the close of Book IV, Gabriel and his troops having put Satan out of the Garden of Eden, Book V opens with the lovely image of the rising of morning, an image combined of Biblical and classical elements:

> Now Morn her rosie steps in th' Eastern Clime
> Advancing, sow'd the Earth with Orient Pearle.
> (*P. L.*, V, 1-2)

The Biblical allusion is to the image of the psalmist, "Light is sowen for the righteous, and gladnesse for the upright in heart" (Ps. 97:11). There is also, in the first line, a reminiscence of the recurring Ἠὼς ῥοδοδάκτυλος of Homer's *Odyssey*. The image prepares a pleasant psychological atmosphere for Adam's cheering of Eve after her dream, their morning hymn, and their visit from a heavenly messenger.

After Eve has related her dream of the night before and Adam has cheered her, the two join in a hymn of praise to God in which they call upon the various orders of creation—angels, stars, planets, sun and moon, and all the creatures of earth—to give praise to the Creator. The framework of the hymn is taken from Psalm 148 and the Apocryphal Song of the Three Children. This framework from Scripture, together with Milton's additions, serves in the speech of Adam and Eve to give a more attractive and dramatically effective picture of Paradise in the early morning than could be given in the narration of the poet. After calling upon beings and things supramundane to praise God, the hymn descends to terrestrial nature. A comparison of the psalm with the hymn of *Paradise Lost* shows how Milton filled in a Scriptural framework with beautiful poetry which is at once lyrically descriptive and earnestly devotional.[11] "Praise ye the Lord from the earth, ye dragons, and all deepes; Fire and haile; snow, and vapour; stormie wind fulfilling his word: Mountaines, and all hilles; fruitfull trees, and all cedars; Beasts, and all cattel; creeping things, and flying fowl . . . Let them praise the Name of the LORD" (Ps. 148:7-10, 13). The order, in Milton's hymn, becomes: "vapour"—"wind"—"trees"—"deepes"—"flying fowl"—"dragons"—"Beasts, and all cattel; creeping things"—"Mountaines, and all hilles."

> Ye Mists and Exhalations that now rise
> From Hill or steaming Lake, duskie or grey,
> Till the Sun paint your fleecie skirts with Gold,

11. Joseph H. Summers, in "'Grateful Vicissitude' in *Paradise Lost*," *Publications of the Modern Language Association*, LXIX (March, 1954), 251-264, emphasizes this hymn, with its portrayal of dynamic nature, as central to Milton's celebration of *change*, "of that movement which is eternal so long as God's creations continue truly to exist" (p. 264). Thus unfallen man recognizes that God is most praised by acceptance of and participation in the creation's constant state of flux and not by static forms.

In honour to the Worlds great Author rise,
Whether to deck with Clouds the uncolourd skie,
Or wet the thirstie Earth with falling showers,
Rising or falling still advance his praise.
His praise ye Winds, that from four Quarters blow,
Breathe soft or loud; and wave your tops, ye Pines,
With every Plant, in sign of Worship wave.
Fountains and yee, that warble, as ye flow,
Melodious murmurs, warbling tune his praise.
Joyn voices all ye living Souls, ye Birds,
That singing up to Heaven Gate ascend,
Bear on your wings and in your notes his praise;
Yee that in Waters glide, and yee that walk
The Earth, and stately tread, or lowly creep;
Witness if I be silent, Morn or Eeven,
To Hill, or Valley, Fountain, or fresh shade
Made vocal by my Song, and taught his praise.
(*P. L.*, V, 185-204)

It is into such a natural setting, a setting in which all Nature recognizes and praises its Maker, that Raphael comes to warn Adam and to relate the story of Satan's rebellion. Paradise was seen in Book IV primarily through the eyes of the Devil, and Adam and Eve were seen as oblivious to the lurking evil in the midst of their innocent bliss. After Eve's dream, however, there is a consciousness that something is not quite right, although Adam's explanation of the dream, based only on his knowledge of human nature within, does not take into account any outside evil influence. Raphael's mission to make Adam aware of this outside influence in the person of Satan is fulfilled within the day after Eve's dream.[12]

12. Milton's handling of setting when a long narrative of action taking place in a setting different from that in which the narrating is being done is interesting. As a dramatist would, he puts in reminders to the reader that the war in Heaven of Books V and VI is being related to Adam by Raphael, as when Raphael says to Adam that the march of the elect angels was like the "Birds in orderly array on wing" who "Came summond over *Eden* to receive / Thir names of thee" (VI, 74-76); but the reader is so caught up in the action of Heaven that the present setting in Eden is all but forgotten. Thus the invocation to Urania which opens Book VII is as necessary to bring the reader back to earth as it is for any other purpose; like the poet, he needs to be returned to his native element.

Half yet remaines unsung, but narrower bound
Within the visible Diurnal Spheare;
Standing on Earth, not rapt above the Pole,
More safe I Sing with mortal voice, unchang'd

Although the main action of Book IX takes place in the light of day, the opposition of light and darkness as representative of good and evil is maintained. The book opens, in accord with the tragic notes of the introduction, at night. Satan returns to the Garden of Eden at midnight; furthermore, he has spent the preceding seven twenty-four hour periods in a "space of seven continu'd Nights" (IX, 63) by staying constantly on the dark side of the earth. The Evil One loves "darknesse rather then light" because his deeds are evil indeed (John 3:19). He returns to Paradise on the eighth night and, discovering where the Tigris River goes underground at the foot of the Mount of Paradise to rise by the Tree of Life within the Garden,

> In with the River sunk, and with it rose
> Satan involv'd in rising Mist.
> (*P. L.*, IX, 74-75)

After Satan has compassed the earth in darkness, entered Paradise, chosen the "wilie Snake" as the instrument of temptation, unburdened himself of one of his devilish soliloquies, and entered the sleeping Serpent to await the morn, one greets Milton's description of the dawn with a sigh of relief mingled with anxiety. The beginning of the day is described in Biblical terms: the

---

> To hoarce or mute, though fall'n on evil dayes
> On evil dayes though fall'n, and evil tongues;
> In darkness, and with dangers compast round,
> And solitude.
> (*P. L.*, VII, 21-28)

In this personal passage, Milton uses Biblical allusions which help explain his meaning and at the same time set a mood for that which is to come: a mood of expectation of the Fall. Milton returns the reader not only to the earth of Adam but also, by anticipation, to the earth of Milton, an earth under a curse and afflicted by the "barbarous dissonance / Of Bacchus and his Revellers" (VII, 32-33), an earth in which a great voice, though neither hoarse nor mute, has fallen on evil days and evil tongues. Bible passages alluded to are: "Remember now thy Creatour in the dayes of thy youth, while the evill dayes come not . . . while the Sunne or the light . . . be not darkened" (Eccles. 12:1-2) and "walke circumspectly, not as fooles, but as wise, Redeeming the time, because the days are evill. . . . And be not drunke with wine . . . but be filled with the Spirit; Speaking to yourselves in Psalms and Hymnes, & spiritual songs, singing and making melody in your heart to the Lord" (Eph. 5:15-19). Although Milton is old and his light is darkened, he is not hoarse; he lives in evil days when others are drunk with wine and walk as fools, but he is not mute. With heavenly aid, he continues to sing, both because of and in spite of his position, "Standing on Earth, not rapt above the Pole."

light which dawns on Eden is "sacred Light" (IX, 192) for "God is light" (I John 1:5) and all things that breathe, as from a great altar, "send up silent praise / To the Creator, and his Nostrils fill / With grateful smell" (IX, 194-197), as when offerings were made on an Old Testament altar and "the LORD smelled a sweet savour" (Gen. 8:21).

But all is not right in Eden. Eve has already been affected by the Satanic dream, and, unaware that Satan's night-hatched scheme to use the Serpent to lead man into sin has already been put into operation, she broaches to Adam in Biblical language her plan "to dress / This Garden" (IX, 205-206; Gen. 2:15) more efficiently by their working separately. After she has won her point over Adam's wiser objections and has begun to work in an isolated area, Satan, "to his wish, / Beyond his hope" (IX, 423-424), spies Eve

> Veild in a Cloud of Fragrance, where she stood,
> Half spi'd, so thick the Roses bushing round
> About her glowd, oft stooping to support
> Each Flour of slender stalk, whose head though gay
> Carnation, Purple, Azure, or spect with Gold,
> Hung drooping unsustaind, them she upstaies
> Gently with Mirtle band, mindless the while,
> Her self, though fairest unsupported Flour,
> From her best prop so farr, and storm so nigh.
> (*P. L.*, IX, 425-433)

Milton compares this "delicious" setting to mythical gardens,

> Or that, not Mystic, where the Sapient King
> Held dalliance with his faire *Egyptian* Spouse.
> (*P. L.*, IX, 442-443)

In the Song of Solomon the Bride speaks of her beloved as having gone "downe into his garden, to the beds of spices, to feed in the gardens, and to gather lillies" (6:2). Milton's identification of the Bride of Solomon's Song with the wise king's Egyptian wife is based on the words of the Bridegroom, "How beautifull are thy feet with shooes, O Princes daughter!" (Song of Sol. 7:1) coupled with the account of Solomon's marriage to the daughter of Pharaoh (I Kings 3:1). Thus the setting in which Eve is found by Satan is given a Biblical background by comparison with the sensual beauty of the garden of Solomon. It is no wonder that Satan, confronted by such beauty, is tortured more "the more he sees / Of pleasure not for him ordain'd" (IX, 469-470) and resolves even fiercer hate and stronger determination to ruin mankind.

Involved in the Biblical comparison to Eve's setting is a double irony. If Adam had maintained his position of authority as "head" and "prop" of Eve, his "fairest unsupported Flour" (IX, 432, 433; I Cor. 11:3), instead of giving in to her desire to work separately, Eve would not be in this place, alone, viewed by the Tempter, and Adam and his posterity might not have been led into sin and death. The Biblical situation is a similar one: if Solomon had not indulged his weakness for "strange women," of whom his "*Egyptian* Spouse" was the first (I Kings 1:11), he and his nation would not have been led into idolatry. Again there is irony in the reference to "dalliance" by a "Sapient King." After Adam has eaten of the fruit with Eve, the pair begin to burn in lust, and Milton echoes the reference to Solomon in the lines:

> Till *Adam* thus 'gan *Eve* to dalliance move.
> *Eve*, now I see thou art exact of taste,
> And elegant, of Sapience no small part.
> (*P. L.*, IX, 1016-1018)

And Adam proceeds to demonstrate how much sapience he has gained from the fruit by his horrifyingly blasphemous joke,

> if such pleasure be
> In things to us forbidden, it might be wish'd,
> For this one Tree had bin forbidden ten.
> (*P. L.*, IX, 1024-1026)

But after sin comes shame, and Adam, like the sinners in the Apocalypse, wishes that he might be covered, not by rocks and mountains, but by the thickest and highest woods; of the face of "God or Angel, earst with joy . . . beheld" he cries out to the forest trees, "Hide me, where I may never see them more" (IX, 1090), echoing the cry of the mighty men of John's vision, who pray to the rocks and mountains, "hide us from the face of him that sitteth on the Throne" (Rev. 6:16). The Biblical allusion emphasizes dramatically the shift that has come about in man's attitude towards his natural setting; the trees which have served as a pleasant shade while Adam communed with his Maker and with Raphael are now thought of only as a means of hiding from God and His messengers of light. Like the Tempter, Adam now loves darkness rather than light because his deeds are evil.

Adam and Eve remain hidden among the thick trees of Paradise, engaging in bitter "mutual accusation . . . but neither self-condemning" (IX, 1187, 1189), until the evening; then the Father sends the Son to the Garden of Eden to judge fallen man. The setting of the judgment scene is established in Biblical language. "The coole of the day" with "soft windes" carrying the sound of the Judge's voice to the guilty pair in their hiding place (Gen. 3:8; *P. L.*, X, 95-101) emphasizes the gentleness and mercy with which the Judge tempers his justice. Later in the same setting Adam and Eve repent in humble contrition for their sin, encouraged to believe that they will be forgiven by remembering the mild and gracious temper of their Judge and his tender care for them in clothing them against the changed climate of an earth that has been put under the curse of sin.

*The Atmosphere of Alternatives*

In addition to his use of the Bible in the establishment of physical setting and psychological mood, Milton uses Biblical allusion in such a way as to create an atmosphere of alternatives, of freedom of choice, both for the actors in *Paradise Lost* and for the reader.[13] During Raphael's visit to Adam's bower in Book V, both Adam and the reader become acutely conscious of man's ability and responsibility to make free choices between alternatives. First it is the reader. He does not have to recognize the Biblical allusion involved, for Milton makes an explicit statement which carries his point. Recognition of the allusion, however, intensifies the atmosphere of the ability of both angels and men to choose good or evil, to obey or disobey their Maker.

13. There are matters on which Milton discusses alternative theories without dogmatically asserting, as poetic statement, either alternative as true, without any Biblical allusions. For example, although his universe in *P. L.* is constructed according to the Ptolemaic system, the Copernican system is suggested as possibly true by Raphael (VIII, 122-178), and although Milton accepts the theory that the sun's course was altered after the Fall, he presents the alternative explanation that the earth's poles were turned "ascanse . . . twice ten degrees and more" (X, 651-691).

> Mean while at Table *Eve*
> Ministered naked, and thir flowing cups
> With pleasant liquors crown'd: O innocence
> Deserving Paradise! if ever, then,
> Then had the Sons of God excuse to have bin
> Enamour'd at that sight; but in those hearts
> Love unlibidinous reign'd, nor jealousie
> Was understood, the injur'd Lovers Hell.
> (*P. L.*, V, 443-450)

Milton is applying the reference to the "sons of God who saw the daughters of men that they *were* fair; and . . . took them wives of all which they chose" (Gen. 6:2) to both Raphael and Adam. The two opposing interpretations of this Biblical passage, both of them referred to in other parts of his epic poems, are (1) that the sons of God represent the fallen angels who took human wives and bred a race of giants before the flood and (2) that the sons of God represent the human descendants of the godly line of Seth who intermarried with the women of the line of Cain.[14] Milton's point in the passage from *Paradise Lost* quoted above is twofold: if ever an angel could have been excused for falling in love with a woman, it would have been when Raphael saw Eve in all her naked beauty as she ministered to his needs at Adam's table; if ever a man could have been excused for lusting after a woman and being jealous of anyone else's enjoying the sight of her, it would have been in this bower scene. "But in those hearts"—the heart of Raphael and the heart of Adam—"Love unlibidinous reign'd, nor jealousie / Was understood." In Book IV, when Satan sees the lovers together, he cannot resist a "jealous leer maligne" (l. 503), for he has chosen to follow evil; Raphael, on the other hand, though possessed of as free a will as Satan, knows neither libidinous love nor jealousy, for he has chosen to follow God and good. A few lines further after the reader has been made conscious that an atmosphere of free alternatives prevails and that it is by choice that

14. See *P. L.*, III, 463-465; *P. L.*, XI, 621-627; *P. R.*, II, 179-181. In the first reference, which is noncommittal, the speaker is Milton; in the second, which adopts the sons of Seth theory, the speaker is Raphael; in the third, which agrees with the fallen angel hypothesis, the speaker is Satan. It may be safe to assume that, as one conscious of the dramatic character of the speakers in his poems, Milton gave what he felt to be the truth to Raphael and what was either unreliable or false to Satan.

Adam and Raphael are good, Adam becomes conscious of his own freedom as he has not been before. In answer to Adam's question, "What meant that caution joind, *if ye be found / Obedient?*" (V, 513-514), Raphael replies:

> God made thee perfet, not immutable;
> And good he made thee, but to persevere
> He left it in thy power, ordaind thy will
> By nature free, not over-rul'd by Fate
> Inextricable, or strict necessity;
> Our voluntarie service he requires,
> Not our necessitated.
>
> (*P. L.*, V, 524-530)

The allusion to the sons of God of Genesis is a means of preparing not only for this pronouncement on free will but also for the free choice of Satan to rebel and the free choice of Abdiel to remain loyal to God, soon to be related by Raphael.

In Book X, having pronounced judgment upon Adam and Eve and the Serpent, the Son, "both Judge and Saviour sent" (X, 209), takes pity on the pair who stand before him naked to an atmosphere now to suffer adverse change because of sin, and he clothes

> Thir nakedness with Skins of Beasts, or slain,
> Or as the Snake with youthful Coate repaid.
>
> (*P. L.*, X, 217-218)

Here the mood of free choice is established by the alternatives Milton refers to as present in the Biblical text alluded to: "Unto Adam also, and his wife, did the LORD God make coates of skinnes and cloathed them" (Gen. 3:21). The reader may take his choice and believe either that God killed the animals to provide coats for the man and woman or that the skins were merely shed to be naturally replaced by new skins for the animals. The pair have both their outward and inward nakedness hidden by the gracious action of the Son, although neither Adam nor Eve has yet shown repentance. The Son "thought not much to cloath his Enemies" (X, 219), an allusion to the text "when we were enemies, we were reconciled to God by the death of his Son" (Rom. 5:10), which emphasizes at once the provident grace of God and the still unrepentant state of the sinners.

Repentance must come as voluntarily as did transgression and, later in Book X, it does come, but not before the mood of alternative choices is emphasized further. The angels hymn the Son, after his ultimate victory over sin and death has been announced by the Father, as

> Destin'd restorer of Mankind, by whom
> New Heav'n and Earth shall to the Ages rise,
> Or down from Heav'n descend.
>
> (*P. L.*, X, 646-648)

The New Heaven and New Earth will either rise out of Chaos like the first Heaven and Earth (*P. L.*, I, 9-10), as Michael later indicates that they will (XII, 546-549), or they will descend from the abode of God, as John, in the Apocalypse, saw them "coming downe from God out of heaven" (Rev. 21:2). Milton, through the hymn of the angels, is maintaining the atmosphere of alternatives, and even emphasizing it, in Book X preceding the repentance of Adam and Eve. Immediately following the hymn are two different theories of how the seasons of cold and heat came to affect the earth. "Some say" (X, 668) that the earth's poles were turned askance from the sun's axle; on the other hand, "Som say" (l. 671) that the sun changed its course.

In the midst of this atmosphere of alternatives in Book X there is the soliloquy of Adam, often quoted as support for Milton's espousal in *Paradise Lost* of the mortalist heresy, in which he revolves the question, "How much of me dies with death? Body only, or both body and spirit?" Adam's statement, "All of me then shall die" (X, 792) does not settle the question. A few lines later he returns to his prior speculation that perhaps the spirit cannot die with the body.

> But say
> That Death be not one stroak, as I suppos'd,
> Bereaving sense, but endless miserie
> . . . . . . . . . . . . . . . . .
> Ay me, that fear
> Comes thundring back with dreadful revolution
> On my defensless head.
>
> (*P. L.*, X, 808-810, 813-815)

Adam's struggle with the problem of death is not a mere dogmatic parallel to Milton's *De Doctrina Christiana,* as it has been supposed.[15] It is a dramatically conceived and expressed presentation of the thoughts of a man caught up in one of the greatest of all mysteries, the mystery of death. Adam is in no position to dogmatize or settle theological matters; his is a human situation of dramatic power not unlike that of Hamlet in his "To be or not to be" soliloquy or Claudio, in *Measure for Measure,* contemplating what lies beyond death. Added to this, the atmosphere of alternatives developed in Book X, partly by means of Biblical allusion, works against the reader's getting any impression of a settled conviction on the part of Adam as to the nature of death.

Finally both Adam and Eve come freely to the place of accepting responsibility for their own sin; Adam can speak sincerely at the close of Book X of the atmospheric changes of the earth as "evils which our own misdeeds have wrought" (l. 1081). Returning to the same Biblical setting in which they were judged, the two voluntarily and humbly confess their faults and seek forgiveness, believing, as they remember the mild compassion with which He judged and clothed them in the cool of the evening, that God will "relent and turn / From his displeasure" (X, 1093-1094).

### *Paradise Regained*

Some of Milton's most beautiful descriptions of setting are in *Paradise Regained.* Such a passage as that describing the morning following the night-long howling storm to which Satan has subjected Christ is unsurpassed in Milton's poetry (*P. R.,* IV, 426-438). There is very little use, however, of Biblical allusion in the establishment of setting in the shorter epic. The setting in the desert is, of course, taken from the Scriptural accounts of the temptation (Matt. 4, Luke 4), and the effect of Christ's aloneness in the wil-

15. Maurice Kelley (*This Great Argument* [Princeton, 1941], pp. 154-155) gives lines from Adam's soliloquy as parallels to the *De Doctrina* discussion of death as of the whole man, body and spirit; and, of course, there are close parallels. The point here is that the dramatic nature of the poem prevents any insistence that the meaning of parallel statements in it and the prose treatise is identical or that Milton intended to indoctrinate the readers of his poem with the theology of his treatise. See Chapter One (pp. 39-40) for a discussion of another instance in which Professor Kelley draws dogma from a dramatic situation.

derness is strengthened by allusions to Biblical stories of others who suffered privation in the desert: Elijah (*P. R.*, II, 266-269, 312-314 with I Kings 17:5-6, 19:5-7), Hagar (II, 308 with Gen. 25-13), and the whole race of Israel (II, 310-312 with Exod. 16:4, 14-15).

Biblical allusion is used for both physical setting and psychological mood in a scene which occurs in the opening of Book II. When the disciples of Christ miss him after his baptism, they begin to doubt "and doubted many days, / And as the days increas'd, increas'd thir doubt" (II, 11-12). Their lack of faith and near despair is emphasized by allusions to the time that Moses was "in the Mount, and missing long" (l. 14) when the people of Israel, through impatience and faithlessness, built a golden calf to worship (Exod. 32) and to the time when Elijah, having been caught up by God in a chariot of fire, was sought by the doubting sons of the prophets of Jericho (ll. 15-19 with II Kings 2:11-18). Then, after listing the names of the cities and towns in which the disciples searched for Jesus (names which call up in the Bible student's mind an image of the Jordan area of a map of Palestine), Milton describes the scene in which Andrew, Simon, and the others discuss the disappearance of the Messiah.

> Then on the bank of *Jordan*, by a Creek:
> Where winds with Reeds, and Osiers whisp'ring play
> Plain Fishermen, no greater men them call,
> Close in a Cottage low together got
> Thir unexpected loss and plaints out breath'd.
> (*P. R.*, II, 25-29)

Both the physical and the psychological setting are drawn from the reprimand of Jesus to the people who had gone to Jordan to hear John the Baptist preach and had been disappointed in him and had not believed his message. Jesus asked, "What went yee out in the wildernesse to see? A reed shaken with the wind?" (Matt. 11:7). Many of those who went to hear John preach did not expect him to be so uncompromising and firm in his message; they expected him to be as variable as the natural scenery of wind-blown reeds on the river bank. Consequently they were disappointed and did not believe. The disciples in *Paradise Regained* "on that high Authority had believ'd" (II, 5), but now that events have not gone as they expected, they have followed the example of the doubting prophets of Jericho in searching for their master, and they have gathered in the same or a similar scene (on the bank of the Jordan where wind-swayed reeds grow) as that in which they first believed John's proclamation that Jesus is the Son of God. Fortunately, as they recall how God has dealt with them thus far, their hope and faith conquer doubt and "they out of their plaints new hope resume" (II, 58).[16]

Thus Biblical allusions are used in both epic poems to suggest physical setting and psychological mood; in *Paradise Lost* such allusions are used also to establish an atmosphere of alternative choices, both for the reader and for the human actors in the poem. The general effect of such use of allusion in both epics is to increase the reader's understanding of the significance of the drama taking place within the physical and psychological setting.

## *ACTION*

Milton uses Biblical allusion for increasing the dramatic effect of the action of the poems in three ways: to emphasize the significance of the present action, to foreshadow forthcoming action within the poem itself, and to place the action of the poem in the broader context of eternity and the inevitability of the ultimate victory of God over evil.

### *Present Action*

After the fallen angels are roused up from the burning lake in *Paradise Lost,* Book I, and the principal ones are described in terms of the names by which they are later to be known to their worshippers, some account is given of the particular blasphemy against the true God connected with the temples of each: Moloch led Solomon, through his wives, to build his idolatrous temple "right against the Temple of God" (I, 402); Peor led the men of

16. With special reference to the psychological setting, it is interesting to note that a pattern of progression from doubt to hope is set here and is repeated with Mary, who begins with "O what avails me now" (II, 66) and ends with "I to wait with patience am inur'd" (l. 102); with Satan, who suggests to his council that he may be overmatched (ll. 145-146) but ends with a confident "The rest commit to me" (l. 233); and even Christ begins with "Where will this end?" (l. 245) and ends with "I content me" (l. 257).

Israel into adulterous relationship with the women of Moab and later had his temple near Moloch's, "lust hard by hate" (I, 417), *et cetera.* Thus it is appropriate that Milton's description of the future anti-God activity of the devils to be adored for deities in their pagan temples be followed by a description of the present action of their building Pandaemonium in Hell with allusions associating it with the great Temple built for God in Jerusalem by Solomon. Mammon and his crew, having quickly discovered that there is gold in the hills of Hell, build in an hour what innumerable hands could scarce perform in an age.

> Anon out of the earth a Fabrick huge
> Rose like an Exhalation, with the sound
> Of Dulcet Symphonies and voices sweet,
> Built like a Temple.
>
> (*P. L.*, I, 710-713)

A comparison is made to the shrines of pagan gods built by Alcairo and Babylon "when Ægypt with Assyria strove / In wealth and luxurie" (ll. 721-722), but the circumstances of the building of Pandaemonium, coupled with the preceding emphasis on the future rivalry between the seats of these devils and the Seat of God in Jerusalem, cause the reader familiar with the Bible to make a comparison between this "ascending pile" and the construction of Solomon's Temple. There is no mention of music accompanying the building of the Temple at Jerusalem like that which accompanies the rise of Satan's palace, but the absence of any sounds signifying effort or labor—"there was neither hammer nor axe, nor any toole of iron heard in the house, while it was in building" (I Kings 6:7)—is notable in the construction of both temples. In Pandaemonium are "Doric pillars overlaid / With Golden Architrave" and the roof is "fretted Gold" (I, 714-715, 717); the Temple in Jerusalem was "overlayd . . . within with pure gold" (I Kings 6:21) and the decorative carvings of the Temple were "covered with gold, fitted upon the carved worke" (I Kings 6:35). Such language, associating Pandaemonium (built by Heaven's fallen Architect even as Solomon's Temple incorporated features of heavenly architecture, since it followed the pattern God gave Moses for the tabernacle in the wilderness) with the Temple of God, intensifies at once one's admiration for the industry of the devils and one's horror at their blasphemy in not only building a palace like a temple for the Arch-Enemy but even building it with similarities to the Biblical Temple. The devils far surpass what the most dedicated and devoted men could do in building a temple for God; Solomon's Temple took seven years to build and, though built silently, involved a tremendous amount of labor, while Satan's palace rises to the sound of sweet music in an hour. The allusion heightens, by contrast, the speed of construction and the beauty of Pandaemonium and the amazing power and energy of the fallen angels.

Upon the dissolution of the "*Stygian* Counsel" the leading demons issue forth from Pandaemonium with Satan in the midst in "Godlike imitated State":

> him round
> A Globe of fierie Seraphim inclos'd
> With bright imblazonrie, and horrent Arms.
> Then of thir Session ended they bid cry
> With Trumpets regal sound the great result:
> Toward the four winds four speedy Cherubim
> Put to their mouths the sounding Alchymie
> By Haralds voice explain'd: the hollow Abyss
> Heard far and wide.
>
> (*P. L.*, II, 511-519)

The magnificence of Satan's pomp, the angels, and the sounding of the trumpets recall the Biblical description of the Second Advent of Christ. "They shall see the Sonne of Man comming in the cloudes of heaven with power and great glory. And he shall send his Angels with a great sound of a trumpet, and they shall gather together his elect from the foure windes, from one ende of heaven to the other" (Matt. 24:30b-31). The parallelism between the pomp of Hell and that of Heaven raises Satan in splendor and simultaneously magnifies his blasphemous pride, for his departure from Pandaemonium to initiate the temptation which will lead to man's destruction is accompanied by trumpeting angels comparable to those who are to gather redeemed mankind together when the trumpet sounds at the end of time. There is a point of contrast which the allusion reveals; whereas the Biblical trumpet calls the elect together from the four winds, the demonic trumpets result in the dispersion of the demons into various parts of Hell to pursue various diversions as they await the return of their Chief.

Those of the dispersed fallen angels who are adventurous in nature set out to explore Hell and are identified, by Biblical allusion, with the unclean spirits who afflicted demoniacs in the New Testament, such as the one spoken of by Christ, who, when he has gone out of a man, "walketh through drie places, seeking reste and findeth none" (Matt. 12:43). Milton's roving bands

> With shuddring horror pale, and eyes agast
> View'd first thir lamentable lot, and found
> No rest.
>
> (*P. L.*, II, 615-618)

As the devils wander "O're many a Frozen, many a Fierie Alpe, / Rocks, Caves, Lakes, Fens, Bogs, Dens, and shades of death," encountering "*Gorgons* and *Hydra's*, and *Chimera's* dire" (II, 621-622, 628), they return the reader to the horrifying realization of what Hell really is; such description, using both Biblical and classical allusions, brings one a long way from the marvelous Palace of Hell, "built like a Temple," the eloquent oratory of the devils, and the "Godlike imitated State" of Satan and prepares one for the unspeakably ugly and monstrous offspring of Satan who are soon to confront their father at the gates of Hell. The change from pomp and circumstance to the true hellishness of Hell begins with Satan's issuance from his palace and the allusion which contrasts the demons' reception of the plan to ruin mankind with Christ's gathering of his elect together at his return for the ultimate redemption of mankind.

Biblical allusion adds dramatic power to the action of the closing lines of *Paradise Lost.*

> In either hand the hastning Angel caught
> Our lingring Parents, and to th' Eastern Gate
> Led them direct, and down the Cliff as fast
> To the subjected Plaine; then disappeer'd.
> They looking back, all th' Eastern side beheld
> Of Paradise, so late thir happie seat,
> Wav'd over by that flaming Brand, the Gate

> With dreadful Faces throng'd and fierie Armes:
> Som natural tears they drop'd, but wip'd them soon;
> The World was all before them, where to choose
> Thir place of rest, and Providence thir guide;
> They hand in hand with wandring steps and slow,
> Through *Eden* took thir solitarie way.
> (*P. L.*, XII, 637-649)

There is amplified re-telling here, of course, of the expulsion scene in Genesis in which God "drove out the man; and he placed at the East of the garden of Eden Cherubims, and a flaming sword which turned every way, to keepe the way of the tree of life" (3:24), but there is also allusion to the action, later in Genesis, of the deliverance by angels of Lot and his wife and daughters from the imminent destruction of Sodom: "And when the morning arose, then the Angels hastened Lot, saying, Arise, take thy wife, and thy two daughters ... lest thou be consumed in the iniquitie of the citie. And while he lingred, the men laid hold upon his hand, and upon the hand of his wife, and upon the hand of his two daughters; the LORD being mercifull unto him: and they brought him foorth, and set him without the citie.... But his wife looked backe from behind him, and she became a pillar of salt" (19:15-16, 26). The similarities are immediately apparent to anyone familiar with the story of Lot, and recognition of the similarities leads to an awareness of the dissimilar elements in the action. Lot and his family are being delivered from the destruction of a wicked place because Lot is righteous; Adam and Eve are being driven from the Garden of Eden because they have sinned. Lot, his wife, and his two daughters are commanded not to look back, for looking back would be the equivalent of identifying themselves with Sodom and of regretting the destruction of such a wicked place; Adam and Eve are not so commanded and they do look back, for the hope of regaining Paradise through the promised Seed has been held out to them as well as the prospect of possessing, through righteousness, a Paradise within themselves "happier farr." The backward look of Lot's wife brings her petrification into salt; the backward look of Adam and Eve brings the dropping of "Som natural tears" for the loss of their "happie seat" but also a dependence upon guiding Providence. This dependence has been strengthened by the visions Michael has given Adam as well as by the dreams God has given Eve, whereby they have been shown the good that God will ultimately bring out of the evil of their sin and loss of Paradise. Therefore, although the action is associated with the Biblical expulsion from the Garden, a harsh, punitive, and depriving action by God, Milton has given overtones of hope to the scene by allusion to the story of Lot, who was not expelled as a punishment from God but was delivered through His mercy. The element of hope is heightened when the points of contrast are recognized between the action of the poem and that of the Bible story. Thus, for the reader who knows the Bible, the closing action of *Paradise Lost* does not seem in sad contrast to the hopeful visions of a better world given by Michael; tears are dropped but they are soon wiped away, as Adam and Eve, hand in hand and with Providence to guide them, face a world under the curse of their Fall, but a world to be redeemed by the prophesied Seed of Eve.[17]

In the same action, the descending cherubim, "Gliding meteorous," are compared to the evening mist, rising from a river and gliding over the marshes as it "gathers ground fast at the Labourers heel / Homeward returning" (XII, 631-632). This simile helps to mitigate the sadness of Adam's expulsion from the Garden; his activity has changed little since he worked in the Garden, and now he is to labor to earn his bread by the sweat of his brow. After all, he is returning home to the ground from whence he was taken before he was placed in Paradise. The image of the laborer returning home in the evening is not an unpleasant one. Yet it is indicative of the merging of sadness and hope throughout the closing action of *Paradise Lost* that this image has other connotations. It is part of Adam's curse to be a laborer until, as God said to him, "thou returne unto the ground; for out of it wast thou taken; for dust thou *art,* and unto dust shalt thou returne"

17. One of Joseph Addison's criticisms of the fable of *Paradise Lost* was that it did not have a happy ending. He said, "Milton seems to have been sensible of this imperfection in his fable, and has therefore endeavoured to cure it by several expedients, particularly by the mortification which the great adversary of mankind meets with upon his return to the assembly of infernal spirits . . . and likewise by the vision wherein Adam . . . sees . . . himself restored to a happier Paradise." (*Spectator* paper no. 297 [Feb. 9, 1712], in

(Gen. 3:19). One sense, then, in which Adam is the laborer "Homeward returning" is that he is moving inevitably toward death and the grave in his native dust. Yet although the forces of judgment occupy the ground at his heel, the promised Seed will one day bring judgment upon the head of the one who will bruise his (the Seed's) heel, and by returning to the ground in death, he will conquer death and the grave as "the last Adam . . . made a quickening spirit" (I Cor. 15:45).

In planning the action of *Paradise Regained* Milton did not have to decide what its limitations would be, for the limits are set by the account of the temptation of Christ in the Gospels which were his sources. Apparently he felt, however, a necessity for making clear why certain kinds of temptations were not applied to Christ by the Tempter. To this end he made use of Biblical allusion in Satan's explanation to Belial and the other devils of why Christ was not tempted with women. After his unsuccessful attempt to get Christ to turn stones into bread, Satan returns to his domain in the air to discuss with his "Potentates in Council" the problem of how to bring about the downfall of Christ, a man to whom Adam was "inferior far," "Though *Adam* by his Wives allurement fell" (II, 134). Belial is the only devil who suggests a plan of attack:

> Set women in his eye and in his walk,
> Among daughters of men the fairest found;
> . . . . . . . . . . . . . . . . .
> Women, when nothing else, beguil'd the heart
> Of wisest *Solomon,* and made him build,
> And made him bow to the Gods of his Wives.
> (*P. R.*, II, 153-154, 169-171)

Satan has a quick answer for this suggestion: "But he whom we attempt is wiser far / Then *Solomon*" (II, 205-206). Belial's allusion is to the account in I Kings of Solomon's weakness for strange (i. e., foreign, pagan) women and his sin of building temples for

*Addison's Criticisms on Paradise Lost,* ed. Albert S. Cook [New York, 1926], p. 35.) The Biblical allusions pointed out above do not make the ending happy, but they do constitute another expedient used by Milton, and used successfully, to avoid leaving the reader in a downcast and despondent mood at the end of the poem.

the idolatrous worship of his wives (11:1-4); the argument is, If Solomon, the wisest of men, was led astray by women, why not this man? Satan's answer alludes to the words of Christ to the Pharisees: "The queen of the south shall rise in the judgment with this generation, and shall condemn it: for she came from the uttermost parts of the earth to hear the wisdome of Solomon: and behold, a greater then Solomon *is* here" (Matt. 12:42). Satan's repudiation of Belial's suggestion provides a basis for limiting the temptation to "manlier objects . . . such as have more shew / Of worth, of honour, glory, and popular praise. . . . Or that which only seems to satisfie / Lawful desires of Nature, not beyond" (II, 225-227, 229-230). This decision made, Satan returns to the wilderness to proceed with the temptation. His going, not alone but in company with "a chosen band / Of Spirits likest to himself in guile" (II, 236-237), recalls the unclean spirit Jesus told of in the verses immediately following the quoted reference to Solomon, who, having left his abode in a human being, returns to his house from whence he came and "taketh with him selfe seven other spirits more wicked than himselfe" so that the "last state of that man is worse then the first" (Matt. 12:43-45). When Satan, having been repulsed in Book I, returns with reinforcements in Book II to launch a more elaborate program of temptation, his course of action and the limits within which that action is to take place are set up with the aid of Biblical allusion. The allusions not only emphasize the significance of the present action but also foreshadow future action to take place within the poem.

*Future Action*

Important elements in the human action to take place on the earth are foreshadowed in the demonic action of Book I of *Paradise Lost.* In the roll call of the fallen angels, Milton uses the name of each as he is to be known later in the pagan worship of Canaan, and he refers to Biblical stories of the blasphemies connected with the worship of each. The part Solomon played in establishing these pagan deities in Jerusalem is alluded to three times during the roll call, and the high place which Solomon set aside for the temples of abomination, called in Scripture "the mount of corruption" (II

Kings 23:13), is referred to as "that opprobrious Hill" (I, 403), "that Hill of scandal" (I, 416), and "th' offensive Mountain" (I, 443). Of Solomon himself, who, according to Scripture, was "wiser than all men" (I Kings 4:31) and yet was led astray by his wives, who "turned away his heart... after other gods" (I Kings 11: 3-4), Milton says that Moloch led his "wisest heart... by fraud to build / His Temple right against the Temple of God" (I, 402-403); and the Solomon who had the divine gift of "largenesse of heart" (I Kings 4:29), Milton calls "that uxorious King, whose heart though large, / Beguil'd by fair Idolatresses, fell / To Idols foul" (I, 444-446). In *Paradise Lost* Solomon, quite anachronistically, becomes a type of Adam, foreshadowing Adam's fall. As Solomon, though the wisest of men, was led into sin by Satan, working by fraud through women, Adam falls and completes the sin original as a result of the fraud Satan perpetrates upon Eve, who then practices a similar fraud upon Adam (though he is not deceived). The reader is reminded of Solomon's uxoriousness and his "fair Idolatresses" when Michael shows Adam the "fair Atheists" who are to lead astray the sons of God and bring on the flood. Adam cries out that man's woe ever begins with woman, but Michael replies, "From Mans effeminate slackness it begins" (XI, 634).

A more explicit allusion to Solomon at a crucial point in the poem is that found amidst the tragic notes of Book IX. The Garden of Eden is like that of "reviv'd *Adonis,* or renownd / *Alcinous* ... Or that, not Mystic, where the Sapient King / Held dalliance with his faire *Egyptian* Spouse" (IX, 440, 442-443). The allusion to the garden in the Song of Solomon (6:2) and to Solomon's Egyptian bride (Song of Sol. 7:1; I Kings 3:1, 11:1) points backward to Book I and to the references made there to Solomon's part in the infiltration of pagan worship into Jerusalem, while it points forward to Adam's post-Fall dalliance with his spouse and his punning about "Sapience." The point being made here is that Solomon and his strange wives have not suddenly entered the poem by way of an allusion in Book IX; such allusions have been made strongly and repeatedly in Book I to foreshadow the action of Book IX in which Adam, like Solomon, falls as a result of the fraud practiced by Satan upon the wife Adam loves so well.

Biblical language foreshadows future action within the poem in Book V. Satan has entered the Garden and caused Eve to dream of the smell and taste of the forbidden fruit; when she relates the dream to Adam next morning, he seeks to comfort her with the thought that if she so much abhors having dreamed of doing such a thing, she surely will never consent to commit such an act when awake.

> Be not disheart'nd then, nor cloud those looks
> That wont to be more chearful and serene
> Then when fair Morning first smiles on the World,
> And let us to our fresh imployments rise
> Among the Groves, the Fountains, and the Flours
> That open now thir choicest bosom'd smells
> Reservd from night, and kept for thee in store.
> So cheard he his fair Spouse, and she was cheard,
> But silently a gentle tear let fall
> From either eye, and wip'd them with her haire.
> (*P. L.*, V, 122-131)

For the reader sensitive to Biblical allusion, there is powerful dramatic irony in Adam's assurance that the groves are opening their choicest delights, which they have "Reservd from night" and "kept . . . in store" for Eve. For one thing, night is associated with the Devil in the poem; it is his element, and the too recent influence that he has exerted upon Eve during the night is vividly remembered. But, more important, Adam's last words may well be an echo of a Biblical warning of the coming judgment upon the world because of sin. "But the heavens and the earth, which are now, by the same word are kept in store, reserved unto fire against the day of Judgement and perdition of ungodly men" (II Pet. 3:7). There is one of the garden trees in particular the fruit of which is reserved and kept in store for Eve, and judgment upon all mankind as well as upon the heavens and the earth will be the result of her appetite's succumbing to its "choicest bosom'd smells." But just as Eve now sheds tears as a sign of "sweet remorse" for her dream, the remorse and repentance which she will eventually feel for the actual sin of eating the fruit is foreshadowed as she wipes her tears with her hair. The action calls to mind the woman "which was a sinner" who came to Jesus and wiped the tears which she shed on his feet "with the haires of her head" (Luke 7:37-38). Of course, the whole matter of the Satanic dream, in addition to functioning as a part of Milton's justification of the ways of God to men by making occasion for the warning visit of Raphael, serves to foreshadow the actual temptation and sin of Eve; but the Biblical allusions intensify the dramatic irony by giving ominous overtones of judgment upon a sinful world to Adam's ostensibly comforting words to Eve and by associating Eve with the repentant Magdalene.

Raphael's final warning to Adam at the close of Book VIII is reminiscent of Scripture and foreshadows the way in which Adam will fall from innocence. Adam has admitted to Raphael that Eve is so beautiful and composed of so many winning graces that

> Wisdom in discourse with her
> Looses discount'nanc't, and like folly shewes;
> Authoritie and Reason on her waite,
> As one intended first, not after made
> Occasionally.
> (*P. L.*, VIII, 552-556)

Upon hearing this, Raphael, "with contracted brow," warns Adam against "attributing overmuch to things / Less excellent" (ll. 565-566) and against mistaking passion for love. The angel's final charge is:

> Be strong, live happie, and love, but first of all
> Him whom to love is to obey, and keep
> His great command; take heed least Passion sway
> Thy Judgment to do aught, which else free Will
> Would not admit.
> . . . . . . . . . . . . . .
> stand fast; to stand or fall
> Free in thine own Arbitrement it lies.
> Perfet within, no outward aid require;
> And all temptation to transgress repel.
> (*P. L.*, VIII, 633-637, 640-643)

Raphael's charge alludes to God's exhortation to Joshua to "be strong" (Josh. 1:6) as he replaced Moses as the leader of Israel and to the New Testament principle that "the love of God is that we keep his commandments" (I John 5:3), but it is the allusion to Paul's commendation of one who "standeth stedfast in his heart, having no necessity, but hath power over his own will, and hath so decreed in his heart that he will keep his virgin" (I Cor. 7:37) which hints that in the forthcoming action Adam will allow his passionate love for Eve to sway his judgment and cause him to eat the fruit which otherwise his free will would have rejected. In Book IX, when Adam completes the "mortal Sin / Original" by eating the fruit, it is "Against his better knowledge, not deceav'd, / But fondly overcome with Femal charm" (IX, 998-999); he does not stand steadfast although he has "power over his own will" and is "Free in [his] own Arbitrement," but he feels such necessity that "he resolves through vehemence of love to perish with her" ("Argument," Book IX).[18] Neglecting to keep Raphael's charge to love God "first of all," he puts Eve first.

Biblical allusion is also used in *Paradise Regained* to foreshadow action. Of course, that Christ is going to overcome Satan's temptation is as sure to the reader of *Paradise Regained* as that Adam will fall is sure to the reader of *Paradise Lost;* the progressive unfolding of the action and the particular treatment by the poet, however, make the story dramatically interesting in spite of the outcome's being known from the first. That the Tempter will be completely "foil'd / In all his wiles, defeated and repuls't" is explicitly stated within the first few lines of *Paradise Regained,* but exactly how his defeat is accomplished is only gradually revealed. Frequent reference to the trials of Job, his patience in adversity and his refusal to turn against God though afflicted by evil, emphasizes the quiet mood of the Son of God in his victory

18. E. M. W. Tillyard (*Milton* [London, 1946], p. 263) says of *P. L.*, IX, 999: "The last line is curiously inconsistent with what went before. Adam had made up his mind before Eve exercised her charm on him: her caresses were superfluous." In the total context of Book IX, however, "domestick Adam" (IX, 318) was "overcome with Femal charm" when he allowed Eve to work alone in the Garden that day. He was overcome with Eve's charm (both in the sense of her beauty and sexual attractiveness and in the sense of her speech ["charm" here may have the meaning of "charm" in IV, 642, 651], for he has admitted that "Wisdom in discourse with her . . . like folly shewes" [VIII, 552-553]) from the first day he ever saw her. Adam's deliberate decision to fall with Eve is based on his faulty view of her as "last and best / Of all Gods works" (IX, 896-897) in spite of Raphael's (and God's) insistence that *he* is the superior creature. It is this faulty view of woman that causes "effeminate slackness" in man, for it results in his neg-

over Satan and indicates as well the pattern of verbal debate, similar to that between Job and his "friends," to be followed between Satan and Christ. Milton has the Father Himself first compare Satan's failure to corrupt Job with his failure in the temptation of Christ. Of Satan's forthcoming attempts, God says:

> he might have learnt
> Less over-weening, since he fail'd in *Job,*
> Whose constant perseverance overcame
> Whate're his cruel malice could invent.
> (*P. R.*, I, 146-149)

In the Bible God says of Job, "he holdeth fast his integrity" (Job 2:3), and that is a good description of Christ's conduct in Milton's poem; he never lowers himself to Satan's level nor compromises on even the finer points of truth. James makes the New Testament comment on Job's trials: "Beholde, wee count them happy which endure. Ye have heard of the patience of Job, and have seen the end of the Lord: that the Lord is very pitifull, and of tender mercy" (Jas. 5:11). Just as Satan failed in Job, he will fail in Christ, for though Christ is made of "female Seed" he is "far abler to resist" (I, 151) Satan than Job was; and just as God, through his tender mercy, restored to Job in the end "twice as much as he had before" (Job 42:10), he will be tenderly solicitous of Christ's welfare after the arduous temptation in the wilderness is over. The initial mention of Job in *Paradise Regained,* then, foreshadows the verbal debate form of the temptations, the Job-like steadfastness of Christ, and the Father's loving care to be manifested in "the end of the Lord." Subsequent references to Job in the poem, such as those by Satan (I, 369 ff.) and by Christ (III, 92-95), reinforce the comparison; Satan's reference emphasizes that the worthiness of Job was proved by his trial (in spite of Satan's purpose to imply otherwise), while Christ's reference stresses Job's patience in bearing the burdens Satan put upon him. The reader makes a transference from Job to Christ which

lect of "self-esteem, grounded on just and right / Well manag'd" (VIII, 572-573). Milton's statement that Adam was fondly overcome with female charm is perfectly consistent; although it may not be the immediate cause of his eating the fruit, it is the initial motivation for all his mistakes where Eve is concerned.

would have been made even if the Father's earlier mention of Job had not been included. This initial reference, however, since it contains an explicit comparison, foreshadows the main lines the poem's action will follow to its end.

As references to Job foreshadow the action and its outcome, allusions to Elijah and Daniel point forward to Christ's rejection of Satan's offered banquet and to the eventual satisfaction by divine means of Christ's need for food. Satan's first suggestion that Christ turn stones into bread is rejected, as in the Gospel account, with the Old Testament quotation, "Man lives not by Bread alone, but each Word / Proceeding from the mouth of God" (*P. R.*, I, 349-350 with Deut. 8:3, Matt. 4:14), but Milton adds to Christ's rejection references to the Israelites' being fed manna in the wilderness (I, 350-351; Exod. 16:14-15), to Moses' remaining on Mount Sinai forty days without food (I, 351-352; Exod. 24:18), and to Elijah's being sustained for forty days on two angel-prepared meals (I, 353-354; I Kings 19:1-8). These allusions emphasize Christ's faith that his Father will as surely supply all his needs as He had supplied the needs of other true followers of his Word.

Later, in Book II, when Christ hungers for the first time after forty days of fasting, he lies down to sleep and dreams of food; it is not a lavish banquet such as Satan will shortly spread before him that fills his dreams, however.

> Him thought, he by the Brook of *Cherith* stood
> And saw the Ravens with their horny beaks
> Food to *Elijah* bringing Even and Morn,
> Though ravenous, taught to abstain from what they brought:
> He saw the Prophet also how he fled
> Into the Desert, and how there he slept
> Under a Juniper; then how awakt,
> He found his Supper on the coals prepar'd,
> And by the Angel was bid rise and eat,
> And eat the second time after repose,
> The strength whereof suffic'd him forty days;
> Sometimes that with *Elijah* he partook,
> Or as a guest with *Daniel* at his pulse.
> (*P. R.*, II, 266-278)

Remembering that Elijah's steadfast integrity in the face of the enmity of Ahab and Jezebel caused him to choose rather to be fed by ravens in the desert than to enjoy the feasts of Ahab's court and that Daniel's determination not to defile himself with the unclean meats and wine of the King of Babylon led him to prefer pulse (a kind of grain cereal), the reader expects Christ to follow their example by refusing the food Satan offers and by waiting patiently for whatever his Father will provide. To Satan's question, "Tell me if Food were now before thee set, / Would'st thou not eat?" (II, 320-321), Christ replies, "Thereafter as I like / The giver" (II, 321-322). This answer points directly to the real significance of the Biblical stories alluded to: divine aid came to those in need when their position in the wilderness or in captivity and, consequently, their need was a result of their rejection of the wrong kind of giver. Israel fled from Egypt to escape slavery and idolatry. Elijah fled to Cherith and ate raven's food rather than soften his message to win the favor of Ahab; later he wandered in the wilderness for forty days sustained on two meals rather than favor Jezebel by forsaking God to worship Baal. But the allusion to Daniel, perhaps, carries most weight. Christ's answer that he will eat only what comes from an acceptable giver follows his dream in which he ate "as a guest with *Daniel* at his pulse," and his answer anticipates Satan's attempt to persuade him that his situation is different from Daniel's. Satan says,

> nor mention I
> Meats by the Law unclean, or offer'd first
> To Idols, those young *Daniel* could refuse;
> Not proffer'd by an Enemy, though who
> Would scruple that, with want opprest?
> (*P. R.*, II, 327-331)

But Daniel's refusal of "the portion of the kings meat [and] the wine which he dranke" (Dan. 1:8) was made neither on the grounds that the meat was proscribed by the Law nor that it had been previously offered to idols; although Daniel purposed "in his heart that he would not defile him selfe" (Dan. 1:8), the inference that his determined purpose was because the meat and wine were the gift of the conqueror of Jerusalem and the desecrater of the Temple is more readily drawn from Scripture than any inference that his rejection was because of dietary restrictions. The Biblical allusions, particularly to Daniel, in the feast temptation enforce Christ's contention that the real test of the acceptability of a gift is the *giver* and oppose Satan's plea that the satisfaction of a need is more important than whether or not the satisfaction is offered by an enemy. The allusion to Daniel, who, after ten days on pulse, "appeared fairer and fatter in flesh, then all the children, which did eat the portion of the kings meat" (Dan. 1:15), also foreshadows the final "Heavenly Feast" by which Christ, having refused any gifts from the wrong giver, is refreshed and strengthened as though he had never undergone the days of privation and hunger in the wilderness.

*God's Ultimate Victory*

In addition to emphasizing the present action and foreshadowing future action within the poems, Milton's references to Scripture in both epics foreshadow God's ultimate victory over Satan and evil. Of course, explicit statements of that coming victory occur in both poems, especially in *Paradise Lost,* where Books XI and XII are largely devoted to Michael's foreview of God's overruling grace in the affairs of men, culminating in the new heavens and new earth. But in addition there are many Biblical allusions, even in passages where Satan appears to have the upper hand, which have the dramatic effect of implying that the inevitable consummation of the conflict between good and evil will be a victory for God.

In Book I of *Paradise Lost,* even before Milton's explicit statement that Satan's efforts are futile against God and good, allusions in Satan's speech foreshadow his defeat and God's bringing good out of evil. Satan would never have been able to rise or heave his head above the burning lake of Hell, says Milton, had not

the will
And high permission of all-ruling Heaven
Left him at large to his own dark designs
That with reiterated crimes he might
Heap on himself damnation, while he sought
Evil to others, and enrag'd might see

How all his malice serv'd but to bring forth
Infinite goodness, grace and mercy shewn
On Man by him seduc't, but on himself
Treble confusion, wrath and vengeance pour'd.
(*P. L.*, I, 211-220)

Earlier in the action, when Satan boasts,

That Glory never shall his wrath or might
Extort from me. To bow and sue for grace
With suppliant knee, and deifie his power
Who from the terrour of this Arm so late
Doubted his Empire, that were low indeed,
That were an ignominy and shame beneath
This downfall,
(*P. L.*, I, 110-116)

he is eloquent in his scorn, but his words have an ironic ring for one familiar with God's statement through the prophet Isaiah. "I *am* God, and *there is* none else. I have sworne by my selfe; the word is gone out of my mouth *in* righteousnesse, and shall not returne, that unto mee every knee shall bow, every tongue shall sweare" (45:22b-23). And the New Testament application of this divine oath adds to the irony, for it includes all things in the universe and specifies that the kneeling will be to the Son for the glory of the Father. Paul speaks of the exaltation of Jesus Christ by the Father so that "at the Name of Jesus every knee should bow, of *things* in heaven, and *things* in earth, and *things* under the earth; And that every tongue should confess that Jesus Christ is Lord, to the glory of God the Father" (Phil. 2:10-11). Similarly, Satan's boast,

If then his Providence
Out of our evil seek to bring forth good,
Our labour must be to pervert that end,
And out of good still to find means of evil,
(*P. L.*, I, 162-165)

brings to mind Paul's assurance that "all things worke together for good to them that love God, to them who are the called according to his purpose" (Rom. 8:28) as well as the apostle's confident statement, "the Lord shall deliver mee from every evill worke, and will preserve mee unto his heavenly kingdom" (II Tim. 4:18).

Thus while Satan boasts his words carry allusions to Scriptures assuring the triumph of God and good over evil. When Satan says, however, that the devils "oft times may succeed, so as perhaps / Shall grieve him... and disturb / His inmost counsels from their destind aim" (I, 166-168), he speaks truth in one breath and falsehood in the next. The sins into which Satan led the antediluvian civilization "grieved [God] at his heart" (Gen. 6:6) as did many of the sins of the Israelites; but so far is Satan's sin from ever disturbing God's inmost counsels from their aim that the Christians of the early church, in praying to Him, could speak of the slayers of Jesus as those who were gathered together "to do whatsoever thy hand and counsel determined before to be done" (Acts 4:28). Thus Satan's opening statements of what he will and will not do are contradicted by the Biblical associations his language calls up, and the future supremacy of God and subjection of Satan are forecast even in Satan's proud speeches to the contrary.

When Milton, with the aid of his Muse, calls the roll of the principal devils in Hell, allusions to Biblical stories of their defeat as pagan deities reinforce prior allusions foreshadowing God's future victory over Satan; the God Who can defeat Moloch, Peor, Dagon, and the rest, can and will, in His own good time, defeat the Prince of these devils. Although the devils are successful in establishing their "Seats... next the Seat of God, / Their Altars by his Altar" (I, 383-384) through the weakness of kings like Solomon and Ahaz, God raises up kings like "good *Josiah*" to drive them down to Hell again (I, 418; II Kings 23:13-14); sometimes intervenes supernaturally, as when the symbol of His presence and glory, "the Captive Ark," maimed and shamed Dagon before his worshippers (I, 453-461; I Sam. 5:2-4); and sometimes uses a prophet to work a miracle, as when Naaman, cleansed of his leprosy, turned from the worship of Rimmon to that of Jehovah (I, 467-471; II Kings 5:12-18). The mention of the final plague upon Egypt, in which Jehovah "equal'd with one stroke / Both Egypt's first born and all her bleating Gods" (I, 487-489; Exod. 12:12, 29), and of the followers of Belial in Eli's family and in Sodom (I, 495-496, 503; I Sam. 2:12-17, Gen. 19) remind the reader that the God of the Old Testament brought swift and terrible judgment both upon the pagan deities worshipped and upon the sins of their worshippers whenever He chose to punish them.

In the light of such Biblical allusions, therefore, Book I of *Paradise Lost* is not an eloquent poetic glorification of the independent and revolutionary spirit of Satan and his cohorts. Aside from Milton's comments, which give the alert reader plenty of clues as to how he is to interpret Satan's character and speeches (for example, Satan "with high words, that bore / Semblance of worth not substance, gently rais'd / Their fainted courage," [I, 528-530]), in the midst of Satan's proud utterances and shot through the pomp and ceremony of the hellish procession of demonic dignitaries, there are Biblical allusions which foreshadow the futility of Satan's endeavours and the inevitability of God's final victory over him.

Nor are such allusions restricted to Book I or to Satan's speeches. The last and most effective of the fallen angels' orations in Book II is Beelzebub's. Moloch has counseled open, desperate war as a matter of revenge, win or lose. Belial has answered him with a plea for peace on the grounds that perhaps God will eventually ease the torments of Hell if the devils behave themselves. Then Mammon has won the assembly's assent to his suggestion that the devils acclimatize themselves to Hell and develop the natural resources found therein. Beelzebub now rises, as a front man for Satan, to propose the plan at which Satan hinted in Book I: that the evil powers seek to corrupt the new world which God is creating for his new creature, man. Beelzebub convinces the devils that they cannot hope to be left alone in Hell for peaceful self-development; they must take the initiative and seek a way out, and the best way out seems to be by invasion of the newly created world. The assembly unanimously agrees that his proposal is better than to "sit in darkness here / Hatching vain Empires" (II, 377-378). But during the course of his speech Beelzebub outargues himself without realizing it; his persuasive argument that the devils cannot hope for peaceful self-development in Hell is:

For he, be sure,
In highth or depth, still first and last will Reign
Sole King, and of his Kingdom loose no part
By our revolt, but over Hell extend
His Empire, and with Iron Scepter rule
Us here, as with his Golden those in Heav'n.
(*P. L.*, II, 323-328)

Beelzebub's argument holds true for Hell, but it also holds true for the new world to be invaded; allusions in his speech to the words of the risen Christ, "the first and the last" (Rev. 1:11a, 22:13), who shall reign as the "onely Potentate, the king of kings and Lord of Lords" (I Tim. 6:15), to the prophecies of the Messianic psalms, "Thy throne, O God, *is* for ever and ever: the sceptre of thy kingdome is a right sceptre" (Ps. 45:6) and "Thou shalt breake them with a rod of yron" (Ps. 2:9), and to the words of the Apocalypse concerning Christ, "He shall rule them with a rod of yron" (Rev. 19:15) all point forward to the time when the Son of God, after defeating Satan and the armies of Anti-Christ, shall establish his eternal and universal reign of righteousness.

At the close of Book III and the opening of Book IV, Milton explicitly connects the action of *Paradise Lost* and the final defeat of Satan as described in Revelation. Having escaped from Hell and pushed his way through Chaos, Satan is within the created universe approaching the sun. There, seeing "a glorious Angel stand, / The same whom *John* saw also in the Sun" (III, 622-623) he asks directions to Paradise, "His journies end and our beginning woe" (III, 633). Having Satan directed to Eden by Uriel, identified with the angel whom John saw, is poetically appropriate, for the angel in the Revelation passage alluded to is announcing the final defeat of the Satanically inspired Anti-Christ and his armies at the coming of Christ in power and glory: "And I saw an Angel standing in the Sunne, and he cryed with a loud voice, saying to all the foules that flie in the midst of the heaven, Come and gather yourselves together unto the supper of the great God" (19:17). Uriel, an unwitting agent in Satan's entry into the world, will, in Milton's scheme, have the privilege of announcing the destruction of Satan's power over the earth when Anti-

Christ is defeated at Armageddon, and the allusion to Revelation foreshadows the ultimate defeat of those forces of evil which Satan is now going to Paradise to loose in the heart of man. Reference is made again to the angel of Revelation in the prayer which opens Book IV.

> O for that warning voice, which he who saw
> Th' *Apocalyps,* heard cry in Heaven aloud,
> Then when the Dragon, put to second rout,
> Came furious down to be reveng'd on men,
> *Wo to the inhabitants on Earth!* that now
> While time was, our first Parents had bin warnd
> The coming of thir secret foe, and scap'd
> Haply so scap'd his mortal snare; for now
> *Satan,* now first inflam'd with rage, came down,
> The Tempter ere th' Accuser of man-kind,
> To wreck on innocent frail man his loss
> Of that first Battel, and his flight to Hell.
> (*P. L.*, IV, 1-12)

The passage in Revelation to which Milton refers includes a warning voice which is uttered in a context forecasting the victory of God and the speedy end of the Devil's power: "And I heard a loud voyce saying in heaven, Now is come salvation, & strength, and the kingdome of our God and the power of his Christ: for the accuser of our brethren is cast down, which accused them before our God day and night.... Therefore rejoyce, ye heavens, and ye that dwell in them. Woe to the inhabiters of the earth and of the sea: for the devell is come downe unto you, having great wrath, because hee knoweth that hee hath but a short time" (12:10-12). The passage in the epic, with its Biblical allusion, prefigures the angelic warning to be given to "our first Parents" when Raphael visits Paradise, but it points forward also to the future battle which will result in Satan's being cast out as the accuser and, consequently, his being utterly defeated as the eternal kingdom of God begins.

Although Biblical texts alluded to in Milton's image of God's "golden Scales," Libra of the zodiacal constellations, emphasize God's control of the present situation and Satan's recognition of that control, they also prophesy the ultimate destruction of Satan, the celestial sign practically becoming a permanent symbol of God's power over him. As Satan stands ready, "Like *Teneriff* or *Atlas,*" to combat Gabriel's whole squadron of angels, God intervenes with a heavenly sign. The poet describes the incident in this passage:

> Th' Eternal to prevent such horrid fray
> Hung forth in Heav'n his golden Scales, yet seen
> Betwixt *Astrea* and the *Scorpion* signe,
> Wherein all things created first he weighed,
> The pendulous round Earth with ballanc't Aire
> In counterpoise, now ponders all events,
> Battels and Realms: in these he put two weights
> The sequel each of parting and of fight;
> The latter quick up flew, and kickt the beam;
> Which *Gabriel* spying, thus bespake the Fiend.
> *Satan,* I know thy strength, and thou knowst mine,
> Neither our own but giv'n; what follie then
> To boast what Arms can doe, since thine no more
> Then Heav'n permits, nor mine, though doubld now
> To trample thee as mire: for proof look up,
> And read thy Lot in yon celestial Sign
> Where thou art weigh'd, & shown how light, how weak,
> If thou resist. The Fiend lookt up and knew
> His mounted scale aloft: nor more; but fled
> Murmuring, and with him fled the shades of night.
> (*P. L.*, IV, 996-1015)

Milton has taken the Scriptural statements that God "hath measured the waters in the hollow of his hand, and meted out heaven with the span, and comprehended the dust of the earth in a measure, and weighed the mountaines in scales, and the hills in a balance" (Isa. 40:12), has made the "weight for the winds, and ... weigheth the waters by measure" (Job 28:25), and knows "the balancings of the cloudes" (Job 37:16) as authority for his image of the golden scales.[19] In addition, Milton has identified these

19. As is more often true than can be indicated in these notes, there is a fusion here of Biblical with classical sources of imagery. The golden scales in which Father Zeus placed two fates of death, one for Achilles and one for Hector, are alluded to (*Iliad,* Book XXII). Whereas Hector's doom sank down to Hades, however, Satan's weight goes up; the lightness of Satan's cause defeats him (as lightness defeated Belshazzar). The Biblical image predominates.

scales with the constellation Libra, still to be seen in the heavens between Astrea (Virgo) and Scorpio; thus the sign of Libra becomes symbolic of God's power as Creator. But it is symbolic of more. It is true that God, in the Creation, weighed the "things created," but now He "ponders all events, / Battels and Realms," as Hannah said in her Biblical prayer: "the LORD *is* a God of knowledge, and by him actions are weighed" (I Sam. 2:3). There is a further significance in the light of Biblical allusion. Satan, like Belshazzar, has been "weighed in the balances, and... found wanting" (Dan. 5:27); he is light and weak when compared to the power of God, and like Belshazzar, he is given a sign which forecasts the futility of fighting now and the certainty of defeat later.

That the "celestial Sign" foreshadows his ultimate defeat, Satan would hardly admit, but the point is clear to the reader that if God can so order the outcome of one encounter, He can determine the ultimate outcome of all encounters between good and evil. Milton has, within the framework of his epic, made the sign of Libra a heavenly symbol similar to the Scriptural rainbow (Gen. 9:12-16); as the rainbow signifies God's promise never again to destroy all terrestrial life by water, the constellation of the "golden Scales" symbolizes God's power as Creator, His power of deciding the outcome of the actions of His creatures, and, by extension from the present action of Book IX, His power to defeat Satan whenever it is His will to do so.

At the close of Book X in *Paradise Lost,* Adam and Eve, having realized their individual responsibility for their sin and having ceased accusing one another, consider death as a way out of their misery; Eve further suggests childlessness. But Adam recalls part of what was said to Eve by their Judge: "That thy Seed shall bruise / The Serpents head" (X, 1031-1032). Although Adam does not yet fully realize the prophetic implications of the statement, it is, for the reader, an explicit prophecy of the coming Messiah. There is implicit foreshadowing also, however, in the language Adam uses to help Eve see that their judgment is not so harsh after all. We had expected to die immediately, he says, but in the judgment,

lo, to thee
Pains onely in Child-bearing were foretold,
And bringing forth, soon recompenc't with joy,
Fruit of thy Womb.
(*P. L.*, X, 1050-1053)

The joy in the child that for a woman follows after the sorrows of childbirth is used as a parabolic figure in the Bible; for example, Jesus, speaking of his coming death and resurrection to his disciples, said: "A woman, when she is in travaile hath sorrow, because her houre is come: but as soon as she is delivered of the child, she remembreth no more the anguish, for joy that a man is borne into the world" (John 16:21). Adam's words of comfort and hope, therefore, reach beyond their temporary significance to Eve and suggest the joy to be brought into the world through the fruit of the womb of the Virgin Mary, "Second *Eve*" (V, 387 with Luke 1:42, 2:10-11), and even further into the future, to the joy of believers in the resurrection of Christ from the dead, the special event which Jesus is prophesying by means of the childbirth analogy. The kind of sweeping foreview of events to be given by Michael in Books XI and XII is preceded by this kind of allusive hint at the future outcome of the Fall, a kind of foreshadowing that is responded to by any reader familiar with the Bible.

In *Paradise Regained,* as well as in the longer epic, there are both explicit references to the future victory of God over Satan and foreshadowings which are implicit in Biblical allusions. In the first book of *Paradise Regained* that Satan will be utterly defeated in his efforts to tempt Christ is stated within the first seven lines, and Satan himself speaks of his

dread attending when that fatal wound
Shall be inflicted by the Seed of *Eve*
Upon my head, (*P. R.*, I, 53-55)

thus making it clear that even he does not deceive himself about the final outcome of his struggle against God. Yet he still seeks to do all he can to thwart God's purposes.

Seeking to tempt Christ to run ahead of the slow development of God's purposes and to begin without delay to reign on the throne of David, Satan says, "The happier raign the sooner it begins, / Raign then; what canst thou better do the while?" (*P. R.*, III, 179-180). Christ answers with a Biblical phrase, "All things are best fullfil'd in their due time" (III, 182; Rom. 5:6). Then, after suggesting the sufferings he is to undergo as "just tryal e're I merit / My exaltation" (III, 196-197), Christ asks Satan,

> But what concerns it thee when I begin
> My everlasting Kingdom, why art thou
> Sollicitous, what moves thy inquisition?
> Know'st thou not that my rising is thy fall,
> And my promotion will be thy destruction?
> (*P. R.*, III, 198-202)

Satan replies with what seems at first a counsel of despair (like Moloch's in *Paradise Lost*): if there is worse to suffer, he wants it to come as soon as possible. "Worst is my Port," he says:

> My error was my error, and my crime
> My crime; whatever for it self condemn'd,
> And will alike be punish'd; whether thou
> Raign or raign not.
> (*P. R.*, III, 209, 212-215)

Christ's words emphasize that, as the Bible presents future events, his reign and Satan's ultimate defeat are inextricably bound up together. Although Satan's words deny this fact, even his denial recalls the promise that in his reign Christ will "put downe all rule, and all authoritie & power; for he must reigne, till he hath put all his enemies under his feet" (I Cor. 15:24-25). Quickly shifting his argument, Satan tries to make it appear that he desires Christ's reign because he hopes that "that gentle brow," "that placid aspect and meek regard," would shield him from God the Father's wrath; actually, as Satan knows, Christ reigning in glory will be quite different from Christ the suffering Son of Man, and that wrath which shall cause men to call upon the mountains to fall upon them in the Day of Judgment shall be "the wrath of the Lambe" (Rev. 6:16). Satan's real purpose in tempting Christ to take up his reign prematurely is to cause the Son to disobey the Father by impatient and impulsive action; not only does Satan fail but the language of his own lies recalls the Biblical prophecies that his destruction is directly connected with Christ's return to the earth and his reign on David's throne.

Constantly seeking to arouse doubt in Christ's mind as to whether he is the Son of God in any special sense, Satan alludes to the Biblical designation of angels as "gods" and "children of the most High" (Ps. 82:6) and of Satan himself as "god of this world" (II Cor. 4:4; *P. R.*, IV, 196-203). The term "Son of God," the Devil argues, bears no single meaning;

> The Son of God I also am, or was,
> And if I was, I am; relation stands;
> All men are Sons of God. . . .
> (*P. R.*, IV, 518-520)

But the Old Testament text alluded to (a text repeated in the New Testament in John 10:34) does not give assurance that "relation stands": "I have said, Ye *are* gods: and all of you *are* children of the most High: But ye shall die like men, and fall like one of the Princes" (Ps. 82:6). Immediately after this allusion Satan takes Christ to the pinnacle of the Temple "to know what more thou art then man, / Worth naming Son of God by voice from Heav'n" (IV, 538-539). There Christ stands as proof of his divine Sonship, while Satan, "smitten with amazement," falls. That the prince of the power of the air is defeated at his own game and in his own element suggests his ultimate defeat, a suggestion which is made more explicit by the elect angels and emphasized by further Biblical allusion at the close of the poem.

The circumstances of Satan's defeat in the final book of *Paradise Regained* are emphasized by comparison to Antaeus, who "Throttl'd at length in the Air, expir'd and fell" (IV, 568); Satan's fall, however, is much more remarkable than that of Antaeus. The latter fell through being out of touch with the earth, the element which gave him strength, but Satan, designated many times in both Milton's epics by his Biblical title of "prince of the power of the air" (Eph. 2:2), is in his own sphere of dominion and would be expected to hold his own in the air if anywhere (obviously, that is what he expected). But this defeat is only the beginning. The hymn of the angels states that this defeat of Satan on the Temple prefigures an even greater future defeat:

> But thou, Infernal Serpent, shalt not long
> Rule in the Clouds: like an Autumnal Star
> Or Lightning thou shalt fall from Heav'n trod down
> Under his feet: for proof, e're this thou feel'st
> Thy wound, yet not thy last and deadliest wound.
> (*P. R.*, IV, 618-622)

The final allusion of the angels is to the casting out of devils to take place during Christ's preaching ministry, and it is made a foreview of his ultimate victory over Satan. The angels sing:

> hereafter learn with awe
> To dread the Son of God: he all unarm'd
> Shall chase thee with the terror of his voice
> From thy Demoniac holds, possession foul,
> Thee and thy Legions, yelling they shall flye,
> And beg to hide them in a herd of Swine,
> Lest he command them down into the deep
> Bound, and to torment sent before thir time.
> Hail Son of the most High, heir of both worlds,
> Queller of Satan, on thy glorious work
> Now enter, and begin to save mankind.
> (*P. R.*, IV, 625-635)

The defeat of Satan in the temptation has proved to the devils once and for all that Christ is the Son of God; that is why they fear him. Those demons who possessed the two men dwelling in the tombs cried out to Jesus, "What have we to do with thee, Jesus, thou Sonne of God? Art thou come hither to torment us before the time?" (Matt. 8:29). This striking example of Christ's power over the devils provides a Scriptural foreview of the time when all evil ones shall be tormented in the lake of fire (Rev. 20:15). There may be doubt among men on earth as to the outcome of the war between good and evil, but, according to Milton, neither Heaven nor Hell doubts God's victory, a victory to be gained through the "greater Man." All Hell rues Satan's attempt on Christ, for it has merely made clear the inevitability of Christ's victory. The elect angels hail Christ, by anticipation, as "Queller of Satan" and "victor." Among men only is Christ "unobserv'd" for what he really is as he returns privately to his mother's house.

# IV

## *Dramatic Effectiveness*
## *Language and Character*

IN ADDITION to its use as a means of establishing setting and of forwarding and foreshadowing action, the Bible is used in Milton's epic poems to add dramatic force to language and to add dimensions to the characterizations of the chief actors.

### *LANGUAGE*

Certain dramatic effects are gained in both epics by language which suggests a Biblical incident or statement. The language sometimes suggests a situation in Scripture which is similar to the one being portrayed in the poem, thus adding depth and a background of Biblical connotation to the dramatic situation in the poem; sometimes the Biblical language suggests its context within the Bible, thus adding ironic or other dramatic effects; sometimes the purpose of the Scriptural language is completely reversed from its purpose in the Bible. Since the whole of both *Paradise Lost* and *Paradise Regained* is permeated by Biblical language and since, once the reader is aware of the extra dimension often added by Biblical allusion, an abundance of examples of the uses mentioned above may be found throughout the poems, the passages discussed here will be limited to only a few.

#### *Suggestion of Biblical Situation*

When the Son of God rides forth alone on the third day of the war in Heaven to rout the hosts of Satan, he says to the armies of elect angels:

> Stand still in bright array ye Saints, here stand
> Ye Angels arm'd, this day from Battel rest;

> Faithful hath been your Warfare, and of God
> Accepted,
>
> . . . . . . . . . . . . . . . . . . . .
>
> but of this cursed crew
> The punishment to other hand belongs,
> Vengeance is his, or whose he sole appoints;
> Number to this dayes work is not ordain'd
> Nor multitude, stand onely and behold
> Gods indignation on these Godless pourd
> By mee.
>
> (*P. L.*, VI, 801-804, 806-812)

The imperatives "Stand still" and "stand onely" recall the command of Moses to the Israelites when they were caught between the pursuing armies of Pharaoh and the impassable waters of the Red Sea. "Feare ye not, stand still, and see the salvation of the LORD, which hee will shew you to day: for the Egyptians whom ye have seene today, yee shall see them againe no more for ever. The LORD shall fight for you, and ye shall hold your peace" (Exod. 14:13-14). The similarity between Satan and his followers and Pharoah and the Egyptians has already been suggested by Milton's comment on the obdurate perverseness of the wicked who will not repent even in the face of such miraculous wonders as the Son's restoration of the uprooted hills and gutted valleys of Heaven to their original position and beauty.

> But to convince the proud what Signs availe,
> Or Wonders move th' obdurate to relent?
> They hard'nd more by what might most reclame,
> Grieving to see his Glorie, at the sight
> Took envie.
>
> (*P. L.*, VI, 789-793)

As God's signs and wonders by Moses in Egypt served only to harden the heart of Pharaoh (Exod. 7:14), the power of God through the Son serves only to harden and make envious Satan and his angels. As the elect angels stand still to see the victory of the Son over his enemies, the Messiah drives the fallen angels to the "Chrystal wall of Heav'n, which op'ning wide," rolls inward and discloses a "spacious Gap" through which the rebels throw themselves headlong into the "wastful Deep."

> Disburd'nd Heav'n rejoic'd, and soon repaird
> Her mural breach, returning whence it rowld.
> (*P. L.*, VI, 878-879)

Pharaoh and his hosts were destroyed when the waters of the Red Sea, having rolled back to allow the Israelites to cross on dry land, were caused by God's power to close upon the pursuing Egyptians (Exod. 14:26-28). Although the situations are not exactly parallel, their similarity supports the idea that the language of the Messiah ("Stand still") is intended to recall the Biblical occasion when God overthrew His enemies through Moses as God here casts out the rebel angels through the Son. The Father, through Whose power the victory is effected, is magnified and the mighty figure of the Son in single fight against Satan's armies provides a dramatic illustration of another Biblical text alluded to in his speech: "Vengeance is mine, I will repay, saith the Lord" (Rom. 12:19; *P. L.*, VI, 808).

An imperative expression in Raphael's parting admonition to Adam recalls a similar situation in the Bible and emphasizes the very aspect of Adam's responsibility under God in which he is to fail in the crucial Book IX. Raphael exhorts Adam:

> Be strong, live happie, and love, but first of all
> Him whom to love is to obey, and keep
> His great command; take heed least Passion sway
> Thy Judgement to do aught, which else free Will
> Would not admit.
> (*P. L.*, VIII, 633-637)

After the death of Moses, God chose Joshua to lead the Israelites across Jordan and into the Promised Land; the exhortation from God to Joshua, repeated three times in the commission given him, is "Be strong, and of a good courage" (Josh. 1:6, 7, 9). Although other responsibilities of Joshua are mentioned in Scripture, most emphasis is placed upon the necessity of his keeping "all the Law, which Moses my servant commanded" (Josh. 1:7). In *Paradise Lost* a like emphasis is put upon the necessity for Adam to be obedient to God's command, but Raphael stresses the additional New Testament principle that obedience to God is the result of loving God and that God should be loved first of all, alluding to:

"For this is the love of God, that wee keepe his commandements, and his commandements are not grievous" (I John 5:3).[1] Adam has been telling Raphael of his love for Eve and has even been asking Raphael about the love-life of angelic beings; hence Raphael's exhortation "live happie, and love"; but, because Adam has admitted to having his wisdom, authority, and reason sometimes overpowered by his love for Eve, Raphael's main purpose in the command "Be strong" is to cause Adam to remember his position of authority and his responsibility to put God first. Joshua's commission was one of authority over Israel, an authority under God from which there was no appeal, hence his special need of strength; Adam's commission and need are similar. Adam's breakdown in the maintenance of his authority over Eve when he allows her to work alone in the Garden is the first step in a series of events leading to his own disobedience and the consequent woe to all his sons.

An example of Biblical language suggesting a Biblical situation occurs in *Paradise Regained* when Satan first appears to Christ. Disguised as an aged man in rural weeds, he tempts Christ to turn stones into bread by urging both Christ's own need and the need of others who live in the desert. We "Who dwell this wild," says Satan, are

> Men to such misery and hardship born;
> But if thou be the Son of God, Command
> That out of these hard stones be made thee bread;
> So shalt thou save thy self and us relieve
> With Food, whereof we wretched seldom taste.
> (*P. R.*, I, 341-345)

This particular temptation is based on the Gospels of Matthew and Luke (4:3 in both), but Satan's language recalls from the Bible a similar test put before Christ to prove his divine Sonship. Satan pleads explicitly two reasons (in addition to the implied reason that Christ should prove his divinity) why Christ should turn the stones into bread: that Christ may save himself from

1. Cf. II Tim. 2:1 and Eph. 6:10 ff., Scripture passages in which Paul exhorts Christians to be strong in the face of temptation, the latter following a discussion of the need for husbands to love their wives and also to have them in subjection (Eph. 5:23 ff.).

starvation and that he may relieve the hunger of the poor unfortunate residents of the wilderness. The latter reason, not even implied in Scripture, is the result, of course, of a false show of charitable piety on the part of Satan. The language, however, associates this dramatic situation with Luke's account in which one of the thieves crucified beside Christ "railed on him, saying, If thou be Christ, save thy selfe and us" (23:39). As the thief's raillery reveals his basically unrepentant and selfish attitude and his mocking tone shows that he is interested primarily in his own and his fellow thief's deliverance, so Satan's use of "save thy self and us," though ostensibly expressing interest in Christ's welfare, suggests that his main concern is seeing what tricks he can get Christ to perform and that his plea for relief for the "wretched" is hypocritical mockery (akin to that of Judas Iscariot in John 12:3-6). Recognition of the analogue to the thief's language magnifies the Devil's culpability here, for the thief's "if thou be" test sprang from his despair and disbelief, while Satan's "if thou be" springs not from disbelief but from a desire to implant distrust and doubt in the heart of Jesus. Christ asks, "Why dost thou then suggest to me distrust, / Knowing who I am, as I know who thou art?" (*P. R.*, I, 355-356).

### *Suggestion of Biblical Context*

An effect of dramatic irony is achieved through the use of language from a Biblical context which carries connotations different from, at times even opposed to, the suggestions of the speaker whose speech includes the Biblical allusion. In *Paradise Lost*, Book I, Satan, having reared himself from the lake of fire, says to Beelzebub,

> But wherefore let we then our faithful friends,
> Th' associates and copartners of our loss
> Lye thus astonisht on th' oblivious Pool,
> And call them not to share with us their part
> In this unhappy Mansion [?]
>
> (*P. L.*, I, 264-268)

As he leaves on his mission to the new world, Satan refers again to "this ill Mansion" (II, 462), and Uriel uses unwitting irony in praising Satan's desire to see God's works which has led him to leave his "Empyreal Mansion" (III, 699). "Mansion" may allude to Christ's words of comfort to his disciples, "In my Fathers house are many mansions. . . . I goe to prepare a place for you" (John 14:2). When one remembers Milton's earlier description of Hell as the "place Eternal Justice had prepar'd" for the rebellious spirits (I, 70), the ironic truth that Hell is one of the Father's mansions, though an unhappy one, comes to the reader with a force that Satan does not intend.[2] Further, Satan's reference to his "copartners" and "their part / In this unhappy Mansion" suggests one of the final curses of the Bible: "But the fearefull, and unbeleeving, and the abominable, and murderers, and whoremongers, and sorcerers, and idolaters, and all lyars, shall have their part in the lake which burneth with fire and brimstone" (Rev. 21:8). This is an apt description of Satan's "faithful friends," and though Satan and his "copartners" are soon to invade the new world, Milton's choice of language reminds the reader of the Scriptural assurance that the Devil and all his followers will eventually bear "their part" in the fiery regions "for ever and ever" (Rev. 20:10).

When Satan appears before the throne of Chaos to plead that his only purpose in passing through this realm towards the new world is "once more / [to] Erect the Standerd there of *ancient Night*" (*P. L.*, II, 986), the "Anarch old" answers:

> I know thee, stranger, who thou art,
> That mighty leading Angel, who of late
> Made head against Heav'ns King, though overthrown.
> (*P. L.*, II, 990-992)

In identifying Satan, Chaos uses almost the same words which the demons who possessed the man at Capernaum used to identify Jesus: "Let us alone, what have wee to doe with thee, thou Jesus of Nazareth? art thou come to destroy us? I know thee who thou art, the holy One of God" (Mark 1:24). The ironic difference is that the unclean spirit in the Bible story recognizes the one he iden-

2. The Son of God uses the phrase "prepar'd ill Mansion" with ironic allusion to the Biblical promise of Christ to prepare a mansion for faithful disciples (John 14:2) when he says to the Father that he will soon "rid heav'n of these rebell'd, / To thir prepar'd ill Mansion driven down / To chains of Darkness, and th' undying Worm" (*P. L.*, VI, 737-739).

tifies as an enemy who will deprive him of his dwelling place, while Chaos, not recognizing Satan's enmity towards all, believes his lie that some of the created realms may be re-won to Chaos; the result is, however, the same in both cases. The unclean spirit is cast out by Christ, and the territory of Chaos is even further limited by the journey of Satan, for Sin and Death follow him, constructing the "broad and beat'n" causeway from Hell to the newly created universe. The injection of "stranger" into the Biblical words used by Chaos indicates his failure to recognize the real nature of Satan, who is an enemy to everyone and everything but himself.

Sometimes in the poetry the suggested Biblical context reinforces the statement of the speaker. The Heavenly Father, viewing the invasion of man's world by Sin and Death following the Fall, speaks of how even these horrible monsters, unknown to themselves, fulfill His purposes.

> [They] know not that I call'd and drew them thither
> My Hell-hounds, to lick up the draff and filth
> Which mans polluting Sin with taint hath shed
> On what was pure, till cramm'd and gorg'd, nigh burst
> With suckt and glutted offal, at one sling
> Of thy victorious Arm, well-pleasing Son,
> Both *Sin*, and *Death*, and yawning *Grave* at last
> Through *Chaos* hurld, obstruct the mouth of Hell
> For ever, and seal up his ravenous Jawes.
>
> (*P. L.*, X, 629-637)

The splendid image of the Son destroying God's "scornful Enemies" (l. 625) with one sling of his mighty arm is reminiscent of David, who slew the giant Goliath with one stone from his sling (I Sam. 17:49), but its source is almost certainly the prophetic words of Abigail, spoken to dissuade David from killing her churlish husband, Nabal. "Yet a man is risen to pursue thee, and to seeke thy soule: but the soul of my lord shall be bound in the bundle of life with the LORD thy God; and the soules of thine enemies, them shall he sling out, *as out* of the middle of a sling" (I Sam. 25:29). When these words were spoken to David he was an outcast and exile from Israel, fleeing from Saul who sought his life; Abigail is saying that just as David "fighteth the battels of the LORD" (I Sam. 25:28), as shown by such past victories as that over Goliath with a simple sling, God will fight David's battles for him and destroy all his enemies together as though he slung them out of a sling. The suggestive Biblical connotations in the poem are that the "soules" (lives) of Adam (soon to be an exile from Paradise and now subject to sin and death) and the Son of God are bound together as David's and God's lives were, so that just as God undertook to destroy David's enemies and to place him on the throne of the land from which he had been driven in exile, Christ will undertake to destroy the enemies of Adam and his posterity and to restore man to Paradise in "Heav'n and earth renewd" (X, 638). It is precisely when the actions of Sin and Death make it appear that the victory of evil is assured that God emphasizes the certainty of Christ's triumph for man's sake.

*Reversal of Biblical Purpose*

Language used in Milton's epics suggesting a similar situation in the Bible and suggesting the Scriptural context of the Biblical language has, as this discussion has shown, an ironic effect at times. But a use of Biblical language in which the original purpose of the language is reversed gives a more powerful effect of dramatic irony, when the reversal is recognized, than any use seen thus far. Other fallen angels use reversals of language from the Bible (as do Sin, Eve, and the poet himself), but, as one might expect, Satan is the character whose utterances most often include language reversed in purpose from its use in the Bible.

Satan's first speech to the assembled devils, in which he calls for a "Full Counsel" to "mature" their thoughts of continued war against Heaven, hints at the plan, later decided on, to corrupt God's new Creation. But some plan of guile rather than of force is necessary, Satan thinks.

> Henceforth his might we know, and know our own
> So as not either to provoke, or dread
> New warr, provok't; our better part remains
> To work in close design, by fraud or guile
> What force effected not: that he no less
> At length from us may find, who overcomes
> By force, hath overcome but half his foe.
> (*P. L.*, I, 643-649)

Satan's description of his recommended strategy of underhanded fraud as "our better part" is a reversal in purpose and use of the Scriptural phrase "that good part," taken from the words Christ spoke to Martha when she complained that her sister Mary was not helping with the housework but was, instead, sitting at his feet and hearing his words: "Martha, Martha, thou art carefull and troubled about many things: But one thing is needfull, and Mary hath chosen that good part, which shall not be taken away from her" (Luke 10:41-42). The contrast in the Bible is between the passive listening of Mary and the active service of Martha; the "good part" is to listen and learn from Christ rather than to get so involved in the business of serving, even when it is the Lord one is serving, that he and his teachings are neglected. Satan's point is that "close design . . . fraud or guile" which may even give the appearance of a passive desire to learn from God (it is this approach, one may remember, that fools Uriel when Satan pretends to wish to see mankind only that he may adore his Maker) is better for the devils to choose than the part of active enemies in open conflict against God.[3]

In the debate of the devils in Pandaemonium reversals of Biblical language occur in an especially concentrated form. The ironic effect of the reversals builds from speech to speech as the hellish assembly proceeds in its deliberations.

Moloch's advice that "strange fire" (II, 69) be used by the fallen angels to make war upon Heaven, briefly commented on in Chapter Two, deserves additional comment here. The allusion is to the offering, as an act of unauthorized and self-willed pseudo-devotion, of "strange fire" by Nadab and Abihu, an offering which resulted in the destruction by fire of those priests themselves (Lev. 10:1). Moloch is advocating making war on God with that which brought

3. The allusion to Christ's words to Martha has been recognized and noted by Verity in his edition of *Paradise Lost.* A possibility which has not been pointed out is that Satan's "our better part" may be an allusion to Shakespeare's Falstaff, who, justifying his running from battle, said: 'The better part of valour is discretion: in the which better part, I have saved my life" (*Henry IV*, Part I, V, iv, 121-122). To accept the possibility that Milton had Shakespeare's fat comic in mind would be to support C. S. Lewis' view of Satan as ridiculous, almost comic, and a fool in many of his speeches, a view which he presents in *A Preface to Paradise Lost* (London, 1942), pp. 92-96. Another possible Biblical source for the phrase is I Sam. 23:20.

destruction upon these two chosen sons of Aaron, when they offered it to the Lord although he had "commanded them not"; the ironic question raised by the reversal is, of course, that if strange fire offered in erroneous devotion brought swift destruction upon those who offered it, how much more swiftly would the attempt to attack God's throne with strange fire bring destruction upon the attackers? Again, Moloch's rhetorical question (to be taken up by Belial), which begins "what can be worse / Then to dwell here," includes a reference to the fallen angels as "The Vassals of his anger" (II, 90), an allusion to the Biblical question in Romans 9:22: "What if God, willing to shewe his wrath, and to make his power knowen, indured with much long suffering the vessels of wrath fitted to destruction [?]" Moloch's argument is that since the devils are the slaves of God's anger (with a play on "Vassals" for "vessels") they should not fear to "incense / His utmost ire" because things cannot possibly get worse even if the devils are completely consumed; yet Moloch's language alludes to a passage of Scripture in which God is presented as enduring with "much long suffering the vessels of wrath" even though they are destined to eventual destruction.

Although Belial answers Moloch's speech with scorn and argues eloquently that things could be much worse than they are, he shows a misunderstanding of God similar to Moloch's. Both devils feel that God may be suddenly incensed into destroying them or making things worse for them, as though he did not operate on a long-range plan of "Eternal Providence" but allowed such rebels to spur him into unpremeditated action.[4] Belial, arguing that things could be worse, says,

> What if the breath that kindl'd those grim fires
> Awak'd should blow them into sevenfold rage
> And plunge us in the Flames?
> (*P. L.*, II, 170-172)

4. See *Paradise Lost*, X, 626-632, where God sees Sin and Death on their way to Earth and comments on this particular misconception of His nature on the part of his enemies, who laugh as if God, "transported with some fit / Of Passion," had "At random yeilded up" the new creation to the misrule of Satan's hordes. The truth is that God uses these "Hell-hounds" to fulfill his eternal purposes.

The idea that God's breath kindles the flames of Hell is Biblical, but the text alluded to makes it clear that Hell was not created out of sudden anger; it was prepared of old, according to foreknowledge: "For Tophet *is* ordeined of old; yea, for the king it is prepared; he hath made it deepe *and* large: the pile thereof *is* fire and much wood, the breath of the LORD, like a streame of brimstone, doeth kindle it" (Isa. 30:33).

Belial's reference to "sevenfold rage" almost surely alludes to Nebuchadnezzar, who, in sudden wrath against the Hebrew children for their refusal to bow to his image, was "full of fury, and the forme of his visage was changed against Shadrach, Meshach, and Abednego: *therefore* he spake, and commanded that they should heat the furnace one seven times more than it was wont to be heated" (Dan. 3:19). The implication of Belial's language is that God is an Almighty Tyrant who, if the rebels make war, is likely to fly into a fit of passion and devise new torments on the spur of the moment. The other side of the same coin is Belial's assumption that if the devils bear their doom quietly, God's irresponsible arbitrariness will motivate him to "Not mind us not offending" (II, 212), and that, consequently, "these raging fires / Will slack'n, if his breath stir not thir flames" (II, 213-214). Thus both Moloch's counsel of desperate war and Belial's counsel of "ignoble ease, and peaceful sloath" (II, 227), as Milton calls it, are based, as shown by their reversals of Biblical language, upon the kind of perverted and inadequate view of God that one would expect such fallen angels to have.

But Mammon, who wins the applause of the assembly as a result of his opposition to both Moloch and Belial and his advocacy of self-development in Hell, descends even lower in his attitude towards God; he will not admit that Heaven has anything to offer that Hell does not have:

> for ev'n in heav'n his looks & thoughts
> Were always downward bent, admiring more
> The riches of Heav'ns pavement, trod'n Gold,
> Then aught divine or holy else enjoy'd
> In vision beatific.
>
> (*P. L.*, I, 680-684)

Of any special blessedness in seeing God as the result of purity in heart (Matt. 5:8), therefore, Mammon knows nothing and cares nothing; he is a complete materialist and, as such, is contemptuous of Heaven's King with his "Strict Laws" requiring "warbl'd Hymns" and "Forc't Halleluiah's" (II, 241-243). Heaven has light, but even there God imitates "our Darkness"; we will "his Light / Imitate when we please" (II, 269-270), says Mammon. From Hell's "Desart soile" we can dig gems and gold with which to "raise / Magnificence; and what can Heav'n shew more?" (II, 272-273), he asks.

But nowhere does Mammon reveal his irredeemable perversity of mind more than in his counsel that he and the other devils seek

> Our own good from our selves, and from our own
> Live to our selves, though in this vast recess,
> Free, and to none accountable, preferring
> Hard liberty before the easie yoke
> Of servile Pomp.
>
> (*P. L.*, II, 253-257)

Embedded in Mammon's oxymoronic sarcasm is the sneering reference to "the easie yoke," an allusion to the words of Jesus: "Take my yoke upon you, and learne of me; for I am meeke and lowly in heart: and ye shall find rest unto your soules. For my yoke is easie and my burden is light" (Matt. 11:29-30). In keeping with the character of Mammon, the purpose of the words is reversed; that true freedom which Christ offered to those who would receive and obey him (the kind of freedom championed by Abdiel in Book V, lines 822-830) is inconceivable to Mammon, for he cannot believe that there really is such a thing as an easy yoke. His liberty is license and is summed up in his phrase "to none accountable." He recognizes no superior and thus cannot imagine himself being voluntarily obedient to or responsible to any authority higher than one of his own stripe. He has not learned and will never learn that "whosoever committeth sin is the servant of sinne" (John 8:34).

The speaker who turns the tide from approval of Mammon's proposal to acceptance of the plan "the Author of all ill" had in mind from the beginning is Beelzebub. In addition to the authoritativeness and the air of truth which Biblical allusion gives to his speech, there is included ironic reversal of Biblical language. After his diabolic proposition that God's new Creation be invaded and, if possible, possessed by the devils or, at least, destroyed by God angry to see His new creatures seduced to join the devils' party, his call for a volunteer to make the arduous journey to the new world involves a complete reversal of the purpose served by the language in Scripture.

> But first whom shall we send
> In search of this new world, whom shall we find
> Sufficient?
> (*P. L.*, II, 402-404)

The question is an ironic parallel to the one asked by the Lord in Isaiah's vision: "Also I heard the voice of the Lord, saying, Whome shall I send, and who will goe for us?" (6:8). Isaiah's quick response, "Here am I; send me," is far simpler than Satan's proud acceptance oration (II, 430-466), but the difference which gives the effect of dramatic irony to Beelzebub's question and Satan's volunteering lies in the reversal of purpose in the Biblical language. The question in Isaiah is prompted by the divine desire to send a messenger to the Israelites who, though his message would be rejected by many, would be the means of bringing blessing to those who believed him; Beelzebub's question is motivated by the desire to send to Earth and mankind a representative whose lies will be believed and who will become the means of man's sin and death. Isaiah's sin has been purged by a live coal from God's altar before he volunteers and is commissioned as a messenger of God; Satan's sin has just begun to flourish and the fall into Hell seems to have further inflamed his iniquity. And later in the epic, Satan's ostensibly noble choice to undertake alone the journey to Earth takes on even deeper irony when it is remembered at the time of Christ's voluntary offering of himself as the one to die in man's place for man's sin (III, 213-216, 237-241).

In a manner reminiscent of the dramatic asides and soliloquies of the villains in Elizabethan drama, Satan reveals his true nature in the frank statements of Book IV of *Paradise Lost*. When Satan is talking to himself, he is quite different from the Satan who displays such singleness of mind and unconquerable will before his cohorts in Hell. The soliloquy at the beginning of Book IV, which reveals Satan's character both directly and through his use of Biblical allusion, is reserved for later comment; but in this book his reversal of the purpose of Biblical language is noteworthy.

After having gazed upon Adam and Eve for a long time, Satan speaks with sadness of the woe with which their happiness is soon to be replaced; but he seeks to lay the blame on God, since he is not man's "purposed foe" but God's. Any wrong he does to man is aimed at God, and, therefore, in his twisted reasoning, God is to blame for it. His sarcasm in the lines,

> my dwelling haply may not please
> Like this fair Paradise, your sense, yet such
> Accept your Makers work; he gave it me,
> Which I as freely give,
> (*P. L.*, IV, 378-381)

is intensified by the ironic reversal of purpose which Satan gives to the words of Christ, "Freely yee have received, freely give." Jesus' words had to do with the gift of the Spirit to "Heale the sicke, cleanse the lepers, raise the dead, cast out devils" (Matt. 10:8)—as the disciples had freely received of the power of the Spirit, they were freely to give spiritual help to others less fortunate. Satan, with grim, diabolic humor, indicates his willingness to give freely of sin, suffering, death, and finally Hell as freely as it was given to him. Actually, of course, he deserved his fate; God did not really consign him to Hell "freely," as though for no cause, as Satan implies. Recognition of Satan's reversal of Biblical language increases the bitterness of his heavy sarcasm, making his plan to ruin man appear even more fiendish.

Once Satan has entered into the Serpent in Book IX, the Serpent's beauty and ability to speak combined with Satan's persuasive and flattering eloquence soon brings Eve to the forbidden tree. Satan uses the Serpent's arguments as recorded in Genesis, but additional ones are supplied in Milton's dramatic portrayal. Explaining that he has risen from brute dumbness to human intelligence and articulate speech by eating of the forbidden fruit, Satan, in the Serpent, argues that Eve can rise above human limitations and be as wise as the gods.

So ye shall die perhaps, by putting off
Human, to put on Gods, death to be wisht.
(*P. L.*, IX, 713-714)

The language is patterned after Paul's description of conversion: "Lie not one to another, seeing that you have put off the old man with his deeds; And have put on the new man, which is renewed in knowledge after the image of him that created him" (Col. 3: 9-10). The Biblical image of putting off old garments to put on new occurs in a context which relates it to conversion and baptism, an important step of obedience to God; Satan uses the image, reversing its purpose, to persuade Eve to take the first step of disobedience to God. The Biblical figure is that of a dying and a rebirth—the old man of sin dies; a new man, "renewed in knowledge," comes to life in Christ. Satan, too, relates to dying and rebirth what he is urging Eve to do—death as a human being will be followed by life as a god, he argues. In Satan's last words, his call to action which results in Eve's plucking and eating the fruit, he sums up this argument and bases his imperative invitation on it: "Goddess humane, reach then and freely taste" (IX, 732). The words "Goddess humane" suggest his preceding arguments. He does not need to repeat them. The two words imply: Eve, you are already a goddess, the "Sovran of Creatures" (l. 612) and "Empress of this fair World" (l. 568), but you are still human and limited; if you would put off the limitations of humanity and put on complete godhood as I have put off animal limitations and put on human intellect and speech, "reach then and freely taste."[5] Satan's phrase "freely taste" recalls God's command to Adam, "Of every tree of the garden thou mayest freely eate: but of the tree of the knowledge of good and evill, thou shalt not eate of it" (Gen. 2:16-17); again Satan is reversing the purpose of the Scriptural phrase, this time by using "freely taste" as an invitation to Eve to eat of the one tree to which God's "freely eate" did not apply.

Sin uses a Scriptural phrase as she talks with her son Death while they sit at the gates of Hell awaiting the triumphal return

5. The interpretation of "Goddess humane" set forth above seems to have been conclusively demonstrated to be the correct interpetation by Professor Ants Oras in "'Goddess Humane' ('Paradise Lost' IX. 732)," *MLR*, XLIX (1954), 51-53.

of their Author. The poetic and the Biblical situation are similar, but, more important here, the purpose of the language is reversed.

> O Son, why sit we here each other viewing
> Idlely, while Satan our great Author thrives
> In other Worlds, and happier Seat provides
> For us his ofspring deare? (*P. L.*, X, 235-238)

In the Bible analogue there are, sitting at the gate of a besieged city, four lepers who say to one another, "Why sit we here until we die?" (II Kings 7:3). The lepers have no hope of having their famine relieved either at the gate or within the city; therefore, they elect to go out into the camp of the enemy (Syria) and take their chances on being fed or killed. Their hope is to live, and the result of their venture into the enemy camp is good news to all the city, for the Syrians have retreated and left all their food and clothing behind. Sin's suggestion that she and Death sit no longer at the gate, however, is motivated by her hope that Satan has been successful in tempting man, thus opening the way for the horrible pair to enter God's (the enemy's) new world; the hope of Sin and Death is "carnage, prey innumerable" (X, 268), and the bridge they build is a source of fiendish joy to the inhabitants of Hell since it provides them with a passageway to Earth. In short, the result of the lepers' question and their action in the Bible is life for many who were on the verge of starvation; the result of Sin's question and the consequent action is misery, corruption, and death for what has been a world of life. Then as Sin and Death finish the "stupendous Bridge," Satan appears on his journey back to Hell to report his success in causing man's Fall, praises his off-spring for their work, and gives them the charge: "If your joynt power prevaile, th' affaires of Hell / No detriment need feare, goe and be strong" (X, 408-409). The charge given by Moses to Israel in the wilderness (Deut. 11:8) and by God to Joshua after Moses' death (Josh. 1:6, 9), the charge to "be strong and goe in and possess the land," is reversed in purpose and becomes, in Satan's mouth, a charge to Sin and Death to possess the Earth.

After she and Adam have repented and have been given assurance of forgiveness, Eve assumes that she and her husband will remain in the Garden of Eden. That labor has been enjoined upon them does not seem so bad; as she says,

> while here we dwell,
> What can be toilsom in these pleasant Walkes?
> Here let us live, though in fall'n state, content.
> (*P. L.*, XI, 178-180)

Immediately following these words, ominous signs in Eden, such as an eagle seeking to kill two smaller birds, give indication that all is not well. But that Eve's hope is unrealistic is suggested also by her language, associated with the Pauline statement, "I have learned in whatsoever state I am, therewith to be content" (Phil. 4:11). Eve's idea is that to be fallen is not really so bad after all if one may still live in Paradise. But fallen man cannot stay in Paradise; the Fall has corrupted him and Nature, and he will henceforth corrupt whatever he touches. Eve's words are used to a purpose which is the reverse of Paul's; her suggestion is that lovely surroundings can make one content even though one is fallen, while Paul's point is that the inner peace and strength which Christ gives (Phil. 4:13) make him content no matter what his outer surroundings are. The allusion emphasizes that Eve, and Adam, have yet to learn through the visions given by Michael and through God-given dreams that the external environment is not so important as having a "Paradise within" which can be "happier farr" (XII, 587).[6]

In *Paradise Regained,* as in the longer epic, Biblical language is reversed in purpose for dramatic effect, but there all such reversals

6. Reversals of Biblical language in *Paradise Lost* do not occur in the speech of the actors alone. Milton's comments upon the action sometimes involve such allusions. See, for example, his description of Satan's choice of the Serpent as his instrument: "his final sentence chose / Fit Vessel, fittest Imp of fraud, in whom / To enter, and his dark suggestions hide" (IX, 88-90). In Scripture, Paul the great Apostle to the Gentiles is "a chosen vessell" to God (Acts 9:15). By keeping himself pure a man may be "a vessell unto honour . . . meete for the Masters use" (II Tim. 2:21). The dramatic irony is heightened when another Biblical allusion is recognized: the question of Scripture, "*What* if God, willing to shewe *his* wrath, and to make his power knowen, indured with much long suffering the vessels of wrath fitted to destruction?" (Rom. 9:22). The Serpent is a "Fit Vessel" for Satan because of his "native suttletie" (IX, 93), but he is also a vessel of wrath fitted to destruction.

are by Satan. Reporting to his consistory of demons after the first encounter with Christ, Satan says,

> I, as I undertook, and with the vote
> Consenting in full frequence was impowr'd,
> Have found him, view'd him, tasted him, but find
> Far other labour to be undergon
> Then when I dealt with *Adam* first of Men.
> (*P. R.*, II, 129-133)

There is allusion here to the exhortation of the psalmist: "O taste and see that the LORD is good: blessed *is* the man *that* trusteth in him" (Ps. 34:8). Satan has "tasted" Christ (in the sense of "tested" him) and has found him good, but this is far from bringing Satan to blessing through trust in Christ. All Satan will admit is that Christ will require quite a different approach from that which ensnared the first of men; having tasted Christ, Satan finds him comparatively good but will not admit that he is absolutely good. Not only does he not trust in Christ's claim, therefore, but he still seeks to defeat Christ.

Later in Book II of *Paradise Regained*, after the lavish banquet spread by the devils has failed to attract Christ, Satan seeks to impress him with the need of money to bring him "Honour, Friends, Conquest, and Realms," and his advice echoes Scriptural structure.

> Therefore, if at great things thou wouldst arrive,
> Get Riches first, get Wealth, and Treasure heap,
> Not difficult if thou hearken to me,
> Riches are mine, Fortune is in my hand.
> (*P. R.*, II, 426-429)

Satan is contradicting such Biblical principles as that the power to get wealth comes from God (Deut. 8:17-18) and that one should seek first not money but the kingdom of God and his righteousness (Matt. 6:33); and Satan's imperative advice to "Get Riches ... get Wealth," following the same structural pattern, recalls the imperative of Solomon in Scripture: "Get wisedome, get understanding; forget *it* not; neither decline from the wordes of my mouth" (Prov. 4:5). Christ reveals as specious Satan's reasoning that riches are the *sine qua non* of greatness by references to both Biblical and classical examples to the contrary, and the reader may well remember such Biblical warnings as "He that trusteth in his riches shall fall" (Prov. 11:28) and "be not high-minded, nor trust in uncertaine riches, but in the living God" (I Tim. 6:17). But anticipating these is the dramatic effect of Satan's reversal of purpose in his use of the structure of the familiar proverb, "Get wisedome, get understanding."

During the last temptation when Satan sets Christ on the highest pinnacle of the Temple, he urges:

> Cast thy self down; safely if Son of God:
> For it is written, He will give command
> Concerning thee to his Angels, in thir hands
> They shall up lift thee, lest at any time
> Thou chance to dash thy foot against a stone.
> (*P. R.*, IV, 555-559)

Here Satan uses authoritative Scriptural quotation as a means of getting Christ to cast himself down to prove that God will preserve him according to the promise of the Bible. Satan is using the psalm alluded to for a different purpose from that for which it was written, for he tries to use it to motivate Christ to commit a rash or presumptive act. To reverse the purpose of the Bible passage, Satan omits part of it (as he does in the Bible account of the temptation); the full promise is, "For he shall give his Angels charge over thee: to keepe thee in all thy wayes. They shall beare thee up in *their* hands: lest thou dash thy foote against a stone" (Ps. 91:11-12). The promise then, fully quoted, is that the child of God, whether His Son or one of His other children, will be kept from harm *in all his ways,* i. e., in ways that are wise and befitting a child of God. It is the phrase "in all thy wayes" which Satan omits. Christ's way could not be a way of presumption or a way which would reduce him to the level of a cheap stunt-man. Thus Satan attempts, by the use of Scripture, to tempt Christ to do something which is contrary to the whole spirit of the Scripture verse in its original form.[7]

7. Of Satan's quotation of Scripture in *Paradise Regained,* IV, 555-559, Merritt Y. Hughes, in his 1957 edition of the poem, merely notes: "The lines paraphrase Psalm xci, 11-12" (*John Milton: Complete Poems and Major Prose* [New York, 1957], p. 528). Other editors note the Bible reference but do not comment on Satan's omission; the significance of Satan's use of Scripture here has been, therefore, generally overlooked. Elizabeth Marie Pope (*Paradise Regained: The Tradition and the Poem* [Baltimore, 1947], pp. 82-83),

## *CHARACTER*

### *Satan*

The character in *Paradise Lost* most fully and dramatically delineated by the use of allusions to the Bible and to Biblical characters is Satan. This is not to say that other leading characters —the Son, Abdiel, Adam and Eve, Raphael, Michael, or the lieutenants of Satan—are inadequately delineated. But the very nature of the position which Satan occupies in the epic focuses attention upon him from the beginning; he is the leader of the revolt against God, the Tempter who brings about the Fall, and these roles make him the chief actor on the stage of our attention. Though Milton is careful to make it clear that God is ruling in omniscience and omnipotence over all the universe and that it is only by the permission of God that Satan can do anything, yet, dramatically, Satan's actions are usually the initiating ones, bringing reaction from God, the angels, and man. As Satan acts, he talks, and others, including the poet, make comments to or about him. The Biblical language used by and about Satan is constantly mirroring his character so that the reader may see that character roundly reflected as the poem progresses.

The tremendous size and power of Satan are emphasized in the first book of *Paradise Lost,* and the use of Biblical language height-

---

however, has pointed out that the Devil's crafty twisting in the Biblical temptation of the text alluded to in Ps. 91 was noted by such early theologians as Chrysostom, Jerome, Theophylactus, and Origen, as well as by such commentators as Jeremy Taylor and John Calvin. As Milton presents the final scene between Satan and Christ, however, the real test to which Satan is finally subjecting Christ, the only test to which Christ makes an active response in the whole poem, is the test, "There stand, if thou wilt stand; to stand upright / Will ask thee skill" (IV, 551-552), with allusion to "stand against the wiles of the devill" (Eph. 6:11-14) from a New Testament passage in which "stand" appears four times in four verses. Satan does not really believe Christ can stand on the needle-sharp spire; thus, he is putting him in position so that he must either fall or jump, and Satan's temptation is that he jump. Christ does neither, but, to Satan's amazement, he *stands,* demonstrating divine power for the first time in the poem. He can make such a demonstration, for Satan has not seriously tempted him to stand; his emphasis is on the other alternatives. And, as Pope has shown, Christ can quote the Biblical "Tempt not the Lord thy God" (Deut. 6:16) with application to himself without contradicting Milton's Arianism in *De Doctrina* because there Milton had agreed that in the Bible "the name and presence of God is used to imply his vicarious power and might resident in the Son" (quoted by Pope, p. 105).

ens and intensifies the reader's impression of him. The first words spoken by him (the first by any character in the poem) are allusive to the words spoken by God (through the prophets Isaiah and Ezekiel) to Lucifer after his fall from Heaven: "How art thou fallen from heaven, O Lucifer, sonne of the morning?" (Isa. 14:12) and "Thou hast corrupted thy wisedome by reason of thy brightnesse" (Ezek. 28:17).[8] Satan speaks to Beelzebub:

> If thou beest he; But O how fall'n! how chang'd
> From him, who in the happy Realms of Light
> Cloth'd with transcendent brightnes didst outshine
> Myriads though bright. (*P. L.*, I, 84-87)

The dramatic effect of having Satan speak to one "next himself in power" (l. 79) in language reminiscent of that used by God speaking to Satan in the Bible is to raise one's estimate of Satan's lost estate in Heaven and to magnify the depths of his fall much more than if the words were applied by Beelzebub, for example, to Satan. Other allusions serve to support both the impression of Satan's great character (his courage, will power, and perseverance, even though they are misdirected and later revealed by his soliloquy in Book IV to be affected, are great) and the depth and

8. Merritt Y. Hughes, in the introduction to his 1935 edition of the epic, speaks of Milton's having followed the traditional interpretation of Isaiah 14:12 as referring to the fall of Satan, "although we now know that the prophetic passage referred really to the King of Babylon" (*Paradise Lost* [New York, 1935], p. xxxii). But of course Milton, and anyone else who read the Bible, knew as well as do twentieth century readers that Isaiah was commanded to take up a "proverb against the king of Babylon" (Isa. 14:4); Medieval and Renaissance Christians knew that prophecy is closely connected with history and that the prophets had, first of all, a message for their contemporaries. They were accustomed, however, to looking in the Bible for passages which transcended their historical and dispensational limitations and suggested explanations of the past or disclosures of the future. It is not true, as Professor Hughes' statement implies, that "we" know more about the Bible's statements now than Milton and his contemporaries did; what is true is that we have adopted a literal-minded idea that history will explain everything in the prophets, and we have, therefore, lost the imaginative allegorical vision which responds to prophetic transcendence of historical horizons in the Bible. Perhaps Professor Hughes' recognition of this loss prompted him to omit his comment about what "we now know" in his 1957 edition. For a serious modern presentation of Biblical hermeneutics which seeks to maintain the validity of the "mystical sense of Scripture," see Louis Berkhof, *Principles of Biblical Interpretation* (Grand Rapids, Michigan, 1950), particularly Chapter VII, entitled "Theological Interpretation."

desperateness of his fallen condition. Although the character of Satan is well delineated aside from the use of Biblical allusion, by recognition of Milton's use of the Bible the reader gains deeper insight into the character of Satan in both epic poems.

In *Paradise Lost* Milton provides glimpses of the various facets of Satan's character by having the language used either by or about Satan associate him with familiar villains of the Bible.[9] Thus the Devil is associated by Bible words and phrases with Dives, Nebuchadnezzar, Herod, Esau, Belshazzar, the Pharisees, Pharaoh,[10] and even Judas Iscariot.

The first view of Satan in *Paradise Lost* is in Hell; he stirs and begins to think:

> for now the thought
> Both of lost happiness and lasting pain
> Torments him; round he throws his baleful eyes.
> (*P. L.*, I, 54-56)

The words of Christ in the Bible concerning Dives are, "In hell he lift up his eyes, beeing in torments" (Luke 16:23a). The allusion forcefully emphasizes the contrast between Satan's former and present state; like the rich man in Jesus' story, who was "clothed in purple and fine linnen and fared sumptuously every day" (Luke 16:19), Satan finds himself in a situation completely unlike the place from which he has fallen. But, unlike the rich man of Scrip-

9. Other kinds of Biblical associations suggest elements in Satan's character. When he alights on Hell's "singed bottom," Milton's comment is "Such resting found the sole / Of unblest feet" (I, 236-238), which connects Satan with the raven let out of the ark by Noah. The dove released from the ark "found no rest for the sole of her foote" (Gen. 8:9), but the raven, let out earlier, did not return but was content with the rocky cliffs and blasted trees of a world under judgment. Satan would rather be under judgment in Hell than enjoy the security of Heaven in subservience to God. Cf. also *P. L.*, XI, 856, where the dove is described as "surer messenger" who sought "Green Tree or ground" unlike the raven whose unblest feet rested otherwise. There is an ironic parallel between Milton's description of Satan as "by transcendent glory rais'd / Above his fellows" (II, 427-428) and the psalmist's description of Messiah as "annoynted . . . with the oyle of gladnes above thy fellowes" (Ps. 45:7, quoted in Heb. 1:9). Then as Satan views his prey in Paradise, he is portrayed as taking on the form of a lion and stalking Adam and Eve (IV, 401-402); this form recalls the Biblical simile of Peter, who warned that Satan "as a roaring Lion, walketh about, seeking whom he may devoure" (I Pet. 5:8), and foreshadows Satan's future role as man's enemy.

10. See above in the section on language the discussion of allusions linking Satan and his hosts with Pharaoh and his army.

ture, Satan lifts his eyes to behold "sights of woe, / Regions of sorrow, doleful shades" (I, 64-65) unmitigated by any view of such a place of blessing as Abraham's bosom, and, further unlike Dives, who had a desire to warn his relatives about Hell, Satan ostensibly has no regrets and no requests, no quarter to ask of God. His aim is to "wage by force or guile eternal Warr" (l. 121). Both the similarities and the differences, therefore, between Dives and Satan contribute to the dramatic force of Satan's character as it is being revealed in description, action, and speech.

Later in Book I, as he engages in action ascribed to him in the Bible, Satan is associated with King Nebuchadnezzar of Babylon. As the fallen angels assemble in military order before him, Satan views

> Thir visages and stature as of Gods,
> Thir number last he summs. And now his heart
> Distends with pride, and hardning in his strength
> Glories.
>
> (*P. L.*, I, 570-573)

The numbering of the host recalls the Biblical occasion when "Satan stood up against Israel, & provoked David to number Israel. ... And Joab gave the summe of the number of the people unto David.... And God was displeased with this thing, therefore he smote Israel" (I Chron. 21:1, 5, 7). David's numbering, as such, was not wrong, but the motive behind it was; for the earthly king over God's chosen people to glory in the numbers he ruled was blasphemous, for it suggested that he, not God, was responsible for the greatness of the kingdom and its people. But there is further significance to the Scriptural allusions. Satan's pride and self-glorying is like that of Nebuchadnezzar of Babylon, who, "when his heart was lifted up, and his minde hardened in pride ... was deposed from his kingly throne, and they tooke his glory from him" (Dan. 5:20). The suggestion of the Biblical allusions is that Satan, like David who was punished for numbering his people in pride and like Nebuchadnezzar whose pride resulted in his being driven out to live with the wild beasts, will fall the harder in defeat the more he exalts himself. The allusions highlight dramatically the complete egotism and proud self-centeredness of Satan.

Another association with a Bible villain occurs when Satan, disguised as a "stripling Cherube" (III, 636), approaches the sun to ask Uriel's directions for finding the seat of man within the newly created universe. He asks,

> Brightest Seraph tell
> In which of all these shining Orbes hath Man
> His fixed seat, or fixed seat hath none,
> But all these shining Orbes his choice to dwell;
> That I may find him, and with secret gaze,
> Or open admiration him behold.
> (*P. L.*, III, 667-672)

The contrast between the ulterior motive of Satan in seeking man and his stated reason involves hypocrisy akin to that which led Herod to pretend interest in the whereabouts of the Christ-child, announced by the wise men from the orient (guided to Jerusalem by a star) as "born King of the Jews," because of a desire to worship him, when his real motive was a desire to kill him. Herod sent the wise men to Bethlehem with the charge: "Goe, and search diligently for the yong child: and when ye have found him, bring mee word againe, that I may come and worship him also" (Matt. 2:8). The wise men in the Biblical story, like Uriel by Satan in *Paradise Lost,* were taken in by the dissembling of Herod in spite of their wisdom and were only prevented from returning to report to him by the intervention of God in a dream (Matt. 2:12). The association of Satan with the evil king who perpetrated the slaughter of the innocent children of Bethlehem is dramatically apt both in the dark shadow it throws upon the character of Satan and in the similarity between Satan's mission to destroy the newly created first Adam and Herod's attempt to destroy the newly born second Adam.

Perhaps the fullest revelation of Satan's character occurs in the soliloquy near the opening of Book IV; like the villains on the Elizabethan stage, Satan opens his heart to himself and to the reader. Here is a Satan quite different from the one who stands like a rock of adamant before his followers. As he himself says, his followers little know how dearly he abides his vaunting boasts that he could subdue God himself or "Under what torments inwardly" he groans. Many Biblical allusions add to the dramatic effectiveness of his utterances of "ire, envie, and despair" (IV, 115), but the central one around which the others revolve is that in the following lines:

> O then at last relent: is there no place
> Left for Repentance, none for Pardon left?
> None left but by submission; and that word
> *Disdain* forbids me, and my dread of shame
> Among the Spirits beneath, whom I seduc'd
> With other promises and other vaunts
> Then to submit.
>
> (*P. L.*, IV, 79-85)

By allusion to Scripture, Satan is here identified with Esau, described in the New Testament as a "profane person . . . who for one morsell of meat sold his birthright" and who "afterward, when he would have inherited the blessing . . . was rejected: for he found no place of repentance, though he sought it carefully with teares" (Heb. 12:16b-17). This New Testament description is an interpretation of the Old Testament story of Esau who sold his right of primogeniture to his twin brother Jacob for a mess of red pottage and who, later, wished to inherit the blessing of the Abrahamic Covenant from his father Isaac after the blessing had already been given to Jacob (Gen. 25:29-34, 27:30-41). (Jacob resorted to deception, through disguising himself as Esau, in order to get the blessing, but it was rightfully his anyway once Esau had sold him the birthright.) What caused Esau to weep so bitterly was not deep remorse over having allowed his appetite to overcome his better judgment; rather it was sorrow over losing the blessing which he had thoughtlessly given up by the sale of his birthright. Similarly, although Satan says things in his soliloquy which indicate grief over his sin of pride and opposition to God (as when he says to himself, "Nay curs'd be thou; since against his thy will / Chose freely what it now so justly rues" [IV, 71-72]), there is no genuine repentance over his sin of rebellion. He still disdains submission to God as much as ever, and pride prevents his admission to the rebels that he has lied to them. His sorrow, like Esau's, is a self-pitying sorrow which is concerned not with his sin but with his loss.

Satan's expression of hatred for the sun of the new universe, because it reminds him of the "bright eminence" he enjoyed before he sinned, reveals his emphasis not on how he has sinned but on what he has lost. To the sun he says,

> to thee I call,
> But with no friendly voice, and add thy name
> O Sun, to tell thee how I hate thy beams
> That bring to my remembrance from what state
> I fell, how glorious once above thy Spheare.
> (*P. L.*, IV, 35-39)

The sun, the light of this world, is used often in the Bible as an image representing Christ; in the Old Testament he is figured in prophecy as "the Sunne of Righteousnesse . . . with healing in his wings" (Mal. 4:2a), and in the New Testament he is "the light of the world" (John 9:5), the one whose countenance is "as the Sun shineth in his strength" (Rev. 1:16b). He is the one who said, "For every one that doeth evill, hateth the light" (John 3:20), the one who appeared to John on Patmos with his face shining like the sun and gave John the warning message to the Church of the Ephesians, "Remember . . . from whence thou art fallen, and repent" (Rev. 2:5). Whenever Satan sees anything or anyone in an exalted position, his jealousy and hatred are aroused. The glorious sun, ruling like a god over the new world, causing the brilliant stars to hide their heads in his sight, draws hatred from the sinful pride and ambition of Satan just as the Son, exalted by the Father and ordained to rule as Messiah over the angels, drew Satan's hatred and rebellion. The Biblical allusions of the beginning of Satan's soliloquy emphasize the parallel between his hatred of the Son and of the sun and indicate the reason for his hatred; he "that doeth evill, hateth the light" (John 3:20). Though he is called to remembrance of his former state, he does not repent. He does admit, however, that he was not created as he is; he says of his war against God,

> he deservd no such return
> From me, whom he created what I was
> In that bright eminence, and with his good
> Upbraided none; nor was his service hard.
> (*P. L.*, IV, 42-45)

It is not "whom he created what I am" but "whom he created what I was." Satan is corroborating God's word (through Ezekiel) to himself: "Thou wast perfect in thy wayes, from the day that thou wast created, till iniquity was found in thee" (Ezek. 28:15). In the same Biblical context, Satan was told, "thou hast corrupted thy wisedome by reason of thy brightnesse" (Ezek. 28:17). Satan's words also allude to the promise of James that "God . . . giveth to al *men* liberally, & upbraideth not" (Jas. 1:5) and to John's definition of the love of God as keeping God's commandments "and his commandments are not grievous" (I John 5:3).

Satan realizes, then, that his action was unwise; he matched himself against "Heav'ns matchless King" (IV, 41). He realizes too that God gave him only good and thus gave him the wisdom, "free Will and Power to stand" as faithfully as the "other Powers as great" who did not fall (IV, 63, 66). Neither did God upbraid him with His goodness nor make His service hard with grievous commandments. Why then does Satan not repent and be received again into his place of glory in Heaven? Because, like Esau, he can find "no place of repentance" (Heb. 12:17; Authorized Version margin: "no way to change his mind"), no place "for Pardon left" (IV, 80). Satan's attention, like Esau's, is focused on the lost place of blessing rather than on the sin by which he lost that place. Satan, like Esau, has made his choice long ago, and though he did not realize at the time that the result of his choice would be exclusion from blessing, as Esau did not realize it, such was the case, and he is not now willing to undergo the change of mind necessary for reinstatement. The very willful corruption of his nature which led Satan to make the original choice to rebel will prevent any true reconciliation with God. Even if he could be restored, Satan says, "how soon / Would highth recal high thoughts, how soon unsay / What feign'd submission swore" (IV, 94-96). Therefore Satan makes his declaration of irrevocable purpose:

> So farwel Hope, and with Hope farwel Fear,
> Farwel Remorse: all Good to me is lost;
> Evil be thou my Good.
>
> (*P. L.*, IV, 108-110)

If one remembers at this point the allusion to Esau, one may recall that Esau, while he did not make such a statement as Satan does, immediately following his tears of remorse over the lost blessing, did state his intention of murdering his brother (Gen. 27:41), an intention which would certainly not indicate that Esau's tears represented any real repentance. That Esau was reprobate is indicated by the scathing denunciations by the prophets Obadiah and Malachi of Esau and his descendants and by the familiar phrase, "Jacob have I loved but Esau have I hated" (Rom. 9:13, Mal. 1:2-3). Satan's intention is to do far worse than murder; he is on his way to the Garden of Eden to bring sin and death upon an entire race. That his purposes will eventually bring more wrath down upon his own head is suggested by the allusion in his phrase, "Evil be thou my Good," to Isaiah's warning: "Woe unto them that call evil good, and good evill; that put darknes for light, and light for darknesse, that put bitter for sweet, and sweet for bitter" (5:20).

At the close of Book IV when Satan is taken into custody by the guardian angels and brought before their chief, Gabriel, he is described as a magnificent figure with a stature that reaches the sky (IV, 886-900). But a moment later God intervenes with the sign of Libra in the stars; the weight in the scales which represents Satan's chances in a fight with the elect angels flies upward. Then Gabriel says to Satan:

look up,
And read thy Lot in yon celestial Sign
Where thou art weigh'd, & shown how light, how weak,
If thou resist.
(*P. L.*, IV, 1010-1012)

The allusion to Scripture here associates Satan with Belshazzar, King of Babylon, to whom Daniel, interpreting the handwriting on the wall on the night Babylon was to be overthrown by Darius the Mede, said: "Thou art weighed in the balances, and art found wanting" (Dan. 5:27). The divine evidence in the sky transforms Satan from a mighty, awe-inspiring figure boasting of his prowess into a silent fiend who flees murmuring from Paradise. The Biblical allusion to Belshazzar emphasizes the dramatic change in Satan's attitude. Satan is, of course, a far more courageous character than Belshazzar, whose knees knock from fear when he is confronted by a sign from God (Dan. 5:6), but the association of the two by the reference to being weighed and found too light emphasizes one aspect of Satan's character as it is revealed in Book IV. He who proudly vaunts his undaunted courage while he is surrounded by his followers in Hell is full of doubts and inner turmoil when he is alone, as in the soliloquy at the opening of Book IV; and when he is faced with clear evidence that God has determined the outcome of battle against him, he flies from danger.

Satan's first formal speech to the great host of angels whom he has led off into the north of Heaven includes, as recounted by Raphael, many allusions to Biblical passages emphasizing the power of the Messiah as given him by the Father (*P. L.*, V, 772-802; Phil. 2:10-11; Matt. 28:18; Ps. 2:2-3; Matt. 11:29-30; Heb. 1:3; John 8:33-34). Satan uses these allusions in his speech to give the false impression that a new and different kind of subservience is to be required of the angels under the Messiah than has been required previously under the Father. He skillfully uses rhetorical questions to suggest to the minds of his listeners the humiliation that is being heaped upon him and them by the required "Knee-tribute" and by the submission of their necks to "this Yoke." Will you choose to bow to this Messiah? he asks; then he answers for them:

> ye will not, if I trust
> To know ye right, or if ye know your selves
> Natives and Sons of Heav'n possest before
> By none, and if not equal all, yet free,
> Equally free. (*P. L.*, V, 788-792)

Satan's indignant affirmation that he and all the angels are free, "possest before / By none," is reminiscent of the response of the Pharisees to Christ's statement that faith in his word would bring them to know the truth and that truth would make them free. They answered, "Wee bee Abrahams seed, and were never in bondage to any man: how sayest thou, Yee shall be made free?" (John 8:33). Satan's argument is that he and the other angels do not need to submit themselves to the Son, for they are free and ordained "to govern, not to serve" (V, 802); like the Pharisees, Satan does not realize that the kind of freedom he boasts of is a kind of slavery, involving license to do whatever selfish motivation may lead to. Abdiel says later, in the beginning of Book VI, of Satan's freedom,

"Thy self not free, but to thy self enthrall'd" (VI, 181); the answer of Christ to the Pharisees in the Bible is similar: "Verily, verily, I say unto you, Whosoever committeth sin is the servant [δοῦλος, literally "bondman," "slave"] of sinne.... If the Sonne therefore shall make you free, ye shall be free indeed" (John 8:34, 36). Thus Satan, like the Pharisees who rejected Christ's offer of spiritual freedom even as they boasted of their imagined ancestral freedom, even while he pleads his right to and love of freedom as reasons for rebelling against God and his Messiah, demonstrates that he is enslaved to the sins of self-love and pride which have taken root in his mind. The true freedom, freedom indeed, is found only in love and obedience to God and his Son: this is the Biblical position which Abdiel takes. Satan's proud enslavement to sin and self are summed up in his declaration in Book I, "Better to reign in Hell, then serve in Heav'n" (l. 263), whereas the true freedom of Abdiel is expressed in that faithful angel's answer to such an attitude as Satan's:

> Reign thou in Hell thy Kingdom, let mee serve
> In Heav'n God ever blesst, and his Divine
> Behests obey, worthiest to be obey'd.
> (*P. L.*, VI, 183-185)[11]

The Biblical allusion in Satan's speech concerning freedom associates him with the kind of spiritual pride and blindness with which the Pharisees were afflicted, and Abdiel's statement that Satan is enslaved to himself reflects, implicitly, the reply of Christ to the Pharisees that their freedom was slavery.

A Biblical phrase used twice in Raphael's narration to Adam associates Satan with Judas Iscariot. In the first instance, the phrase is not related to Satan specifically because he has not yet fallen from his high estate, but it is clear that he is the one who is soon to break the command of the Father that all knees in Heaven bow to the Son. At the great convocation, the Father proclaims the Son as His anointed vicegerent and says:

11. Abdiel's declaration, which so exactly opposes Satan's, includes an allusion to Romans 9:5b—"Christ came, who is over all, God blessed for ever"; the allusion is in accord with Abdiel's earlier defense of Messiah as worthy to be served both by virtue of his superior nature and by virtue of God's command (V, 822-840; VI, 174-178).

> him who disobeyes
> Mee disobeyes, breaks union, and that day
> Cast out from God and blessed vision, falls
> Into utter darkness, deep ingulft, his place
> Ordaind without redemption, without end.
> (*P. L.*, V, 611-615)

The phrase "his place" is repeated by Raphael immediately preceding his account of the Creation when he speaks of Lucifer as having fallen "with his flaming Legions through the Deep / Into his place" (VII, 134-135). In the Bible Judas is described as one who "by transgression fell, that he might go to his owne place" (Acts 1:25). Satan is, of course, the first of all traitors, and Hell is more appropriately spoken of as "his place" than as anybody else's. Luke states that "Satan entered into Judas surnamed Iscariot" (22:3), John reports the same in his gospel (13:2, 27), and John records also that Jesus called Judas "a devill" (6:70-71). Judas is the only one other than Satan of whom the phrase "his own place," referring to Hell, is used. As this allusion is recognized, the Satan of Milton's epic takes on some of the characteristics of Judas: his dissembling nature, as when he draws a third of the angels into the north on the pretext of desiring to provide entertainment in reception of the newly anointed King, is like that of Judas, who gave the appearance of loving Jesus but betrayed him with a kiss; and the fatal course of Satan's existence tends toward self-destruction as a result of his part in the destruction of man in Adam, a course similar to that of Judas, whose betrayal of Christ resulted in his own suicide. If the reader catches the slight hint of a connection between Satan and Judas, he glimpses occasionally, under all the eloquent oratory and sometimes admirable expression of independence, the mean and sneaking figure of Judas Iscariot the Betrayer.

Satan, therefore, as seen through Biblical allusion in *Paradise Lost,* has the proud vanity of Nebuchadnezzar, the cold-blooded wickedness (masquerading as piety) of Herod, the unrepentant materialism and self-pity of Esau, the cowardliness (covered by boasting until faced with signs of divine omnipotence) of Belshazzar, the blind pride of the Pharisees in a freedom which is spiritual slavery, and the fatal self-seeking disloyalty of Judas Iscariot.

While the Satan of *Paradise Regained* has not the mighty stature nor the oratorical eloquence of the Satan of *Paradise Lost,* he is the same old Serpent, having lost nothing of his talent for guile, fraud, and lying insinuation. He has perhaps even gained in these more subtle talents through the aeons since his fall from Heaven. In his first approach to Christ in *Paradise Regained,* his speech is marked by a Biblical allusion which helps to form the reader's estimate of his dramatic character, an allusion which includes and reinforces a word previously used in the same speech and used often in his original rebellion against God in *Paradise Lost*—the word *new.* Asking Christ what he is doing out in the wilderness alone, Satan continues,

> I ask the rather, and the more admire,
> For that to me thou seem'st the man, whom late
> Our new baptizing Prophet at the Ford
> Of *Jordan* honour'd so, and call'd thee Son
> Of God; I saw and heard, for we sometimes
> Who dwell this wild, constrain'd by want, come forth
> To Town or Village nigh (nighest is far)
> Where ought we hear, and curious are to hear,
> What happ'ns new.
>
> (*P. R.*, I, 326-334)

Satan's initial strategy in tempting away from allegiance to God the hosts of heavenly angels was to suggest that God's exaltation of the Messiah was something new which would result in other innovations that would be detrimental to him and his peers. He spoke to Beelzebub of the "new Laws" being imposed and of how this should lead to "new minds" and "new Counsels" in those who would be obliged to kneel to the anointed Son (*P. L.*, V, 679-682); later he scoffed at Abdiel's statement that he and all the spirits of Heaven were created by the Son as "strange point and new" (*P. L.*, V, 855).

Now, intending to implant distrust in the heart of Christ, he hints that the newness of John the Baptist's ministry suggests that his honoring of Christ as Son of God is a matter to provoke curiosity but not serious credence without a more miraculous sign to attest it (*P. R.*, I, 342-343). Satan does not mention, of course, that he also saw and heard the descending dove and the voice from

Heaven (*P. R.*, I, 79-85), for his purpose is to tempt Christ into making a display of his power as proof of his Sonship to God. In his curiosity and the motive for it, Biblical allusion associates Satan with the Athenians and visitors who came to hear the preaching of the Apostle Paul. After bringing Paul to the Areopagus, the philosophers and others asked, "May wee know what this new doctrine, whereof thou speakest, is?" (Acts 17:19). And Luke, the writer of Acts, adds parenthetically, "For all the Athenians and strangers which were there spent their time in nothing else, but either to tel, or to heare some new thing" (Acts 17:21). As Paul preached his sermon on Mars Hill to demonstrate that the God he preached and the doctrine he taught were not "new" things, so Christ points out, in answer to Satan's pretense of wonder at his deserted state, that it is not a new thing for God to protect and provide for his anointed servants in the wilderness. He mentions the examples of Israel, Moses, and Elijah, and asks, "Why dost thou then suggest to me distrust[?]" (I, 355). Satan's pose as a curious rural swain who merely seeks information about this wanderer is broken as Christ makes it clear that he not only recognizes Satan but knows the purpose of his approach: to tempt Christ to distrust his Father as he tempted the angels and Eve. Yet, although Satan's curiosity is a pose, the Biblical allusion which associates him with the Athenians of Acts adds to the delineation of his character as a worldly-wise sophist, who implies that anything new to his knowledge or experience is suspect.

Satan's character as an ingenious liar is emphasized in his first temptation of Christ in *Paradise Regained* by his reference to two Old Testament stories. After Christ has seen through his disguise, Satan admits his identity, but claims that he, too, is in the service of God: "For what he bids I do," he says (I, 377). His two examples of having done God's bidding are his trial of Job and his misleading of King Ahab.

> I came among the Sons of God, when he
> Gave up into my hands *Uzzean Job*
> To prove him, and illustrate his high worth;
> And when to all his Angels he propos'd
> To draw the proud King *Ahab* into fraud
> That he might fall in *Ramoth*, they demurring,

I undertook that office, and the tongues
Of all his flattering Prophets glibb'd with lyes
To his destruction, as I had in charge.
(*P. R.*, I, 368-376)

That Satan is misrepresenting the case of Job is evident from the poem; earlier God the Father has mentioned that Satan

fail'd in *Job*
Whose constant perseverance overcame
Whate're his cruel malice could invent.
(*P. R.*, I, 147-149)

Therefore, what Satan tries to mislead Christ into regarding as an example of his obedient and successful carrying out of the orders of God has already been spoken of by God as Satan's failure. That Satan's "cruel malice" indeed invented the trials of Job is made clear by Satan's words to God in the Biblical account of Job's trials: "But put foorth thine hand now, and touch all that hee hath, and hee will curse thee to thy face" (Job 1:11) and "touch his bone and his flesh, and hee will curse thee" (Job 2:5). Although no reference in the poem opposes Satan's version of the downfall of King Ahab as clearly as that which opposes his version of Job's sufferings, the reader familiar with the Bible easily sees through Satan's perversion of the Old Testament account. According to Satan, God proposed that Ahab be tricked into going to battle at Ramoth-Gilead; actually, "the LORD said, Who shall perswade Ahab, that he may goe up and fall at Ramoth Gilead?" (I Kings 22:20). According to Satan, the angels all demurred and would not attempt the task; actually, other suggestions were made before Satan's as "one sayd on this manner, and another sayde on that manner" (I Kings 22:20b). According to Satan, he was charged by God to glib the tongues of Ahab's prophets with lies; actually, the lying was Satan's idea and God permitted him to carry it out, saying "goe forth and doe so" (I Kings 22:22b). But the most important element in the story, though it is not even mentioned by Satan, is that God sent a true prophet, Micaiah, to Ahab to warn him that defeat and death awaited him at Ramoth-Gilead; only after Ahab had refused to believe God's message did Micaiah tell him that God had allowed a lying spirit to enter the mouths of the other prophets. Ahab, however, still would not believe Micaiah and so went to his destruction in battle. Christ gives a brief answer to Satan's use of the examples of Job and Ahab (I, 424-429), but only a knowledge of the Scriptures themselves (a knowledge which Milton doubtless assumed for his reader) reveals how cleverly Satan trims and twists Bible texts. Christ sums up the aspect of Satan's character emphasized by these references when he accuses Satan of being "compos'd of lyes / From the beginning" (I, 407-408), an allusion to the words of Christ in the Gospel of John: "When he speaketh a lie, hee speaketh of his owne; for he is a liar and the father of it" (John 8:44b).

Christ makes an explicit allusion to Scripture in *Paradise Regained* which shows Satan's character in its dominant feature: selfish pride. Satan has offered to deliver up Parthia to Christ and thus assure him of reigning over all Israel, including the ten tribes whose offspring still serve in pagan territory. Christ answers:

> But whence to thee this zeal, where was it then
> For *Israel*, or for *David*, or his Throne,
> When thou stood'st up his Tempter to the pride
> Of numbring *Israel*, which cost the lives
> Of threescore and ten thousand *Israelites*
> By three days Pestilence? such was thy zeal
> To *Israel* then, the same that now to me.
> (*P. R.*, III, 407-413)

The reference is to the time when "Satan stood up against Israel, & provoked David to number Israel. . . . So the LORD sent pestilence upon Israel: & there fell of Israel, seventy thousand men" (I Chron. 21:1, 14). Such an appeal by Satan to the pride of life and the love of authority over large numbers reflects his own character as it has been revealed in *Paradise Regained*, but even more strikingly in *Paradise Lost* (I, 571 ff.), and Christ refers to its reflection in the Bible. Pride, which has been Satan's own downfall, is the downfall of any whom he can infect with it as he did David; Christ, however, though he is the rightful heir to David's throne, is not to be infected by such an appeal to pride.

Satan is not the magnificent Titan in *Paradise Regained* that he is in the longer epic, not even when he is addressing his consistory of devils in the middle air. This difference is partly explained by the quite different nature of the two epic poems; the more diffuse epic, involving a tremendous panorama of scenery and action throughout the entire solar system and even beyond, requires a colossal figure of strength, while the briefer, quieter epic, consisting mostly of verbal debate with a minimum of action and change of setting, requires a less imposing but more intellectualized Devil. In *Paradise Regained* Satan is seen more often as the lying sneak that he is because Christ explicitly shows up again and again the fallacies of his reasoning, whereas in *Paradise Lost* Satan's misuse of Scripture and reason is more implicit and must be caught by the reader (with help from Milton's occasional comments and from Biblical allusion). The Biblical allusions used by and about Satan in *Paradise Regained* are from contexts more directly related to him than are those alluded to in *Paradise Lost;* although there are not so many dramatic identifications of Satan with other Bible characters in the shorter epic, there are many cross references between the Satan of *Paradise Regained* and his Biblical original. In spite of the differences, however, Milton's Satan is essentially the same in both epics, particularly as he is revealed through allusions to Scripture.

### *The Son of God*

The characterization of the Son in *Paradise Lost* is quite different from the characterization of Christ in *Paradise Regained;* Christ is more fully delineated and more vividly realistic as a dramatic character in the later poem. In the longer epic Milton had somewhat the same problem in presenting the Son as a character in the drama as he had in presenting the Father, for the Son was in a preincarnate manifestation and was not the man Christ Jesus of the New Testament (although some allusions used by and about the Son in *Paradise Lost* identify him with the Jesus of the Gospels). In *Paradise Regained,* however, Milton had a historical person to present, a person who had been portrayed from four different points of view, but with a unified purpose, in the four Gospels; also there existed a rich Christian tradition about the Christ of the temptation in the wilderness as a character in a dramatic situation.[12] There was no comparable tradition about the preincarnate Son of God, nor, in the absence of clear Scriptural background, could there have been.

The Son is first described in *Paradise Lost,* Book III, in the language of the New Testament and, in keeping with the function of this part of the poem as a theological explanation of what has happened and of what is going to happen, the language is theological.

> Beyond compare the Son of God was seen
> Most glorious, in him all his Father shon
> Substantially express'd, and in his face
> Divine compassion visibly appeerd,
> Love without end, and without measure Grace.
> (*P. L.*, III, 138-142)

The allusions to the Son as the express image of the Father (Heb. 1:3), as one of divine compassion (Matt. 9:36), and as one who possesses unmeasured love and grace (John 1:14, 3:34, 13:1) associate him with the doctrinal view of Jesus in the Gospels and Epistles, but they do not aid the reader to visualize him, nor do they give him any distinctive dramatic character. When the Son begins to speak to the Father, however, his language recalls Biblical heroes whose characters illustrate dramatically the abstract qualities of compassion, love, and grace. The Son thanks the Father for his promise that "Man . . . shall find grace" (l. 131) and then asks:

> For should Man finally be lost, should Man
> Thy creature late so lov'd, thy youngest Son
> Fall circumvented thus by fraud, though joynd
> With his own folly? that be from thee farr,
> That farr be from thee, Father, who art Judge
> Of all things made, and judgest onely right.
> (*P. L.*, III, 150-155)

The plea is like Abraham's intercession for his nephew Lot after God had revealed that Sodom, the wicked city in which Lot lived, was to be destroyed. Abraham said to God: "That be farr from thee, to do after this manner, to slay the righteous with the wicked, and

12. See Pope, *Paradise Regained,* Chapter II, "The Exalted Man."

that the righteous should be as the wicked, that be far from thee; Shal not the Judge of all the earth doe right?" (Gen. 18:25). Abraham pled that Lot, though he had chosen to live in a wicked city among sinful people, might not perish along with the reprobate Sodomites who had corrupted Lot's family; the Son is pleading that man, though he will fall as a result of Satan's fraud and his own folly, may not be destroyed finally with Satan and his followers, who, unlike man, are "self-tempted, self-deprav'd" (III, 130). The situations are similar. But most important, the Son is identified with a Biblical character interceding for another human being in a dramatic situation fraught with important consequences, not only for the human being but also for the reputation of God as One who always does right.

Coupled to this plea is the Son's statement of the consequences should God abolish His creation and unmake, because of the Devil, what he had made for his own glory:

> So should thy goodness and thy greatness both
> Be questiond and blaspheam'd without defense.
> (*P. L.*, III, 165-166)

Although there is no similarity in the language used, the argument here recalls that used by Moses when God was about to destroy the idolatrous Israelites in the wilderness. Moses argued that since God had just delivered these people from Egypt with great signs and wonders, if He should now annihilate them for imitating the idolatrous calf-worship of Egypt, the Egyptians would mockingly ask, "For mischiefe did he bring them out, to slay them in the mountaines, and to consume them from the face of the earth?" (Exod. 32:12; cf. Num. 14:12-19). Both Abraham and Moses[13]

13. Although the connection indicated above between the Son and Moses seems rather tenuous, it is supported by the identification of the Son with Moses which is the dramatic effect of the Son's language when he cries out to the armies of the elect angels,

> Stand still in bright array ye Saints, here stand
> Ye Angels arm'd, this day from Battel rest
> . . . . . . . . . . . . . . . . . . . . . . . . . . . . . . . . . . . .
> stand onely and behold
> Gods indignation on these Godless pourd
> By mee. (*P. L.*, VI, 801-802, 810-812)

Any clear impression of the Son in the war in Heaven is rare; he rides forth in "The Chariot of Paternal Deitie" (VI, 750) like a dazzling swift-moving were, among many other things, compassionate and understanding intercessors with God on behalf of sinful men; therefore, the association of the Son, by Biblical allusion, with these Old Testament heroes gives more concretely dramatic effect to the characterization. Without such allusions, as subtly suggested as they are, the character of the Son would be as undifferentiated dramatically as that of the Father.

Allusions in the dramatic characterization of the Son connect him not only with Abraham and Moses but also with the Jesus of the New Testament. Issuing forth from Heaven to create the new universe, the Son is described in general, abstract terms. He is "Girt with Omnipotence, with Radiance crown'd / Of Majestie Divine, Sapience and Love" (*P. L.*, VII, 194-195), attended by winged chariots from the armory of God; Heaven's gates swing open to let him forth as the "powerful Word . . . coming to create new Worlds" (VIII, 208-209). But when the Son speaks, though he is called "th' Omnific Word," his first words are the words of Jesus of Galilee:

> Silence, ye troubl'd waves, and thou Deep, peace.
> (*P. L.*, VII, 216)

The words remind one of the very human Jesus, so tired that he slept in a storm-tossed ship, who, nevertheless, when he was awakened by his fearful disciples, manifested his divine power over the forces of nature. "And he arose, and rebuked the wind, and said unto the sea, Peace, be still. And the winde ceased, and there was a great calme" (Mark 4:39). The Miltonic image is appropriately much grander than the Gospel story of Christ in a fishing boat stilling a lake storm. Milton's epic pictures the Son, in all the preincarnate glory of the Father, commanding the wild and surging "vast immeasurable Abyss" of Chaos. But that Milton's Son speaks in the words of the Galilean emphasizes the essential

---

vision, an allegorical figure of winged Victory at his right hand. The words "Stand still" not only mark a sudden pause in the whirlwind action; they also gain the effect of associating the Son with Moses and the wonders wrought through him by God at the Red Sea. This allusion has been discussed in the section on language in this chapter. It is mentioned again here to show that there is evidence for allusive identification of the Son with Moses in *Paradise Lost*.

identity of dramatic character between the eternal Word of the epic (and of the Gospel of John) and the Son of Man of the Synoptic Gospels.

As he converses with Adam just prior to the creation of Eve, the Son tests Adam's reactions by a method like that used by the Biblical Christ to test Philip at the feeding of the five thousand. Telling Raphael the story of his creation, Adam says that after he had named all the creatures of land, sea, and air, he still felt there must be somewhere a mate to partake with him of the pleasures of Eden and to provide companionship for him. When he expresses his desire for companionship to his Maker, a mildly humorous dramatic interchange occurs between them. God asks Adam why he cannot be happy with one of the creatures he has named or even in solitude since God himself is "alone / From all Eternitie" (VIII, 406). Adam says that God, since He is perfect within Himself, has no need of companionship or propagation but that if God should feel such a need He could elevate one of his creatures to his own level, an act which Adam cannot perform. The Son answers Adam's last respectful appeal:

> Thus farr to try thee, *Adam*, I was pleas'd,
> And finde thee knowing not of Beasts alone,
> Which thou hast rightly nam'd, but of thy self,
> Expressing well the spirit within thee free,
> My Image, not imparted to the Brute,
> Whose fellowship therefore unmeet for thee
> Good reason was thou freely shouldst dislike,
> And be so minded still; I, ere thou spak'st,
> Knew it not good for Man to be alone,
> And no such companie as then thou saw'st
> Intended thee, for trial onely brought,
> To see how thou could'st judge of fit and meet.
> (*P. L.*, VIII, 437-448)

The trial of Adam is similar to the trial of Philip's faith by Jesus. When Jesus, in the Bible, asks Philip whether he knows where bread may be bought for the hungry multitude, John, the writer of the story, says parenthetically, "And this he said to proove him: for he himselfe knew what he would doe" (John 6:6). Although the dialogue between Adam and his Maker is the product of Milton's imagination rather than of close adherence to the Genesis account of Eve's creation and events immediately preceding that creation, it is a dramatically credible and convincing dialogue. And the allusion to Christ's gentle test of his disciple's faith adds to the warm, understanding, "human" character of the Son as Milton portrays him in the Garden of Eden.

In addition to establishing a relationship between the character of the Son as Mediator and as Creator in *Paradise Lost* and the Christ of the Gospels, Milton establishes an explicit relationship between the character of the Son as Judge in the epic with the Christ of the Bible. In Milton's account of the judgments upon Adam, Eve, and the Serpent, after all the sentences had been pronounced by the Son, who came as both Judge and Saviour, the Son

> disdain'd not to begin
> Thenceforth the forme of servant to assume,
> As when he wash'd his servants feet, so now
> As Father of his Familie he clad
> Thir nakedness with Skins of Beasts . . .
> . . . . . . . . . . . . . . . .
> And thought not much to cloath his Enemies.
> (*P. L.*, X, 213-217, 219)

The framework for Milton's passage is, of course, that of Genesis: "Unto Adam also and to his wife did the LORD God make coates of skinnes and cloathed them" (3:21). But allusions identify the Son and the function in which he is here engaging with the Saviour of the New Testament. Paul speaks of Christ as having been in the form of God but having condescended to take "upon him the form of a servant" and be made "in the likenesse of men" (Phil. 2:7); the particular servitude mentioned is that recounted by John as having occurred at the Last Supper when Judas Iscariot was also present. "He riseth from supper, and layed aside his garments: and tooke a towell, and girded himselfe, After that he powreth water into a bason, and beganne to wash the disciples feete, and to wipe them with the towell wherewith he was girded" (John 13:4-5). Milton refers to the Son as "Father of his Familie" in accord with the Biblical statement ascribed to Christ, "Behold I and the children which God hath given me" (Heb. 2:13b). The reference to the Son's clothing his enemies is an allusion both to the fact of Judas' having been served in the foot-washing by his Master and to Paul's statement that "when we were enemies, wee were reconciled to God, by the death of his Sonne" (Rom. 5:10). The Son, as seen in this part of the poem, combines stern judgment, compassionate sympathy for man's plight, and tender concern for man's comfort. The latter quality is most emphasized by the allusion to Christ's humble service of foot-washing.

Although Biblical allusions used in portraying the character of Christ in *Paradise Regained* occur primarily in his own speech, there also are allusions in Satan's remarks about Christ; and in one allusion used by both Christ and Satan, the latter contradicts Christ's view of the matter alluded to. From his first speech in the poem, the extraordinary yet modest character of Christ is revealed. Before he speaks, he has been described by Satan and by God the Father as the promised Saviour, the promised Seed of the woman; his simple, modest character is the more striking, therefore, because of what has preceded it. He feels an inner assurance that he exists for a great purpose and he has often been told this—by his mother, by those who saw him as a young child, and most recently by John the Baptist—but he admits that these inner feelings and outer reports ill sort with his present state. His statement about his childhood is phrased to contrast, by allusion, with the Apostle Paul's familiar saying, "When I was a child, I spake as a child, I understood as a child, I thought as a child: but when I became a man, I put away childish things" (I Cor. 13:11). Christ says,

> When I was yet a child, no childish play
> To me was pleasing, all my mind was set
> Serious to learn and know, and thence to do
> What might be publick good.
> (*P. R.*, I, 201-204)

The contrast of his childhood with the normal childhood of the great Apostle to the Gentiles heightens the reader's conception of Christ's serious nature and character. The allusion which immediately follows is to Christ's statement concerning his purpose for coming into the world:

my self I thought
Born to that end, born to promote all truth,
All righteous things.
(*P. R.*, I, 204-206)

In answer to Pilate's question, "Art thou a king then?" Jesus answered, "Thou sayest that I am a King. To this end was I borne, and for this cause came I into the world, that I should bear witnesse unto the trueth" (John 18:37). This eloquent statement of purpose from Christ's lips, which occurs in the Bible just before his death, is alluded to in Milton's poem just before his temptation, as he reminisces about his childhood. With dramatic force the allusion emphasizes not only his high seriousness but also the lifelong consistency of this seriousness.

Christ's own view of his experience among the doctors in the Temple indicates his quiet modesty. According to his account, he read and so grew in the knowledge of the Scriptures that

e're yet my age
Had measur'd twice six years, at our great Feast
I went into the Temple, there to hear
The Teachers of our Law, and to propose
What might improve my knowledge or their own;
And was admir'd by all.
(*P. R.*, I, 209-214)

The story as Luke tells it is that the parents of Jesus, having been lost from him for three days, "found him in the Temple, sitting in the midst of the Doctours, both hearing them, and asking them questions. And all that heard him were astonished at his understanding and answeres" (Luke 2:46-47).

Satan deliberately exaggerates the same incident, for, remarkable as the story is, it is not as extreme as Satan, trying flattery, suggests. By referring to the childhood experience of Christ he aims to persuade Christ to be famous by worldly wisdom if not by an earthly throne and kingdom. Christ's addiction to knowledge, Satan says,

by that early action may be judg'd,
When slipping from thy Mothers eye thou went'st
Alone into the Temple; there was found
Among the gravest Rabbies disputant

> On points and questions fitting *Moses* Chair,
> Teaching not taught. (*P. R.*, IV, 215-220)

The Gospel narrative does not indicate that Jesus slipped away from his parents; he stayed behind in Jerusalem when the family group began their journey back to Nazareth, and the fact that his parents lost him was not attributable to his truancy as much as to their carelessness in assuming that he was "in the company" somewhere (Luke 2:43-44). Christ's unassuming, modest account is much closer to that of the Bible; he went "to hear" the teachers, not to dispute with them, he was proposing "what might improve" his knowledge first and theirs second, and, though all were astonished at his "understanding and answeres," he is not represented in the Bible as "Teaching not taught." Further, Satan's allusion to "*Moses* Chair" is a sardonic suggestion of a similarity between Christ's knowledge and the hairsplitting quibbles of the scribes and Pharisees, who preached but did not practice the Law (Matt. 23:1-3). Christ's character is enhanced by the contrast between his and Satan's versions; modestly truthful yet conscious of his own excellence, he is the opposite of the know-it-all but do-nothing Pharisees.

As indicated earlier, however, this quiet modesty of Christ in *Paradise Regained* results from no doubt on his part as to his supernatural birth and high calling. In his opening soliloquy he recalls the accounts his mother has given him of the Annunciation with its prophecy that he would sit on David's throne, of the supernatural events surrounding his birth, and of the prophecies of Simeon and Anna. All that Mary has taught him culminates in his discovery within the Bible of his identity.

> This having heard, strait I again revolv'd
> The Law and Prophets, searching what was writ
> Concerning the Messiah, to our Scribes
> Known partly, and soon found of whom they spake
> I am. (*P. R.*, I, 259-263)

The "I am" would stand out in this context as an echo of Jesus' declaration in the Gospel of John, "Verely, verely, I say unto you, Before Abraham was, I am" (8:58), but the position of the phrase (at the beginning of a line following a run-on line with a caesura immediately following the phrase) throws it into even more prominence. Both in John and in *Paradise Regained* the phrase is connected with Jehovah's Old Testament identification of himself to Moses: "Thus shalt thou say unto the children of Israel, I AM hath sent me unto you" (Exod. 3:14). That Christ is conscious not only of his supernatural origin and his divine nature but also of the full responsibility upon him as the Messiah is indicated by his description of the life that lies ahead of him:

> Through many a hard assay even to the death,
> E're I the promis'd Kingdom can attain,
> Or work Redemption for mankind, whose sins
> Full weight must be transferr'd upon my head.
> (*P. R.*, I, 264-267)

Christ is consciously identifying himself with the prophecies of the Messiah as a suffering Saviour before a reigning King; the last two lines refer to Isaiah's statement of the Messiah, "and the LORD hath layd on him the iniquitie of us all" (Isa. 53:6b). Knowing himself and his mission as he does (a mission "to our Scribes / Known partly" [261-262]), Christ is not to be misled by Satan into believing that there is some short cut or easy way to attain the throne of David and rulership over Israel.

In overcoming Satan's temptations to eat of the banquet, Christ is aided by this firm knowledge of who and what he is and by his quiet submission to his Father's will, which is his meat. He has no fear of the sting of famine, "Nor mind it, fed with better thoughts that feed / Mee hungring more to do my Fathers will" (II, 258-259), as Christ puts it. One is reminded of the occasion when the disciples, concerned because they could not understand why Jesus was not as hungry as they, were told, "My meat is to doe the will of him that sent mee, and to finish his worke" (John 4:34). Satan cannot find a chink in such an armor of trust in God. When he seeks, with his philosophy of "the sooner the better," to instill impatience in Christ, the quiet patience of the Son of God baffles him completely. Christ says,

> All things are best fullfil'd in their due time,
> And time there is for all things, Truth hath said:

If of my raign Prophetic Writ hath told
That it shall never end, so when begin
The Father in his purpose hath decreed,
He in whose hand all times and seasons roul.
(*P. R.*, III, 182-187)

The reference to Truth is to Ecclesiastes (3:1 ff.), but the emphasis on the fulfillment of God's purposes "in due time" recurs often in the Bible (Titus 1:3, I Tim. 2:6, Rom. 5:6). And Christ's answer in Milton's poem is almost identical with the Biblical one (given by Christ to his disciples when they, somewhat impatiently, questioned him about the establishment of his kingdom after his resurrection): "It is not for you to know the times or the seasons, which the Father hath put in his owne power" (Acts 1:7).

It is precisely this knowledge of himself and his powers, coupled with complete submission to the Father and willingness to wait in patience for the unfolding of divine Providence, that makes the Christ of *Paradise Regained* a perfect foil to Adam in *Paradise Lost.* Adam did not keep the knowledge of himself and his role before his consciousness at crucial moments and thus he lost Paradise. Christ, as portrayed in *Paradise Regained,* knows himself and his role perfectly, and he keeps this knowledge before him constantly in overcoming Satan. Such complete and unquestioning obedience as the Son gives the Father is beyond the understanding of the originator of all rebellion; Satan, since he cannot conceive of such patient endurance springing from noble motives, even suggests that Christ may be only timid about seeking to hasten the fulfillment of the prophesied kingdom. Satan says,

The wisest, unexperienc't, will be ever
Timorous and loath, with novice modesty,
(As he who seeking Asses found a Kingdom)
Irresolute, unhardy, unadventrous.
(*P. R.*, III, 240-243)

The reference to Saul (I Sam. 9:20-21), who was so shy that he had to be brought out of hiding to be anointed king over Israel, is dramatically ironic in the light it throws, by contrast, on the character of Christ. Saul was extremely modest, at least in outward appearance, when he became king over Israel, but it was not long before he became a proud, arrogant ruler, whose disobedience to

God brought about his personal downfall and the failure of his house to succeed to the throne (I Sam. 15:24-31). Christ, on the other hand, so far from being timid and unhardy, is exhibiting "the better fortitude / Of Patience and Heroic Martyrdom" (*P. L.*, IX, 31-32). He is not seeking a kingdom at present because, knowing God's purposes, he is willing to wait for God's own "due time" for setting him on the throne of David. Meanwhile he will suffer patiently and obediently whatever occurs.

The character of Christ in *Paradise Regained* is summed up in Book IV by a Biblical metaphor applied to Christ by both Milton and Satan. Milton uses a series of similes at the opening of Book IV to show both the vanity and the continued persistence of Satan's attempts to corrupt or overcome Christ. Like a man who has been outwitted time after time by a more cunning opponent, he still, "to salve his credit, and for very spight," continues to clash with the same foe to his own deeper shame. Like a swarm of flies about the winepress in vintage time, who, no matter how many times they are beaten off, return again and again, Satan persists. Or like

> surging waves [which] against a solid rock,
> Though all to shivers dash't, the assault renew,
> Vain battry, and in froth or bubbles end,
> (*P. R.*, IV, 18-20)

Satan dashes himself against the rock-like Christ. Satan himself says to Christ, immediately preceding the scene on the pinnacle of the Temple,

> opportunity here I have had
> To try thee, sift thee, and confess have found thee
> Proof against all temptation as a rock
> Of Adamant, and as a Center, firm
> To the utmost of meer man both wise and good,
> Not more.
> (*P. R.*, IV, 531-536)

The identification of Christ with a rock is common to both Testaments. Paul brings together the Old Testament types picturing God as a rock, especially the rock which provided water in the wilderness, and applies them to Christ as the New Testament antitype when he says that the Israelites "did all drinke the same spirituall drinke (for they dranke of that spirituall Rock that followed them: and that Rocke was Christ)" (I Cor. 10:4). A more familiar Scriptural rock, that upon which Christ said he would build his church, has been a center of controversy for centuries as to whether it represents Peter, Christ, or Peter's statement of faith; Milton was convinced that it refers to Christ in the personal sense and to Peter's faith in another sense.[14] Because of this conviction, it seems certain that the passages quoted from *Paradise Regained* allude to this more familiar text. When Peter declared his faith in Jesus as the Christ, the son of the living God, Christ said, "Thou art Peter[Πέτρος],and upon this rocke [πέτρα] I will build my Church; and the gates of hell shall not prevaile against it" (Matt. 16:18). Satan, like some of his followers described by Jude as "raging waves of the sea, foaming out their owne shame" (Jude 13), finds that all his assaults on the Son of God are "Vain battry," yet he is still not willing to concede that Christ is more than the "utmost of meer man." But that he and "Hell . . . in all her gates" (IV, 623-624) cannot prevail against this Rock is proved to him when Christ stands on the highest spire of the Temple while Satan himself falls.

One aspect of Christ's character in *Paradise Regained* needs defense; some critics see Christ in his attitude toward the common people as more like an austere, aristocratic Milton than the meek and lowly Christ of the Gospels. Christ's repudiation of Satan's suggestion that he seek glory and the admiration of the world has been referred to as unlike the Christ of the Bible.[15]

14. Milton wrote, "Nor does the celebrated text, Matt. xvi, 18, 19, which is perverted by the Pope to form the charter of his authority, confer any distinction upon Peter beyond what is enjoyed by other professors of the same faith. For inasmuch as many others confessed no less explicitly than Peter that Christ was the Son of God (as is clear from the narrative of the evangelists), the answer of Christ is not, *upon thee Peter,* but *upon this rock I will build my church,* that is, upon this faith which thou hast in common with other believers, not upon thee as an individual; seeing that, in the personal sense of the word, the true rock is Christ, nor is there any other foundation, whence also faith in Christ is called the foundation." ("Of Christian Doctrine," trans. Bishop Sumner, in *The Student's Milton* [New York, 1947], ed. Frank Allen Patterson, p. 1037.)

15. E. M. W. Tillyard (*Milton* [London, 1946], p. 305), for example, says of Milton's Christ in *Paradise Regained*: "In the last two lines of the poem alone,

hee unobserv'd
Home to his Mothers house private return'd

For what is glory but the blaze of fame,
The peoples praise, if always praise unmixt?
And what the people but a herd confus'd,
A miscellaneous rabble, who extol
Things vulgar, & well weighed, scarce worth the praise.
They praise and they admire they know not what;
And know not whom, but as one leads the other;
And what delight to be by such extoll'd,
To live upon their tongues and be thir talk,
Of whom to be disprais'd were no small praise?
His lot who dares to be singularly good.
(*P. R.*, III, 47-57)

Yet the Jesus of the New Testament is described in Mark as having looked upon the people "as sheepe not having a shepherd" (Mark 6:34). He had compassion on them and tried to teach them many things, but that the people were "confus'd" was simply a fact. Although "herd" and "rabble" are harsher terms than Jesus used of the common people, they are not as harsh as those he used of the proud and hypocritical (as in Matt. 23:13-33). John records the words of Jesus to a Samaritan woman who was questioning him as to whether one should worship in Jerusalem or at Mount Horeb; the words are quite similar to those Milton gives Christ: "Yee worship ye know not what: we know what we worship: for salvation is of the Jews" (John 4:22). Jesus later gave this woman the water of life, but first he was brutally frank with her about her ignorance and sin. Luke represents Jesus as having pronounced a special blessing on those who were not only "disprais'd" but were even hated by the mass of men: "Blessed are ye, when men shall hate you, and when they shall separate you *from their company*, and shall reproch you, and cast out your name as evill for the Sonne of mans sake. . . .Woe unto you when all men shall speake well of you: for so did their fathers to the false prophets" (Luke 6:22, 26). Not only, therefore, has any apparent inconsistency in

---

does he bear any relation to the Jesus of the Gospels. His classical education and contempt for the people (he calls them a 'herd confus'd, a miscellaneous rabble') do not sit well on the carpenter's son who had compassion on the multitude. Christ in fact is partly an allegorical figure, partly Milton himself imagined perfect." One need not reject Tillyard's last sentence, but one must regret his first; as this study shows, Milton's Christ bears a rather close relationship to the Christ of the Gospels, considered as a dramatic figure.

attitude toward people between the Christ of the Gospels and the Christ of Milton's poem been exaggerated, but even a passage which has been chosen to show such inconsistency can be demonstrated to be based on the principles of and expressed in the language of the Biblical Christ.

The characterization of the Son of God in *Paradise Lost* is heightened dramatically by Biblical allusions which associate him with Abraham, Moses, and especially the Christ of the New Testament. The characterization of Christ in *Paradise Regained* is made consistent with the Christ of the Gospels by allusions which emphasize both his unassuming, humble patience and his calm, fearless passivity under the hand of his Father, characteristics which are based on his assurance of who he is, what his mission is, and what the limitations of his adversary are.

*Adam and Eve*

The human actors in *Paradise Lost* are only two. Other human beings are seen in the major epic only by means of prophetic vision, and in *Paradise Regained* the purely human characters do not play important roles. Adam and Eve, then, provide the background for a discussion of Milton's use of Biblical allusion for dramatic effect in the presentation of human character.

That Adam is noble, wise, and fit to bear rule over all the creatures of the new world is made evident from the first view of him in *Paradise Lost,* Book IV, although there the emphasis is on his position of rule over his mate. Adam is described as of admirable stature and appearance; he is the "goodliest man of men since borne / His Sons" (IV, 323-324). His courteous speech to Eve (though it informs the Devil of the prohibition of the Tree of Knowledge) is tender and loving; but it is when speech and action are in combination in a more dramatic situation that the character of Adam is most clearly seen. The scene in Book IV serves primarily to forward the action: Adam and Eve, by their conversation, give the eavesdropping Satan the information that there is a forbidden tree in the Garden and that Eve has a Narcissus-like attraction to her own beauty. Knowing these things, Satan can plan his attack. He will tempt them to reject God's "envious commands"

(IV, 524) by first planting "discontented thoughts, / Vain hopes, vain aimes, inordinate desires" (IV, 807-808) in the mind of Eve while she sleeps. The later scene in which Adam and Eve discuss the beauty of the night as they observe their nightly devotions to God, beautiful as it is, does not add much to the reader's conception of the character of either. In Book V, however, when Raphael appears at Adam's bower to warn him of the Devil, the more dramatic situation and the allusions sharpen Adam's character.

Having sped in flight from Heaven to Earth through the "vast Ethereal Skie," appearing like a Phoenix to the fowls of Earth's atmosphere, Raphael returns to his own shape as a winged Seraph when he alights in Paradise:

> six wings he wore, to shade
> His lineaments Divine; the pair that clad
> Each shoulder broad, came mantling o're his brest
> With regal Ornament; the middle pair
> Girt like a Starrie Zone his waste, and round
> Skirted his loines and thighes with downie Gold
> And colours dipt in Heav'n; the third his feet
> Shaddowd from either heele with featherd maile
> Skie-tinctur'd grain. (*P. L.*, V, 277-285)

The description of Raphael is drawn from that of the seraphim seen by Isaiah in his vision in the Temple. Above the throne of God the prophet saw the seraphim: "each one had sixe wings: with twaine he covered his face, and with twain hee covered his feete, and with twaine he did flie" (Isa. 6:2). As a part of his vision of God's glory, the seraphim so impressed Isaiah when they ascribed holiness unto the Lord that he cried out, "Woe *is* me; for I am undone, because I *am* a man of uncleane lips, and I dwell in the midst of a people of uncleane lips" (6:5). But Adam makes no such reaction; he is sinless and does not feel the shame felt by a fallen man in the presence of a heavenly being.[16] Even though

16. Later, after the Fall, when Michael comes to visit Paradise on a sterner mission, Adam's fallen condition is intensified if the contrast between his reception of Raphael and his reception of Michael is recognized. In Book V Adam sees without fear or inferiority glories such as humbled Isaiah in the dust, but when Michael comes, Adam is not able to see the glorious apparition accompanying Michael, for "doubt / And carnal fear that day dimm'd *Adams* eye" (*P. L.*, XI, 211-212).

Adam is not shamed or awed by the approach of Raphael, however, since he is human, he shows the proper reverence for his heavenly guest and is conscious of the honor being paid him by such a visit. Although Adam's conduct is similar to that of a monarch receiving a very high dignitary representing another realm, that he is a man entertaining an angel is emphasized by Biblical allusion which associates him with Abraham, who entertained angels on the plains of Mamre immediately preceding the divine destruction of Sodom and Gomorrah. The approach of Raphael

> *Adam* discernd, as in the dore he sat
> Of his coole Bowre, while now the mounted Sun
> Shot downe direct his fervid Raies to warme
> Earths inmost womb, more warmth then *Adam* needs.
> (*P. L.*, V, 299-302)

Adam walks forth to meet his "god-like Guest" with "submiss approach and reverence meek, / As to a superior Nature, bowing low" (ll. 359-360). The allusions recall the story of Abraham's heavenly visitors. "And the LORD appeared unto him in the plaines of Mamre: and he sate in the tent doore in the heate of the day; And he lift up his eyes and looked, and, loe, three men stood by him: and when he saw *them,* hee ranne to meet them from the tent doore, and bowed himselfe toward the ground" (Gen. 18:1-2). Like Abraham, Adam instructs his wife to provide the very best in food and hospitality that is available (V, 313 ff. with Gen. 18:6) and invites his guest to rest in the shade until the heat of the day is past (V, 365 ff. with Gen. 18:4). The dramatic situation in the poem is similar to that in the Bible—the heavenly visit brings news of blessing (Abraham and Sarah will have a son through whom the world will be blessed, while Adam and Eve will fill the new world with sons) and of impending judgment (on Sodom and Gomorrah for their sin, on man if he heeds the Tempter)—but more important is the dramatic impact of the association of Adam with Abraham. Without some such association, Adam might continue to be a perfect superman physically, mentally, and spiritually, a character with whom it would be hard to sympathize and whose reality as a character would be difficult to accept. The association with Abraham, however, prepares the way for Adam's very human questions and admissions which are to come later in Books V, VI, VII, and VIII. This initial association of Adam with the Biblical Abraham foreshadows the Adam who pleads with God for a mate in language reminiscent of Abraham's plea for Lot, the Adam who too readily hearkens to his wife as Abraham did when Ishmael was conceived, and, finally, the Adam who, in spite of earlier follies, is able by faith to look down through the centuries and see the day of Christ as Abraham saw his day and rejoiced (*P. L.*, XII, 276-277; John 8:56).

Adam is never more dramatically human than when he pleads with his Maker for a mate. Though he has seen and named all the creatures of earth, he has not found the companion whom he feels he needs in order to enjoy fully the good things God has provided for him. He asks plaintively how one can enjoy such bounty in solitude, or if one could enjoy it alone, how one could find contentment. God asks how Adam can speak of solitude when the whole realm of nature is filled with living creatures; He even seems to order Adam to be content with one of the beasts for a companion. Adam, though with humble deprecation, continues to implore:

> Let not my words offend thee, Heav'nly Power,
> My Maker, be propitious while I speak,
> (*P. L.*, VIII, 379-380)

and he proceeds to argue eloquently for man's need of a human mate just as the other species have mates of their own "kinde." The language of Adam's importunate plea recalls Abraham's request that God spare the righteous in the city of Sodom. "Oh let not the Lord be angry, & I will speak: Peradventure there shall thirtie be found there. And God said, I will not doe *it, if* I find thirtie there. And hee said, Behold now, I have taken upon me to speake unto the Lord: Peradventure there shalbe found twenty. . . .Oh let not the Lord be angry, and I will speake yet but this once: Peradventure ten shalbe found there" (Gen. 18:30-32). This new association of Adam with Abraham emphasizes the persistence of Adam, a persistence for which God praises him: "Good reason was thou freely shouldst dislike, / And be so minded still" (VIII, 443-

444). The allusion by contrast also raises Adam far above Abraham. With courtly grace and an eminently respectful and self-deprecating air, Adam pleads the difference between his own nature and God's nature as his main argument for being given a mate, just as Abraham respectfully and humbly based his plea on the nature of God ("Shall not the Judge of all the earth doe right?" [Gen. 18:25b]). When one considers imaginatively the intellectual strain of having to defend one's desires on the basis of one's own nature and that before the Maker Himself, not to mention the difficulty of maintaining such a delicate balance as Adam maintains (and Abraham did) in his courtesy which never becomes impudence even in insistence, and when one further recognizes that Adam's plea is based partly on an appeal to the nature of God Himself, one can appreciate the praise of C. S. Lewis for the poise and self-assurance of the Patriarch of the Race.[17] The Biblical allusion emphasizes both the similarities and the contrasts between Adam's and Abraham's importunity before the Lord. Adam's straightforwardness raises him, by contrast, above Abraham. Abraham repeats respectful introductory phrases as a means of gradually reducing the required number of righteous persons for the city to be spared instead of making known frankly his real wish: that Lot and his family be spared. Adam, on the other hand, is fully as respectful and reverent as Abraham in addressing himself to God, but, more straightforwardly, he makes one clear request: a human consort to partake of the pleasures of Paradise with him.

Book VIII closes with Raphael's warning to Adam to put God first and take heed lest passion sway him to do what otherwise his free will would not allow. He has warned Adam to weigh himself with Eve and value himself properly so that Eve "will acknowledge ... her Head" (VIII, 574) in him. The admonitions of Raphael to "Be strong" and "stand fast" indicate that the supreme test for Adam is to come soon.

Book IX opens with the statement that the poet's notes must be changed to tragic:

> No more of talk where God or Angel Guest
> With Man, as with his Friend, familiar us'd

17. *A Preface to Paradise Lost*, pp. 114-115.

> To sit indulgent, and with him partake
> Rural repast.
> (*P. L.*, IX, 1-4)

The lines recall the association of Adam with Abraham. Adam is no longer to enjoy the relationship with angel guests that Abraham, the "Friend of God" (Jas. 2:23), enjoyed. He is no more to plead, face to face with God, as Abraham pled. No further opportunity of enjoying a meal with heavenly visitors will be provided for Adam. The Fall is imminent, and the way it will come about is soon evident.

In spite of Raphael's warnings about his relationship with Eve, Adam gives in to her request that she be allowed to work separately during the day. This separation is the very thing Satan had wished for but not dared to hope for (IX, 421-424), and the deception and sin of Eve is soon thereafter an accomplished fact. While Eve, exulting in the forbidden fruit, considers whether she should, by withholding the fruit from her husband, render herself equal or perhaps even superior to him, Adam awaits her return.

> *Adam* the while
> Waiting desirous her return, had wove
> Of choicest Flours a Garland to adorne
> Her Tresses, and her rural labours crown
> As Reapers oft are wont thir Harvest Queen.
> (*P. L.*, IX, 838-842)

The simile presents a happy rural picture as Adam, promising great joy to his thoughts of Eve's return, weaves the garland; but the passage is heavy with dramatic irony. Eve's "rural labours" having included plucking the forbidden fruit, it is appropriate that Adam crown her "Tresses" with a garland symbolic of such labors, for those very tresses have been explicitly designated (in Book IV) as the symbol of her subjection to her husband, a subjection she has renounced. Since he is the one responsible for having lapsed in his duty as her authority, Adam should be the one to crown Eve for her day's labor. The irony is deepened when the comparison of Adam to "Reapers" recalls the Biblical idea of one's reaping the results of one's errors and sins: "Be not deceived; God is not mocked; for whatsoever a man soweth, that shall he also reape"

(Gal. 6:7). Adam is a reaper with a vengeance whose "Harvest Queen," he soon discovers, has brought him a bitter harvest and astounds him by the trespass she has committed. Yet, persisting in his faulty view of himself and of woman which has led to this scene, he chooses to die with Eve rather than to live without her. His first words upon learning of her sin are spoken not aloud to her but silently to himself.

> O fairest of Creation, last and best
> Of all Gods Works, Creature in whom excell'd
> Whatever can to sight or thought be formd,
> Holy, divine, good, amiable, or sweet!
> (*P. L.*, IX, 896-899)

Thus putting the woman even above himself as "best" of God's works, Adam puts his love for her above his love for God and resolves to die with her before he ever speaks to her.

When Adam does speak, it is to discuss the possibility that they may not die after all. He reasons that God would be loath to abolish man,

> least the Adversary
> Triumph and say; Fickle their State whom God
> Most Favors, who can please him long?
> (*P. L.*, IX, 947-949)

This would be "Matter of scorne, not to be given the Foe" says Adam (l. 951). Here, just before the Fall, Adam is using his native instinct and powers of reasoning to determine what God's nature is like, and, as in the case of his discussion of the nature of God when he asked for a mate (at least the discussion was uncorrected by God), Biblical allusions indicate that he may be right. Adam's intelligence, untainted by sin, which enabled him to name the animals, birds, and fish, helps him to know by reason what was láter to be revealed supernaturally about God. Moses, in a song in which he speaks in the person of God, says: "I would scatter them into corners, I would make the remembrance of them to cease from among men: Were it not that I feared the wrath of the enemie, lest their adversaries should behave themselves strangely, *and* lest they should say, Our hand is high, the LORD hath not done all this" (Deut. 32:26-27). Again Moses pled with God on behalf of Israel, "Now *if* thou shalt kill *all* this people as one man, then the nations which have heard the fame of thee will speake, saying, Because the LORD was not able to bring the people into the land which hee sware unto them, therefore hee hath slaine them in the wildernesse" (Num. 14:15-16). Adam senses and expresses in language allusive to these Scriptures that God is not going to allow the Devil "Matter of scorne" against him, but Adam cannot foresee the misery and pain that his sin and the consequent "long day's dying" will bring into the world before the Son destroys the power of sin and death. The latter vision awaits his repentance and the visit of Michael. Meanwhile the dramatic effect of the allusions to the Bible in Adam's pre-Fall discussion is to increase the tragedy of his fall by emphasizing the intellectual powers he enjoys, even to the extent of coming to Biblically accurate conclusions about the nature of God and what God is likely to do once Adam and Eve have both fallen.

Once Eve has eaten of the Tree of Knowledge, it becomes an idol, a substitute for the God she has worshipped; she addresses the Tree as "Sovran, vertuous, precious of all Trees" (IX, 795), speaks of her purpose to return each morning to offer praise and song to the Tree, and as she turns to leave, she bows in "low Reverence" (IX, 835). Once Adam has partaken with Eve, he too has praise for "this vertuous Tree" (IX, 1033). His shockingly jocular statement that

> if such pleasures be
> In things to us forbidden, it might be wish'd,
> For this one Tree had bin forbidden ten,
> (*P. L.*, IX, 1024-1026)

is followed by language suggestive of a Biblical situation involving idolatry and sinful levity. Adam's invitation to Eve is

> But come, so well refresh't, now let us play,
> As meet is, after such delicious Fare.
> (*P. L.*, IX, 1027-1028)

The allusion is to the idolatry of Israel. After the Israelites had promised to keep whatever commandments God would give them, Moses went up into Mount Sinai to receive the decalogue. While he was communing with God, Aaron led the people to make a golden calf and to worship it. "And they rose up early on the morrow, and offered burnt offerings, and brought peace offerings; and the people sate downe to eate and drinke, and rose up to play" (Exod. 32:6). The Old Testament incident was judged worthy by Paul of incorporation into a warning in one of his epistles: "Neither be ye idolaters, as were some of them; as it is written, The people sate downe to eate & drinke, and rose up to play" (I Cor. 10:7). The lustful and salacious play of Adam and Eve is as "meet" (as Adam says) to follow their forbidden feast, since it is connected with their idolatrous attitude toward the Tree, as was the play of the Israelites following their idolatrous festivities around the golden calf. Idolatry, since it removes God from the center of the spiritual consciousness and substitutes some *thing*, leads to thoughtless frivolity and to the degradation of human dignity; what has been lovely and tender between Adam and Eve has become animal desire.

Another Biblical allusion emphasizes the sinfulness of what has been a holy relationship between Adam and Eve.

> There they thir fill of Love and Loves disport
> Took largely, of thir mutual guilt the Seale,
> The solace of their sin. (*P. L.*, IX, 1042-1044)

The allusion associates Eve with the harlot warned against in Proverbs, who says to a foolish young man, "Come, let us take our fill of love until the morning: let us solace ourselves with loves" (7:18). The guiltiness of the "play" of Adam and eve is reinforced by the comparison of Adam to Samson, who "rose . . . from the Harlot-lap / of *Philistian Dalilah,* and wak'd / Shorn of his strength" (IX, 1061-1063). This Biblical simile sums up strikingly what the other Biblical allusions have been suggesting about the change in Adam's character. Adam has fallen much lower than Samson because he was higher to start with; from the first of men in physique, intelligence, and devotion to God, Adam has fallen to a lecherous, low-minded cracker of jokes and an idolater as a result of disobedience, and Biblical allusions dramatically intensify his loss of stature.

The formerly placid mental state of Adam and Eve is now disrupted by sin:

> Anger, Hate,
> Mistrust, Suspicion, Discord . . . shook sore
> Thir inward State of Mind, calme Region once
> And full of Peace, now tost and turbulent.
> (*P. L.*, IX, 1123-1126)

As described later in Book X, Adam sees miseries growing around him in Eden. The poet describes him, however, as feeling "worse . . . within, / And in a troubl'd Sea of passion tost" (X, 717-718). The two passages from the epic show that Adam and Eve, in their inward mental state as fallen creatures, fit Isaiah's description of the wicked. "But the wicked are like the troubled sea, when it cannot rest, whose waters cast up myre and dirt. *There is* no peace, sayth my God, to the wicked" (57:20-21).

But not only is Adam's fall into the depths of sin and despair emphasized by Biblical allusions; they intensify the drama of his development to self-insight, involving an admission that he is most at fault, and to a spirit of genuine love towards Eve. Touched by Eve's penitence and willingness to take all God's wrath on her own head, Adam shows her compassionate human understanding:

> But rise, let us no more contend, nor blame
> Each other, blam'd enough elsewhere, but strive
> In offices of Love, how we may light'n
> Each others burden in our share of woe.
> (*P. L.*, X, 958-961)

The allusion is to Paul's advice, "Beare ye one anothers burdens; and so fulfill the law of Christ" (Gal. 6:2).

One of the most strikingly dramatic characterizations of Adam occurs in Book XI when his words associate him with his future son, Cain. Told by Michael that he must leave Paradise, Adam submits to God's will, but says,

> This most afflicts me, that departing hence,
> As from his face I shall be hid, deprivd
> His blessed count'nance; here I could frequent,
> With worship, place by place where he voutsaf'd
> Presence Divine, and to my Sons relate;
> On this Mount he appeerd, under this Tree
> Stood visible, among these Pines his voice
> I heard, here with him at this Fountain talk'd:

So many grateful Altars I would reare
Of grassie Terfe, and pile up every Stone
Of lustre from the brook, in memorie,
Or monument to Ages, and thereon
Offer sweet smelling Gumms & Fruits and Flours.
(*P. L.*, XI, 315-327)

Not only do Adam's words "from his face I shall be hid" link him with Cain, who lamented when God drove him out from his presence, "from thy face shall I be hid" (Gen. 4:14), but also Adam's expressed purpose to build an altar on which to offer "Fruits and Flours" associates him with the Cain who "brought of the fruit of the ground an offering unto the LORD" (Gen. 4:3) and had his offering rejected. Abel's sacrifice of a lamb was accepted, but Cain's offering of fruits displeased the Lord. This allusion to Scripture emphasizes Adam's spiritual ignorance (as contrasted with his spiritual wisdom before the Fall) before Michael reveals the future to him. Adam, like his sons, needs revelation rather than reason to know how to approach God, and he is later shown by Michael the enormous load of sin and guilt to be accumulated by his offspring and expiated by Christ's sacrifice on the cross (XII, 416-417).

Before Michael's revelation Adam is like Cain, ready to worship in what seems a rational way, and he is prone to place too much importance on his geographical location, as though God were not omnipotent and omnipresent. After the revelation from Michael, Adam is again like Abraham, whose faith was such that Christ said of him, "Abraham rejoyced to see my day: and he saw it, and was glad" (John 8:56). When Adam first catches a glimpse of the unfolding purpose of God to bring Messiah the Saviour into the world through the seed of Abraham, he says:

now first I finde
Mine eyes true op'ning, and my heart much eas'd,
Erwhile perplext with thoughts what would becom
Of mee and all Mankind; but now I see
His day, in whom all Nations shall be blest.
(*P. L.*, XII, 273-277)

After having been identified with Abraham in Book V by Biblical allusion, having had the depths of his fall intensified by allusions culminating in a simile associating him with Samson in Book IX, having been identified with the false worship of Cain in Book XI, Adam is in Book XII once again associated with Abraham as a man of faith.

Finally, Adam stands in clear contrast to Satan at the close of *Paradise Lost.* Through the visions Michael has given him, Adam says, he has learned that "suffering for truths sake / Is fortitude to highest victorie, / And to the faithful Death the Gate of Life" (XII, 569-571), and he adds that he has been taught this by the example of Christ the Redeemer. Michael's answer is, "This having learnt, thou hast attained the summe / Of wisdom; hope no higher" (XII, 575-576). Before iniquity was found in him and he was cast out from God, Lucifer was told, "Thou sealest up the summe, full of wisedome, and perfect in beautie" (Ezek. 28:12). Satan began with the sum of wisdom which Adam has just attained: love and obedience to God, no matter what they may involve, even suffering and death. Selfish pride, jealousy, and envy of the Messiah (according to *Paradise Lost*) brought about the corruption of Satan's wisdom and his irrevocable fall from God's favor; yet, now that Satan has successfully caused man's fall from God's favor, man has been restored through the Messiah, and it is love and emulation of the Messiah as Redeemer that has brought Adam to attain the sum of wisdom from which Satan fell. Although Satan caused Adam to lose Paradise, he has brought about events which, as overruled by Providence, give Adam and his posterity the possibility of a Paradise within, "happier farr."

As the reader's first view of Adam in *Paradise Lost* is one in which Adam's dominant role of authority is emphasized, partly by Biblical allusion, Eve's yielding, voluntary submissiveness and subjection are symbolized in her physical appearance and by allusion.

> Shee as a vail down to the slender waste
> Her unadorned golden tresses wore
> Dissheveld, but in wanton ringlets wav'd
> As the Vine curles her tendrils, which impli'd
> Subjection, but requir'd with gentle sway,
> And by her yeilded, by him best receivd,
> Yeilded with coy submission, modest pride,
> And sweet reluctant amorous delay.
> (*P. L.*, IV, 304-311)

There is allusion here to I Corinthians 11, which makes women's long hair symbolic of their subjection to men; another Biblical allusion in this passage, which has been hinted at earlier in the poem (V, 215-219) and is to be picked up and repeated in a later passage, is the comparison of the woman to a vine. In the simile quoted above, Eve's hair is compared to the vine; but long hair is the woman's symbol of her husband's authority over her (I Cor. 11:10), and the vine-like quality of the hair suggests the dependent submissiveness of the woman. In Book IX when Eve broaches her ill-fated plan that she and Adam work separately in their task of dressing the Garden, her reference to the vine is an ironic commentary on her first attempt at independently suggesting what her husband should do.

> Let us divide our labours, thou where choice
> Leads thee, or where most needs, whether to wind
> The Woodbine round this Arbour, or direct
> The clasping Ivie where to climb, while I
> In yonder Spring of Roses intermixt
> With Myrtle, find what to redress till Noon.
> (*P. L.*, IX, 214-219)

The vine has already been connected in the poem with Eve's subjection to her husband; the allusion here is to the psalmist's simile: "Thy wife shalbe as a fruitfull Vine by the sides of thine house" (Ps.128:3). The dramatic irony lies in Eve's suggesting that Adam go teach the woodbine and the ivy where and how to climb when she, the main vine Adam has the duty and responsibility of directing, most needs him with her. The "Patriarch of Mankinde" ends by telling his vine to go her own way, warning her to do her part, for "God towards thee hath done his part" (l. 375)—but Adam, who was made for dominion, has not done his part, a lapse of responsible authority which he is to regret when the Judge reminds him that bearing rule was his "part / And person" had he known himself aright (X, 155-156).

Another Biblical allusion, repeated as a means of characterizing Eve, highlights her tenderness and sensitivity while associating her with a sinful woman of the Bible. Language used to describe Eve before the Fall (but only after her dream) and after the Fall (but only after she has become conscious of the enormity of her guilt) associates her with the penitent sinner, Mary Magdalene. The Biblical statement is: "And, behold, a woman in the citie, which was a sinner, when she knew that Jesus sate at meat in the Pharisees house, brought an Alabaster boxe of ointment, and stood at his feete, behinde him, weeping, and began to wash his feete with teares, and did wipe them with the haires of her head, and kissed his feet, and anointed them with the oyntment" (Luke 7:37-38). In Book V, after Eve has been comforted by Adam, the poet says:

> So cheard he his fair Spouse, and she was cheard,
> But silently a gentle tear let fall
> From either eye, and wip'd them with her haire.
> (*P. L.*, V, 129-131)

These tears are the gracious signs of "sweet remorse" (l. 134) and the wiping of them with her hair is enough to foreshadow dramatically the character development of Eve to the point where (after she has really, not just in a dream, sinned and suffered) she will experience genuine remorse and repentance over her sin against God and her husband. After the Fall, in spite of the harshest things Adam can think of to say to her, Eve will not be repulsed in her efforts to make peace with him. She

> with Tears that ceas'd not flowing,
> And tresses all disorderd, at his feet
> Fell humble, and imbracing them, besaught
> His peace, and thus proceeded in her plaint.
> (*P. L.*, X, 910-913)

Milton's description of the scene makes it similar to the Biblical scene; Eve, like the sinful woman in Luke, is behind Adam as she clasps his feet, her tears flowing, her hair in disorder. Since Adam sinned against God only and Eve has sinned against both God and Adam, she is willing to ask that all the punishment for their sin be transferred to her alone: "Mee mee onely just object of his ire" (X, 936). Like the sinful woman at the feet of Jesus, Eve will not cease weeping until Adam has made peace with her. Magdalene was rewarded by the words of Jesus, "Go in peace" (Luke 7:50), and Eve persists until Adam relents with "peaceful words" and upraises her (X, 946).

Milton's Eve is not to be judged too harshly. She is first in the transgression in both *Paradise Lost* and the Bible, but in the epic she is also first in a penitent attitude. Although she is identified with Mary Magdalene in at least two allusions, it should be remembered that it is Mary the penitent, receiving the forgiveness of her Lord, that is revealed in the Bible, not Mary the sinner. And, as Adam himself admits, Eve was the "infirmer Sex" committed to his care and exposed by him to the Tempter (X, 956-957). The final portrait of Eve is in accord with her position of loving subjection to her husband; she no longer desires to part from him even for a brief time. When she laments the necessity of leaving Paradise, her "Native Soile" (XI, 270), Michael reminds her that, although she was created in Paradise, her husband is properly her native soil: she was taken out of him and for him. At the close of the poem, Eve, the repentant sinner, now at peace with God and with Adam, can say to her husband:

> In mee is no delay; with thee to goe,
> Is to stay here; without thee here to stay,
> Is to go hence unwilling; thou to mee
> Art all things under Heav'n, all places thou,
> Who for my wilful crime art banisht hence.
> This further consolation yet secure
> I carry hence; though all by mee is lost,
> Such favour I unworthie am voutsaft,
> By mee the Promis'd Seed shall all restore.
> (*P. L.*, XII, 615-623)

The dramatic elements of setting, action, language, and character have been seen in this and the preceding chapter as enhanced in effectiveness through Milton's use of the Bible in his epic poems. The purpose Milton expressed in his *Reason of Church Government Urged Against Prelaty* of painting out and describing "whatsoever hath passion or admiration in all the changes of that which is called fortune from without, or the wily subtleties and refluxes of man's thoughts from within . . . with a solid and treatable smoothness" was accomplished in both his "diffuse" and his "brief model" epic as a result of his "industrious and select reading, steady observation, insight into all seemly and generous arts and affairs" and "devout prayer to that eternal Spirit, who . . . sends out his seraphim, with the hallowed fire of his altar, to touch and purify the lips of whom he pleases";[18] and that much of Milton's "select reading" was in the Scriptures is attested by the manifold use he made of specific references and allusions. That such allusions would be recognized and responded to Milton could be as sure of as (or, considering the "fit audience" for whom he wrote, more sure of than) the Elizabethan dramatists before him who had made allusions to Scripture an integral part of their dramatic art.

18. Patterson, *The Student's Milton*, pp. 525-526.

# V

## *Epic Unity of Theme*

THUS FAR, Milton's use of the Bible in his epic poems has been seen aiding in the poetic communication of truth and reality, giving pleasure and instruction through allusions to the original, and Latin, Scriptures as well as to the English Bible, and adding dramatic power to the already dramatically forceful portrayal of setting, action, language, and character. All of these uses of the Bible and their effects are, of course, fused into the epic structure as integral parts of the two poems; in this study the uses of the Bible have been artificially extracted for purposes of analysis, just as parts of a great painting might be microscopically examined by means of photographs of small sections in detail. It is hoped that the detailed analysis, together with the synthesis of Biblical patterns, may enable the reader to return to the poems with a greater appreciation of them as unified wholes, as epics. It is the purpose of the present chapter, then, to show how Milton makes his use of the Bible contribute to and heighten the thematic unity of each epic in spite of, and even because of, the diversity and variety involved in his Biblical allusions, and how Milton maintains this thematic unity from one epic to the other.[1]

*Paradise Lost,* since it is more clearly in the traditional epic genre than *Paradise Regained,* involves uses of Scripture in accord with conventions peculiar to the epic form; peculiarly epic uses of Biblical allusion are not found in *Paradise Regained.* There are, however, phrases reiterated throughout both which give unity of theme to the individual epics and which also make thematic connections between the major and the minor epic more vital and

1. Milton's epics have structural unity in the Aristotelian sense, including one main action with a beginning, middle, and end; the term "unity" as it is used in this chapter, however, is not unity in the Aristotelian sense but simply unity of theme.

unifying. Each poem is a complete whole, while the two share a common theme. But before this point is pursued further, some of the elements of *Paradise Lost* previously discussed should be recalled.

It is obvious that many of the cited passages from *Paradise Lost,* although they are dealt with under various headings dictated by the discussion of Biblical allusions, have their roots in epic necessity and convention: the supernatural machinery of angels and demons, the scenes in Heaven and Hell, the dialogues between persons of the Godhead, the space devoted to the speeches of heroic characters (Books II, V, and VI), the long catalogues of names, the beginning *in medias res* with the later recounting of earlier events of the story, the description of mighty antagonists in single combat (Abdiel and Satan in Book VI), the maintenance of a highly dignified and serious style, and the repetition of certain epithets, phrases, and syntactical formulas.[2] This last epic characteristic of reiteration will be discussed later. First there is a need to examine perhaps the most characteristic mark of the epic style: the use of the figure of speech known as the epic simile, a figure so successfully employed by Milton that he attains a sublimity of high seriousness and at the same time a unity in variety rarely attained by any other writer. As one scholar has said, "To decorate his verse in the Homeric manner and to lift the imagination to embrace a whole age of history, Milton uses figures which have come to designate a type because of their sublimity, a type which is known as the Miltonic figure. Milton's power to form expansive similes of the epic type testifies to the application of Longinus' definition of the sublime as 'a certain excellence and perfection of language.'"[3]

Milton's sublime, elevated style has often been praised and has sometimes been explained. The quoted critic sees Milton's unflagging sublimity as primarily the result of his having followed classi-

2. For example, God is "Eternal Father" in *P. L.*, V, 246; VI, 96; VII, 136-137, 516-517; X, 32, 68. "So saying" appears as a participial transition in *P. L.*, IV, 536, 797; V, 82, 331; VI, 189; VIII, 300, 644; IX, 179, 780, 834, 990; X, 272, 410. Biblical phrases are also reiterated as is later seen.

3. Ivar Lou Myrh, *The Evolution and Practice of Milton's Epic Theory* (Nashville, 1942), p. 52.

cal and Renaissance concepts of the epic; C. S. Lewis sees it as, to a great extent, the result of abrupt jolts from one idea to another (such as T. S. Eliot makes without transitions) provided with apparently smooth logical and syntactical connections which push the reader forward while affecting him with "subterranean" meaning;[4] Marianna Woodhull sees it as an almost inevitable result of Milton's having chosen the epic form rather than the form of tragedy;[5] and E. M. W. Tillyard sees it as largely the result of Milton's exercise of and belief in the human will "stretched and sustained to the utmost" to govern a large amount of material by a "powerful predetermination."[6] B. Rajan considers Milton's style, with its quality of "superhuman permanence," as the result not of the more obvious adornments of the verse, the "subordinate effects," but of the constant "ground swell which supports them";[7] Arnold Stein seeks to sum up his evaluation of Milton's "answerable style" as one which involves, chiefly, "a sober realization of the now under the great promise of Time";[8] and F. T. Prince attributes the sublimity of Milton's style to his use of Tasso's principle of

4. *A Preface to Paradise Lost* (London, 1942), pp. 44-50.

5. *The Epic of Paradise Lost* (New York, 1907), p. 41 and *passim.*

6. *The English Epic and Its Background* (London, 1954), pp. 4 ff. In attempting to lay aside any discussion of form and to define "the spirit of the epic," Professor Tillyard lists four essential qualities which a work must have in order to be considered an epic: (1) high seriousness and high quality, involving the use of words in a distinguished way; (2) "amplitude, breadth, inclusiveness"—a diffusion which is the opposite of intense concentration in a short space, as in tragedy; (3) "control commensurate with the amount included," with all material "governed by a powerful predetermination"; (4) a choric expression of the "feelings of a large group living in or near [the writer's] times." All four of these qualities are present in *P. L.* to an eminent degree, but, Tillyard feels, the second and fourth qualities are lacking in *P. R.* (p. 446). But even in terms of Tillyard's definition *P. R.* cannot be denied a choric quality in the light of Elizabeth Marie Pope's *Paradise Regained: The Tradition and the Poem* (Baltimore, 1947), which shows conclusively that Milton is expressing essentially the serious convictions of a multitude of thoughtful men in or near his own times. As for the second quality Tillyard lists (he excludes Job as an epic, as well as *P. R.*, for lacking this quality), whether or not *P. R.* does have it depends on the degree of "amplitude, breadth, inclusiveness" one requires. That Tillyard requires more than Milton's minor epic has should not prevent others from requiring less, and *P. R.* seems to have a valid claim to the title of epic even on Tillyard's terms.

7. *Paradise Lost and the Seventeenth Century Reader* (London, 1947), p. 125.

8. *Answerable Style: Essays on Paradise Lost* (Minneapolis, 1953), p. 160.

*asprezza,* "roughness," the use of metrical techniques developed by Tasso which, though never satisfactorily exemplified in Tasso's own work, became the "unmistakable model of Milton's blank verse."[9]

It seems clear, as these critics would doubtless admit, that the complete explanation for Milton's sublimity lies in no one of these attempts at explanation but in a combination of all of them with something more. The something more could probably be assigned no satisfactory name but might be called the indomitable strength and dignity of the spirit of John Milton. To these partial explanations of his epic sublimity in *Paradise Lost,* however, may be added one more demonstrable factor: Milton's use of the Bible as a source of, and a supplement to, the traditional epic simile, a use which goes far towards explaining how his epic similes have established a type known as the "Miltonic figure."

## *EPIC SIMILES*

The first epic simile in *Paradise Lost* characterizes and gives a visual image of the tremendous figure of Satan as he lies on the burning lake of Hell, expressing to Beelzebub his defiance of the God who has cast him out of Heaven.

> Thus Satan talking to his neerest Mate
> With Head up-lift above the wave, and Eyes
> That sparkling blaz'd, his other Parts besides
> Prone on the Flood, extended long and large
> Lay floating many a rood, in bulk as huge
> As whom the Fables name of monstrous size,
> *Titanian,* or *Earth-born,* that warr'd on *Jove,*
> *Briarios* or *Typhon,* whom the Den
> By ancient *Tarsus* held, or that Sea-beast
> *Leviathan,* which God of all his works
> Created hugest that swim th' Ocean stream:
> Him haply slumbring on the *Norway* foam
> The Pilot of some small night-founder'd Skiff,
> Deeming some Island, oft, as Sea-men tell,
> With fixed Anchor in his skaly rind
> Moors by his side under the Lee, while Night
> Invests the Sea, and wished Morn delayes:

9. *The Italian Element in Milton's Verse* (London, 1954), p. 57.

> So stretcht out huge in length the Arch-fiend lay
> Chain'd on the burning Lake. (*P. L.*, I, 192-210)

The simile expands from swift hints at the size of Satan—through mention of the Titans, Briarios the hundred-handed giant, and the monster Typhon—to the Biblical Leviathan, hugest of all sea creatures; then a complete picture is given of sailors in a small skiff, unsuspectingly moored to the side of this terrible sea serpent, unable to see and wishing for daylight, and the reader almost loses sight of Satan to whom the simile refers. But the words "So stretcht out huge in length the Arch-fiend lay / Chain'd" return the reader abruptly to the flashing, hate-filled eyes and colossal bulk of Satan "Prone on the Flood." Even without recognition of the Biblical allusions in this passage, definite effects are gained: Satan is visualized as of tremendous size, and although he lies chained on the lake of fire, the "Head up-lift" and fiery eyes make one decidedly uneasy in his presence. The uneasiness is increased to fearful apprehension by the image of the seamen with their anchor fixed in a monster's "skaly rind" while they await daylight—at what moment will the beast arouse himself and kill them all? But then the reader is quickly reminded that Satan is the subject and that, terrifying as he is, he is chained to be released only by the "high permission of all-ruling Heaven" (I, 212). Thus there is here, on the surface, a delicate balance between feelings of fear at the size and potential danger of Satan and feelings of security in the knowledge that "th' Omnipotent" is he who cast out "th' infernal Serpent" (I, 34, 39). Recognition of the Biblical allusion, however, deepens and broadens these effects while it elevates into Scriptural truth a scene which might otherwise be merely mythology and folklore.

The Leviathan is mentioned several times in the Bible. The primary allusion in Milton's simile is most likely to the prophecy of Isaiah: "In that day the LORD with his sore and great and strong sword shall punish Leviathan the piercing serpent, even Leviathan that crooked serpent; and he shall slay the dragon that *is* in the Sea" (27:1). That is, even in the figure of speech used to magnify the power and size of Satan, there is allusion to the Biblical promise of his eventual defeat as the "crooked serpent." There is allusion also to the questions God asked of Job when he wished to humble him; Job's insignificance in comparison with God is emphasized by reference to Leviathan, created and controlled by God but feared by Job. "Canst thou draw out Leviathan with an hooke? or his tongue with a corde *which* thou lettest downe? . . . Shall not one bee cast downe even at the sight of him? . . . His scales are his pride, shut up together as with a close seale. . . . He beholdeth all high things; he is a king over all the children of pride" (Job 41:1, 9, 15, 34).

Even the image of the sailors and their precarious condition is in language allusive to the Biblical experience of Paul and other disciples in the terrible storm which wrecked their Rome-bound prison ship. Paul knew that they had to be "cast upon a certain Iland" (Acts 27:26); then "about midnight, the shipmen deemed that they drew neere to some countrey" (Acts 27:27b) and, afraid the ship would run aground, "they cast foure ancres out of the sterne, and wished for the day" (Acts 27:29). If the language reminiscent of the Bible is recognized and the angel's promise to Paul during the storm that no lives would be lost (Acts 27:22-24) is remembered, there is, even in the suspense of the image of sailors moored to the side of a dangerous monster, assurance of God's providence and protection.[10] The simile gives variety by momen-

10. T. S. Eliot, in a lecture read before the British Academy in March, 1947 (*Milton: Annual Lecture on a Master Mind,* from Proceedings of the British Academy, XXIII [London, 1947], 15-16), says that while he is not happy about certain matters of detail in the simile under discussion, he thinks that much "extraneous matter" is happily introduced. "Any writer, straining for images of hugeness, might have thought of the whale, but only Milton could have included the anecdote of the deluded seamen without our wanting to put a blue pencil through it. We *nearly* forget Satan in attending to the story of the whale; Milton recalls us just in time. Therefore the diversion strengthens, instead of weakening, the passage." Mr. Eliot, however, sees in such combinations of "extraneous matter" in Milton's similes "a kind of inspired *frivolity,* an enjoyment by the author in the exercise of his own virtuosity, which is a mark of the first rank of genius." I believe that the discussion of the Biblical allusions in the Leviathan simile demonstrates that none of the matter is really extraneous, but that out of the variety comes sublimity through the Biblical overtones of God's inevitable victory over evil and thematic unity because of the allusions to a Bible passage emphasizing God's provident care for his people in distress. Milton is, perhaps, enjoying his own virtuosity in "a kind of inspired *frivolity";* the indications of the Biblical allusions are, however, that Milton is also going seriously about his business of asserting eternal providence and justifying

tarily taking the reader away from the burning lake to the "*Norway* foam," away from the Arch-fiend to a slumbering, but potentially deadly, sea monster, away from the "darkness visible" of Hell to the pitch-black darkness of the sea at night,[11] away from the fallen angels to a group of human beings who are anxiously wishing for the morning which seems so slow in coming. But when the reader is brought back again to the setting of *Paradise Lost,* especially if he has recognized the Biblical allusions, he is both more aware of Satan's terrible nature and frightful possibilities as the enemy of man and more conscious of God's overruling control and providence than he would be without the expanded heroic figure of the Leviathan.[12]

When Satan, by divine permission, rears himself from the lake, makes his way to the "Beach / Of that inflamed Sea" (I, 300),

---

the ways of God to men in this Leviathan simile—and even in the "anecdote of the deluded seamen." Perhaps, without his realizing it, Mr. Eliot's real reason for not wanting to "put a blue pencil through it" is his own subconscious recognition of the Biblical echoes of Milton's language.

11. In his lecture (p. 15), Mr. Eliot speaks of the inappropriateness of "night-founder'd Skiff" (*P. L.,* I, 204). He maintains that the phrase is inappropriate even though Professor Tillyard has pointed out that *night-founder'd* is used in *Comus* (I, 483), for there it refers to travelers on land and here it refers to seamen at sea. Eliot says, "A *founder'd* skiff could not be moored, to a whale or anything else," because of the literal meaning of *foundered.* But the skiff is not foundered in the literal sense of filled with water and sinking; it is filled with *night* and sunk in *night.* The use of "night-founder'd" as an adjective here intensifies the helplessness of the seamen, so bound by darkness that their skiff is unnavigable, their location unknown.

12. Leviathan is mentioned again in Raphael's account of Creation:

> there Leviathan
> Hugest of living Creatures, on the Deep,
> Stretcht like a Promontorie sleeps or swimmes,
> And seems a moving Land.
> (*P. L.,* VII, 412-415)

After the simile in Book I, the reader cannot fail to connect this image with Satan "stretcht out huge" on the lake of fire. Following the description of Leviathan in Book VII, Milton describes the "Eagle and the Stork" building their "Eyries" on cliffs and cedar tops (VII, 423-424) and "the prudent Crane" steering on her annual voyage (VII, 430-431). The allusions are to Job 39:27, 28, which verses emphasize man's ignorance of the instincts guiding animals and birds, and to Jer. 8:7, which contrasts the instinctive knowledge of the seasons possessed by the stork, the crane, etc., with man's ignorance of God's judgments. Even amidst the beautiful poetry describing the creation of fish and fowl, therefore, Milton includes forebodings of man's fall through Biblical allusions recalling Satan, the Serpent, and contrasting animal instinct with man's free will.

and seeks to arouse his legions, he sees them lying on the infernal waves,

> Thick as Autumnal Leaves that strow the Brooks
> In *Vallombrosa,* where th' *Etrurian* shades
> High overarch't imbowr; or scatterd sedge
> Afloat, when with fierce Winds *Orion* arm'd
> Hath vext the Red-Sea Coast, whose waves orethrew
> *Busiris* and his *Memphian* Chivalrie,
> While with perfidious hatred they pursu'd
> The Sojourners of *Goshen,* who beheld
> From the safe shore their floating Carkases
> And broken Chariot Wheels, so thick bestrown
> Abject and lost lay these, covering the Flood,
> Under amazement of their hideous change.
> (*P. L.,* I, 302-313)

Again there is the swift, glancing comparison suddenly expanded into a picture complete in itself: the not unpleasant image of autumnally colored leaves gently falling and floating on Italian brooks shifts to one of violently scattered brown sedge on the waters of the Red Sea, and suddenly there, tossed on the waves of that sea, are the dead bodies and broken chariots of the Egyptians who pursued the Israelites and were destroyed by God.

The allusion is to the story of God's miraculous opening of the Red Sea to allow the Israelites to pass through on dry land and of his destruction of the Egyptians (called "perfidious" because of Pharaoh's broken promise to let Israel leave Egypt in peace) when they attempted to follow the route of God's people through the sea. "And the Egyptians pursued, and went in after them to the midst of the Sea, even all Pharaohs horses, his charets, and his horsemen. . . . The LORD took off their charet wheeles, that they drave them heavily: So that the Egyptians said, Let us flee. . . . And the Lord overthrewe the Egyptians in the midst of the sea. . . . Thus the LORD saved Israel that day out of the hand of the Egyptians and Israel saw the Egyptians dead upon the sea shore" (Exod. 14:23, 25a, 27b, 30). The shift from the image of leaves which have fallen in the natural course of things to sedge torn up along the sea coast by fierce winds to the "floating Carkases / And broken Chariot Wheels" of the enemies of God's people emphasizes the "hideous change" which has taken place in these "Angel Forms" (I, 301). The change is underscored by Satan's reference to his legions as "the Flowr of Heav'n, once yours, now lost" (I, 316) and his sarcastic allusion to their taking their ease in slumbering now in Hell as they formerly did in the "Vales of Heav'n" (I, 321). But the peculiar aptness of the explicit analogy between Satan's host and the armies of Pharaoh comes home to the reader later in the poem when Biblical allusions in Book VI identify Satan and his rebels with Pharaoh and his troops and the Son of God and his elect angels with Moses and the Israelites; the effect is to stress the omnipotence and supreme control of God above and behind the action of the poem as it is stressed in the Bible story (*P. L.*, VI, 788-815 with Exod. 14:8, 13-14; VI, 860-862, 878-879 with Exod. 14:22-28). In Book I we are *in medias res* and the epic simile gains its effect in elevating God, the Victor over these demons, by showing the abject and confused condition into which the demons have fallen; but later, when allusions are made to the same Biblical passage in Raphael's narration in Book VI of events preceding, chronologically, the action of Book I, Biblical allusions which have already added sublimity and variety are seen to add unity by the repetition of the theme of God's sovereignty, omnipotence, and justice by which he brings good out of evil and punishes the perpetrators of the evil.[13]

13. A final repetition of the Biblical allusion to the destruction of the Egyptians in the Red Sea occurs in Michael's foreview of the future in Book XII. The language is similar to that of the allusions in Book VI: Pharaoh's "stubborn heart" is "as Ice / More hardn'd after thaw" (XII, 193-194) as Satan and his followers are "hardn'd more by what might most reclame" (VI, 791); Pharaoh is "th' obdurate" (VI, 790). The language is also similar to that used in the epic simile of Book I (ll. 307 ff); the Israelites in both instances are "sojourners" (XII, 192; I, 309); Pharaoh pursues "in his rage" (XII, 194) and "with perfidious hatred" (I, 308); the image of the "Chariot wheels" broken miraculously is repeated (XII, 210; I, 311). The main point, however, is that the final allusion in *P. L.* to the overthrowing of the Egyptians is in a context which connects it with God's preservation of the "Race elect" (XII, 214) for the express purpose of bringing forth "that destind Seed to bruise/ The Serpent" and "achieve Mankinds deliverance" (XII, 233-235). The earlier allusions take on more importance by hindsight after the final repetition, and the consistency of Milton's allusions to this particular Bible passage, connoting, as they do, God's power to win over evil in his eternal providence—past (in Book I), present (in Book VI), and future (in Book XII)—lends thematic unity as well as epic sublimity and variety to Milton's poem.

In answer to Satan's call, "Awake, arise, or be for ever fall'n" (I, 330), an ironic echo of the Biblical "Awake thou that sleepest, and arise from the dead, and Christ shall give thee light" (Eph. 5:14), the demons rise from the burning lake.

> As when the potent Rod
> Of *Amrams* Son in *Egypts* evill day
> Wav'd round the Coast, up call'd a pitchy cloud
> Of *Locusts,* warping on the Eastern Wind,
> That ore the Realm of impious *Pharoah* hung
> Like Night, and darken'd all the Land of *Nile*:
> So numberless were those bad Angels seen
> Hovering on wing under the Cope of Hell.
> (*P. L.*, I, 338-345)

The allusion is to the plague of locusts brought upon Egypt because of Pharaoh's obdurate refusal to let the Israelites leave his land. "And Moses stretched foorth his rod over the land of Egypt, and the LORD brought an East-winde upon the land all that day, and all that night; and when it was morning, the east wind brought the locusts. And the locusts went up over al the land of Egypt, and rested in all the coastes of Egypt: very grievous were they; before them there were no such locusts as they, neither after them shall be such. For they covered the face of the whole earth, so that the land was darkened" (Exod. 10:13-15a). As Moses stretched out his "potent Rod," so Satan waves his "uplifted Spear" (I, 347) to direct the winged host; and in a very real sense, as Milton's explicit statements have already made clear ("all his malice serv'd but to bring forth / Infinite goodness, grace, and mercy" [ll. 217-218]), Satan is unwittingly directing his evil angels to serve God's ultimate purposes just as Moses directed the grievous locusts to serve God's purposes in Egypt. The image is striking and elevating to the imagination, and Milton's use of language makes one see and almost feel the circular, soaring motion of the angels as they spring up upon the wing: "round the Coast," "up," "warping on the Eastern Wind," "ore the Realm . . . hung." Together with the simile associating the host of angels with the barbarous Goths who "Came like a Deluge on the South," which follows a few lines later (I, 354), the simile of the locusts prepares the way for the description of the devils and their future wholesale invasion of Earth while it adds the pleasure of diversity for the reader. And, perhaps most important, the dominant chord of Book I and of the whole poem is struck again: God is sovereign and as He controlled and used the evil brought by the locusts to bring forth good for Israel, so He will control and bring forth good out of the evil to be loosed on the earth by the devils.[14] In the catalogue of devils, immediately following the passage under consideration, almost every name used connotes the defeat of some pagan deity by Jehovah, and thus the theme of God's inevitable victory is continued.

One of the most striking of the Miltonic figures in *Paradise Lost*[15] is that used in connection with the stairway to the Gate of Heaven from the outside rim of the universe, seen by Satan just after his passage through Limbo:

> farr distant hee descries
> Ascending by degrees magnificent
> Up to the wall of Heaven a Structure high
> . . . . . . . . . . . . . . . . .
> The Stairs were such as whereon *Jacob* saw

14. The locusts appear again in Book XII, ll. 185-188. Among other plagues, Michael says, "Herb, or Fruit, or Graine, / A darksom Cloud of Locusts swarming down / Must eat, and on the ground leave nothing green" before Pharaoh will let the Israelites leave Egypt. Milton here substitutes "darksom Cloud" for "pitchy cloud" (I, 340) of the first allusion, but the emphasis is still on the fact that God is above and behind the locusts, using them as a means of bringing deliverance to his people who, in turn, will bring forth "great *Messiah*" (XII, 244), "in whom all Nations shall be blest" (XII, 277).

15. Two illustrative examples of the sons of Belial in Book I, which are passed over here because they are not expanded into complete pictures like the epic simile but which suggest the theme of divine retribution for evil and of evil overcome by good, are those of "*Ely's* Sons, who fill'd / With lust and violence the house of God" (I, 495-496) and of "that night in *Gibeah,* when the hospitable door / Expos'd a Matron to avoid worse rape" (I, 503-505). Eli's sons, Hophni and Phinehas, referred to in the Bible as "sons of Belial" (I Sam. 2:12), were both destroyed in one day as a judgment of God (I Sam. 2:34, 4:11), and the Benjamites, who refused to deliver up the members of their tribe who were such sons of Belial that they attempted sodomy and rape and killed the concubine of a visiting Levite, paid with the lives of 25,000 fighting men (Judg. 20:46) and were prohibited from taking wives of other Israelite tribes (Judg. 21:1). Yet God replaced the doting Eli and his wicked sons with the devoted Samuel, and the eventual outcome was a stabilized kingdom under David and Solomon; Israel's civil war against Benjamin resulted in a more united nation as the other tribes repented of their harsh treatment of Benjamin (Judg. 21:6, 15).

> Angels ascending and descending, bands
> Of Guardians bright, when he from *Esau* fled
> To *Padan-Aram* in the field of *Luz,*
> Dreaming by night under the open Skie
> And waking cri'd, This is the Gate of Heav'n.
> (*P. L.,* III, 501-503, 510-515)

The Biblical account from which Milton drew this simile concerns Jacob's flight to avoid being killed by his brother shortly after he had deceived Isaac into blessing him as though he were Esau. "And he dreamed, and behold, a ladder set up on the earth, and the top of it reached to heaven: and behold the Angels of God ascending and descending on it. . . . And Jacob awaked out of his sleep, and he said, Surely the LORD is in this place; and I knew it not. And he was afraid, and said, How dreadfull *is* this place? this is none other, but the house of God, and this *is* the gate of heaven. . . . And he called the name of that place Bethel: but the name of that citie was called Luz, at the first" (Gen. 28:12, 16-17, 19). Perhaps what is most notable about the Biblical simile of the stairs is the contrast between Jacob and Satan. When Jacob sees the stairway he is overwhelmed by a sense of fear and reverence as he looks *up* toward Heaven from the earth; when Satan sees the stairway, and even stands on the lower steps, he looks *down* "with wonder at the sudden view / Of all this World at once" (III, 542-543) and is seized by a malign envy (ll. 552-553). When God lets down the stairway so that Jacob may see it, the man is stirred by his vision to worship and make vows to God (Gen. 28: 20-22); Milton mentions only two possible reasons for the stairway being let down before Satan: "to dare / The Fiend by easie ascent, or aggravate / His sad exclusion from the dores of Bliss" (III, 523-525). But the simile of the stairs has significance with relation to the epic as a whole.

Milton says, "Each Stair [the stair which Satan saw and the stair which Jacob saw] mysteriously was meant" (III, 516); that is, there is a figural significance. The mysterious meaning of Jacob's ladder is made clear by Jesus: "Verily, Verily, I say unto you, Hereafter ye shall see heaven open, & the Angels of God ascending and descending upon the Sonne of man" (John 1:51). The Son of Man, Christ Jesus, is the ladder, the stairway, from Earth to Heaven, "the Way, the Trueth, and the Life" (John 14:6); whether one came up from the earth and over the sea of jasper "Wafted by Angels" (l. 521) like Lazarus (Luke 16:22) or "Rapt in a Chariot drawn by fiery Steeds" (l. 522) like Elijah (II Kings 2:11), one must climb the stairway of the Son of Man. One may get even to the "foot / Of Heav'ns ascent" (l. 486) after seeking "In *Golgotha* him dead, who lives in Heav'n" (l. 477), but if one is trying to "pass disguis'd" in the weeds of a friar (l. 480) instead of in the "wedding garment" of faith in Christ (Matt. 22:12-13), he will be blown "transverse ten thousand Leagues awry" (l. 487) into Limbo. Satan stands on the "lower stair" that ascends "by steps of Gold to Heav'n Gate" (l. 541), a stair which represents Christ as does Jacob's stairway, turns his back on Heaven, and "without longer pause / Down right into the Worlds first Region throws / His flight precipitant" (III, 561-563). Satan's leap from the stair, which has neither dared him to ascend nor aggravated his "sad exclusion" from Heaven, is a disdainful act which precedes the full expression of his disdain from his own mouth in the soliloquy of Book IV. He has rejected the Son as the Messiah in Heaven, spurned him as Jacob's Ladder on the rim of the world, and is soon to express his hatred for the Son as the Sun of Righteousness.

An epic simile in Book IV has been condemned as "too outrageous," "too strained," and as an "absurdity" by a critic as eager, normally, to praise Milton as C. S. Lewis.[16] It is the simile in which Milton contrasts the pleasant smells of Eden which attract Satan with the stink of burning fish which put Asmodeus to flight in the apocryphal story of Tobit. Because the context of the passage (it follows an especially beautiful epic simile without Biblical allusions) may help explain what Milton is doing, it is quoted here with the epic simile drawn from the Apocrypha. Gentle gales are bringing "Native perfumes" of Eden to Satan's nostrils:

> As when to them who saile
> Beyond the *Cape of Hope* and now are past
> *Mozambic,* off at Sea North-East windes blow
> *Sabean* Odours from the spicie shoare
> Of *Arabie* the blest, with such delay
> Well pleas'd they slack thir course, and many a League

16. *A Preface to Paradise Lost,* p. 42.

Cheard with the grateful smell old Ocean smiles.
So entertaind those odorous sweets the Fiend
Who came thir bane, though with them better pleas'd
Then *Asmodeus* with the fishie fume,
That drove him, though enamourd, from the Spouse
Of *Tobits* Son, and with a vengeance sent
From *Media* post to *Ægypt*, there fast bound.
(*P. L.*, IV, 159-171)

Of the reference to Asmodeus, Professor Lewis says, "Milton wants to make us feel the full obscenity of Satan's presence in Eden by bringing a sudden stink of fish across the sweet smell of the flowers, and alluding to one of the most unpleasant Hebrew stories. But the pretence of logical connection (that Satan liked the flowers of Paradise *better* than Asmodeus liked the smell of burning fish) is too strained. We feel the absurdity."[17] But Milton is not feinting with "pretence of logical connection"; there is a logical connection, one of contrast rather than of comparison: a contrast that is intensified if the preceding comparison is kept in mind. The image there is of sailors, tired and perhaps mentally depressed from the effort of rounding the Cape of Good Hope, so pleased and cheered with the "Odours from the spicie shoare / Of *Arabie* the blest" that even "old Ocean," so recently their enemy in the struggle against its currents at the Cape, seems to smile. Satan has also sailed "Beyond the *Cape of Hope*"; after his long, arduous journey through Chaos to the new world, after having declared "So farwel Hope" (IV, 108), he has arrived at the foot of the mount of Paradise where the air carries sweet smells that are able to drive away "All sadness but despair" (l. 156). Like the sailors who slack their course to enjoy the scent from shore, Satan journeys on "pensive and slow" (l. 173). But what of Asmodeus and the "fishie fume"? The reference to Tobit 8:1-4 emphasizes, by contrasting Satan and Asmodeus, the similarity between Satan and the sailors of the preceding simile. They have struggled against the forces of God's world, though not against God; Satan has struggled against the forces of God's world (he even wishes to destroy the world and man) and against God Himself. Yet within sight and smell of the abode he hates, he finds himself entertained by

17. *Ibid.*

the very sweets of which he has come to be the "bane" (l. 167), the destroyer (from Old English *bana,* "slayer"). Asmodeus came to the bridal chamber of Sara "enamourd," but found himself hating the smell of her chamber because of the burning heart and liver of the fish. Therefore, although Satan came to destroy the sweets, he is pleased with them; Asmodeus came to love Sara and, displeased by the stink, was driven away. Satan was "better pleas'd" because he stayed to carry out his mission, whereas Asmodeus fled. Satan's hate is a far stronger motive than Asmodeus' love because Satan will stay to destroy that which pleases him, while Asmodeus allowed that which displeased him to cause him to leave what he loved. The "better" (which seems so illogical on the surface) is simply Miltonic irony, similar to Satan's statement in *Paradise Regained* that he came to Jordan while John was baptizing, "though not to be Baptiz'd" (*P. R.*, IV, 512). Finally, though Satan does not flee like Asmodeus and is not "fast bound" like Asmodeus but instead "At one slight bound" overleaps all "bound" (l. 181) of Paradise, the allusion to Asmodeus and his fate foreshadows the ultimate fate of Satan to be bound and cast into the lake of fire forever (Rev. 20:2, 10). God may defeat evil by putting its instrument to flight or by letting the evil do its work in order to bring good out of the evil. The latter course brings greater glory to God and is the course taken with regard to Satan's entrance into the Garden of Eden and, consequently, into the heart of man.

Finding only one gate, Satan disdains "Due entrance" (IV, 180) and leaps over the wall of trees into Paradise. Milton follows his description of this action by two Biblical epic similes.

> As when a prowling Wolfe,
> Whom hunger drives to seek new haunt for prey,
> Watching where Shepherds pen thir Flocks at eeve
> In hurdl'd Cotes amid the field secure,
> Leaps o're the fence with ease into the Fould:
> Or as a Thief bent to unhoord the cash
> Of some rich Burgher, whose substantial dores,
> Cross-barrd and bolted fast, fear no assault,
> In at the window climbes, or o're the tiles;
> So clomb this first grand Thief into Gods Fould:
> So since into his Church lewd Hirelings climbe.
> (*P. L.*, IV, 183-193)

The allusion is to the discourse on the Good Shepherd in John's Gospel.[18] The words are spoken by Jesus: "Verily, verily, I say unto you, Hee that entereth not by the doore into the sheepefold, but climbeth up some other way, the same is a theefe, and a robber. . . . Verily, verily, I say unto you, I am the dore of the sheepe. . . . The theefe commeth not but for to steale, and to kil, and to destroy. . . . I am the good shepheard: the good shepheard giveth his life for the sheepe. But he that is an hireling, and not the shepheard, whose owne the sheepe are not, seeth the woolfe comming, and leaveth the sheepe, and fleeth: and the woolfe catcheth them, and scattereth the sheep. The hireling fleeth, because he is an hireling, and careth not for the sheepe" (10:1, 7, 10a, 11-13).

Just as Satan turned his back on the stairway to Heaven's Gate, and cursed the sun (both Biblical symbols of Christ), he disdains the "doore of the sheepe" into Paradise because he is a wolf, come to scatter the sheep, and a thief, come to steal, to kill, and to destroy; therefore he "climbeth up some other way." Satan is called the "first grand Thief" so to enter God's fold, because he has been followed by a long line of successors, some even masquerading as shepherds though they were "wolves" (Acts 20:29), "theeves and robbers" (John 10:8), and hirelings (John 10:12-13). Thus Milton not only gives the reader, through the similes of the wolf and the thief, images which powerfully affect the imagination and emphasize the outrageous disdain connected with the Devil's intrusion into God's world and man's Garden; Milton also suggests that Satan's act is the seminal violation of order in this new universe. When Michael informs Adam that after the apostles have fulfilled their ministry and have left the Bible behind them, "Wolves shall succeed for teachers, grievous Wolves" (XII, 508) to pervert the Bible and to force "Spiritual Lawes by carnal power . . . / On every conscience" (XII, 521-522), the reader may remember the earlier figure of the wolf from whom all the enemies of God's sheep have descended. The complete pictures brought to mind, in Book IV, by the images of the wolf and the thief divert the reader momentarily from Satan and Paradise only to bring him back more vividly

18. Allusions are also present to Acts 20:29 and Ezek. 22:27. Milton doubtless recalled Virgil's simile comparing Turnus, as he attacks the Trojan camp, to a hungry wolf circling a sheepfold (*Aeneid,* IX, 59-64).

aware than ever of the significance for the present and for the future of Satan's mode of entrance to man's abode. And the images being taken from the discourse of Jesus on himself as the Good Shepherd brings a suggestion, which does not need to be stated, that no matter what evil this "first grand Thief" may accomplish, the Good Shepherd, who "giveth his life for the sheepe" (John 10:11), will overrule it and bring out of it good for the sheep to the glory of the Father.[19] The echo of the wolf simile in Book XII by Michael is closely followed by the promise of the coming Christ

> In glory of the Father, to dissolve
> *Satan* with his perverted World, then raise
> . . . . . . . . . . . . . . .
> New Heav'ns, new Earth, Ages of endless date
> Founded in righteousness and peace and love,
> To bring forth fruits Joy and eternal Bliss.
> (*P. L.*, XII, 546-547, 549-551)

At the close of Book IV, as Satan gives signs of wishing to fight the angelic forces rather than to obey Gabriel's stern order to get out of Paradise, the angels prepare for battle. As Milton describes it,

> th' Angelic Squadron bright
> Turnd fierie red, sharpning in mooned hornes
> Thir Phalanx, and began to hemm him round
> With ported Spears, as thick as when a field
> Of *Ceres* ripe for harvest waving bends
> Her bearded Grove of ears, which way the wind
> Swayes them; the careful Plowman doubting stands
> Least on the threshing floore his hopeful sheaves
> Prove chaff.
> (*P. L.*, IV, 977-985)

The visual image of the host of spears moving together to the diagonal port position is made perfectly clear by the simile of the field of wheat bending in the direction of the wind; why, then, does

19. Satan is called the "Thief of Paradise" in the closing hymn of the angels in *Paradise Regained* (IV, 604), where Christ is being praised for having "frustrated the conquest fraudulent" and "regain'd lost Paradise" (IV, 608-609). In such a context, the echo of the thief simile marking Satan's first entrance to Eden is appropriate, for the theme of God's overruling Satan's evil is being repeated.

Milton expand the image to include "the careful Plowman"? The plowman, in Scripture, stands for the servant of God (as in I Corinthians 9:10 and Luke 17:7), but he also stands for the Son of God (described in Matthew 13:37 as "he that soweth the good seede" and connected in Luke 9:62 with "the plough").[20] The Biblical principle that "hee that ploweth, should plow in hope; and he that thresheth in hope should be partaker of his hope" (I Cor. 9:10) is alluded to here, and Milton shifts the identification of the plowman from the servant to God. There is doubt that the elect angels and their spears unaided can effect Satan's expulsion from Eden; thus God, immediately following this simile and the description of Satan's tremendous might, intervenes and doubles the strength of Gabriel's forces to "trample . . . as mire" (l. 1010) the Fiend. But there is more significance still to the simile of the plowman. The reference to "chaff" (l. 985) recalls Christ's words to Peter, shortly before that disciple's denial of his Lord: "Simon, Simon, behold Satan hath desired *to have* you, that he may sift *you* as wheat: but I have prayed for thee, that thy faith fail not" (Luke 22:31-32). Satan's sifting, or threshing, of Peter as wheat resulted in the taking away of only the chaff of Peter's overconfident assurance that he would remain, in his own strength, faithful to Christ. Again the theme of Satan's evil becoming the occasion for good to God's people through God's power is hinted at: if Satan and the angels had fought without God's intervention and if Satan had won, only chaff would be gone, and the wheat would be even more pure, just as the elect angels who did not fall with Satan are praised by the Father as those who "in thir state, though firm, stood more confirmd" (XI, 71). But why is a plowman rather than a reaper associated with grain ripe for harvest? Perhaps the allusion is to the prophetic promise of God that in the days of the millennial reign of the Messiah, "the plowman shall overtake the reaper, and the treader of grapes him that soweth seed; and the mountaines shall drop sweet wine, & all the hils shall melt" (Amos 9:13); when the

20. There is also, as literary precedent for Milton's connection of God and his servants with a plowman, Langland's *Piers the Plowman*, in which Piers is successively a layman, a priest, a bishop, and Christ himself (cf. "*Petrus, id est Christus*" in Passus XV). Cf. also Hugh Latimer's "The Sermon of the Plough."

seasons so merge into one another, the "Eternal Spring" of Paradise will be regained. Thus, through Milton's Biblical allusions in his extended epic similes in Book IV of *Paradise Lost,* whether Satan is entering Paradise or being expelled from it, the theme of God's ultimate victory over Satan and the restoration of the blissful seat by "one greater Man" runs quietly as a strong, prevailing undercurrent beneath the uncertain turbulence of the surface action of the epic.

One final Miltonic simile based on the Bible remains to be considered.[21] It, like others discussed earlier, is a twofold simile, drawn from two different Bible stories, the second being expanded more than the first. As Michael and his bands of guardian angels descend to Paradise, they form a glorious apparition, although Adam is blind to the glory of it through the results of sin, "doubt / And carnal fear" (XI, 212), which dim his eyes.

> Not that more glorious, when the Angels met
> *Jacob* in *Mahanaim,* where he saw
> The field Pavilion'd with his Guardians bright;
> Nor that which on the flaming Mount appeerd
> In *Dothan,* cover'd with a Camp of Fire
> Against the *Syrian* King, who to surprize
> One man, Assassin-like had levied Warr,
> Warr unproclaim'd.
>
> (*P. L.*, XI, 213-220)

The Biblical description of Jacob's meeting with the angels is about as brief as Milton's and is even less easily visualized: "And Jacob went on his way, and the Angels of God met him. And when Jacob saw them, he saide, This is Gods hoste; and he called the name of that place Mahanaim" (Gen. 32:1-2). But although Jacob saw the angels and named the place Mahanaim, meaning "two bands," indi-

21. One simile has been passed over because of its having been mentioned as a means of characterizing Adam in an earlier chapter. It is that simile in Book IX in which Adam is compared, as he rises from his lustful and degrading sexual orgy with Eve, to "*Herculean Samson*" rising from the "Harlot-lap / Of *Philistean Dalilah* . . . Shorn of his strength" (IX, 1059-1062). The reference is to Judg. 16:4-20; but that Adam will be eventually victorious over his sin and shame through Christ, the last Adam, is suggested when it is remembered that, even though Samson was blinded and enslaved, "the haire of his head began to grow againe" (Judg. 16:22) and God gave him a greater victory in his death than he had ever won in his life (Judg. 16:30).

cating that his own band was reinforced and protected by the angelic band, his guilty conscience and fear of meeting Esau (whom he had tricked out of their father's blessing years before) dimmed his appreciation of the beauty of the angels and weakened his faith in their protection. Upon hearing that Esau was coming to meet him with four hundred men, Jacob was so afraid that he divided the human company into two bands and acted as though the divine company did not exist (Gen. 32:6-8). Thus the comparison between Adam and Jacob, both afflicted by fear and doubt even in the presence of angels, is appropriate.

The second simile alludes to the story of the King of Syria's attempt to attack the prophet Elisha. Dothan, where Elisha and his servant were, was surrounded during the night with horses and chariots and a great host. "And when the servant of the man of God was risen early & gone forth, behold, an host compassed the citie, both with horses and charets. And his servant said unto him, Alas, my master! how shall we doe? And hee answered, Feare not: for they that bee with us *are* more than they that bee with them. And Elisha prayed, and said, LORD, I pray thee open his eyes, that hee may see. And the LORD opened the eyes of the young man, and he saw: and, behold, the mountaine was full of horses, and charets of fire round about Elisha" (II Kings 6:15-17). As Adam is like Jacob in not fully appreciating the band of angels he sees, he is also like Elisha's servant, who was not conscious of the presence of divine help until his eyes were opened by God (as Adam's eyes are to be opened by Michael). But in this second part of the twofold simile, the allusion to Elisha and the Syrian king, there is a more important point of comparison with the action of *Paradise Lost*. The Syrian king came, "Assassin-like," to levy "Warr unproclaim'd" on "One man"; this is exactly what Satan has done to Adam. Satan did not come with a host of his demons, but he came with all the superior advantage of his supernatural power and with the element of surprise on his side to destroy "One man" and, in him, the race. God gave man an angelic guard who did all they could to protect him from Satan, but once Satan had Eve as his instrument, all was lost for Adam. Yet now that Adam has fallen, been judged, and repented, as the angel bands come to dispossess him of Paradise,

Milton uses similes based on Scriptural sources in which angel bands appeared for the purpose of guarding and shielding man, not for punishing or penalizing him. In spite of the shock of disappointment which Adam and Eve feel (and which the reader feels with them) at their being expelled from Paradise, the underlying connotation of Biblical allusion is that it is ultimately a good thing that man should be sent "from the Garden forth to Till / The Ground whence he was taken, fitter soile" (XI, 97-98).

Rather than leave man in Paradise to pluck the fruit of the Tree of Life "and eat, / And live for ever, dream at least to live / For ever" (XI, 94-96), God decrees that man should not only be sent forth but also prevented from returning. Paradise is to be guarded with maximum security so that foul spirits cannot prey on the Garden trees "With whose stol'n Fruit Man once more to delude" (XI, 125). Although man's leaving Paradise is a sad banishment, it is also a providential blessing; only by leaving the physical Paradise, for one thing, can man possess the Paradise within him, "happier farr" (XII, 587). Man will be far better through having learned from experience that God is not on "this Rock onely; his Omnipresence fills / Land, Sea, and Aire, and every kinde that lives" (XI, 336-337). And aiding in giving the reader assurance that things are turning out best for Adam after all are the references identifying Michael's angelic armies with Biblical guardians and protectors of man's happiness and welfare rather than with ministers of vengeance.[22] The same hosts of angels take on a terrifying aspect in the closing lines of the poem, but it is a terror mitigated by the image of their leader, Michael, "hastning . . . / Our lingring Parents" (XII, 637-638) by walking hand in hand with them out of the Eastern Gate and down the mount of Paradise to the plain of Eden. This final image of Michael and Adam and Eve, with its similarity to the story of the angels' hastening Lot and his wife and daughters out of Sodom (Gen. 19), is more suggestive of deliverance than of banishment. Again the unifying theme of God's power to bring good out of evil is heard softly in the background, as it has been

22. The expression "Guardians bright" in the passage under discussion (XI, 215) is verbally identical with that used earlier to describe the angels Jacob saw on the stairway to Heaven (III, 512), angels which were there, Milton implies, to guard Jacob in his flight from Esau. And part of the

heard in many passages in the poem, and especially underlying the Biblical allusions in the epic similes. Shortly before the end of *Paradise Lost,* Adam gives loud and clear emphasis to this theme which has so often appeared in the minor key:

> O goodness infinite, goodness immense!
> That all this good of evil shall produce,
> And evil turn to good; more wonderful
> Then that which by creation first brought forth
> Light out of darkness! (*P. L.*, XII, 469-473)

## *EPIC REITERATION*

In addition to the strengthening of the thematic unity of the major epic by the use of Biblical epic similes, there are certain allusions reiterated often enough throughout both *Paradise Lost* and *Paradise Regained* to unify the poems through common themes, so that the sequel becomes a part of the original epic thematically although not structurally or stylistically.[23]

Each of the epics opens with allusions to a Biblical truth which becomes central for both. Milton's song,

> Of Mans First Disobedience, and the Fruit
> Of that Forbidden Tree, whose mortal tast
> Brought Death into the World, and all our woe,
> With loss of *Eden,* till one greater Man
> Restore us, and regain the blissful Seat,
> (*P. L.*, I, 1-5)

is echoed by the sequel,

> I who e're while the happy Garden sung,
> By one mans disobedience lost, now sing
> Recover'd Paradise to all mankind
> By one mans firm obedience fully tri'd,
> (*P. R.*, I, 1-4)

---

function of Michael's troops is to guard Adam in his enforced flight from the scene of his crime.

23. A. S. P. Woodhouse, who has examined carefully the artistic pattern of both *P. L.* (in "Pattern in *Paradise Lost,*" *UTQ,* XXII [January 1953], 109-127) and *P. R.*, says of the latter epic: "Its pattern is of a different order and self-contained, but is not therefore independent" ("Theme and Pattern in *Paradise Regained,*" *UTQ,* XXV [January 1956], 167). The contention of the section above and following in my discussion is that a vital part of the pattern of *P. R.* which links it to, rather than makes it independent of, *P. L.* is the reiteration of key Biblical phrases.

and the opening notes of both songs allude to the Biblical statement that "by one man sinne entered into the world, and death by sinne; and so death passed upon all men. . . . For as by one mans disobedience many were made sinners, so by the obedience of one, shall many be made righteous" (Rom. 5:12, 19).

Following the opening lines, there are many allusions in both poems to the same sources in Scripture, especially to man's disobedience in *Paradise Lost,* since that is the main action of the longer epic, and especially to the obedience of One Man in *Paradise Regained,* which is a poetic demonstration of the loyal obedience of the God-man under the most trying circumstances, obedience in accord with his promise in *Paradise Lost,* Book III. "Man disobeying" (*P. L.*, III, 203) in the epic on the Fall is countered by the Son's "Filial obedience" (*P. L.*, III, 269) in the epic on Christ's overcoming of Satan's temptations. At the close of Book VI of *Paradise Lost* Adam is warned to profit by having heard from Raphael "By terrible Example the reward / Of disobedience" (VI, 910-911). At the opening of the crucial Book IX full allusion is made to the source once again in language that connects the allusion to the poem's opening lines, as Milton changes his notes to tragic to speak of

> foul distrust, and breach
> Disloyal on the part of Man, revolt,
> And disobedience . . .
> . . . . . . . . .
> That brought into this World a world of woe,
> Sinne and her shadow Death.
> (*P. L.*, IX, 6-8, 11-12)

After man's disobedience and eventual repentance, Michael appears to reveal the future to Adam and gives a theological explanation of the Biblical text on "one mans disobedience" and the "obedience of one." Christ can be the Saviour, Michael says.

> But by fulfilling that which thou didst want,
> Obedience to the Law of God, impos'd
> On penaltie of death, and suffering death,
> The penaltie to thy transgression due
> . . . . . . . . . . . . . . . . .
> The Law of God exact he shall fulfill
> Both by obedience and by love.
> (*P. L.*, XII, 396-399, 402-403)

And, for those who believe in his redemption, "his obedience / Imputed becomes theirs by Faith" (XII, 408-409). Finally Adam can say "henceforth I learne, that to obey is best" (XII, 561). The reader of *Paradise Lost,* through the reiterated allusions to the passage in Romans which contrasts the curse that one man's disobedience brought with the blessing that the obedience of One provides, is made aware of the unified theme of the epic; furthermore, when he comes to read *Paradise Regained* and finds allusion to the same passage in the opening lines of the shorter epic, he is conscious of the continuation of the theme of the effects of disobedience overcome by the effects of obedience.

The Genesis account of the Fall neither identifies Satan with the Serpent nor mentions Satan's being embodied in the Serpent when Eve is tempted. The Biblical statement is made that "the Serpent beguiled Eve through his subtiltie" (II Cor. 11:3), but it is only in the last book of the Bible that Satan is clearly identified as "that old Serpent, called the Devil, and Satan" (Rev. 12:9, 20:2), Apparently taking as his authority the Apocalyptic identification of Satan as a Serpent, Milton calls Satan "th' infernal Serpent" in his very first reference to him in *Paradise Lost* and "Infernal Serpent" in his penultimate reference to him in *Paradise Regained* (*P. L.*, I, 34; *P. R.*, IV, 618). It is interesting to trace Milton's use of the word "serpent" throughout the two poems as Satan deteriorates from the magnificent demigod of *Paradise Lost,* Book I, to the serpentine Tempter of Book IX, and finally to the disgusting, crawling serpent of Book X; from Book XI on to the end of *Paradise Lost,* Satan's designation as Serpent is connected with the promise that the Seed of the woman will bruise his head.[24] In *Paradise Regained* Satan is simply

24. "Serpent" is used with reference directly or indirectly to Satan only once each in *P. L.,* Books I, II, and IV (ll. 34, 652, and 347 respectively); it is used twice in Book VII (ll. 482, 495), thirteen times in Book IX (ll. 86, 161, 182, 413, 455, 560, 615, 647, 764, 785, 867, 930, 1150), thirteen times in Book X (ll. 3, 84, 162, 165, 174, 495, 514, 580, 867, 879, 927, 1032, 1034), and four times in Book XII (ll. 150, 234, 383, 454). Satan is referred to as "Serpent" once in each of the four books of *P. R.* (I, 312; II, 147; III, 5; IV, 618), the last time being the same phrase ("Infernal Serpent") as the first reference to him in *P. L.* He is also called "Snake" (*P. L.* IX, 613, 643), "Adder" (IX, 625), and "Worm" (IX, 1068). Interesting too is the carryover of the comparison of Satan to a star in *P. L.*, VII, 133 and X, 426, 450, to *P. R.*, IV, 619. His starry brightness, however, is "false glitter" (*P. L.*, X, 450).

the "old serpent" of Scripture with all his wiles and wickedness intact but with most of his eloquent bombast and imposing stature gone. But even when Satan is most impressive and apparently heroic in *Paradise Lost,* it should be remembered that he is introduced in the poem as "th' infernal Serpent."

Milton makes particularly effective use of repetitions of the statement in Genesis that "the Serpent was more subtill than any beast of the field which the LORD God had made" (3:1a). Raphael first uses the line (Milton substitutes a superlative for the Scriptural comparative) as he describes the living creatures created by God on the sixth day:

> The Serpent suttl'st Beast of all the field,
> Of huge extent somtimes, with brazen Eyes
> And hairie Main terrific, though to thee
> Not noxious, but obedient at thy call.
> (*P. L.*, VII, 495-498)

When Satan re-enters the Garden and searches for a creature which might serve his wiles best, he finds and chooses "The Serpent suttlest Beast of all the Field" (IX, 86). When the Biblical line is repeated the third and final time in the epic, it is varied to form Eve's amazed address to the Serpent:

> Thee, Serpent, suttlest beast of all the field
> I knew, but not with human voice endu'd.
> (*P. L.*, IX, 560-561)

These three references to the Serpent as "suttlest beast"—the innocent irony of Raphael's designation of the Serpent as "Not noxious, but obedient at thy call" (VII, 498), the poet's explanation of Satan's choice of the Serpent as his instrument (IX, 86), and Eve's unsuspecting surprise at the Serpent's voice (IX, 560)—form the crux of the many allusions to Satan as "Serpent" listed here both in text and in notes, for it is in these three references that the Devil and his instrument become inextricably identified in the reader's mind. Neither the angels (X, 1-5, 19-21) nor man (IX, 1067-1069) nor woman (IX, 1149-1150) can ever afterward have a simple admiration for the Serpent as such; he has become, though a beast, identified as Satan. He too must be judged, and from being the "suttlest" of beasts he becomes the lowest of them "accurst / Above all Cattel, each Beast of the Field" (X, 175-176) to crawl on his belly and eat the dust. Throughout the remainder of *Paradise Lost* and throughout *Paradise Regained* the Serpent is Satan and Satan is the Serpent and, as Satan's daughter was serpentine in her lower parts, Satan and his followers are transformed periodically into crawling serpents. After Book X (and including X, 1032-1034), all the references to the Serpent in *Paradise Lost* are connected with the promise of his future bruising by the Seed of the woman.[25] Thus mention of the Serpent shifts from an evocation of fearful anticipation on the part of the reader in *Paradise Lost*, Books I through IX, to hope of redemption through Christ in Books X through XII and on through *Paradise Regained.*

Allusions are made frequently and with increasing significance in both epics to the Biblical statements that Satan is, since the Fall, "the prince of the power of the aire" (Eph. 2:2), that Christ has triumphed over Satan in his own domain of the air at the resurrection when he "ascended up on high [leading] captivitie captive" (Eph. 4:8), and that Christ will triumph completely over Satan at his Second Advent:[26] "For the Lord himselfe shall descend from

25. Reiteration of the Scriptural phrases "seed of the woman" and "woman's seed" occurs frequently in *P. L.*, beginning with God's judgment of the Serpent in X, 180, and continuing through the poem (X, 499, 965, 999, 1031; XI, 116, 155; XII, 125, 148, 233, 260, 273, 327, 379, 395, 450, 543, 600, 623). Edward S. Le Comte (*Yet Once More* [New York, 1953], p. 165) says that so many repetitions of the "seed" theme in Book XII indicate that Milton "put a merely mechanical trust in the letter of Scripture" to overcome the preponderant gloom of the final books by repeated allusion to the promise of the Redeemer. The variation of structure and context of the reiterations, however, keep them from being "merely mechanical"; but even if they are considered mechanical, they achieve the desired effect in the mind of the Bible-centered Christian, which is to emphasize the fortunate aspects of the Fall. The many allusions of *P. L.*, Book XII, are echoed three times in *P. R.*, Book I (ll. 54, 64, 151), twice by Satan himself and once by God the Father.

26. The triumph of Christ is also suggested by the use of a Biblical line as a form of address. God's mode of address to His saints in Book V —"Thrones, Dominations, Princedoms, Vertues, Powers" (l. 601)—is anticipated in the action of *P. L.* by Satan's address to his fallen hosts, "Princes, Potentates" (I, 315) and "Powers and Dominions, Deities of Heav'n" (II, 11). The Biblical allusion is both to Paul's portrayal of Christ as the one by and for whom all things were created "whether they be Thrones, or Dominions, or Principalities, or Powers" (Col. 1:16) and to the Biblical identification of Satan as "prince of the power of the aire" (Eph. 2:2). The reiteration of God's exact form of address by Satan as he incites rebellion (V, 772) intensifies his blasphemous disloyalty while it suggests, through Biblical

heaven with a shout, with the voyce of the Archangell, and with the trumpe of God: and the dead in Christ shall rise first: Then we which are alive & remaine shall be caught up together with them in the clouds, to meete the Lord in the aire: and so shall we ever be with the Lord" (I Thess. 4:16).

The key word Milton uses to evoke these Biblical truths of Satan's present reign in the air and of Christ's final triumph over him in his own realm is "air." Since the scope of his major epic is so all-inclusive, Milton begins his allusions to these passages in the speeches of the devils in Hell as they plan for a better domain before a created earth with an atmosphere of air ever existed. He continues to use these allusions to show how Satan and his offspring and followers came into possession of the air, to emphasize the changes that were wrought in the air and on the earth by man's sin, and to foreshadow, even from Book II, Christ's ultimate triumph in the air. Then allusions to the same texts are used in *Paradise Regained* to demonstrate that, although Satan and his cohorts have possession of the air, Christ's standing firm against every temptation of the Devil gives infallible assurance that Christ will triumph over Satan in his resurrection and second coming as prophesied in the Bible and alluded to in both epics.

Being winged creatures, once the devils have raised themselves from the fiery lake of Hell, they are in the "air" of Hell much more than on the land (*P. L.*, I, 226, 516, 545, 767; II, 528, 540, etc.).

---

allusion, the irony of his position as a rebel against his own Creator. When the same words are applied by the faithful Abdiel to "all the Spirits of Heav'n" as having been created by the Son (V, 840), the full impact of Satan's willful disobedience and its inevitable consequences are felt. When Satan rolls out the mighty line for his last time (X, 460), he has been anticipated by Milton's use of the words to describe those who accompanied the Son to Heaven's Gate as he descended to judge Adam, Eve, and the Serpent (X, 86-87). Satan's metamorphosis into a real serpent follows almost immediately after his final reiteration of the line (X, 460), and God soon predicts the Son's victory over Satan, Sin, and Death; Satan's presumption in using the divine words is appropriately rewarded. Not in the order of Milton's presentation, but in the order of strict chronology, the initial treachery of Satan is stressed by his imitation of God's form of address, there is a long period in which he uses only shortened and modified versions of God's words, and, finally, there is his use of the full formula again to signalize his "victory," a victory which is shown explicitly to be what the Biblical allusions of the heavenly titles have implied all along: a Pyrrhic victory.

But the overwhelming response to Beelzebub's plan for invading the new universe indicates that the fallen angels dislike (to use litotes) the atmosphere of Hell and, although they would like to believe such advisers as Belial and Mammon, that they have not really believed it possible for them to settle down there, get acclimated, and live happily ever after. As soon as the vote of the assembly has been cast in favor of his plan, Beelzebub speaks of the devils' hope of being once more lifted up, perhaps nearer their ancient seats, perhaps to some mild zone of light, where

> the soft delicious Air,
> To heal the scarr of these corrosive Fires
> Shall breath her balme,
> (*P. L.*, II, 400-402)

instead of remaining in this horrible place where "the parching Air / Burns frore, and cold performs th' effect of Fire" (II, 594-595). That Satan, too, shares the hope of possessing a more pleasant climate and one in which he can do more injury to the works of God is shown by his promise to Sin and Death to win a better kingdom for them and to give them the privilege to "Wing silently the buxom Air" of Earth and "be fed and fill'd (II, 842-843). Finally, after struggling through Chaos and winging through the "dun Air sublime" (III, 72) of the outside rim of the universe, Satan enters the solar system, winding with ease "Through the pure marble Air his oblique way" (III, 564). Although he gets entangled in his own lies when he is caught in Paradise by Gabriel's forces, Satan is known by the reader to be giving a genuine reason when he says, his words alluding to the Biblical phrase, "prince of the power of the aire" (Eph. 2:2), that he has come to Eden

> here in hope to find
> Better abode, and my afflicted Powers
> To settle here on Earth, or in mid Aire.
> (*P. L.*, IV, 938-940)

But before being surprised by the guardian angels, Satan has successfully gained entrance to Adam's bower in the form of a toad and has caused Eve to dream of the forbidden fruit. In her account of the dream to Adam, Eve quotes the bright being (Satan) of her dream as having said of the fruit,

> Taste this, and be henceforth among the Gods
> Thy self a Goddess, not to Earth confind,
> But sometimes in the Air, as wee.
> (*P. L.*, V, 77-79)

Later, in his actual temptation of Eve, Satan echoes the suggestion that Eve has a right to power in the air as well as on the earth. He expresses surprise that God has said "Of all these Garden Trees ye shall not eate" although Adam and Eve are "Lords declar'd of all in Earth or Aire" (IX, 657-658). Of course, Satan is lying and knows it; that one tree only is prohibited and that Adam is the one who has dominion he has learned long ago. There is the subtle insinuation that God has been unfair, and little by little Eve adopts Satan's point of view that God has indeed been unfair to deny her and her husband anything. Satan's purpose is to gain both the earth and the air for his province; he accomplishes it by the temptation and fall of Eve and the consequent fall of Adam, and one method by which he brings about Eve's sin is to implant in her the inordinate desire to be a goddess of the air. It is a vain hope for her, but her belief in it and her action upon that belief brings about the fulfillment of Satan's hope. No sooner has sin entered in power than it follows in body (X, 585-586) and Sin and Death launch out on their bridge-building voyage to Earth, Death upturning "His Nostril wide into the murkie Air, / Sagacious of his Quarrey from so farr" (X, 279-281). Meeting them, Satan gives the pair a charge blasphemously similar to that given Adam by God:

> right down to Paradise descend:
> There dwell & Reign in bliss, thence on the Earth
> Dominion exercise and in the Aire,
> Chiefly on Man, sole Lord of all declar'd.
> (*P. L.*, X, 398-401)

Through repetition of allusions to Satan's dominion in the air, Milton has brought the reader from Hell, where the devils merely hoped to gain a better abode (better both in the sense of its being more pleasant and of its forming a base of destructive operations against the works of God), to Earth, where the Fall has occurred and Satan, Sin, and Death have invaded the once pure air. Changes are bound to take place and they are not long in coming. The

Judge takes pity on Adam and Eve because they stand before him "naked to the aire, that now / Must suffer change" (X, 212-213), and Adam soon finds that night is not as it was

> ere man fell
> Wholsom and cool, and mild, but with black Air
> Accompanied, with damps and dreadful gloom.
> (*P. L.*, X, 846-848)

Soon other signs in Nature serve as bad omens to Adam; the first signs of enmity and violence between other creatures takes place in the air.

> Nature first gave Signs, impress
> On Bird, Beast, Aire, Aire suddenly eclips'd
> After short blush of Morn.
> (*P. L.*, XI, 182-184)

Adam sees an eagle pursue two smaller, beautifully colored birds toward the east; then a lion stalks a hart and hind toward the Eastern Gate. Adam recognizes "this double object in our sight / Of flight pursu'd in th' Air and ore the ground" (XI, 201-202) as prognosticators of "some furder change" (XI, 193). The change is, of course, that he and Eve are to be banned from the Garden, but a very significant change has already taken place: Satan and his evil offspring have begun their pernicious influence in the air.

All the references in *Paradise Lost* to Satan's power in the air, however, are not favorable to him. Milton has given hints and even explicit statements that point forward to Christ's victory in the air, a victory over Satan in Satan's own realm. The first allusion is a mere hint in an epic simile used to describe the impending battle between Satan and Death at the gates of Hell:

> as when two black Clouds
> With Heav'ns Artillery fraught, come rattling on
> Over th' *Caspian*, then stand front to front
> Hov'ring a space, till Winds the signal blow
> To joyn thir dark Encounter in mid air:
> So frownd the mighty Combatants
> . . . . . . . so matcht they stood;
> For never but once more was either like
> To meet so great a foe.
> (*P. L.*, II, 714-719, 720-722)

If this image of the two clouds encountering in "mid air" (with its hint that neither Satan nor Death will ever but once again meet a foe so great) is remembered when Christ announces his coming victory over Satan in Book III, the effect of the allusion is even more powerful. Christ promises,

> I through the ample Air in Triumph high
> Shall lead Hell Captive maugre Hell, and show
> The powers of darkness bound.
>
> (*P. L.*, III, 254-256)

When the Son as Judge pronounces the curse on the Serpent and announces that the Seed of the woman will bruise the Serpent's head, Milton makes the fullest and most explicit of his allusions to the texts in Scripture concerning Satan's princedom in the air, Christ's triumph over Satan in the air, and Christ's deliverance of those who have been enslaved by Sin and Death ("Captivity led captive," X, 188 with Eph. 4:8). The poet says of the Son of God's statement about the Serpent's future defeat:

> So spake this Oracle,[27] then verifi'd
> When *Jesus* son of *Mary* second *Eve*,
> Saw Satan fall like Lightning down from Heav'n,
> Prince of the Aire; then rising from his Grave
> Spoild Principalities and Powers, triumpht
> In open shew, and with ascention bright
> Captivity led captive through the Aire,
> The Realme it self of Satan long usurpt,
> Whom he shall tread at last under our feet;
> Eevn hee who now foretold his fatal bruise.
>
> (*P. L.*, X, 182-191)

In addition to those already noted, there is allusion here to Colossians: "having spoyled principalities and powers, he made a shew

27. Reiterations of "oracle" in *P. L.* and *P. R.* are interesting to note. The first reference (*P. L.*, I, 12) is to the Temple in Jerusalem; the reference above from Book X is to Christ himself as the Word, the Logos, of God. The term is used by Christ of himself and of the Spirit in *P. R.* (I, 460, and I, 463, respectively) as a rebuke to Satan, who had claimed to be a friend of man through "oracles . . . Whereby they may direct their future life" (*P. R.*, I, 395-396). Christ shows the great disservice Satan has done man by his so-called oracles which mix "somewhat true to vent more lyes" (*P. R.*, I, 433) and announces that "Oracles are ceast" (*P. R.*, I, 456) now that God has sent his Son as "living Oracle" and his Spirit as "inward Oracle" (*P. R.*, I, 460, 463). Satan, with his Serpent wiles, seeks to pick

of them openly, triumphing over them in it" (2:15). One last allusion in *Paradise Lost,* that by Michael in Book XII (the book in which all repetitive Biblical allusions in the poem find their culmination), speaks of Christ's triumph.

> Then to the Heav'n of Heav'ns he shall ascend
> With victory, triumphing through the aire
> Over his foes and thine; there shall surprise
> The Serpent, Prince of aire, and drag in Chaines
> Through all his realme, & there confounded leave.
> (*P. L.*, XII, 451-455)

As *Paradise Regained* opens, the clock is turned back to time preceding that of the victory in the final visions of Adam in *Paradise Lost,* to the time of the life of Christ when Satan still possessed his realm of air. Satan speeds to "his place . . . in mid air" (*P. R.*, I, 39) upon witnessing the baptism of Jesus, and addresses his "gloomy Consistory":

> O ancient Powers of Air and this wide world
> For much more willingly I mention Air,
> This our old Conquest, then remember Hell
> Our hated habitation. (*P. R.*, I, 44-47)

He further expresses the hope that "that long threatn'd wound" from the Seed of the woman will not take away all the devils' power, freedom, and being "In this fair Empire won of Earth and Aire" (I, 63). But Satan's fair empire of earth and air was won by fraud, by his deception of Eve and her temptation of Adam; he is soon to discover that the man with whom he has now to deal will overcome all his temptations and deceptions and will thus make it absolutely certain that Satan is going to lose his realm through man as he gained it through man.

Although Satan boasts to Christ that he enjoys

> Large liberty to round this Globe of Earth,
> Or range in th' Air,
> (*P. R.*, I, 365-366)

---

this reference up later and use it to tempt Christ to "be as the Oracle" to Kings and nations (*P. R.*, III, 13); again he seizes on Christ's praise of Socrates (III, 96 ff) to make the subtle suggestion that the oracles must be accurate after all since "well-inspir'd the Oracle pronounc'd [Socrates] Wisest of men" (IV, 275-276).

and shows his dominion of the air by transporting Christ through the air and giving him visions "multiplyed through air" (IV, 41), actually Satan is so utterly defeated in his own boasted realm when Christ stands upright on the pinnacle of the Temple that he is aptly compared to Antaeus, who, although "Throttl'd . . . in the Air" (IV, 568) as Satan is, was defeated because he was out of touch with his own element, the earth. Satan is foiled in the territory of which he is the self-proclaimed prince. The effect is to emphasize that Satan's dominion of the air is a usurper's rule; the true ruler is the Son of God as demonstrated by his standing while Satan falls.

When Satan falls, a globe of elect angels hasten to minister to Christ and bear him through the "blithe Air" (IV, 585), happy in the assurance that Satan's ultimate doom is sealed; this victory of Christ in the wilderness makes sure all his future victories. The angels address Satan in their song and prophesy his doom on the basis of his failure to tempt the Son of God into any disobedience or even imprudence.

> But thou, Infernal Serpent, shalt not long
> Rule in the Clouds: like an Autumnal Star
> Or Lightning thou shalt fall from Heav'n trod down
> Under his feet: for proof, e're this thou feel'st
> Thy wound, yet not thy last and deadliest wound
> By this repulse receiv'd. (*P. R.*, IV, 618-623)

The fact that Christ's triumph in the wilderness has not finished the work of redemption is made clear by the hymn; indeed, that Christ has not even begun that part of his work which shall save mankind but has merely proved his ability to defeat Satan and "re-install" man in Paradise "when time shall be" (IV, 616) is stated in the final words of the angelic host: "Queller of Satan, on thy glorious work / Now enter, and begin to save mankind" (IV, 634-635).

Milton's epic similes are formed in language that elevates the material of *Paradise Lost* to a level of high seriousness and those which are drawn from the Bible are especially effective in this way as well as in providing a stimulating variety of background for the action of the epic and in stressing the dominant theme of the epic: that God rules the universe in eternal providence in such a way as to bring good out of evil. It is the acceptance of this theme that makes God's ways appear justified and justifiable to men. In addition, the chains of reiteration in Biblical allusions, notably of this last chain formed by links of reference to Satan's and Christ's relationship to the earth and the air, bind into one theme the individual epics and even bind the two epics together into a thematic whole, though not a structural or stylistic whole. *Paradise Lost* is a complete whole and so is *Paradise Regained;* the latter epic, however, supplements and reinforces the great truths of the former. Milton must have been especially happy that in writing *Paradise Regained* he had not only continued the great theme of the obedience of one man overcoming what had befallen because of the disobedience of one; he had also produced a poem which would not leave

> the better fortitude
> Of Patience and Heroic Martyrdom
> Unsung
>
> (*P. L.*, IX, 31-33)

but would portray this particular kind of heroism in its highest manifestation: the "patient Son of God" undergoing temptation in "calm and sinless peace" (*P. R.*, IV, 420, 425).

## Conclusion

THE SHEER cumulative weight of the evidence presented on the preceding pages should aid one in evaluating Milton as a Biblical poet, and, even if there were no other benefits to be gained from the study than this merely mechanical one of making the Biblical saturation of Milton's mind and, consequently, of his great epic poems more evident, this study should be worthwhile. A greater end than this, however, was envisioned from the beginning and some elements of this greater end were indicated in the introduction; it is hoped that the more important result of bringing the student of Milton to a fuller appreciation of the nature, extent, and poetic effect of the Biblical saturation of *Paradise Lost* and *Paradise Regained* has been achieved. There remain a few general conclusions to be drawn from what has gone before; but first a basic principle which has been mentioned several times in the preceding chapters needs emphasizing again. Although Biblical words, phrases, idiom, structure, repetitions, and epithets are pervasive and pregnant with suggestion throughout Milton's epics, nowhere does the reader need more than a fraction of the thorough knowledge of the Bible which the poet himself enjoyed in order to get the meaning of a passage. Like Milton's classical allusions, most of the Biblical ones are accompanied by enough information in the poem to supply the significant surface meaning without recognition of the particular Biblical incident, person, or principle being alluded to. The allusions in general require no such annotation, or even reserach into obscure secondary works, which, say, the poetry of T. S. Eliot sometimes requires. It is true, however, that the deepening and broadening of the meaning of Milton's poems require a better than casual knowledge of the Bible. If the seed of suggestion Milton sows falls upon good ground, it will bring forth a hundredfold. But even if the seed falls by the wayside and never takes root, there is enough material in the poems to carry the reader along with Milton's meaning. An example is Satan's speech in *Paradise Lost,* Book I, (ll. 570-573). Since Milton says that Satan hardens his heart and glories in his pride, the clue for the interpretation is explicit; however, the implications of the Biblical allusion, which associates Satan with the proud Nebuchadnezzar of Babylon, greatly enrich the reader's understanding of Satan when the allusion is recognized.

Above all, a careful study of Milton's use of the Bible in his epic poems reveals the artist's great mind acting as a prism through which the light of the Bible passes to be broken up into all the colors of the rainbow: he communicates the authority of Biblical truth, instills confidence in the ultimate triumph of God and good, dramatically develops character and action, orders emotion, and raises awe and admiration for the Almighty, especially as He is manifested in His Son. The theme which runs through all Milton's uses of the Bible in his epics is "The Lord God omnipotent reigneth!" (Rev. 19:6). Even when the main purpose of Biblical allusion is to communicate authoritative reality, there is the underlying, figural, foreshadowing connection between persons, events, and places in God's transcendent universal scheme of eternal providence. Milton's linguistic skill is used to affect the reader's attitude towards the characters of his epic drama in relation to God's purposes; Satan's name, the names of the human pair, of Eden, emphasize the nature and cause of the loss of Paradise but at the same time suggest the eternal life and happier Paradise which will be the final result. Milton's use of the original Scriptures underscores such important elements as Heaven's far-reaching view of events taking place on the little globe of earth and the nature of Christ's victory over Satan. His use of the Bible for dramatic effect intensifies the theme of God's omnipotent providence, especially in the delineation of character. Satan is doomed to defeat like the Biblical villains with whom he is associated by allusion; Adam, though he falls, is assured of salvation for himself and for his posterity by his identification with faithful Abraham and the second Adam; Eve, more sinned against than sinning, since she is the weaker vessel who should have been ruled by Adam, is connected with Mary, the "second *Eve,*" from whose womb will come the promised Seed to bruise the Serpent's head. Particularly in the similes and reiterated allusions of his peculiarly epic uses of the Bible, Milton has sounded and resounded the *motif* of God's ultimate victory. The connotation of every Biblical simile, and even many of the classical similes, is defeat for Satan and victory for God and for man through Christ; reiterations of Biblical phrases throughout both epics suggest, over and over, the means by which man will regain lost Paradise and overcome the Tempter.

Milton himself, the man and the poet, comes through clearly as a result of his use of the Bible in his epic poems. The vast knowledge of the Bible in four languages, the consummate skill with which he selected and arranged his allusions to the Bible, and the delicate, sensuous, yet universal beauty that the Biblical account of Adam and Eve in the Garden of Eden takes on in the major epic increase one's admiration for the superbly sustained discipline which Milton achieves. And in both epics, an impression of the firm moral principles of this Christian humanist and his rather Hebraic manliness, though communicated in other ways as well, is reinforced by his use of the Bible.

One of his most impressive intellectual and artistic feats is the transmutation of Biblical, classical, and historical allusions into something peculiarly Miltonic, a something which is artistically a new creation, greater than the sum of its parts. That his mind could be so filled with classical, theological, scientific, Scriptural, and historical lore is amazing; but more amazing still is the ability of his mind to carry so much material in solution until the artistically appropriate moment and then to fuse that rapidly flowing intellectual and emotional turbidity and crystallize out of it periods of such structural wholeness and thematic unity as that period which opens Book IX of *Paradise Lost* (ll. 1-41). The period is not a mosaic formed of diverse elements fitted together; rather, it is a unified creation in which elements (including the personal) which were once diverse have been structurally, psychologically, and metrically assimilated into a Miltonic whole.

The man who strove to form of his own life a "true poem" and was conscious from an early age of possessing the *os magna soniturum,* the mouth formed for great utterances, became, for more than a century after the publication of his major works, almost an Authorized Version himself.[1] He is far from that today. But, in the light of his use of the Bible in his epic poems, the fact that neither Milton nor the Authorized Version of the English Bible (however much either or both may have been ignored) has ever been successfully equaled or supplanted by imitators or rivals seems peculiarly appropriate.

1. An interesting example of the fusing of Milton and the Bible in the mind of a poet as late as the nineteenth century is discussed by Professor Ants Oras in "The Multitudinous Orb: Some Miltonic Elements in Shelley," *MLQ*, XVI (1955), 247-257. After comparing Milton's "Chariot of Paternal Deitie" in *P. L.*, VI, 749-850, with Shelley's *Prometheus Unbound*, IV, 236-283, and after analyzing the parallels in both poetic passages with the common Biblical source, the first chapter of Ezekiel, Professor Oras concludes: "Milton and the Bible seem, at least occasionally, to have been mingled for Shelley in an inextricable total impression, with the imagery and phraseology of Milton tending to predominate."

# *Bibliography*


### Bibles

Biblia Hebraica. Eorundem Latina Interpretatio Xanti Pagnini Lucensis, Recenter Benedict Ariae Montani Hispal. & quorundam aliorum collato studio, ad Hebraicam dictionem diligentissimè expensa. Antverpiae, Ex officina Christophori Plantini. M. D. LXXXIIII.

Novum Testamentum Graecum, cum vulgata interpretatione Latina Graeci contextus lineis inserta: Quae quidem interpretatio cùm à Graecarum dictionum proprietate disedit, sensum, videlicet, magis quàm verba experimens, in margine libriest collocata: atque alia Ben. Ariae Montani Hispalensis operâ è verbo reddita, ac diverso characterum genere distincta, in eius est substituta locum. Antverpiae, Ex officina Christophori Plantini. M. D. LXXXIIII. (This Greek New Testament is bound with the Hebrew Old Testament listed above; together they constitute the Antwerp Polyglot of 1584.)

Biblia Sacra. Vulgate Editionis, Sixti V. et Clementis VIII. Londoni: Sumptibus Samuelis Bagster, n.d.

The Holy Bible, Conteyning the Old Testament and the new: newly translated out of the Originall tongues: & with the former translations diligently compared and revised by his Maiesties special Commandement. Appointed to be read in the Churches. Imprinted at London by Robert Barker, Printer to the Kings most Excellent Maiestie, Anno Dom. 1612.

### Bible Reference Works

Berkhof, Louis. *Principles of Biblical Interpretation.* Grand Rapids, Mich.: Baker Book House, 1950.

Butterworth, Charles C. *The Literary Lineage of the King James Bible.* Philadelphia: University of Pennsylvania Press, 1941.

Daiches, David. *The King James Version of the English Bible: An Account of the Development and Sources of the English Bible of 1611 with Special Reference to the Hebrew Tradition.* Chicago: The University of Chicago Press, 1941.

Young, Robert. *Analytical Concordance to the Bible.* Grand Rapids, Mich.: Wm. B. Eerdmans Publishing Company, 1955. 22nd American ed.

### Editions of Milton

Hughes, Merritt Y. (ed.). *John Milton: Complete Poems and Major Prose.* New York: The Odyssey Press, 1957.

————. *Paradise Lost.* New York: The Odyssey Press, 1935.

————. *Paradise Regained, the Minor Poems, and Samson Agonistes.* Garden City, N. Y.: Doubleday, Doran & Company, 1937.

Masson, David (ed.). *The Poetical Works of John Milton.* 3 vols. London: Macmillan and Co., Ltd., 1910. First published, 1874.

Patterson, Frank Allen (ed.). *The Student's Milton.* New York: F. S. Crofts & Co., 1947. First published, 1930.

________. *The Works of John Milton.* 18 vols. New York: Columbia University Press, 1931.

Todd, Henry John (ed.). *The Poetical Works of John Milton.* 6 vols. London: Bye and Law, 1801.

Verity, A. W. (ed.). *Milton: Paradise Lost.* 2 vols. Cambridge: The Cambridge University Press, 1936. First published, 1910.

EDITIONS FROM WHICH OTHER AUTHORS ARE CITED

Brooke, C. F. Tucker and Nathaniel Burton Paradise (eds.). *English Drama, 1580-1642.* Boston: D. C. Heath and Co., 1933. (Marlowe.)

Coffin, Robert P. Tristram and Alexander M. Witherspoon (eds.). *Seventeenth Century Prose and Poetry.* New York: Harcourt, Brace and Co., 1946. First published, 1929. (Sir Thomas Browne.)

Corrie, George E. (ed.). *The Works of Hugh Latimer.* Cambridge: The Cambridge University Press, 1844-45.

Neilson, William Allan and Charles Jarvis Hill (eds.). *The Complete Plays and Poems of William Shakespeare.* Cambridge, Mass.: Houghton Mifflin Co., 1942.

Palmer, George Herbert (ed.). *The Odyssey of Homer: The Text, and an English Version in Rhythmic Prose.* Boston: Houghton Mifflin Co., 1899.

Skeat, Walter W. (ed.). *The Vision of William Concerning Piers the Plowman.* 2 vols. Oxford: The Clarendon Press, 1886.

Vergilius Maro, Publius. *Aeneid.* Translated by C. Day Lewis. New York: Oxford University Press, 1952.

BOOKS

Auerbach, Erich. *Mimesis: The Representation of Reality in Western Literature.* Translated by Willard Trask. New York: Doubleday & Co., Inc., 1957. First published, 1946, Berne, Switzerland.

Banks, Theodore Howard. *Milton's Imagery.* New York: Columbia University Press, 1950.

Barker, Arthur. *Milton and the Puritan Dilemma.* Toronto: The University of Toronto Press, 1942.

Bowra, C. M. *From Virgil to Milton.* London: Macmillan & Co., Ltd., 1948.

Bush, Douglas. *Paradise Lost in Our Time: Some Comments.* Gloucester, Mass.: Peter Smith, 1957. First published, 1945.

________. *The Renaissance and English Humanism.* Toronto: The University of Toronto Press, 1939.

Conklin, George Newton. *Biblical Criticism and Heresy in Milton.* New York: King's Crown Press, 1949.

Cook, Albert S. (ed.). *Addison's Criticisms on Paradise Lost.* New York: G. E. Stechert & Co., 1926.

Darbishire, Helen. *Milton's Paradise Lost.* London: Oxford University Press, 1951.

Fletcher, Harris Francis. *Milton's Rabbinical Readings.* Urbana: University of Illinois Press, 1930.

________. *The Use of the Bible in Milton's Prose.* Urbana: University of Illinois Press, 1929.

Hanford, James Holly. *A Milton Handbook* (4th ed.). New York: Appleton-Century-Crofts, Inc., 1954. First published, 1926.

Johnson, Samuel. *Lives of the English Poets,* ed. George Birkbeck Hill. 3 vols. London: Oxford University Press, 1905.

Joseph, Sister Miriam. *Orthodoxy in Paradise Lost.* Quebec: Les Presses Universitaires Laval, 1954.

Kelley, Maurice. *This Great Argument: A Study of Milton's De Doctrina Christiana as a Gloss upon Paradise Lost.* Princeton: Princeton University Press, 1941.

Le Comte, Edward S. *Yet Once More: Verbal and Psychological Pattern in Milton.* New York: Liberal Arts Press, 1953.

Lewis, C. S. *A Preface to Paradise Lost.* London: Oxford University Press, 1942.

Myhr, Ivar Lou. *The Evolution and Practice of Milton's Epic Theory.* Nashville, Tenn.: The Joint University Libraries, Vanderbilt University, 1942. (A summary of a doctoral thesis.)

Oras, Ants. *Milton's Editors and Commentators from Patrick Hume to Henry John Todd (1695-1801): A Study in Critical Views and Methods.* London: Oxford University Press, 1931.

Pope, Elizabeth Marie. *Paradise Regained: The Tradition and the Poem.* Baltimore: The Johns Hopkins Press, 1947.

Prince, F. T. *The Italian Element in Milton's Verse.* London: Oxford University Press, 1954.

Rajan, B. *Paradise Lost and the Seventeenth Century Reader.* London: Chatto & Windus, 1947.

Stein, Arnold. *Answerable Style: Essays on Paradise Lost.* Minneapolis: University of Minnesota Press, 1953.

———. *Heroic Knowledge: An Interpretation of Paradise Regained and Samson Agonistes.* Minneapolis: University of Minnesota Press, 1957.

Thorpe, James (ed.). *Milton Criticism: Selections from Four Centuries.* New York: Rinehart & Co., Inc., 1950.

Tillyard, E. M. W. *The English Epic and Its Background.* London: Chatto & Windus, 1954.

———. *Milton.* London: Chatto & Windus, 1946.

———. *Studies in Milton.* London: Chatto & Windus, 1951.

West, Robert H. *Milton and the Angels.* Athens: University of Georgia Press, 1955.

Willey, Basil. *The Seventeenth Century Background.* New York: Doubleday & Co., Inc., 1953. First published, 1934.

Woodhull, Marianna. *The Epic of Paradise Lost.* New York: G. P. Putnam's Sons, 1907.

## Articles and Essays

Allen, Don Cameron. "Milton's Amarant," *Modern Language Notes,* LXXII (1957), 256-258.

Baxter, Wynne E. "Milton Bibles," *Notes and Queries,* III (1911), 109-110.

Cormican, L. A. "Milton's Religious Verse," *A Guide to English Literature,* ed. Boris Ford, III, 173-192. London: Penguin Books Ltd., 1956.

Eliot, T. S. *Milton: Annual Lecture on a Master Mind* (Henriette Hertz Trust, read 26 March 1947), from the Proceedings of the British Academy, Vol. XXXIII. London: Geoffrey Cumberlege Amen House, 1947.

Hanford, James Holly. "The Dramatic Element in Paradise Lost," *Studies in Philology,* XIV (1917), 178-195.

Huxley, Aldous. "Accidie," *Great Essays,* ed. Houston Peterson, pp. 367-371. New York: Pocket Books, Inc., 1954.

———. "The Multitudinous Orb: Some Miltonic Elements in Shelley," *Modern Language Quarterly,* XVI (1955), 247-257.

Oras, Ants. "'Goddess Humane' ('Paradise Lost' IX. 732)," *Modern Language Notes,* XLIX (1954), 51-53.

Potter, George. "Milton Bibles," *Notes and Queries,* III (1911), 70.

Summers, J. H. "'Grateful Vicissitude' in *Paradise Lost,*" *Publications of the Modern Language Association,* LXIX (1954), 251-264.

Whiting, G. W. "Without Thorn the Rose," *Review of English Studies,* X (1959), 60-62.

Woodhouse, A. S. P. "Pattern in *Paradise Lost,*" *The University of Toronto Quarterly,* XXII (1953), 109-127.

————. "Theme and Pattern in *Paradise Regained,*" *The University of Toronto Quarterly,* XXV (1956), 167-182.

UNPUBLISHED WORKS

Sims, James H. "Marlowe's Looking-Glass View of Scripture." Unpublished paper, read before the Southeastern Renaissance Conference at Chapel Hill, N. C., April, 1958. Abstract published in "Renaissance Conference," *The South Atlantic Bulletin,* XXIV (May 1958), 10.

Walker, Fred B. "*Milton's Use of the Bible in His Shorter English Poems.* Unpublished M. A. thesis, University of Florida, 1947 (177 pp.).

# *Index of Biblical References*

THIS INDEX lists the Biblical references by line number for both Milton's epics and includes an abbreviated indication of the editors and commentators who have noted each Biblical allusion. Where no abbreviation follows the reference, no previous identification of the reference has been discovered.

Collaborators, contributors, and former editors whose Biblical annotations are included in Todd's edition are indicated by a lower case initial following the abbreviation for Todd. Information on those whose contributions are in Todd (except for Greenwood) may be found in Ants Oras, *Milton's Editors and Commentators* (London, 1931). Abbreviations of the names of books of the Bible are those found in Webster's New Collegiate Dictionary. Line numbering is that of F. A. Patterson in *Student's Milton.* The order is book and line numbers in Milton, chapter and verse numbers in the Bible.

| | |
|---|---|
| T–Henry John Todd | Tg–John Gillies |
| M–David Masson | Tgr–Greenwood |
| V–A. W. Verity | Th–Patrick Hume |
| H–Merritt Y. Hughes | The–John Heylin |
| Ta–Joseph Addison | Tn–Bishop Newton |
| Tbe–Richard Bentley | Tp–Zachary Pearce |
| Tbo–Bowle | Tr–J. Richardson and Son |
| Tc–Calton | Ts–Stillingfleet |
| Td–Charles Dunster | Tth–Robert Thyer |

## PARADISE LOST

### Book I

| Line | Reference |
|---|---|
| 1 | Rom.5:19 |
| 2 | Gen.2:17 |
| 3–5 | Rom.5:12,19(V) |
| 4 | I Cor.15:45,47 |
| 5 | Ps.23:3 |
| 6 | Exod.34:2-3; Wisd.7:27, 8:4(H) |
| 7 | Deut.4:10, Exod.19:18 |
| 8 | Exod.3:1(T); Exod.24: 12-18(M) |
| 9 | Gen.1:1, John 1:1 |
| 10 | Ps.2:6 |
| 11 | Isa.6(T); Neh.3:15, 8:6(M) |
| 12 | Ps.28:2(V) |
| 17–19 | I Cor.6:19, 2:12-13(V) |
| 21 | Gen.1:2, Luke 3:22 (T,V); Luke 11:36 |
| 26 | Rom.3:1-4(T); Ps.51:4 |
| 27–28 | Ps.139:7-8 |
| 32 | Gen.2:16-17 |
| 34 | Rev.12:9 |
| 35b–36 | I Tim.2:14, II Cor.11:3, Gen.3:20 |
| 36 | Ps.56:3(V) |
| 37–38a | Rev.12:9 |
| 38b–39 | Isa.14:13 |
| 40–42 | Isa.14:13-15 |
| 43 | Rev.12:7 |
| 45 | Luke 10:18(V) |

| Line | Reference |
|---|---|
| 47 | Rev.17:8, 19:20, 20:3 |
| 48 | II Pet.2:4(V); Jude 6 (V,H) |
| 54 | Jude 6 |
| 56 | Luke 16:23 |
| 63 | Job 10:22(V); Matt.6: 23, Luke 11:35 |
| 68–69 | Rev.20:10 |
| 70–71 | Matt.25:41 |
| 81 | Matt.12:24 |
| 82 | Job 1:6 |
| 84 | Isa.14:12 |
| 85 | I John 1:5, Rev.21:23 |
| 86 | Ezek.28:17 |
| 101 | Heb.12:22 |
| 111–12 | Phil.2:10-11, Isa.45:23 |
| 117 | Ps.104:4(Tn) |
| 128 | Eph.2:2 |
| 162b–63 | Rom.8:28 |
| 166–67 | Gen.6:6 |
| 184 | Rev.20:10 |
| 186 | Eph.2:2 |
| 188 | Matt.13:39 |
| 201 | Job 41:1(Tn,V); Ps. 74:14(V); Job 41:34 |
| 205–208 | Acts 27:29 |
| 206 | Job 41:15(V) |
| 210 | Rev.21:8 |
| 211–13 | Job 1:12, 2:6 |
| 217 | Ps.76:10 |
| 229 | Rev.20:10 |
| 237–38 | Gen.8:9 |
| 267 | Rev.21:8 |
| 268 | John 14:2, Matt.25:41 |
| 280 | Rev.20:10 |
| 306–11 | Exod.14:23-30 |
| 309 | Gen.45:10; Gen.47:27 (V) |
| 310–11 | Exod.14:25,30 |
| 330 | Eph.5:14 |
| 337 | Rom.6:16(V) |
| 338–43 | Exod.10:12-15(Tn,V, H) |
| 339 | Exod.4:16-20(M) |
| 361–63 | Ps.9:5-6, Rev.3:5(Tg) |
| 365–66 | Job 1:7, 2:2 |
| 367–71 | Rom.1:20,23,25(Tn,V) |
| 373 | Deut.32:17, I Cor.10: 20 |
| 382 | I Pet.5:8(T,V) |
| 386–87 | I Kings 6:23(Th,V); Exod.20:18(V); Ps.80: 1(V,H); II Kings 16: 10-18(H) |
| 387b–391 | Jer.7:30, II Kings 21: 4-5, Ezek.7:20, 8:5-6 (Tn); Exod.25:22, II Kings 19:15(V); II Cor.6:14 |
| 392–396a | II Sam.12:26-29, Judg. 11:12-18(M); Ps.106: 37-38, Amos 5:26(V); Lev.18:21, II Kings 23:20(Th) |
| 396b–97 | II Sam.12:27(Tn,H) |
| 398–99 | Judg.11:12-18, Deut. 3:12(H) |
| 399b–402 | I Kings 11:7, 4:29-31 (Tn,V) |
| 403 | II Kings 23:13(V,H) |
| 404–405 | Jer.7:31(Tn); Jer.19: 5(H) |
| 406 | I Kings 11:7(V) |
| 407–11 | Num.32(V) |
| 408–409 | Num.21:26(V,H); Ps. 135:11, 136:19(H) |
| 410 | Isa.16:8-9(V) |
| 412–14 | Num.25:9(Tn,V,H) |
| 418 | II Kings 23:10-14(Tn, H) |
| 419–20 | Gen.2:14, 15:18(Tn); I Sam.30:10(H) |
| 422 | Judg.2:11-13 |
| 433 | Isa.12:2, I Sam.15:29 |
| 438–39 | Jer.7:18(V); I Kings 11:5 |
| 443 | II Kings 23:13(Tn) |
| 444–46a | I Kings 4:29-31a(V); I Kings 11:1-3 |
| 454–57a | Ezek.8:12-14(Tn,V) |
| 458–61 | I Sam.5:2-5(Tn,V,H) |
| 464–65 | I Sam.5:1-2 |
| 467 | II Kings 5:12-18(V,H) |
| 471–76 | II Kings 5:17, 16:10, II Chron.28:22-23(Tn, V) |
| 483–84 | Exod.12:35(Tn,V); Exod.32:4(V,H) |
| 484b–85 | I Kings 12:28(Tn,V,H) |
| 486 | Ps.106:20(Tn,V) |
| 487–89 | Exod.12:12,29(Tn,H); Num.33:3-4(Tn) |
| 494b–96 | I Sam.12:12-17(Tn,V, H) |
| 500b–505 | Gen.19:4-11, Judg.19: 22-28(Tn,V,H) |
| 508-509 | Deut.32:17, Isa.66:19 (V); Gen.10:2(H) |

534 Lev.16:8(Tn,V,H)
571a I Chron.21:1-2, II Sam. 24:1
571b–73 Dan.5:20(Tg)
591–92 Ezek.28:17
632–33 Rev.12:4(Tn)
645 Luke 10:42(V)
657 Rev.20:1-3
658–59 Rev.20:3, Jude 6
664–65 Gen.3:24
666–67 Ps.21:1-2, 18:13
678–79 Matt.6:24(H)
682 Rev.21:21(Tn,V)
684 Matt.5:8(V,H)
694a Gen.11(V)
710–13 I Kings 6:7
778 Gen.6:4

BOOK II

10 Luke 1:51, Neh.1:11
11 Col.1:16(Tn); Rom. 8:38
66 Rev.4:5
69 Lev.10:1, Num.3:4, 26:61, II Pet.2:4
88 Matt.18:8, Mark 9: 43-44, Jude 7
90 Rom.9:22(Tbe)
95–96 Deut.4:24, Heb.12:29
112–13 Num.11:7
139 Deut.4:24, Ps.104:4(H)
150 Isa.45:7
169 Rev.20:3,10
170 Isa.30:33(Tn,V)
171–72 Dan.3:19
189–90 Zech.4:10, Prov.15:3
191 Ps.2:4(Tn,V,H)
256 Matt.11:30
263 Ps.18:11,13, 97:2(Tn, V,H); II Chron.5:13-6: 1(H)
294 Rev.12:7
323a–25 Rev.1:11, 21:6, 22:13 (V,H)
326b–28 Ps.2:9(V,H); Esth.5:2 (Th); Ps.45:6
348–50 Ps.8:5, Heb.2:6-7
351a–53 Heb.6:17(Tn);Gen. 22:16, Isa.45:23(V); Isa.13:12-13, Heb. 12:26
369–70 Gen.6:7(Tg)
377 Ps.107:10-11
385b–86a Ps.76:10, Gen.50:20
402 Isa.6:8
405 Rev.20:3
406 Exod.10:21(V,H)
427–28 Ps.47:7, Heb.1:9, II Cor.11:14
462a John 14:2
516 Ezek.37:9(V); Matt. 24:31
565 Col. 2:8
576 Rev.19:20, 20:10(V)
594 Ecclus. 43:20-21(Tn,V)
602–603 Job 24:19(Tn)
615–18 Matt.12:43, Luke 11: 24(V)
622–25 Rev.20:14, Isa.45:7
629 Job 1:6, 2:1, I Pet. 5:8(H)
653a I Cor.15:56(T,V)
673 Rev.6:2(V,H); Job 18:14(V)
692 Rev.12:3-4(V,H)
701 I Kings 12:11(V)
721–22 Heb.2:14(Tn,V); I Cor.15:25-26(V,H)
731 Ps.2:4
734 Heb.2:14
751 Isa.14:13-14
757–60 Jas.1:15(H); Ezek.28: 15, I John 3:8
781–83 Jas.1:15
843 Ps.49:14(Tg,V)
857–58 II Pet. 2:4
864–65 Ezek.28:15, I John 3:8
868–69 Rom.5:14,21
884–88 Matt.7:13b
891 Job 41:32(Tg,V)
990 Mark 1:24
994 Ezek.31:16(T)
1026 Matt.7:13
1027b Luke 16:26

BOOK III

1 Gen.1:3
3–4 I John 1:5, I Tim.6:16 (Tn,V,H)
6 Wisd.7:25-26(Tn)
8a Job 38:19(Th)
9–12 Gen.1:3-5(V,H)
10 Ps.104:2
11–12 Gen.1:2
51–53a Eph.1:18(T); II Cor.4:6
58–59 Ps.14:2, 102:18-19
62–63 Heb.1:2-3(Th,V,H)

64 John 1:14, 3:16
66 Gen.2:8
70 Luke 16:26
80 John 1:14, 3:16
85–86 Gen.3:15, I Sam.25:39, II Chron.6:23, Neh.4:4, Ps.7:16, Joel 3:4, Judg. 9:57, Esth.9:25
98–99 Eccles.7:29(Tg)
136 I Tim.5:21(V,H)
139–40 Heb.1:3(Th,H)
141 Matt.9:36, Ps.86:15
142 John 1:14, 3:34, 13:1
149 Rom.1:25, 9:5
153–54 Gen.18:25(Tn,V)
168–69 Matt.3:17(Tn,V,H); John 1:18, Rev.19:3, I Cor.1:24(Tn)
170 John 1:1-3(V,H); I Cor.1:24(H); Eph.3:7
173–75 John 1:12-13, Eph. 2:8-9
180 Ps.139:4(H)
183–88 John 15:16, I Thess. 2:13, Matt.22:14
189 Ezek.36:26(Tg,V)
193 Isa.59:1, Ps.34:15
197 Matt.10:22(Th,V); Heb.3:14
198a II Pet.3:19
198b–200 Heb.3:7-8,11-13
206 Gen.3:5(V)
208 Josh.6:17-18
209 I Cor.15:22a
212 Heb.2:14
215 I Pet.3:18(Tn,V)
217–18 Rev.8:1(Tn,V,H); Heb.9:15(H)
225 Col.2:9(T,V); John 3:35(H)
231 II Tim.1:9, Ps. 88:13(Tr)
233 Col.2:13(V,H); Eph.2:15
234–37 Heb.10:8-10
243b–44 John 5:26(Tn,V)
248–49 Ps.16:10, Acts 2: 26-27 [incorrectly noted as Acts 2:20-21 in T] (Tn,V,H)
251–54 Col.2:15, Ps.68:18 (Tn,V,H)
253 I Cor.15:55
255 Eph.4:8
256 Luke 22:53, Col.1:13
259 I Cor.15:26(Th,V,H); Rev.20:14(V)
265 Ps.16:11(T)
269–71 Ps.40:6-8(Tn); Heb. 10:5-7
278–79 Rom.8:32
284 Isa.7:14, Matt.1:23, John 1:14(H)
285–89 I Cor.11:3, 15:22(Tn, V,H)
290–94 Rom.5:18-19
290b–92 Rom.4:5-8
293–94 Rom.6:4-5
295–97 Heb.2:14-17
297b Matt.20:28
299 Matt.20:28(Tg)
306 Phil.2:6(V); John 5:18, 10:30(H)
317–18 Matt.28:18(Tn,V)
319 Eph.4:15(V)
320 Col.1:16(H)
321–22 Phil.2:10(Tn,V,H)
323–26 Matt.25:30-32(Th,V,H)
324–25 I Thess.4:16(Th,V,H)
327–28 Rev.20:11(Th,H)
329 I Cor.15:51-52(T,V)
330–31 John 5:22
334–35 II Pet.3:12-13(Tn,V)
335 Rev.21:1(Tn,V)
341a I Cor.15:28(Th,V.H)
341b–42 Ps.97:7, Heb.1:6(Tn, V,H)
343 John 5:23(Tn)
351–52 Rev.4:10(Tn)
353 I Pet.1:4, 5:4(Th)
357–58 Ps.36:8, Rev.7:17, 22:1-2(Th,V,H)
363 Rev.4:6(V,H)
365 Rev.5:8(Tg)
372 Rev.19:6
373–75 I Tim.1:17
375 Jer.17:3
377 Exod.33:18-23(Tgr)
382 Isa.6:2(Th,V,H)
383 Col.1:15, Rev.3:14 (Tn); Heb.1:2-3(H)
384 John 3:16
385–86 II Cor.4:6
387 John 1:18, 14:9(Tn)
389 John 3:34
390–91 Col.1:16, John 1:2
401 II Cor.1:3
406–407 Ps.85:10

409–10 Rom.4:25
440–41 Job 1:7, I Pet.5:8
451 Matt.6:5
463–64 Gen.6:4(Tn,V)
466–67 Gen.11:2,4(V,H)
477 John 19:41(V); John 19:17(H)
484–85 Matt.16:19(V)
503–507 Rev.21:12, Tob. 13:16 (T)
510–15 Gen.28:11-17(Tn,V,H)
511 John 1:51
515 Gen.28:17
521 Luke 16:22(Tn,V,H)
522 II Kings 2:11(T,V,H)
525 Rev.4:1(T)
538b–39 Job 28:3(Tg)
580–81 Gen.1:14(H)
597–98 Exod.25:7; Exod.28:17-24(H)
622–23 Rev.19:17(Tn,V,H)
634–39 II Cor.11:14
648 II Esdras(V)
649–51 Zech.4:10, Tob.12:15, Rev.1:4,5,6, 8:2(V)
658 Job 2:1(H)
671–72 Matt.2:8
693 Job 33:3(T)
702–704 Ps.111:2-4, Ps.8 (Tgr,H)
706 Prov.3:19(H)
708–709 Heb.11:3
712–13 Gen.1:3(H)

Book IV

1–5 Rev.12:7-12(Tn,V,H)
9 Job 1:6
10 Rev.12:10(Tn,V); Matt.4:3
27–28 Gen.2:8
37 John 3:20
38–39a Rev.2:5
44–45 Jas.1:5(T,V); I John 5:3
79–80 Heb.12:17(Tg,V,H)
110 Isa.5:20
132 Gen. 2:8(H)
134 Ezek.28:13-14(V)
166–71 Tob.6, 7, 8:1-4 (T,H)
183–87 John 10:1(Tn,H); Acts 20:29, Ezek.22:27
192 John 10(V)
193 Acts 17:5(T)
194–95 Gen.2:9, Rev.2:7 (Th,V,H)
196 Isa.34:11(V)
209–10 Gen. 2:8
213–15 II Kings 19:12, Isa. 37:12(V,H); Gen.2:8
216–22 Gen.2:9(H)
223–33 Gen.2:10(Tn,V,H)
250 Ps.84:1(V)
256 Gen.3:18(Tn,V)
292 Gen.1:26
301–308 I Cor.11:14-15(Tn,H)
314 I Cor.12:24(Tn,V)
361–62 Ps.8:5, Heb.2:7 (Tn,V,H)
381–83 Isa.14:9(Tg,V,H)
402 I Pet.5:8(V)
418–19 Acts 17:25(Tg,V)
421–24 Gen.2:16-17(Tn)
430–33 Gen.1:28(Tn,H)
440–41 Gen.2:23(V); I Cor. 11:9
443 I Cor.11:3(H)
483 Gen.2:23(Tn,V,H)
499 Ps.75:12(Tn)
523–26 Gen.3:5
549 Dan.8:16, 10:21, Luke 1:19(H)
561 I Chron.25:8, 26:13, 27(V)
569 Exod.24:18(V)
641 Song of Sol.2:17(T)
691 Gen.2:8
717 Isa.66:19, Gen.10:2 (V)
724–25 Ps.74:16-17(T,V)
733 Gen.1:28(V)
735 Ps.127:2(T,H); I Thess.5:10
741–43 I Cor.7:4-5
743 Eph.5:32(Tp,V,H)
744–49 I Tim.4:1-3(Tn,V)
748 Gen.1:28(H)
750 Eph.5:32(Tp,V,H)
761 Heb.13:4(T,V)
782 Exod.6:18, Num. 3:19(H)
788 Num.26:15(H)
939–40 Eph.2:2(H)
965 Jude 6(H)[recorded as Jude 1:6]
966 Rev.20:3(Th,V)
974 Ezek.1:24, 11:22 (Tn); Ps.18:10(T)

980–85 John 4:35b, Luke 22: 31, I Cor.9:10, Amos 9:13
988 Wisd.18:16(Tn)
997–99 Isa.40:12, Job 28:25, 37:16(Tn,V,H); I Sam. 2:3, Prov.16:2
1000 Job 26:7(Th)
1010 Isa.10:6(Tg,V)
1012 Dan.5:27(Tn,V,H)

Book V

2 Ps.97:11(T)
17–25 Song of Sol.2:10-13(V)
54–56 II Cor.11:14
77–78 Gen.3:5(V)
79 Eph.2:2(V)
128 II Pet.3:7
129 Jer.20:7(Tn,V)
130–31 Luke 7:38
139 Luke 1:78, Job 38:12 (V)
153–208 Ps.148, Song of Three Children (Tn,V,H)
155 Wisd.13:3-5(Tn)
156 I Pet.1:8
162 Rev.7:15(Tn)
166 Rev.22:16
202 Ps.137:6
221–23 Tob.5:4-6
229 Exod.33:11, Jas.2:23
246–47 Matt.3:15
249 Ps.104:4(H)
254 Ezek.1:1(V)
269–70 Isa.30:24(V)
277–85 Isa.6:2, Ezek.1, 10 (Tn,V,H)
298–302 Gen.18:1(Tbe,V,H)
321–22 Gen.2:7(V)
385–88 Luke 1:28, I Cor.15:45 (V,H)
398–99 Jas.1:17(H)
403 Jas.1:17
407–409 Ps.78:25(Tn,V); Luke 24:39-43
426–28 Matt.26:29, Rev.22:2 (Tn)
429–30 Exod.16:14-15, Ps.78:25 (H)
435 Tob.12:19(Tn); cf. Gen.18, 19
446–47 Gen.6:2(Tn)
460 Ps.104:4
469–70 Rom.11:36
471 Wisd.1:14(T)
478 I Cor.15:39-49(T)
501 Isa.1:19
503 Acts 17:28(Tn)
504 Deut.23:24, Lev.25:19 (V)
582–85 Job 1:6, I Kings 22:19–22(Tn,V)
588 Rev.9:16
598 Exod.19:18(Tn,V)
600 Heb.1:5(T)
601 Col.1:16
602–605 Ps.2:6-7, Gen.22:2 (Tn,H)
606 Ps.110:1, Eph.4:15(V); Col.2:10
607a Gen.22:16(Tn,V,H)
607b–608 Phil.2:10-11, Heb. 1:3-5(Tn,V,H)
625–26 Job 38:7
633–35 Matt.26:29
637 Ps.36:8-9(Tn,V,H)
643 I Kings 8:27, Isa.57:15 (V)
645 Rev.21:25(V,H)
647 Ps.121:4(Tn,H)
652 Rev.22:1-2
658 Job 1:6
664 Dan.9:25(H)
685–88 John 8:44(Tn,V)
689 Isa.14:12(Tn,V,H); Jer. 4:6(V)
708 Rev.22:16, Isa.14:2(H)
710 Rev.12:3-4, Jer.16:17
711–12 Ps.54:7, Matt.20:15, Prov.30:17(Tp); Ps. 33:18, Prov.5:21, 15:3, Heb.4:12-13
713 Rev.4:5(Tn,V,H); Zech.3:9(H)
716 Isa.14:12(T,V)
718 Ps.2:1,4(Tn)
720 Heb.1:2
725–26 Isa.14:13
734 Dan.10:6, Matt.28:3 (Tn)
736–37 Ps.2:4
739–40 Matt.28:18
756–57 Isa.14:13
760 Isa.14:12
765 Dan.9:25
766 Isa.14:13(Tn,V)
772 Col.1:16
781–82 Phil.2:10-11

| Line | Reference |
|---|---|
| 784 | Heb.1:3 |
| 789–92 | John 8:33-34 |
| 805 | I Chron.5:15(H) |
| 815–18 | Ps.45:6, Phil.2:10-11, Rom.14:11 |
| 822 | Rom.9:20(Tg) |
| 830 | Col.2:10 |
| 835–40 | Col.1:16-17(Tn,V,H) |
| 839 | Ps.8:5 |
| 846–48 | Ps.2:12(Tn); Isa.55:6-7 (Tg) |
| 853–55 | Num.16:22, 27:16, Col. 1:16(V,H) |
| 864–65 | Ps.12:4(Tg,V); Ps.45:4 (Tbe) |
| 872 | Rev.19:6(Tn,V); Rev. 1:15 |
| 882–83 | Matt.11:29-30 |
| 886–87 | Ps.2:9, 45:6 |
| 890 | Num.16:26(Tn,V); Josh.7:12 |
| 893 | Heb.12:29 |
| 896 | I Cor.4:2 |

Book VI

| Line | Reference |
|---|---|
| 18 | I Macc.6:39(T) |
| 23–27 | Jude 24 |
| 29–30 | I Tim.6:12(Tg); Matt. 25:21, II Tim.4:7(V,H); Ps.62:7, II Tim.2:15 (M) |
| 32 | John 1:9, 14:6(H) |
| 33 | Ps.69:7(V,H) |
| 36 | II Tim.2:15(Tg,V,M) |
| 44–48 | Rev.12:7-8(Tn,V,M,H); Dan.12:1(H) |
| 54 | I Pet.2:4 |
| 56–60 | Exod.19:16-18(Tn,V,H) |
| 73–76 | Gen.2:20 |
| 87 | Gen.7:13 |
| 88–89 | Isa.14:13 |
| 137–39 | Matt.3:9 |
| 156 | Rev.12:4 |
| 167 | Heb.1:14(Tn,V) |
| 184 | Rom.1:25, 9:5 |
| 200–203 | I Thess.4:16 |
| 213 | Eph.6:16 |
| 260 | Rev.20:1-2 |
| 297 | I Pet.1:8 |
| 321 | Jer.50:25(V) |
| 357 | I Kings 11:7 |
| 359 | II Kings 19:22(Tg,V,H) |
| 365 | II Kings 17:31(Th,M, V,H) |
| 371 | Isa.29:1(V,M.H); Ez. 8:16(M); Gen.14:1, Dan.2:14(M,V,H) |
| 374–75 | I Tim.5:21 |
| 447 | II Kings 19:37, Lev.11: 13, Isa.37:38(Tn,M, V,H) |
| 521 | Job 38:12 |
| 526–27 | Eph.6:11 |
| 535 | I Chron.6:26 |
| 539–40a | II Pet.2:17(H) |
| 542–46 | Eph.6:14-17 |
| 680 | Heb.1:3 |
| 681–82 | Col.1:15(V,H) |
| 684 | John 5:19(H) |
| 699 | Luke 13:32, I Cor.15:4, 57 |
| 708 | Heb.1:2 |
| 709 | Ps.45:7(Tg,V) |
| 713 | Ps.45:3-4(Tn) |
| 719–20 | II Cor.4:6 |
| 724–34 | John 17:1-23, Matt. 3:17, 17:5(M,V,H); I Cor.15:24, 28, Ps.139: 21(Tn,M,V) |
| 738 | Rev.20:1-2, Jude 6(Th, V,H); John 14:2, Matt. 25:41 |
| 739 | II Pet.2:4, Mark 9:44, Isa.66:24(Th,M,V,H) |
| 748–49 | Matt.28:1, I Cor.15:4 |
| 749–50 | Ezek.1:4, Isa.66:15 (Tn,V,H) |
| 751–56 | Ezek.1:5,6,13,16,19, 10:12(Tn,V,H) |
| 757–59 | Ezek.10:16,22,26-28 (Tn,V,H) |
| 760 | Eph.6:11(T,V) |
| 761 | Exod.28:30(V,H) |
| 765 | Ps.18:8, 50:3(Tn) |
| 767–69 | Jude 14, Ps.68:17(Tn, V,H); Rev.5:11(V) |
| 771 | Ps.18:10(Tgr,V,H); II Sam.22:11(V,H); Ezek. 1:26 |
| 776 | Matt.24:30(Tg,V) |
| 779 | Rom,12:5, Col.1:18 (Tgr,V,H); Col.2:10 |
| 789–91 | Exod.14(Th) |
| 801 | Exod.14:13-14(Tg,V) |
| 808 | Deut.32:35, Rom.12:19 (Tn,V,H); Ps.94:1, Heb.10:30(H) |
| 814–15 | Matt.6:13 |

| | |
|---|---|
| 832–33 | Job 26:11(Th); Dan. 7:9(T) |
| 842–43 | Rev.6:16(Tn,V,H) |
| 845–48 | Ezek.1:6,12,13,18,20 |
| 853 | Ps.78:38(Tn) |
| 855–56 | Matt.25:33,41(Tn) |
| 859 | Job 6:4, Isa.51:20 (Tn) |
| 866 | Rev.20:1 |
| 874–75 | Isa.5:14(T,V) |
| 876–77 | Mark 9:43-45 |
| 880–92 | Rev.4:11, 12:10(V) |
| 885 | Rev.7:9(V) |
| 888 | Rev.6:11(Tn); Rev. 5:12 |
| 891 | I Tim.3:16, Heb.1:3 (Tg,V,H) |
| 909 | I Pet.3:7(Tn,V,H) |

Book VII

| | |
|---|---|
| 8–12 | Prov.8:23-30(Tn,V,H) |
| 13 | II Cor.12:2,4 |
| 24–26 | Eph.5:16-19, Eccles. 12:1 |
| 28–29 | Ps.17:3 |
| 43–44 | II Thess.2:3-4 |
| 46 | Gen.2:17(V,H) |
| 56–58 | Ps.140:9-11 |
| 78–80 | Eccles.12:13 |
| 79 | Rev.4:11(V) |
| 97 | Job 36:24(Tg,V) |
| 98 | Gen.1:16 |
| 99–100 | Josh.10:12-14(V) |
| 103 | Gen.1:2-3(Th) |
| 106 | Matt.26:40 |
| 113 | Isa.6:6 |
| 114 | I Cor.2:9 |
| 121 | Eccles.7:20(Tp); Ps. 106:29,38(Tth,V); Job 5:9(T) |
| 122–23 | I Tim.1:17, Matt.24:36 (Tn,V) |
| 129–30 | I Cor.8:1(T) |
| 131 | Isa.14:12(M,V) |
| 135 | Acts 1:25(Tn,V) |
| 137 | Rev.4:2(V,H) |
| 144 | Job 7:10, Ps.103:16 (Tn,V) |
| 145–46 | Jude 6(T,V) |
| 163–64 | Col.1:16-17(T,H); John 1:1-3(V) |
| 165–66 | Gen.1:2(Tn); Luke 1:35(Tn,V) |
| 167 | Jer.5:22, Ps.104:9(T) |
| 182–83 | Luke 2:13-14(Tn,V, H); Job 38:7(H) |
| 186 | I Pet.3:18(V) |
| 194 | Ps.18:39(V,H); Ps. 30:11(V) |
| 196 | Heb.1:3(V,H) |
| 197–231 | Ps.104:1-9 |
| 200 | Jer.50:25(V,H) |
| 201 | Zech.6:1(M,V,H) |
| 204 | Ezek.1:20(V) |
| 205–208 | Ps.24:7-9(T,V,H) |
| 210–15 | Ps.24:1-2 |
| 216 | Mark 4:39(Tn) |
| 224 | Ezek.1:16(H) |
| 225 | Prov.8:27(Tr,M,V,H) |
| 230 | Job 38:11 |
| 232–35 | Gen.1:2(Tn,V,H); Luke 3:22(V) |
| 238 | II Pet.2:4 |
| 239 | Ps.89:11, Prov.3:19(V) |
| 242 | Job 26:7(H) |
| 243–52 | Gen.1:3-5(Tn,V,H) |
| 247–48 | Ps.19:4(V,H) |
| 249–50 | Gen.1:4(H) |
| 251–52 | Gen.1:5 |
| 253–60 | Job 38:4,7(Tn,V) |
| 258–59 | Ps.148:2,5 |
| 261–64 | Gen.1:6-8(Tn,M,V,H) |
| 268–69 | Gen.7:11, Ps.104:3, 148:4, II Pet.3:5(Th); Ps.24:2(T) |
| 274–75 | Gen.1:8(Tn) |
| 282–91 | Gen.1:9-10, Ps.104: 6-8(Tn,V,H) |
| 307–309 | Gen.1:10-11(Tn,H) |
| 309–38 | Gen.1:11-13(V) |
| 311–12 | Gen.1:11(M) |
| 317–18 | II Esdras 6:44(T) |
| 331–36 | Gen.2:4-6(Tn,V,H) |
| 337 | Gen.1:12-13 |
| 339–45 | Gen.1:14-19(Tn,V,H) |
| 346–53 | Gen.1:16-18(Tn) |
| 372–73 | Ps.19:5(Tp) |
| 374–75 | Job 38:31(Th,M,V,H) |
| 384 | Ps.136(T) |
| 386 | Gen.1:19 |
| 387–98 | Gen.1:20-22(Tn,V); Ps.104:25, 114:25 (T,M) |
| 412 | Ps.114:26(T); Job 41:1 |
| 423–24 | Job 39:27-28(V) |
| 430 | Jer.8:7(V) |
| 448 | Gen.1:23 |
| 450–58 | Gen.1:24-25(V,H) |

452–53 Gen.1:24(Tp)
463 Job 39:1, Ps.29:9(Tn)
471 Job 40:15, 41:1(M,H)
482 Prov.30:24(Tn)
486 I Kings 4:29(V)
493 Gen.2:19-20(V)
495 Gen.3:1(V)
519–34 Gen.1:26-2:7(Tn,V,H)
527–28 Heb.1:3(V)
535–39 Gen.2:8,9,15(Tn,V,H); II Esdras 3:6(T,M,H)
540–42 Gen.2:16-17
548–50 Gen.1:31(Tn)
562 Job 38:7
565–67 Ps.24:7(Tn,M,V,H)
569–71 Ps.8:4
581–82 Gen.2:2
585–86 Ps.45:6, Isa.6:1, Jer. 17:12, Lam.5:19, Heb. 1:8
591–93 Gen.2:2-3(Tn,V,H); Exod.20:11(V); Heb. 12:2
599–600 Rev.8:3-5(Tn,V,H)
619 Rev.4:6(Tn,M,H); Rev.15:2
622–23 Acts 1:7
628 Ps.8:6-8(Tg,V,H)
634 Ps.146:1(V)
638 Isa.48:3-5

BOOK VIII

15 Heb.11:3, Ps.8:3
19 Ps.147:4(Tr,V,H)
52–53 I Cor.14:35
66–68 Ps.19:1-3, Rom.1:20
69 Gen.1:14
77–78 Ps.2:4,59:8
102 Job 38:5(Tn,V,H); Ps. 19:3-4
119–22 Isa.58:8-9
168 Eccles.12:13
185 Matt.6:34
215–16 Ps.119:103(Tg)
218 Ps.45:3(Tn,V)
225 Rev.22:9(Tn,V)
225b–26 I Pet.1:12
238–40 Ps.103:20
281 Acts 17:28(Tg,V)
296 John 14:2
297 I Cor.15:45
299 Gen.2:8
300–303 Gen.2:15, Acts 8:39 (Tn)
306–309 Gen.2:9
316 Exod.3:14, John 8:58 (Tgr)
320–22 Gen.2:15-17(Tp,H)
323–30 Gen.2:17(Tn)
326 Gen.2:9
338–41 Gen.1:28(V)
343–44 Gen.2:19
354–55 Gen.2:19-20(Tn,H)
379–80 Gen.18:30(Tn,V,H)
402 Gen.2:8
413 Rom.11:33(Th,V)
437 Prov.17:3, John 6:6
441 Gen.1:27
444 Gen.2:18(Tn,V)
453 Gen.2:21-22(Tn,V,H); Dan.10:17(T)
460–61 Num.24:4(V)
462 Gen.2:21(Tn)
465–68 Gen.2:21(Tn,M)
469–71 Gen.2:22
494–99 Gen.2:23-24(Tn,V,H); Matt.19:4-6, Mark 10: 6-8(V,H)
500 Gen.2:22(Tn)
502 I Cor.8:7, Heb.10:2 (Tp)
508 Heb.13:4(V,H)
511 Song of Sol.6:10(T)
568–69 Eph.5:28-29, I Pet. 3:7(Tn,V)
574 I Cor.11:3(V,H)
594 Gen.2:20
598–99 Eph.5:31-32
633 Josh.1:6, Eph.6:10
634–35 I John 5:3(Tn,V,H)
640–42 I Cor.7:37

BOOK IX

1–4 Exod.33:11(T,V); Jas. 2:23
11–12 Rom.5:12,19
58 Job 1:7(T,V)
71–73 Gen.2:10(V,H); Gen. 2:9
73–76 Rev.21:6, Jas.3:11
80 Job 38:10(Tn)
85 Eph.6:11
86 Gen.3:1(Tn,V,H)
88–89 Acts 9:15, II Tim.2:21, Rom.9:22
91b Eph.6:11
149 Gen.2:7
154–56 Gen.1:26, Heb.1:14

| Line | Reference |
|---|---|
| 156 | Ps.104:4(Th); Heb.1:7 |
| 157 | Ps.91:11(T,V,H) |
| 174–76 | Deut.13:13, I Sam.2: 12, Job 41:24, Luke 16:8(T,V); Gen.2:7, 19 |
| 177–78 | Gen.2:7 |
| 192 | I John 1:5(V) |
| 195–97 | Gen.8:21(Tn,H); Lev. 1:9(V) |
| 205–206 | Gen.2:15 |
| 215–17 | Ps.128:3 |
| 264 | Gen.3:1(H) |
| 265–66 | Gen.2:21-22(V) |
| 273 | Gen.18:12 |
| 291 | Gen.3:20 |
| 334 | Rom.8:16(Tn) |
| 383 | I Pet.3:7 |
| 404 | I Tim.2:14 |
| 442 | Song of Sol.6:2(V,H) |
| 443 | I Kings 3:1(V); Song of Sol.7:1(H) |
| 463 | Matt.6:13 |
| 467–68 | Job 1:6, 2:1(Tn) |
| 549 | Matt.4:3 |
| 560–61 | Gen.3:1, II Cor.11:3 |
| 618 | Ps.104:16(Tn) |
| 651–52 | Gen.3:3 |
| 654 | Rom.2:14(Tr,V) |
| 656–57 | Gen.3:1(Th,V) |
| 659–63 | Gen.3:2-3 |
| 685 | Gen.3:4-5(Tn,V) |
| 697–98 | Gen.3:5 |
| 705–10 | Gen.3:5 |
| 713–14 | Col.3:9-10(V) |
| 732 | Gen.2:16-17, Rev.21:6 |
| 741 | Gen.3:6(V,H) |
| 777–81 | Gen.3:6 |
| 811–13 | Ps.10:11, 94:7, Job 22:13-14(V,H); Isa. 47:10 |
| 838–42 | Gal.6:7 |
| 891 | Job 17:8(V,H) |
| 914–15 | Gen.2:23 |
| 928 | Gen.3:3(V) |
| 947–49 | Deut.32:26-27(Tg,V); Job 1:6(M); I Pet. 5:8(V) |
| 955–59 | Gen.2:24b, Eph.5:28 |
| 996–98 | Gen.3:12, I Tim. 2:14 (V); Gen.3:17(T) |
| 1027–28 | Exod.32:6, I Cor.10:7 |
| 1042–44 | Prov.7:18(T,V,H) |
| 1053 | Gen.3:7a |
| 1058–59 | Ps.109:29(V,H) |
| 1059 | Judg.13:2,25, 16:4-20 (H) |
| 1070–74 | Gen.3:7a |
| 1088–90 | Rev.6:16(V) |
| 1110–13 | Gen.3:7(M,V) |
| 1125–26 | Isa.57:20-21 |
| 1155 | I Cor.11:3(V) |

### Book X

| Line | Reference |
|---|---|
| 3–4 | Gen.3:12-13, II Cor.11:3 |
| 9–12 | Gen.1:26(The) |
| 31–33 | Exod.33:9-10, I Kings 8:10-11, Ezek.10:4, Rev.4:5(V) |
| 35 | Jer.46:27 |
| 39 | Luke 16:26 |
| 51–52 | Eccles.8:11(T) |
| 56 | John 5:22(Tn,V,H) |
| 59 | Ps.85:10(Tn) |
| 60–61 | I Tim.2:5-6, Isa.63:16 |
| 62 | I John 5:27(Tn) |
| 64–67 | Heb.1:3(V,H) |
| 69 | John 4:34(T) |
| 70–71 | Matt.3:17 |
| 74 | Gal.4:4(H) |
| 86–87 | Eph.1:21, Col.1:16 |
| 92–95 | Gen.3:8-21(Tn,M,V) |
| 95–99 | Gen.3:8(H) |
| 101–103 | Gen.3:9(Tn) |
| 116–17 | Gen.3:10 |
| 121–23 | Gen.3:11 |
| 137–43 | Gen.3:12 |
| 145 | Gen.30:2, II Kings 5:7(T) |
| 149–50 | I Cor.11:8-9 |
| 155 | I Tim.2:12 |
| 158–62 | Gen.3:13 |
| 175–81 | Gen.3:14-15(V,M,H) |
| 184–91 | Luke 10:18(H); Eph. 2:2,18(V,H); Col.2:15 (V); Ps.68:18(V,H); Rom.16:20(T,M); Eph. 4:8(T) |
| 192–95 | Gen.3:16-19(T,H) |
| 197–208 | Gen.3:17-19 |
| 214–15 | Phil.2:7(Th,V,H); John 13:5(Th,H) |
| 216a | Heb.2:13b |
| 216b–17 | Gen.3:21(Tn,H) |
| 218 | Rom.5:10(Tp) |
| 222–23 | Isa.61:10, Ezek.16:8 (Tn,V,H) |

235 II Kings 7:3
253–54 Luke 16:26
327 II Cor.11:14
372–75 II Cor.4:4
381 Rev.21:6(Tn,M,V,H)
383 Eph.6:12(T)
399 Rom.5:14,17,21
402 John 8:34, Rom.6:23
407 Rom.5:12
409 Deut.31:7-8(Tn); Deut.11:8
425 Isa.14:12
450–52 I Cor.11:14
460 Col.1:16
473 Matt.7:13
496–99 Gen.3:15
514 Gen.3:14
529 Rom.12:9(Tn,M)
546 Hos.4:7(Tg)
585–86 Rom.6:6(Tp)
588–90 Rom.6:8(V,H)
600–601 Prov.27:30(T)
616 Ps.22:16, Isa.56:11, Phil.3:2, Rev.22:15 (Tn)
633–34 I Sam.17:49; I Sam. 25:29(T)
635–36 Hos.13:14(Tr); I Cor. 15:55(Tr,H); Rev. 20:14
638 II Pet.3:7,10-13(V); Rev.21:1-2(H)
641–42 Rev.19:6(Th,V,H)
643–44 Rev.15:3, 16:7(Tn,V)
646–47 Rev.21:2(Tn,V)
651 Gen.3:14, 6:7(H)
711 Gen.1:30(V)
717–18 Isa.57:20(Tgr,H)
722 I Cor.11:7
730 Gen.1:28(V,H)
743–44 Job 33:6(T,V); Isa. 45:9(T,V,H)
762 Isa.45:10(V,H)
770 Gen.3:19
779–80 Job 37:5(T)
784–85 Gen.2:7(Tn,V)
798–801 II Tim.2:13, Heb. 16:18(V)
815–16 Rom.7:20(Th,V)
817 II Esdras 7:48(Tn)
826–27 Rom.1:32
899 Gen.2:18(H)
910–12 Luke 7:38, Matt.28:9
926 Gen.3:15(Tn)
930–31 Ps.51:4(Tg)
936 I Sam.25:24(Tn)
960–61 Gal.6:2
1031–32 Gen.3:15
1050–53 Gen.3:16, John 16:21, Luke 1:42
1054–55 Gen.3:19
1058–59 Gen.3:21
1060–61 Ps.34:5, I Pet.3:12, Ps.119:36,112
1088–89 Jas.5:16a, I John 1:9
1089–90 Isa.16:9
1091 Ps.51:17
1093–96 Joel 2:13-14, Neh.9:17

Book XI

1–2 I Chron.20:5, Luke 18: 13(V); Exod.25:18 (H); Neh.9:2
3 Zech.12:10, Jas.4:6
4 Ezek.11:9(T,H);Ezek. 36:26(T)
5–6 Rom.8:26(Th,H)
17–18 Ps.141:42, Rev.8:3-4(T, V,H); Rev.9:13(V)
20–21 Heb.7:24-25, 12:2, Rev.3:21
23–25 Ezek.20:41, Rev.5:8 (T); Heb.4:14
26–27 Mark 4:20, Heb.13:15
32–34 Rom.8:26, I John 2:1-2 (Tn,V,H)
37–38a Lev.3:5(The); Eph. 5:2
38b–42 Rom.5:10,21
40–43 Phil.1:21,23
44 John 17:11,21,22(Th, H)
45 Num.11:25, Mark 9:7
46 Job 42:8-9
50–53 Lev.18:25(Ts,V)
65 Dan.12:2, Luke 14:14
66 II Pet.3:13
70 II Pet.2:4
74–76 Exod.19:16-19, I Cor. 15:22(V); Exod.20:18, I Thess.4:16(Tn); Matt.24:31(H)
78 I Pet.1:4, 5:4
79 Rev.7:17, 22:1(Tg)
80 I John 1:5b, John 8:12, Luke 16:18, Eph. 5:8
84 Gen.3:22-24(Tn,H)
93–98 Gen.3:22-23(V)

116 Gen.3:5
118–22 Gen.3:24(V,H)
128–29a Ezek.10:12-14(Tn,M)
129b–30 Ezek.1:18(H)
141–42 Jas.1:17
155 Gen.3:15(V)
157–58 I Sam.15:32(Tn,V,H)
159–60 Gen.3:20(Tn,V,H)
164–65 Gen.2:18
171–72 Gen.3:17-19(V)
180 Phil.4:11
199–200 Gen.3:19, Eccles.3:20
203 Matt.8:13
204 Isa.16:3(Tbo)
213–15 Gen.32:1-2(Tn,M,V,H)
216–20 II Kings 6:13-17(Tn,M,V,H)
230–31 Ecclus.19:30(T)
232–33 Ps.93:1(T)
256–57 I Pet.4:8
307–10 Luke 18:5-7(H)
316 Gen.4:14(Tg,H)
327 Gen.4:3
332 Exod.33:22-23
336–37 Jer.23:24(T,H); John 4:21(H); Ps.139, Acts 17:28-29(V)
356–57 Dan.10:14(T,V,H)
358–60 Gen.6:3(Tg); Rom. 5:20
362–64 Phil.4:11
374–75 Heb.4:11, 5:8
376 Phil.3:11
377 Ezek.8:3, 10:2, 40:2, II Chron.26:5(T,M,V,H)
381–84 Matt.4:8, I Cor.15:45-47(Tn,H)
392 I Kings 9:28(H)
416 Ps.36:9(Tg,V,H)
420–22 Dan.10:8, Rev.1:17 (T,V,H)
427 Exod.32:30, John 5:16 (Tn)
430–47 Gen.4:1-16(H)
434–35 Gen.4:2-3(Tn); I John 3:12
436–42 Gen.2:2,4, Heb.11:4
441–42 Judg.6:21, I Kings 18:38, II Chron.7:1(H)
443–44 Gen.4:5
445–46 Gen.4:8
456–57 Gen.4:7(Th)
458 Heb.11:4(Tn,V)
479 Luke 16:20(H)
508 Gen.1:26(V)
520–24 Rom.1:21,24(Tg)
550–52 Job 14:14(Tg,H,V); Heb.9:27
557–63 Gen.4:20(V,H)
564 Gen.4:22(V)
573–74 Gen.6:1-2(M,H)
577–78 Gen.4:26
581–82 Gen.6:1-2
582b–83 I Tim.2:9, I Pet.3:3-4
587 Gen.6:2b
607–608 Ps.84:10(T,V,H)
621–23 Gen.6:2(Tn,V)
661 Gen.34:20, Deut.16:18, 21:19, Zech.8:16 (Tn)
665 Gen.5:21-24(M,H); Jude 14(M)
670–71 Gen.5:24(Tr)
688 Gen.6:4(Tn,M,V,H)
700 Jude 14(Tn,M,V,H)
701 Gen.5:24, Heb.11:5 (T,V)
704–709 Jude 14(Tn)
706 Ecclus.48:9(T)
707b Gen.5:24(Tn)
715–18 Luke 17:26-27
719 Gen.7:6(H)
719ff. Gen.6:9-9:17(H)
721 Heb.11:7b
723–25 I Pet.3:19-20(Tn,V,H)
730–31 Gen.6:14-16(Tn,V)
735 Gen.7(Tn,V)
736–37 Gen.7:7,13,16(H)
765–66 Matt.6:34(Tn,V,H)
812–13 Heb.11:7b
817–18a Gen.6:8
818b–21 Gen.6:14, Heb.11:7
824–27 Gen.7:11(Tn)
828–29 Gen.7:19
833 Gen.15:18(T,V)
836–38 Lam.2:7, Ezek.24:21, II Macc.5:19
842–43 Gen.8:1, Prov.25:23 (V,H)
848–49 Gen.8:2(Tn)
851 Gen.8:4(V)
852 Gen.8:5
855 Gen.8:7
857–58 Gen.8:8-9(V)
859–60 Gen.8:10-11
861–62 Gen.8:13,18,19

| Line | Reference |
|---|---|
| 864–65 | Gen.9:13-14 |
| 866 | Rev.4:3 |
| 867 | Gen.9:11-17(V) |
| 875 | Gen.6:9 |
| 884–85 | Gen.6:6(Tn,V) |
| 886–87 | Gen.6:11-12(Tn,V) |
| 890 | Gen.6:8(Tn,V) |
| 892–93 | Gen.9:11(Tn,V) |
| 895–98a | Gen.9:14-16(Tn,V) |
| 898b–900 | Gen.8:22(Tn,H) |
| 900–901 | II Pet.3:12-13(Tn,H) |

Book XII

| Line | Reference |
|---|---|
| 21 | Exod.29:40(T) |
| 24 | Gen.10:9(H) |
| 33 | Gen.10:8-10(M,V); cf. Jer.16:16, Lam.4:18, Ezek.13:18,20(Tn) |
| 34 | Gen.13:13, 38:7 |
| 36 | Gen.10:9(V) |
| 38–62 | Gen.11:2-9(V,H) |
| 51 | Gen.11:5(Tn) |
| 52–53 | II Chron.18:22(Tr,V) |
| 52 | Ps.2:4(Tn) |
| 59 | Ps.37:13, 59:8, Prov. 1:26(Tn) |
| 61 | Gen.11:8 |
| 62 | Gen.11:9(M,V) |
| 83–84 | John 8:34, II Cor. 3:17(Tg) |
| 95–96 | Matt.18:7(T,V) |
| 101–104 | Gen.9:21-25(Th,M, V,H) |
| 111 | Deut.14:2, Ps.135:4 |
| 114 | Josh.24:4-3, Gen.14:13 (V,H) |
| 115 | Josh.24:2(T,M,V) |
| 116 | Gen.9:28(Tn) |
| 118 | Heb.3:12, I Tim.4:10 (V) |
| 120 | Gen.14:19, Judith 5:7-9(T) |
| 120–21 | Gen.12, Acts 7(T,V) |
| 121–25 | Gen.12:1-3,7(H) |
| 127 | Heb.11:8(T,V,H) |
| 129–30 | Gen.12, Acts 7(V) |
| 129–38 | Gen.12:5,6(H) |
| 130 | Gen.11:31(Tn) |
| 139–42 | Josh.13:5-6(H) |
| 139 | Num. 34:7-8(V,H) |
| 139b | Num.34:3(M,V); Deut.3:8-9(T,M) |
| 141 | Num.34:6(M) |
| 142 | Ps.89:12(V) |
| 143 | Jer.46:8(H) |
| 146 | Num.34:12(V,H); I Chron.5:23(V) |
| 147–48 | Gen.12:1-3(T) |
| 148b–50 | Gen.3:15 |
| 151–52 | Gen.17:5, Gal.3:9 (M,V) |
| 152 | Gen.17:5(Tp) |
| 155–57 | Gen.46:6 |
| 160ff. | Gen.45, 46(V) |
| 164–65 | Exod.1:7-8 |
| 166–67 | Exod.1:9-14 |
| 168 | Exod.1:16 |
| 169–71 | Exod.5:1 |
| 172 | Exod.12:36(V,H) |
| 173–90 | Exod.7; Exod.12(V,H) |
| 173–74 | Exod.5:2 |
| 176 | Exod.7:20 |
| 177–78 | Exod.8:6,17,24 |
| 179 | Exod.9:3,6 |
| 180–81 | Exod.9:8-10 |
| 181b–83 | Exod.9:23-25 |
| 185–88 | Exod.10:14-15,21-23 |
| 188 | Exod.10:21(Tn) |
| 189–90 | Exod.12:29-30 |
| 191 | Exod.29:3(Ta,V,H) |
| 193–94 | Exod.8:8,15 |
| 195–96 | Exod.14:28 |
| 196–99 | Exod.14:21-22 |
| 201–14 | Exod.13:21-22, 14:19-20(V,H) |
| 203 | Exod.13:22 |
| 204–205 | Exod.14:19 |
| 206–207 | Exod.14:19-20(Tn) |
| 210 | Exod.14:25(Tr,H) |
| 211–13 | Exod.14:26-28 |
| 214–19 | Exod.13:17-19(Th, V,H) |
| 224–26 | Exod.24, Num.11:16-24(V,H) |
| 227–30 | Exod.19:16,19,20(H) |
| 232–34 | Heb.8:4-7, Gal.3:16-22 |
| 236–37 | Exod.20:18-19(H) |
| 241–42 | Deut.18:15-19(V,H); Acts 3:22(V) |
| 243 | Heb.9:19,24(Th); Acts 10:43 |
| 247–49 | Exod.25:8-9(H) |
| 250–52 | Exod.25:10-11,16-21, 37 |
| 251–52 | Heb.9:4 |
| 253–54 | I Kings 6(V) |
| 256–58 | Exod.40:34-38(V) |
| 258–60 | Exod.23:23(T,V) |

| Lines | References |
|---|---|
| 263–67 | Josh.10:12-13(V,H) |
| 267–69 | Gen.32:28(V,H) |
| 273–74 | Gen.3:5(Th,V) |
| 276–77 | John 8:56(Th); Gen. 12:3, 22:18(H) |
| 285–306 | Rom.3:20, 4:22-25, 5:1, 13,21, 7:7-8, 8:15, 10: 5, Heb. 7:19, 9:13-14, 10:1-5, Gal.3:4(Tn,M, V) |
| 290a | Rom.3:19-20; 7:7-8 (H) |
| 291 | Heb.10:1(H) |
| 292–93 | Heb.9:13-14 |
| 293 | I Pet.1:18-19 |
| 294a | I Pet.3:18 |
| 294b–95 | Rom.4:3 |
| 296 | Rom.5:1 |
| 297–98a | Gal.2:16 |
| 298b–99 | Rom.10:5(H) |
| 300–306 | Gal.3:22-26 |
| 307–309 | Deut.34, Josh.1(Th,V) |
| 310–14 | Heb.4:8-9, Acts 7:45 (Tn,M,V) |
| 320 | Judg.2:16 |
| 322–24 | II Sam.7:16(M,V,H); Ps.139:34-36(T,M); Luke 1:32 |
| 324–25 | Isa.11:10, Ps.89:36-37 (T,M,V); Acts 10:43 |
| 327 | Gen.3:15(T) |
| 328 | Gen.22:18(T) |
| 330 | Luke 1:32(T) |
| 332 | I Kings 6:7, II Chron.3, 4(V,H) |
| 339–43 | II Chron.36:15-18 |
| 342–43 | II Kings 17:24 |
| 344–45 | Jer.25:12(V) |
| 346–47 | Jer.33:20, Ps.89:29 (T,H) |
| 349 | Ezra 1:1-2, Neh.2:1,5 |
| 353–56 | II Macc.5(V) |
| 360–72 | Matt.2:1-2, 9-4, 9-11, Luke 2:8-18(M,V) |
| 362 | Matt.2:1-2 |
| 363 | Matt.2:11 |
| 364 | Luke 2:11-12 |
| 365 | Luke 2:8 |
| 366 | Luke 2:16 |
| 367 | Luke 2:13-14 |
| 368 | Luke 1:27 |
| 369a | Luke 1:35 |
| 369b–71 | Ps.2:8, Isa.9:7, Zech. 9:9(T); Isa.9:7, Dan. 7:13-22, Matt.19:28, Luke 1:32-33, Rev.2: 25-27(M) |
| 375 | Rom.10:15 |
| 379–80 | Gen.3:15, Luke 1:28 (Tg,V) |
| 381–82a | Luke 1:31-35b |
| 382b | John 1:1,14 |
| 383–85 | Gen.3:15 |
| 394–95 | I John 3:8(Tr,M) |
| 396–97 | Rom.5:19 |
| 399 | Rom.6:23, Ezek.18:4 |
| 400 | Rom.5:14 |
| 401 | Rom.3:24-26 |
| 402 | I Pet.2:22, John 15:10, II Cor.5:21 |
| 403–409a | Heb.5:8-9 |
| 403b–404a | Rom.13:10(Th,M.V, H); John 6:38 |
| 405 | I John 4:2, II John 7 |
| 406a | Heb.13:13 |
| 406 | Gal.3:13, Deut.21:23 (M,V) |
| 407–408 | John 5:24, 6:47, 11: 25-26 |
| 409 | Rom.3:22, 4:5-6,23-25 |
| 409b–10 | Gal.2:16(M); Rom. 10:4; Titus 3:5 |
| 411 | John 15:18, Luke 22: 65 |
| 412b–13 | Gal.3:13(M); John 20:25 |
| 414 | Acts 3:13-15 |
| 415–17 | Col.2:14(Tn,M) |
| 418 | Eph.1:12 |
| 419a | Isa.53:20 |
| 419b–20 | Rev.1:18(T) |
| 420b–21 | Rom.6:9(Tg,M,V); Matt.28:1(Tg,M); Matt.20:19 |
| 424a | I Tim.2:6(T) |
| 424b–27 | Titus 2:14 |
| 425 | John 1:12 |
| 427a | Jas.1:17 |
| 427b–29 | Rom.1:4 |
| 430 | Gen.3:15 |
| 431–32 | I Cor.15:26, 55-57 |
| 433 | Gen.3:15 |
| 434b | I Cor.15:51, I Thess. 4:13-15(T) |
| 437–38 | Acts 1:2-3 |
| 440–42 | Matt.28:19-20 |
| 442–43 | Acts 22:16, Rom.6:4 |
| 444–45a | Phil.2:5,8 |

| | |
|---|---|
| 445 | Isa.59:20, Rom.11:26 (T) |
| 446–50 | Gal.3:7-9 |
| 446 | Matt.28:19-20(M) |
| 446–65 | Gal.3:7,18,16, Rom. 4:16, Col.2:15, Luke 21:27, 24:26, John 5: 28-29, Rev.11:18, 20:2 (M,V,H) |
| 451–53 | Eph.1:20-21, 4:8-10 (M,V) |
| 454–55 | Rev.20:1-2(V) |
| 456 | Luke 24:26 |
| 457–58 | Acts 2:33, Heb.12:2, Eph.1:20 |
| 459 | Rev.14:13,19 |
| 460 | II Tim.4:1, Luke 21:27 |
| 461–62 | John 5:28-29(T,H); Rev.11:18(T); I Cor. 3:14, 4:2 |
| 462b | Matt.25:34 |
| 473 | Gen.1:2-3 |
| 477 | II Cor.4:15(M,V) |
| 478 | Rom.5:20, Gal.5:6 (M,V,H) |
| 484–85 | John 16:2-3(V) |
| 486–87 | John 14:18,23, 15:26, 16:2-3(M,V,H) |
| 487a | Luke 24:49(Tn,M,V) |
| 487b–88a | John 14:17 |
| 488b | Rom.3:27 |
| 489a | Gal.5:6(M,V) |
| 489b | Jer.31:33, Heb.8:10 (H) |
| 490–92 | John 16:13, Eph.6:11-16(Tn,M,V,H) |
| 493 | Ps.56:11(Tn,M,V) |
| 494 | Rev.2:10b |
| 495 | II Cor.1:7 |
| 497b–98 | Acts 2:4, Mark 16:17-18(Th) |
| 500–501 | Acts 2:1-4(V); Acts 10:44-46 |
| 505 | Heb.12:1, I Cor.9:24 (V); II Tim.4:7 |
| 508 | Acts 20:29(Tn,M,V, H) |
| 509 | I Tim.3:16 |
| 511 | I Pet.5:2-3(M) |
| 513 | John 17:17 |
| 514 | I Cor.2:14(Tn,M); I John 2:27 |
| 519–20 | I John 2:20, Acts 2:4, John 14:16 |
| 522–24 | Jer.31:33(T,M,V) |
| 525–26 | II Cor.3:16-17(T,M, V,H) |
| 527 | I Cor.3:17, 6:19(T,V, H) |
| 531–33 | John 4:23(T,V,H); II Tim.3:12 |
| 539 | Rom.8:22(Tg,M,V) |
| 540 | Acts 3:19(Tn,M,H) |
| 543 | Gen.3:15 |
| 544 | II Pet.3:18 |
| 545–47 | Matt.24:30, II Thess. 1:7-8, Matt. 16:27, 26:64(Tg,M,V) |
| 546b–49 | II Pet.3:11-13(Tn,M) |
| 555 | Rev.10:6 |
| 559 | I Thess.4:4(H) |
| 561 | I Sam.15:22(Tn,M) |
| 562 | Eccles.12:13, John 14:15 |
| 564 | I Pet.5:7(Tn,M) |
| 565–68 | Ps.145:9, Rom.12:21, I Cor.1:27(T,M,V,H) |
| 569–73 | I Pet.2:21 |
| 571 | Rev.2:10 |
| 573 | Rom.9:5 |
| 575–76 | Job 28:28, Ps.111:10, Prov.9:10, Ezek.28:12 |
| 581–84 | II Pet.1:5-7, I Cor.13: 2,13(M,V,H) |
| 592–93 | Gen.3:24 |
| 600–601 | Gen.3:15, Gal.4:4-5 |
| 602 | Gen.5:5(V) |
| 611 | Num.12:6(Tn) |
| 623 | Gen.3:15 |
| 628 | Gen.3:24 |
| 630 | I Macc.10:42(Tn); Ezek.47:11(M) |
| 631 | Gen.3:19 |
| 633 | Gen.3:24(V) |
| 637–38 | Gen.19:16(V) |
| 638b | Gen.3:24 |
| 641–43 | Gen.3:24 |
| 649 | Job 30:3, Ps.107:4 |

## PARADISE REGAINED

### Book I

2–4 Rom.5:19(Tn,H)
5 Matt.4:3, Heb.2:18, I Thess.3:5
6 Eph.6:11
7 Deut.32:10
8–9 Matt.4:1(Tn); Luke 4:1(H)
18–19 Isa.58:1, Heb.12:18-19 (Td); Matt.3:1-6(M)
20 Matt.3:2
21–22 Matt.3:5
22b–24 Matt.3:13, Mark 1:9
26 John 1:33(Tn)
26b–27a John 1:15
27–28 Matt.3:14(Tn)
29–32 Matt.3:16-17(H)
33–34 Job 1:6-7, I Pet.5:8 (Td,H)
39 Matt.12:43; Acts 1:25, Eph.2:2
44 Eph.2:2, 6:12(Td, H)
53–55 Gen.3:15(H)
55–58 Ps.90:4(H)
64–65 Gal.4:4
67–68 Luke 2:52(H)
70–71 Mark 1:2-3
73–74 I John 3:3(Tn,H)
75 Matt.3:5
76 Mark 1:9
77–78 John 1:31, Matt.3:14-15
80 Matt.3:14
80b–81a Mark 1:10
81b–82 Matt.3:16, Mark 1:10, Ps.78:23, Rev.4:1(Td)
83 Matt.3:16, Mark 1:10, Luke 3:22(Tn)
84–85 Matt.3:17
92–93 II Cor.4:6
97 I Tim.3:7
119 Luke 4:1-2(Tn)
120 Isa.11:5(H); Eph. 6:11
123 Matt.4:1, Luke 4:1
126–28 Matt.4:1
133–40 Luke 1:26-38(H)
147–90 Job 2-3, Jas.5:11
151 Gen.3:15, Gal.4:4
158–60 I Cor.15:54-57, Col. 2:14-15, Phil. 2:8-11, Heb.2:10-15
161 I Cor.1:27(Td,H); Ps.8:2(Td)
162 John 16:33(Td); Rev.17:14
166–67 Heb.5:8-9
176 John 10:15(H); Matt. 11:27, Luke 10:22
184 John 1:28(Tn,M)
189 Matt.4:1, Luke 4:1
190–91 Mark 1:35, Matt. 14: 35(T)
201–202 I Cor.13:11(Tn)
204 John 18:37(Tn,H)
206 Ps.119:103(Td)
207 Ps.1:2(Td,H)
209–14 Luke 2:46-50(H)
211–12 Luke 2:46
214 Luke 2:47(Tn)
238–41 Luke 1:32-33(Td)
240–54 Matt.2, Luke 1, 2(H)
242–47 Luke 2:8,11-16
248 Luke 2:7
249–54 Matt.2:1-2,9-11
255–58 Luke 2:25-36(Tn,H)
260–62 Luke 4:16-21
263 John 8:58, Exod.3:14
266–67 Isa.53:6(Tn,H)
270–71 John 1:31,33(Tn)
270–79 Mark 1, Luke 3(H)
271–72 Isa.40:3-4, Luke 3:4-5
274 Matt.21:25
275–77 John 1:29-34
278–79 Matt.3:11,14
280–86a Matt.3:16,17
281 Ps.24:7-9(Td,H)
286b–87 Gal.4:4(Tn,H)
289 Matt.21:23-27
290–91 Matt.4:1, Luke 4:1
293 Luke 2:52(Tc,M); Mark 13:32(M)
294 Rev.22:16(Tn,M,H)
299 Matt.4:1, Luke 4:1
303 Matt.4:2, Luke 4:2
308–309 Matt.4:2, Luke 4:2, John 4:32-34
310 Mark 1:13(Td,H); Isa.65:25(H)

| | |
|---|---|
| 312 | Num.21:6(H) |
| 327–29 | John 1:34 |
| 333–34 | Acts 17:21 |
| 342–43 | Luke 4:3 |
| 344 | Luke 23:39 |
| 349–50 | Matt.4:14, Luke 4:4, Deut.8:3(Td,H,M) |
| 350–52 | Exod.16:14-15, 24:18 (H) |
| 353–54 | I Kings 19:1-8(M,H) |
| 360 | Jude 6(H) |
| 365 | I Pet.5:8, Job 1:7, 2:2 |
| 366 | I Kings 8:27(Td); Eph.2:2 |
| 368 | Job 1:6,11, 2:5(M,H) |
| 371–76 | I Kings 22:19-23(Tn, M,H) |
| 407–408 | John 8:44b(H) |
| 428 | I Kings 22:6(Td,M,H) |
| 441 | I Tim.3:7 |
| 442–43 | II Thess.2:10-11 |
| 451–52 | Jas.2:19 |
| 456 | I Cor.13:8 |
| 460 | John 1:14(Tc); Acts 7:38(Td) |
| 462–64 | John 16:13(H) |
| 465 | II Cor.11:4 |
| 488 | Isa.1:12(Td) |
| 488b–89 | I Cor.9:13 |
| 490 | Lev.7:16, 22:18, Num.15:3,8(Td) |
| 490b–92 | Num.23:5; Num.20(H) |
| 495–96 | John 19:11 |

Book II

| | |
|---|---|
| 3–5 | Isa.53:7, John 1:29,36, 41(Td); Matt.3:17, Mark 1:11, Luke 3:22, John 1:34 |
| 7 | John 1:39-42(M,H) |
| 9–10 | John 1:41 |
| 11–12 | Matt.28:17 |
| 14 | Exod.32:1(Td,M) |
| 15 | I Kings 17:1(Tn,M,H) |
| 15–16 | II Kings 2:11(Td) |
| 18–19 | II Kings 2:15-18(H) |
| 20 | John 1:28, Matt.4:15 (Td) |
| 21 | Deut.34:3(H); Gen. 33:18, John 3:23(T, M,H) |
| 26 | Matt.11:7 |
| 27 | Matt.4:18-22 |
| 31–33 | John 1:41,45,49 |
| 34 | John 1:14(Tn,H) |
| 35–36 | Acts 1:6(H) |
| 44 | Ps.2:2(Td) |
| 46–47 | Num.9:26(Td) |
| 51–52 | John 1:29,36 |
| 57 | Acts 28:20, I Tim.1:1 |
| 59 | Isa.65:1 |
| 68 | Luke 1:28(H) |
| 74–75 | Luke 2:7 |
| 75–78 | Matt.2:13-16(H) |
| 79–80 | John 1:46(Tn); Matt. 2:22-23 |
| 83 | Luke 2:23 |
| 83–84 | John 1:29,36 |
| 85 | Matt.3:17 |
| 88–91 | Luke 2:34-35(Td,H) |
| 96–97 | Luke 2:42-46 |
| 98–99 | Luke 2:49(Td,H) |
| 99b–100 | Luke 2:19,50-51(H) |
| 103–105 | Luke 2:19,51(Tn) |
| 111–12 | John 14:10 |
| 112 | John 4:34 |
| 114 | John 18:37 |
| 117–18 | Eph.2:2, 6:12 |
| 131 | Ps.34:8 |
| 147 | Rev.12:9 |
| 151–52 | Tob.3:8, 6:14(Tn,H) |
| 154 | Gen.6:2 |
| 169–71 | I Kings 11:1-8(H) |
| 179–80 | Gen.6:2(Tn,M,H) |
| 205–206 | Matt.12:42, Luke 11:31 |
| 231 | Luke 4:2 |
| 236–37 | Matt.12:4-5(Td) |
| 243–44 | Luke 4:2 |
| 259–60 | John 4:34(Tn,H); Matt.5:6(Td) |
| 261 | Ps.4:4(Tn) |
| 266–69 | I Kings 17:5-6(Tn, M,H) |
| 270–76 | I Kings 19:4-8(Tn,H) |
| 278 | Dan.1:8-19(T,M,H) |
| 308–10 | Gen.21:10,17-19(H) |
| 309 | Gen.25:13(Tn,M,H) |
| 310–12 | Exod.16:4,14-15,35 (H) |
| 312 | I Macc.2:58, Ecclus. 48:1-2(Td) |
| 312–14 | I Kings 19:5,7 |
| 324–25 | Heb.1:2(H) |
| 328–29 | Deut.14:3-20, Lev.11, I Cor.10:28(H); Lev. 11:18, I Cor.8:10-11, Dan.1:8 |

366 Matt.4:3
384 Ps.78:19(H)
385–86 Luke 22:42-43, Matt. 26:53(Td)
404 Matt.4:3
414 Matt.13.55
415 II Cor.8:9
416 Job 18:12(Td,H)
418 Matt.21:23
420–21 John 6:26
427 I Tim.6:17, Prov.4:5-7, 11:28, 13:7
429 Deut.8:17-18
439 Judg.6:15, 11:1-2, Ps.78:70-71(Tn,M, H)
442 Luke 1:33(H)
450–52 II Cor.8:9
477 Eph.3:16
481 Acts 20:35
482 John 10:15,17

Book III

5 Eph.6:11, Rev.12:9
13–15 Lev.8:8, Num.27:21 (M,H); Exod.28:30, Deut.33:8, I Sam.28:6, Ezra 2:63, Neh.7:65 (M)
31 Luke 3:23(Tn,M)
52 John 4:22
56–57 Luke 6:22,26
60–68 Job 1:8(Tn)
68–69 Joel 2:3(Td)
92 II Pet.1:6(T)
95 Jas.5:11
104 Matt.6:1, II John 8
106–107 John 5:30-32, 7:18, 8:50(H); John 8:14, 18
108 Matt.4:3
110–20 Rev.4:11(H)
111 Isa.43:7, Ps.96:8
112–13 Isa.6:3, Luke 2:14
114 I Cor.10:31, Acts 12: 23, Rev.11:13, 14:7
117 Mal.2:2
122 John 1:1-3, II Pet. 3:15(H)
124–25 Ps.107:8-9, Rom.2:4
129 Acts 17:25
134–35 I Cor.4:7
152–53 Luke 1:32-33, Acts 2:29-30
154 Luke 3:23
160–61 II Macc.5(Tn,M)
162–63 I Macc.1:21-24(H)
165–66 I Macc.3:57-58, 5:24
169 I Macc.10:18-21
170 I Macc.2:1
171 II Kings 10:16
175 Ps.69:9, John 2:17(Td, H)
178 Isa.9:6-7
182 Titus 1:3, I Tim.2:6, Rom.5:6
183 Eccles.3:1(Tn,M,H); John 17:17
185–87 Acts 1:7(Tn,H)
188–92a Luke 9:22, 17:25
193–94 Heb.5:8
195–97 Heb.2:9-10
214–15 I Cor.15:24-25, Rev. 20:1-4,10
221–22 Isa.25:5(T)
226 Rev.5:2,4,9-10,12
229–31 Col.1:19
234–35 Luke 2:41(Tn,H)
242 I Sam.9:20-21, 10:1 (Tn,H)
245–46 Matt.4:8
249 Matt.13:11(H)
251–52 Matt.4:8(Tn); Luke 4:5
265–66 Matt.4:3,8
275–76 Jonah 2:3(Tn)
277 Dan.2:32,38(Tn)
279 II Kings 17:1-6(M)
281–83 Dan.4:30, II Kings 17, 24, 25, II Chron.36 (Tn,M,H)
284 Ezra 1, 2(Tn)
359 John 4:9(H)
373–80 II Kings 27:6(H)
374–76 II Kings 18:11(Tn)
384 Gen.15:18, I Kings 4:21(Tn,M,H)
387 II Chron.32:8, Jer.17:5 (Td,H); Col.2:18(T)
396–97 John 7:6(Tn,H)
398 II Pet.3:9
409 I Chron.21:1,14
414–17 I Kings 12:28(H)
417 I Kings 11:5, 16:31-32, 18:19, II Kings 17(Tn, M); I Kings 16:31(H)
427–31 I Kings 12:29(H)
433–35 Isa.43:1-2,5-6

| Line | Reference |
|---|---|
| 436 | Isa.11:15-16(Tn,H); Rev.16:12(Tn) |
| 438 | Ps.74.15(Td) |
| 440 | Rom.5:6, Titus 1:3 |

Book IV

| Line | Reference |
|---|---|
| 1 | Isa.22:5, Esth.3:15, Micah 7:4, Luke 9:7, 21:25(Td) |
| 8–9 | Luke 11:21-22(T) |
| 17 | I Cor.10:4, Jude 13, Matt.16:18 |
| 44–45 | Rev.18:7(H) |
| 88–89 | Matt.4:8(Td) |
| 103–104 | Luke 4:6(Td,H) |
| 107–108 | Luke 1:32-33 |
| 128–29 | Heb.2:14-15 |
| 131 | Matt.15:24 |
| 144–45 | John 8:34 |
| 147–50 | Dan.4:11(Tn,H);Matt. 13:32(Tn); Dan.2:35 (H) |
| 149 | Dan.2:44(Tn); Ps.2:9 (T) |
| 151 | Luke 1:33(Tn) |
| 152 | Acts 1:7 |
| 153 | Matt.4:3 |
| 162–67 | Matt.4:8-9, Luke 4:5-7 |
| 175–77 | Deut.6:13(H); Matt. 4:10, Luke 4:8 |
| 185b | Rev.17:14, 19:16(H) |
| 185–86 | I Tim.6:15(Td,H); Rom.9:5(Td) |
| 193–94 | Luke 4:8, Matt.4:10 |
| 197 | Ps.82:6; Job 1:6(H) |
| 203 | II Cor.4:4(Td,H) |
| 216–19 | Luke 2:46-47 |
| 219 | Matt.23:2(Tn,H) |
| 221 | Matt.16:3(Td) |
| 287–89 | Jas.1:17(Td); Ps.36:9 (T) |
| 310–12 | Acts 17:23-30 |
| 321 | Eccles.12:12(Tn,M,H) |
| 336–37 | Ps.137:1-3(Tn,M,H) |
| 341–43 | Jude 16(T) |
| 350 | II Tim.3:16 |
| 352 | Rom.2:14-15 |
| 362 | Prov.14:34(Td) |
| 363 | Josh.6:5,20 |
| 366 | Eph.6:16(Td,H) |
| 380 | Gal.4:4(Tn); Luke 3:23 |
| 382–93 | Isa.47:11-13 |
| 391–92 | Heb.7:3 |
| 397 | Matt.4:11, Luke 4:13 |
| 408 | Matt.4:3 |
| 424 | Eph.6:16 |
| 425 | Isa.26:3, Eph.2:14 |
| 441 | Eph.6:12 |
| 443 | II Cor.2:11 |
| 455 | Job 26:11(Tth,H) |
| 480 | Ps.45:6, Heb.1:8, Num. 24:7 |
| 495 | Matt.4:9 |
| 499 | Rev.12:12 |
| 500–501 | Luke 20:41-44 |
| 503–504 | Luke 1:26-31 |
| 505–506 | Luke 2:8-14 |
| 510–511 | Matt.3:5-6 |
| 512–13 | Matt.3:17 |
| 518 | Ps.82:6-7, John 10:34-36 |
| 525 | Gen.3:15 |
| 527 | I Pet.5:8 |
| 532 | Luke 22:31, Rev.3:10 |
| 533 | I Cor.10:4, Heb.4:15, Matt.16:18 |
| 539 | Matt.3:17 |
| 545–50 | Matt.4:5, 27:53(Td, M); Luke 4:9(M) |
| 551 | Eph.6:11-14 |
| 552 | John 2:16 |
| 555–59 | Matt.4:5-6, Luke 4:9-11 |
| 556–59 | Ps.91:11-12(M,H) |
| 560 | Matt.4:7, Luke 4:12 |
| 561 | Deut.6:16(M,H); Rom. 14:4 |
| 571 | I Cor.10:12 |
| 581b–82 | Matt.4:11, Mark 1:13 |
| 589 | Rev.22:2 |
| 590 | Rev.21:6 |
| 594–95 | Heb.4:15, Matt.4:3 |
| 596 | Heb.1:3, Col.1:15 |
| 597 | John 1:18(T,H) |
| 597b–98 | John 1:9 |
| 599 | John 1:14, II Cor.5:1 (Td); Phil.2:7 |
| 603 | Isa.14:13-14 |
| 604 | John 10:1(T) |
| 604b–605 | Luke 10:18, Rev.12:9 |
| 611 | Ps.124:7(Td,H) |
| 616–17 | Rev.22:2-3, 20:10 |
| 618 | Rev.12:9 |
| 620 | Luke 10:18(Tn,H); Mal.4:3(H) |
| 620–21 | Rom.16:20(Td) |
| 622 | Rev.13:3, 19:20; Rev. 20:10(H) |

624 Matt.16:18, Isa.3:26, Rev.9:11(Tn); Job 26:6, 28:22, 31:12(H)
626–27 II Thess.2:8
628 Rev.18:2(Td)
629–32 Matt.8:28-32, Rev.20:1-3(Td,H)
633 Mark 5:7, Heb.1:2
634 John 4:34, 17:4
635 Matt.11:29(Td);Matt. 18:11, Luke 9:56, 19:10, I John 4:14
637 Matt.4:11(T)
638 Acts 15:3, Rom.15:24
639 Luke 1:56, 4:14-41

# *Index of Selected Subjects*

UNDER each subject heading are listed line references to Milton's epics, chapter and verse references to the Bible, a symbol for the use Milton made of the Bible in connection with each subject, and the numbers of the pages of this book on which each subject is discussed. Book and line references to the poetry are to *Paradise Lost* except when *PR* (for *Paradise Regained*) appears before the number of the book. Standard abbreviations are used for the books of the Bible. Symbols for the categories of Milton's use of the Bible are as follows: AR—Authoritative Reality; LV—Linguistic Versatility; DE—Dramatic Effectiveness; EP—Epic Unity of Theme.

ADAM: associated with Abraham (V.229-302, 313ff.; VIII.379-380; XII.276-277 with Gen.18:1-2, 4, 6, 30-32; John 8:56; DE), 202-204; —with Cain (XI.315-327 with Gen.4:3, 14; DE), 209-210; —with Joshua (VIII.633-637 with Josh.1:6-9; DE), 153-154; —with Moses (IX.947-949 with Deut. 32:26-27; Num.14:15-16; DE), 206-207; attains sum of wisdom (XII.575-576 with Ezek. 28:12; DE), 211; compared to a reaper (IX.838-842 with Gal.6:7; DE), 205-206; dissociated from Abraham after the Fall (IX.1-4 with Jas.2:23; DE), 204-205; escorted into Paradise (VIII.295-303 with I Cor.15:45; John 14:2; AR), 37-38; expulsion of associated with Lot's from Sodom (XII.637-649 with Gen.3:19, 24, 19:15-16, 26; I Cor. 15:15; DE), 127-130; fall of foreshadowed (VIII.633-637, 640-643 with Josh.1:6; I John 5:3; I Cor.7:37; DE), 134-135; fallen character of (IX.1024-1028, 1123-1126 with Exod. 32:6; Isa.57:20-21; I Cor.10:7; DE), 208-209; reassociated with Abraham (XII.273-277 with John 8:56; DE), 210-211; repentance of (X.958-961 with Gal.6:2; DE), 209; sum of wisdom learned by (XII.561-573, 581-587 with I Sam.15:22; Eccles.12:13; John 14:15; I Pet. 2:21, 5:7; II Pet.1:5-8; Ps.145:9; Rom.9:5, 12:21; I Cor.1:27-28; Rev.2:10; AR), 48-49

ALTERNATIVES, atmosphere of (V.443-450; X.217-219, 645-647 with Gen.6:2, 3:21; Rom.5:10; Rev.21:2; DE), 119-122

ANGELS: armor of (VI.525-528, 535-546 with Eph.6:11, 14, 16-17; LV), 78-79; nature of (V.221-223, 469-503 with Tob.12:15, 19; Rom.11:36; I Cor. 15:37-49; Acts 17:28b; AR), 28-31

BEASTS, Jesus among during wilderness temptation (*PR* I.303-313 with Mark 1:12-13; Num.21:6; AR), 61

BRIDGE THROUGH CHAOS, Biblical basis for (II.1021-1030 with Matt.7:13; AR), 58-59

CHAOS, KING OF, associated with demons (II.990-992 with Mark 1:24; DE), 156-157
COMPASSES, golden, used in creation (VII.224-227 with Prov.8:27; AR), 33-34
CREATION, revelation of God through (VIII.67-69 with Ps.19:1-3; Rom.1:20; AR), 35-36
DEVILS: association of with N.T. demons (II.615-618 with Matt.12:43; DE), 127; Biblical language used ironically by (II.376-378 with Ps.107:10-11; AR), 16; creation of man discussed by (II.344-353 with Ps.8:4-5; Heb.2:6-7, 6:17, 12:26; AR), 15; defeat of foreshadowed (I.402-403, 416, 443-446 with I Kings 4:29-31; II Kings 23:13; DE), 131-132; –(I.110-116 with Isa.45:22-23; Phil.2:10-11; DE), 139-140; –(I.162-168 with Gen.6:6; Rom. 8:28; II Tim.4:18; DE), 140-141; –(II.323-338 with Rev.1:11a, 19:15, 22:13; Ps.45:6, 2:9; I Tim.6:15; DE), 142-143; –(III.622-623 with Rev. 19:17; DE), 143; –(IV.1-12 with Rev.12:10-12; DE), 143-144; –(IV.996-1015 with Isa.40:12; Job 28:25, 37:16; I Sam.2:3; Dan.5:27; DE), 145-146; efforts of to be thwarted by God (II.385-386; III.84-86 with Ps.76:10; Gen. 5:20a; Ps.7:16; AR), 17-18; final defeat of alluded to in Satan's speech (I.264-268 with John 14:2; Rev.21:8; DE), 155-156; names of blotted out in Heaven (I.360-364 with Ps.9:5-6b; Rev.3:4-5, 12b; AR), 12-13; origin of as angels (I.373 with Deut.32:17; I Cor.10:20-21; AR), 13-14; perverted idea of God expressed by (II.69, 90, 170-172 with Lev.10:1; Rom.9:22; Isa.30:33; Dan.3:19; DE), 159-161; –(I.680-684; II.253-257 with Matt. 11:29-30; John 8:34; DE), 161-163; revenge planned by (II.323-328 with Rev.22:13; Ps.2:9, 45:6; AR), 16
EDEN: Biblical description of (IV.215-223, 229-234 with Gen.2:9-10; AR), 22-23; Biblical setting of (IV.724-725; V.1-2 with Ps.74:16a, 97:11; DE), 112-113; –(V.185-204 with Ps.148:7-13; DE), 113-114; –(IX.194-197 with Gen.8:21; DE), 116; –(IX.205-206 with Gen.2:15; DE), 116; –(IX.442-443, 1015-1018, 95-101 with Song of Sol.7:1; I Kings 3:1, 1:11; Gen.3:8; DE), 116-117; meaning of (IV.209-211 with Gen.2:8; AR), 22
EPIC REITERATION: *Air* as realm of Satan's dominion and defeat (II.400-402, 594-595, 842-843, 714-722; III.72, 254-256, 564; IV.938-940; V.77-79; IX. 657-658; X.182-191, 279-281, 212-213, 398-401, 847-848; XI.181-183, 193, 201-202; XII.451-455; *PR* I.39, 44-47, 63, 365-366; *PR* IV.41, 568, 585, 618-623, 634-635 with Eph.2:2, 4:8; I Thess.4:16; Col.2:15; EP), 241-248; *Disobedience* of man theme (I.1-5; IX.6-8, 11-12; XII.396-409; *PR* I.1-4 with Rom.5:12, 19; EP), 237-239; *Serpent* as subtlest beast theme (I.34; *PR* IV.618 with II Cor.11:3; Rev.12.9, 20:2; EP), 329; –(VII.495-498; IX.86, 560-561 with Gen.3:1a; EP), 240-241
EPIC SIMILES: angels like field of grain (IV.977-985 with Amos 9:13; Matt.13:37; Luke 9:62, 17:7, 22:31-32; I Cor.9:10; EP), 232-234; –like guardian bands of Jacob and Elisha (XI.213-220 with Gen.31:1-2, 32:6-8; II Kings 6:15-17; EP), 234-235; devils like locusts of Egyptian plague (I.338-345 with Exod. 10:13-15; EP), 225-226; –like Pharaoh's armies (I.302-313 with Exod. 14:23-30; EP), 223-224; Satan like Asmodeus (IV.159-171 with Tob.8:1-4; EP), 228-230; –like Leviathan (I.192-210; VII.412-416 with Isa.27:1; Job 41:1, 9, 15, 34; Acts 27:22-29; EP), 219-222; –like a wolf (IV.183-193 with John 10:1, 7, 10a, 11-13; Acts 20:29; EP), 230-232; stairs to Heaven like Jacob's ladder (III.501-503, 510-515 with Gen.28:12, 16-17, 19-22; John 1:51; EP), 226-228
EVE: independence from Adam asserted by (IX.214-219 with Ps.128:3; DE), 212; language of Paul used ironically by (XI.178-180 with Phil.4:11; DE), 167; repentant state associated with Mary Magdalene (V.129-131; X.910-

913, 946 with Luke 7:37-38, 50; DE), 212-213; sin of foreshadowed (V.122-131 with II Pet.3:7; Luke 7:37-38; DE), 133-134; subjection of to Adam symbolized by hair (IV.304-311 with I Cor.11:10; DE), 211-212; takes the fruit (IX.777-781 with Gen.3:6; AR), 44; tempted by the Serpent (IX.647-652, 656-658, 659-663, 684-690, 703-709 with Gen.3:1-5; AR), 41-44

FATHER, the deity, praised by angels (III.372-382 with Isa.6:2; I Tim.1:17; Rev.19:6; AR), 19-20

GREEK, transliterations of: abyss (I.657-659; II.404-410 with Rev. 20:1-3; LV), 67-68; amarant (III.351-364 with I Pet.1:4, 5:4; Rev.4:4, 6, 10; LV), 76-77; demoniac (*PR* IV.625-630 with Mark 5:15; LV), 85-86; eremite (*PR* I.8-15 with Matt.4:1; Mark 1:12; Luke 4:1; LV), 83-84; hyaline (VII.617-625 with Rev. 4:6, 11, 15:2; LV), 82-83; myriads (I.86-87, 101, 622 with Luke 12:1; Heb.12:22; LV), 67; panoply (VI.525-528, 760-782 with Luke 11:21-22; Eph.6:11-13; LV), 78-79; tartarus (II.858-869; VI.54; VII.238 with I Pet.2:4; LV), 72-74; Urania (VII.1-7 with Matt.6:14, 26, 32; LV), 80-81

GREEK, variant translations based on: anxiety (VIII.180-187 with Matt.6:31, 33-34; LV), 87-89; Evil One (IX.463; *PR* IV.194 with Matt.6:13a; LV), 94-95; grace (*PR* I.66-69 with Luke 2:52; LV), 95-96; tread (*PR* IV.620-621 with Rom.16:20; LV), 96-97

HEAVEN: Biblical setting of (III.1 with Gen.1:3; III.3-4 with I John 1:5, I Tim. 6:16; III.6-8 with Wisd.7:25-26, Job 38:19; III.375-382 with Ps.104:2, Isa. 6:2; DE), 109-111

HEBREW, transliterations of: Adam (IV.323; IX.175-178 with Gen.2:19; LV), 69-71; Eden (IV.27-30, 208-216; IX.340-341 with Gen. 2:8; LV), 75-76; Eve (XI.158-161 with Gen.3:20; LV), 69-71; Messiah (*PR* II.50 with Dan. 9:25-26; LV), 84-85; Satan (I.81-82; II.629-631 with I Kings 11:25; LV), 69

HEBREW, variant translations based on: breathe (IV.641 with Song of Sol.2:17; LV), 93-94; brooded (I.19-22; VII.233-237 with Gen.1:2; Deut.32:11; Jer.23:9; LV), 92-93; expanse (VII.261-275 with Gen.1:6-8; LV), 91; wind (X.92-103 with Gen. 3:8-9; LV), 89-90

HELL, Biblical setting of (I.45-48 with Luke 10:18, 16:23, II Pet.2:4, Jude 6, Rev.20:1-2; I.280 with Rev.20:15; I.70-72 with Matt.22:13, 25:41; II.614-617 with Matt.12:43, Luke 11:24; DE), 107-108

HOLY SPIRIT, Biblical authority for (I.17-20 with Gen.1:2, I Cor.2:11b-13, 6:19; I.27-28 with Ps.139:7-8, I Cor.2:10b; AR), 17-18

IDOLATRY, deteriorating influence of (I.367-371 with Rom.1:23-25; AR), 13; –(IX.795, 835, 1033 with Exod.32:6; I Cor.10:7; DE), 207-208

LATIN BIBLE, allusions to: adhere (VIII.498 with Gen.2:24; LV), 100-101; fire and ice (II.596-603 with Job 24:19; LV), 97-98; minims (VII.482 with Prov.30:24; LV), 100; palpable darkness (II.404-407 with Exod. 10:21; LV), 98-99; peccant (XI.67-71 with II Pet.2:4-9; LV), 101-102; play (VII.10 with Prov.8:30; LV), 99-100; substance (III.139-140 with Heb.1:3; LV), 99

LIGHT, creation of before the sun (VII.243-252, 370-373 with Gen.1:3-5; Ps.19:1, 4, 5-6; AR), 34-35

MAN: created upright by God (III.98-99 with Eccles.7:29; AR), 18; –in God's image (IV.291-292 with Gen.1:27; AR), 23-24; how knowledge of God gained by (VIII.277-282 with Acts 17:28; AR), 36

MARRIAGE RELATIONSHIP: abused by man after Fall (IX.1042-1044 with Prov. 7:18; DE), 208; enjoyed by man before fall (IV.739-743, 758-762, 765-766 with Eph.5:31-32; I Cor.7:4-5; Heb.13:4; AR), 25-26

PALESTINE, setting of (*PR* II.25-29 with Matt.11:7; DE), 123

PARADISE LOST, authority of opening lines of (I.1-13 with Gen.1:1, 2:17;

Exod.3:1, 19:18, 24:12-18, 34:2; Deut.4:10; Neh.3:15; Ps.2:6, 23:3, 28:2; Isa.8:6; John 1:1; Rom.5:12, 19; I Cor. 15:45-47; AR), 10-12

RAPHAEL, appearance of (V.277-285 with Isa.6:2-5; DE), 201-202

SATAN: associated with Athenians of Acts (*PR* I.326-334 with Acts 17:19-21; DE), 182-183; —with Belshazzar (IV.1010-1012 with Dan.5:27; DE), 178-179; —with Dives (I.54-56 with Luke 16:23a; DE), 172-173; —with Esau (IV.42-45, 79-85 with Ezek.28:15, 17; Jas.1:5; I John 5:3; Heb.12:16b-17; DE), 174-178; —with Herod (III.667-676 with Matt.2:8, 12; DE), 174-175; —with Judas Iscariot (V.611-615 with Acts 1:25; Luke 22:3; John 13:2; John 13:27, 6:70-71; DE), 180-181; —with Nebuchadnezzar (I.570-573 with I Chron.21:1, 5, 7; Dan.5:20; DE), 173-175; —with the Pharisees V.788-792 with John 8:33-36; DE), 179-180; —with the Second Advent of Christ (II.511-519 with Matt.24:30b-31; DE), 125-126; —with the unrepentant thief on the cross (*PR* I.341-345 with Matt.4:3; Luke 4:3, 23:29; DE), 154-155; character of revealed by speech (I.84-87, 643-649 with Isa.14:12; Ezek.28:17; Luke 10:41-42; DE), 158-159, 171-172; evil declared good by (IV.108-110 with Isa.5:20; DE), 177; failure of in tempting Christ foreshadowed (*PR* I.146-149 with Job 2:3; Jas.5:11; DE), 135-136; —(II.402-404 with Isa.6:8; IV.378-381 with Matt.10:8; DE), 163-164; —(X.408-409 with Josh.1:6-9; Deut.11:8; DE), 166; language of Scripture perverted by (PR II.129-133 with Ps.34:8; DE), 167-168; —(*PR* II.426-429 with Deut.8:17-18; Matt.6:33; Prov.4:5, 11:28; I Tim.6:17; DE), 168-169; —(*PR* IV.555-559 with Ps.91:11-12; DE), 169; revealed by Christ as a liar (*PR* I.368-376 with Job 1:11, 2:5; I Kings 22:20, 22; DE), 183-185; —(*PR* I.407-408 with John 8.44b; DE), 185; —(*PR* III.407-413 with I Chron.21:1, 14; DE), 185-186

SERPENT, language of Scripture used ironically by (IX.713-714, 732 with Col. 3:9-10; Gen.2:16-17; DE), 164-165

SIN AND DEATH: Biblical basis allegory of (II.648-653, 666-673, 762-767, 777-787 with I Cor.15:56; Ps. 23; Job 18:4; Ezek. 28:15-16; Rev.6:2a,8; Jas. 1:13-15; AR), 55-57; language of Scripture used ironically by (X.235-238 with II Kings 7:3; DE), 165-166

SON OF GOD: associated with Abraham (III.150-155 with Gen.18-25; DE), 187-188; —with Christ of N.T. (VII.216; VIII.437-447; X.213-217, 219 with Mark 4:39; John 6:6; Gen.3:21; Phil.2:7; John 13:4-5; Heb.2:13b; Rom. 5:10; DE), 189-192; —(*PR* I.203-205, 209-214 with John 18:37; Luke 2:46-47; DE), 192-193; —(*PR* IV.215-220 with Matt.23:1-3; Luke 2:43-44; DE), 193-194; —(*PR* I.259-263 with John 8:58; Exod.3:14; DE), 194-195; —(*PR* I.263-267; *PR* II.258-260 with Isa.53:6b; John 4:34; DE), 195; —with David (X.629-637 with I Sam.24:29; DE), 157-158; —with Moses (III.165-166 with Exod.32:12; cf. Num.14:12-19; DE), 188-189; —(VI.801-804, 806-812 with Exod.14:13-14; DE), 151-153; —with Paul (*PR* I.201-204 with I Cor.13:11; DE), 192; birth of as Jesus foreshadowed (X.1050-1053 with John 16:21; DE), 146-147; character of (III.138-142 with Heb. 1:3; Matt.9:36; John 1:14, 3:34, 13:1; DE), 187; characterized by Satan (*PR* I.70-93 with Matt.3:13-17; Mark 1:9-11; Luke 3:21-22; II Cor.4:6; AR), 50-51; chariot of in war in Heaven (VI.751-759 with Ezek.1:20, 6, 13, 16, 18, 22, 26-28, 10:12; AR), 32-33; compared to Biblical Rock (*PR* IV.17-19, 531-536 with Matt.16:18; I Cor.10:4; Jude 13; DE), 197-198; —to Saul by Satan (*PR* III.240-243 with I Sam.9:20-21, 15:24-31; DE), 196-197; converses with Adam in Paradise (VIII.314-331 with Exod.3:14; Ezek.1:28; John 8:58; Col.1:16; Heb.12:2; Rev.1:17; AR), 37-39; echoes N.T. language of Paul (VI.808 with Rom.12:19; DE), 152-153; fallen pair and Serpent judged by (X.55-62, 116-117, 121-123, 137-143, 162, 197-208 with Gen.3:9-19; Ps.85:10; John 5:22; Gal.3:13; John 5:27; I Tim.2:5-6; AR), 45-47; only begotten of Father (III.80 with John 1:18; AR), 18; own death and resurrection prophesied by (III.245-259, 265 with Ps.16:10, 11; I Cor.15:26, 56; Col.1:13, 2:15; AR), 18-19; patience in temptation shown by (*PR* III.182-187 with Eccles.3:1; Acts 1:7; Rom.5.6; I Tim.2:6; Titus 2:6; DE), 195-196; praised by angels (III.383-389 with John 1:18, 3:16, 3:34; II Cor.4:6 AR), 20; Solomon contrasted with by Satan (*PR* II.169-171, 205-206 with I Kings 11:1-4; Matt. 12:42; DE), 130-131; temptation to seek fame rebuffed by (*PR* III.47-57 with Matt.23:13-33, Mark 6:34, Luke 6:22-26, John 4:22, DE), 199-200; triumph of over Satan foreshadowed (*PR* IV.517-520 with John 10:34; Ps.82:6; DE), 149; ultimate victory prophesied (*PR* IV.625-635 with Matt.8:29; Rev.20:15; DE), 149-150; victory over temptations foreshadowed (*PR* II.266-278 with I Kings 17:3-6; Dan.1:8,15; DE), 137-138

STAIRS TO HEAVEN, Biblical basis for (III.510-515 with Gen.28:12, 16, 17; John 1:51; AR), 60

TEMPLE, building of Pandaemonium associated with (I.710-713 with I Kings 6:7, 21-35; DE), 124-126

TEMPTATIONS OF CHRIST, order of (*PR* I.45-46; *PR* IV.563-571, 395-397 with Matt.4:11; Luke 1:3, 4:13; Heb.4:15; AR), 62-63

THAMMUZ, Biblical authority for (I.446 with Ezek.8:13-14; AR), 14

TREE OF LIFE, location of in Paradise (IV.195 with Gen.2:9; AR), 22

VIRGIN MARY, life of Jesus reviewed by (*PR* II.86-108 with Luke 2:19, 34-35, 46, 48-51; AR), 51-53; as "second Eve" (X.1050-1053, V.387 with Luke 1:42, 2:10-11), 147

WOMAN, subjection to man symbolized (IV.304-308 with I Cor.11:3, 7-10, 14-15; AR), 24-25